Fezzes in the River

Fezzes in the River

*Identity Politics and European Diplomacy
in the Middle East on the
Eve of World War II*

SARAH D. SHIELDS

OXFORD
UNIVERSITY PRESS

OXFORD
UNIVERSITY PRESS

Oxford University Press, Inc., publishes works that further
Oxford University's objective of excellence
in research, scholarship, and education.

Oxford   New York
Auckland   Cape Town   Dar es Salaam   Hong Kong   Karachi
Kuala Lumpur   Madrid   Melbourne   Mexico City   Nairobi
New Delhi   Shanghai   Taipei   Toronto

With offices in
Argentina   Austria   Brazil   Chile   Czech Republic   France   Greece
Guatemala   Hungary   Italy   Japan   Poland   Portugal   Singapore
South Korea   Switzerland   Thailand   Turkey   Ukraine   Vietnam

Published by Oxford University Press, Inc.
198 Madison Avenue, New York, NY 10016

www.oup.com

Library of Congress Cataloging-in-Publication Data
Shields, Sarah D., 1955–
Fezzes in the river : identity politics and European diplomacy
in the Middle East on the eve of World War II / Sarah D. Shields.
p.   cm.
Includes bibliographical references and index.
ISBN 978-0-19-539331-6
1. Turkey—Politics and government—1918–1960.
2. Turkey—Administrative and political divisions—History—20th century.
3. Turkey—Ethnic relations—History—20th century.
4. Turks—Ethnic identity.
5. Arabs—Turkey—Ethnic identity.
6. Turkey—Foreign relations—Europe.
7. Europe—Foreign relations—Turkey.
8. World War, 1939–1945—Turkey. I. Title.
DR477.S54   2011
940.53'25561—dc22
2010023719

1 3 5 7 9 8 6 4 2

Printed in the United States of America
on acid-free paper

To William, with many thanks

CONTENTS

Acknowledgments   ix
Note on Names and Translations   xi

Introduction: Saydo's Argument   3
1. Fezzes and Hats   17
2. The League Takes the Case   48
3. The League Decides   78
4. Transition to Independence   112
5. Independence   143
6. Registrations Begin   176
7. Martial Law   204
Conclusion   232

Appendix I   251
Appendix II   253
Note on Sources   255
Abbreviations   257
Notes   259
Bibliography   289
Index   297

ACKNOWLEDGMENTS

I have been fortunate to be a member of a terrific department that has provided time to write, funding for research, and an intellectual community to challenge my work. Many thanks to all of them, not least my chairs Lloyd Kramer and Fitz Brundage. The University of North Carolina has not only provided time for me to think and research and write but also the financial support to make this all possible. Those grants have come from UNC's University Research Council, the Provost's Office, the College of Arts and Sciences, the Institute for Research in the Social Sciences, the Center for Global Initiatives, and the Institute for the Arts and Humanities.

This project has received support from many other generous organizations. My sincere thanks go to the National Endowment for the Humanities and the American Philosophical Society. I received the Delta Delta Delta Fellowship at the National Humanities Center (NHC), which provided everything a geek could want: a wonderful staff, remarkable colleagues, time to think, and woods to admire. Thanks very much to the staff, Kent Mulliken, Lois Whittington, Joel Elliot, Marie Brubaker, Karen Carroll, Geoffrey Harpham, and the incomparable NHC librarians Eliza Robertson, Jean Houston, and Betsy Dain. Thanks also to my historian colleagues during the 2006–2007 NHC fellowship year, who read and critiqued earlier drafts and pointed me in new directions: Robert Beachy, Chris Browning, Glenda Gilmore, Jan Goldstein, Jud Herrman, Randal Jelks, Alice Kessler-Harris, Ben Kiernan, Sheryl Kroen, Fred Paxton, Bill Sewell, James Sweet, Di Wang, and Rachel Weil.

I owe a great deal to the archivists and librarians of many collections who have helped me locate the materials on which this study is based: Alfred Guidi and Jacques Oberson at the League of Nations Archives, Michael Van Fossen at the University of North Carolina, and the helpful staffs at the French Foreign Ministry archives in Nantes, the British National Archives in London, the U.S. National Archives in College Park, Maryland, the Prime Ministry Archives in

Ankara, the Hafez al-Assad Library in Damascus, the Cultural Center Library in Antakya, and Princeton University Special Collections.

I have benefited from conversation with colleagues in many places while working on this book, including Lisa Pollard, James Gelvin, Joshua Landis, Michael Hunt, and the History Department at Mustafa Kemal University in Antakya. Many, many thanks go to those who have taken the time to read previous versions, make helpful suggestions, ask difficult questions, and provide continuing support: Laurie Maffly-Kipp, Jane Thrailkill, Sheryl Kroen, John Sweets, Zeynep Turkyilmaz, Kathryn Burns, Yektan Turkyilmaz, Peter Sluglett, Marko Dumančić, Joy Reeder, and Brett Merryman. Many thanks to Süha Ünsal, Öktay Özel, and the now-defunct Nüvis, for carrying out the oral history project related to this research. Thanks also to Koray Cengiz and my other friends in Antakya who have hosted me and those who have taken time to tell me about their own experiences, especially Zeki Ural. I appreciate Mihrac Ural's permission to use family photographs, and Mehmet Saplama's agreement to let me include his photographs. Thanks to Bill Nelson for the maps and to Jane Merryman for the index. Thanks also to Susan Ferber, Joellyn Ausanka, the board at Oxford University Press, and my anonymous readers for their suggestions toward improving this book.

My friends have listened to my big questions with even greater patience, and helped me work through many of my ideas; thanks go to Ömür Kayıkcı, Hala Khdeer, Sahar Amer, Martine Antle, and Lisa Lindsay. Katie and Ian allowed themselves to be dragged from archive to archive nearly every summer for most of high school, when they might well have preferred other activities. They have always been unfailing in their patience and support for me and my projects, for which I am much more than grateful. And to William, who has lived with this book, has read too many drafts without complaint, has been consistently encouraging and endlessly helpful, I owe more than I can express. This book is dedicated to him, with the greatest thanks, for his love, his insight, and his presence.

NOTE ON NAMES AND TRANSLATIONS

The problems created by fracturing the commonalities of the past are evident on every page of this book and have created a serious challenge for the author. Most of the cities in the contested Sanjak gradually acquired two different names. Was the altercation at Karim's café in Rihaniye (transliterated from Arabic) or in Reyhanlı (Turkish spelling)? I have tried to provide place names consistently as they appear in 2010 international usage to make it easier for readers to actually locate them on maps. The index will provide alternative names.

Even more difficult, and central to the whole project, is the problem of personal names. The same four Arabic letters, for example, would be used to identify Muhammad in Syria and Mehmet in Turkey; four other Arabic letters could indicate Cemil in Turkey and Jamil in Syria. What should I call these men? The spelling I choose could, unfortunately, appear to assign an identity with which Muhammad/Mehmet or Cemil/Jamil might disagree. Hyphenating names would be completely unwieldy. I ask the reader's indulgence if I have provided inaccurate cues through the spellings of individual names. I hope it will remind readers of the common origins of the people of the Sanjak, the arbitrariness with which they were asked to "identify" themselves into mutually exclusive and externally constructed categories, and the confusion that resulted when people who had long been allowed multiple identities were informed that they could henceforth belong only to *either* one group or another.

Fezzes in the River

Introduction

Saydo's Argument

In the early afternoon of May 10, 1938, a chauffeur named Saydo sat chatting in front of a café in the town of Reyhanlı, in the Sanjak of Alexandretta. Haydar Hassan Musto and a group of friends saw Saydo, approached his table, and began screaming at him. Witnesses described the scene that followed: harsh words, blows, and revolvers brandished in the air. When prosecutors questioned the witnesses, however, most were unable to recount the crescendo of words as Haydar insulted Saydo's mother, demanded that Saydo declare himself to be an Arab, threatened to kill him if he claimed to be a Turk, and taunted him about the brimmed hat he was wearing. The witnesses were unable to recount the argument about whether Saydo should declare himself an Arab or a Turk because it had taken place in a language they did not understand: neither Arabic nor Turkish, but Kurdish.[1]

In Saydo's argument, the main participants were Kurds, but one Kurd was demanding that the other claim to be an Arab instead of registering as a Turk. Saydo's argument suggests that nationalism in the Middle East was somehow fluid—that people were not convinced they had single, fixed identities, or that their identities had to determine their political outlooks. This study examines how people in the Sanjak of Alexandretta struggled to articulate their complex set of allegiances and beliefs when the League of Nations demanded, in 1937, that every man declare his "identity."

Although Saydo's argument took place thousands of miles from Europe, it was one of the countless ripples reverberating from the Europeans' reinvention of the world at the end of World War I. The war had been catastrophic, leaving more than eight million people dead, another 21 million wounded, and making refugees of uncounted millions more. As diplomats, generals and politicians contemplated the future, they searched for clues on how to proceed. Like forensic investigators at an arson site, European statesmen shifted through the ashes of their old order to try to discover the causes of the inferno that seemed to have

Antioch, circa 1940. Courtesy of: Mehmet Saplama.

engulfed the world and forever transformed it. Their varied analyses of the causes of the war, added to their perceptions of the consequences of the peace, would produce over the next decades an array of ideological impulses ranging from a new liberalism, through communism, fascism, and Naziism.

That wide range of ideologies reflects the complexities of the questions facing Europe's leaders at the end of the Great War. What caused the war? How could Europe cope with frustrated nationalists, like the gunman who killed Francis Ferdinand? What kind of government—indeed, what type of state—should replace the expansive and autocratic empires just defeated? What should happen to the Asian and African colonies of the defeated powers? How could the colonial competition that had exacerbated European animosities be brought under control? To the urgency of finding answers in the ashes was joined the exciting possibilities inherent in vast reconstruction.

U.S. President Woodrow Wilson articulated the exhilarating potential of the new opportunities, insisting that the postwar settlements would constitute "a readjustment of those great injustices which underlie the whole structure of European and Asiatic society." Those great injustices, for Wilson, were rooted in the absence of democratic rule. The new postwar order would put all governments "in the hands of the people and taken out of the hands of coteries and of sovereigns, who had no right to rule over the people. It is a people's treaty, that accomplishes by a great sweep of practical justice the liberation of men who never could have liberated themselves. . . . The men who sat around the table in Paris knew that the time had come when the people were no longer going to consent to live under masters, but were going to live the lives that they chose themselves, to live under such governments as they chose themselves to erect. That is the fundamental principle of this great settlement."[2] It was a liberatory impulse that had led to the postwar settlements, he insisted, consonant with the demand for "self-determination of peoples" that he had articulated during his 1917 speech to the U.S. Congress.

The League of Nations was constructed as the embodiment of the new order and the repository of its hopes. Here, statesmen could work out their disagreements without recourse to war; in its chambers, people's grievances could be addressed before they escalated into revolution. Among the first projects of the League of Nations would be to legitimize the territorial settlements that resulted from the defeat of the enormous empires and to agree on a means for dealing with their colonies. Working from a set of assumptions about the superiority of nationalism and self-determination as the future of civilized Europe, the League of Nations carved out new nation-states, trying to satisfy potentially destabilizing nationalists where possible and creating a series of treaties to protect "minorities" when it became clear that each group claiming to be a nation could not be awarded an independent state.

But in the territories of the defeated Ottoman Empire, as in other areas of Asia and Africa, the statesmen controlling the League of Nations were loath to take "self-determination of peoples" so far that it would end their hold on colonial territories. Explaining that local populations were hardly civilized enough to be qualified to determine their own futures, the League of Nations assigned a European power to each of the new post-Ottoman states and to all of the former African and Asian colonial possessions. The League of Nations assigned the territories as mandates and assigned the mandatory power the task of helping them attain the level of discernment and administration required to become independent. The new system of mandates was to be administered through the League, though with extremely limited oversight.

The Sanjak of Alexandretta, where Saydo's argument took place, had been occupied by French troops at the end of World War I. In 1920, the League of Nations had included the Sanjak in the mandate for "Syria," one of many new countries the victorious European states carved out of the ruins of the Ottoman Empire, and assigned France the task of administering Syria while elevating its people to that lofty level of civilization at which they could become capable of ruling themselves. The years that followed were marked by repeated efforts by the Syrians to throw off French control. Finally, at the end of bloody riots in 1936, France negotiated a treaty of independence for the whole of its Syrian territories. Turkey continued to insist, however, that the Sanjak not be included within the new, independent Syrian state because of its large Turkish-speaking population, which should guarantee it a special status apart from the Arab Syrian state. Having only recently been forced to accept the loss of Mosul province to Iraq, the Turkish regime insisted on doing anything necessary to hold on to the Sanjak. France initially refused Turkey's claim, arguing that the League of Nations had given France the mandate for Syria, and that the mandate prohibited Paris from alienating any of Syria's territory. Both governments agreed to refer the case to the League of Nations for resolution.

The Republic of Turkey thus staked its claim to the Sanjak not on geopolitical grounds but on an assertion about identity: the population of the Sanjak, they argued, was Turkish. With this identity came a host of affective commitments; indeed, the story goes that the founder and hero of the new Turkey, Mustafa Kemal (later Atatürk), had been overcome on hearing Turkish spoken in the Sanjak while he was stationed there during World War I. He had vowed all those years before to include the Sanjak in his new state as soon as he was able. Most striking, however, was not that Turkey presented statistics to prove its claim, numbers the French could easily dispute, but instead the twin assumptions on which the claim was based. Turkey's argument before the Council of the League of Nations implied both that the *identity* of the population should determine the future of the territory and that a neighboring power had the right to intervene over issues of identity. Underpinning this claim was an assertion about the primacy of linguistic affiliation: Turkey could claim neighboring territory because the people there *spoke Turkish*. Under the Ottoman, Hapsburg, and Russian empires, claims had been made and territories defined on the basis of the power of the ruling family. Linguistic groups had lived for centuries divided among competing empires, and each empire had always contained more than one linguistic group. Now the Turks were playing by new rules—rules in which linguistic identity marked "national" affiliation, which in turn would determine territorial destiny.

But, as this book shows, these were not rules that Atatürk's new Turkish Republic had created. Rather, nationalism was the fundamental assumption behind the League of *Nations*; the League's ideology of nationalism provided a blueprint for allocating both power and territory. Thus, Turkish claims that the Sanjak should have special treatment because it was home to a preponderance of Turks resonated among the European states deliberating at the League's headquarters in Geneva. Irredentist claims, in which one country asserted its right to territory on the basis of the inhabitants' identity, had become the daily fare of the League of Nations by the time the French and Turkish governments brought up the question of the Sanjak of Alexandretta. Indeed, by 1936, when the dispute first garnered international attention, Germany had already left the League after its own territorial claims based on linguistic identity were frustrated. With the radical new ethnolinguistic definition of political identity, the League's problem in the Sanjak became simple: once it had devised a process to define accurately the people of the Sanjak, the League of Nations would know how to allocate the Sanjak's territory.

This new, widespread acceptance of the notion that the language of a territory's population indicated a distinct ethnic identity that defined its political affiliation was a marked departure from previous notions of belonging, and not only in the Ottoman Empire. Throughout Europe, states incorporated diverse linguistic groups, while at the same time excluding many people who spoke the majority language of the state; many tongues could be heard within Germany's borders, for example, and German was spoken by people who were citizens of other states. Censuses taken by the newly defeated Ottoman Empire had reflected only religious groups; linguistic groups like Turks, Kurds, and Arabs never made sense under Ottoman imperial ideology. The Ottoman Empire that had ruled the Sanjak for centuries before Saydo's argument was hardly Turkish. It was a polyglot, multiethnic empire, home to many religious groups, and held together by its ruling family, the descendants of Osman. That remarkable diversity was quite evident in the Sanjak of Alexandretta, where people often spoke more than one language, where Kurds married Turks, Arabs married Kurds, and the church steeples were easily visible from neighboring minarets. This is not to

assert that the Ottoman Empire was a stranger to discord but that Ottoman conflicts during its first six hundred years of existence played out along lines not
defined by language. As the story of Saydo suggests, the lines dividing "ethnic
groups" were still porous in 1938, with Kurdish-speakers in this court case arguing over whether to "be" Turks or Arabs.

This new focus on the pivotal role of language and identity in political deci-
sion-making accompanied the notions of popular sovereignty and liberal democracy that emerged victorious with the defeat of the old-style Ottoman and
Hapsburg empires during World War I. In the postwar world, it was "the people"
who would rule themselves and determine their own destinies. But who were
"the people"? The nationalism mobilized to answer this question was a European corollary of the Enlightenment notion that legitimate rule comes from the
consent of the governed. Each territory's people were to be permitted to plot its
own collective political trajectory. First, the collective ("nation") had to be identified, and defined (in the new ideological world of the 1920s and 1930s) on the
basis of the common identities of the population. The reasoning was curiously
circular: the "nation-building" of the League of Nations began by positing (or
"planting") a national identity, which the League then had to affirm, verify, and
validate, all the while asserting that this identity was, a priori, an already-extant
foundation for the "nation" that the League then insisted would naturally represent the people with this national identity.

In the lands of the Habsburgs and the Ottomans, however, this nation-building
project was complicated by centuries in which mixed populations had lived in
close proximity, a multilinguistic history that had left its legacies in the multiple
vernaculars of the population. Each state the League created from the empires'
ruins contained not only the "nation" that defined it, but a host of other groups
speaking different languages. What was to be done about those whose identity
did not match that of the anointed "people" in the new states? The fate of "minorities" became arguably Europe's greatest crisis during and after World War I,
leading to massacres, expulsions, ethnic cleansing, and genocide. When the
League of Nations legitimized Europe's long-standing desire for hegemony over
territories to its south and east by giving the European Great Powers the mandates
that provided control over Asia, Africa, and the Middle East, the League brought
the "minorities question" with it in its baggage.

After France (then in control of Syria) and Turkey turned to the League in
1936 with their dispute over the Sanjak of Alexandretta, the contestation of the
identity of the population would become a crucial determinant of the Sanjak's
fate. In the League's understanding of the universal human condition, each individual had one identity, which was imagined to be fixed, impermeable, and fundamental. The League planned to decide whether the Sanjak "belonged" in Syria
or in Turkey by analyzing the preponderance of the people: was more of the

population "Syrian" or "Turkish?" It would be necessary to count the numbers of Turks, Arabs, Kurds, and others who lived within the Sanjak.

Yet as Saydo's argument suggests, identity on the ground in the 1930s Middle East was much more complicated than the League of Nations had imagined. The province of Alexandretta was called home by people who spoke Arabic, Turkish, Armenian, Kurdish, and Greek, and whose community worship took place on Fridays, Saturdays, and Sundays. Moreover, religious differences embraced far more variety than Muslims, Jews, and Christians. Christian groups included the Orthodox, Catholics, Armenians, and Protestants; Muslims were predominantly Sunni or Alawi. To say that these groups had simply "coexisted" over four centuries of Ottoman rule, though, would imply that they were somehow mutually exclusive. Instead, they had mingled, merged, and crisscrossed as linguistic and religious identities intersected. By the time the Ottoman Empire was defeated at the end of World War I, the people of the Sanjak of Alexandretta had affiliations that were overlapping and multiple, comprising a society that could be likened to a mosaic only if some of the tiles could be layered atop adjoining tiles.

Nonetheless, European political ideologies *required* the nation, and the Turkish government made its argument about the Sanjak by claiming that "the Turks" there constituted a majority. The new Turkish republic, established in 1923, was based on the same kind of nationalist ideology that was so much in vogue in Europe during the interwar period. It was founded by a group of nationalist officers led by Mustafa Kemal who rejected the treaty imposed on the Ottoman Empire by the victorious World War I powers. After defeating the World War I allies in Turkey's war of independence, the group created a modern republic in the central lands of the former Ottoman Empire. The new Turkish republic adapted its Ottoman past, defining its new identity as Turkish, modern, secular, and Western-leaning. Indeed, by the 1930s, nationalism was such a central element in the ideology of the new state that the Turkish government created a foundational myth to explain its interest in the Sanjak, and pressed the Sanjak into service as a stage on which to perform national identity. The Turkish government's "invention of tradition" included not only new narratives about the origins and significance of the Turks but also the "rediscovery" of specifically Turkish folk music and poetry and the creation of new national habits: anthems, flags, even costumes. The Sanjak's Turkish nationalists not only wore but even enforced the wearing of the symbolic Western-style brimmed hats that had come to connote the new Turkishness. This was, indeed, the sort of hat Saydo was wearing when he was accosted by Haydar.

Syrian political identity, by contrast, was chiefly anticolonial, aimed less at the creation of a Syrian nation than at eliminating the hated French occupation. Historians have debated the nature and extent of Syrian or Arab nationalism. However, like many groups in the late Hapsburg Empire who had claimed for themselves a separate identity and political future, some Ottoman Arab elites by the early 1900s were calling for recognition of their Arabness, even if not independence. After the defeat of the Ottoman Empire, while Turkey was remaking itself as a nationalist republic, Arab populations were straining against the European control institutionalized as the League of Nations mandates, and their collective political efforts worked not so much to define who they were as to eliminate the foreign European occupiers.[3]

When Turkey made its claim to the Sanjak, then, it was France, not Syria, that determined the course and the outcome of the struggle. The 1936 treaty giving Syria its independence had been neither ratified nor implemented. The Syrian government-in-training, led by Jamil Mardam, had no control over the country and little room to maneuver. Focusing their emerging ideology and their activism on gaining Syria's sovereignty left the Damascus government unprepared for a struggle based on internal identities and, in any case, hardly a fair match for the organized nationalism of the government in Ankara. During the course of the struggle over the Sanjak, Syrian and Arab nationalist ideologies grew, especially under the leadership of Zaki al-Arsuzi, who would later become one of the major thinkers behind the Ba'ath party. But when Saydo met his antagonist, the Damascus government-in-waiting was ill-prepared to advanced nationalist claims to territory based on ideologies not yet developed.

Saydo's argument, related in the documents of the League of Nations Special Tribunal, is only one of many cases adjudicating the violence that accompanied the effort to register people to vote in the first elections of the independent Sanjak. Collectively, the court testimonies demonstrate that national identities were neither fixed nor mutually exclusive during the decades immediately following the destruction of the Ottoman Empire. Over and over, witnesses brought before the Special Tribunal recounted stories of the Sanjak's people changing their identities for political or economic reasons. As I pondered these cases, my conviction grew that the people of the Sanjak of Alexandretta had multiple and porous identities, and that examining the court records and the context in which they were embedded would tell a new story about how people perceived their collective identities.

The question of national identity in the Sanjak is not—and was not—merely an academic enterprise. Disputes over identity worsened over the three-year course of the Sanjak dispute. Turkish nationalists and Syrian nationalists hardened their positions and tried to find adherents within local communities, with violent consequences. By the time the League of Nations ended its role in the affair in 1938, demonstrations and harassment had given way to arson and murder. The process of displaying nationalism had become deadly.

Yet the bloody spectacle on the Sanjak stage had no role whatsoever in the outcome of the contest. Instead, the Sanjak's fate was decided by a backroom deal in Geneva made while the League was discussing the question in official session. The outcome was a travesty of the League's stated principles about self-determination, as the French colonial occupiers collaborated with the Ankara regime to circumvent the established electoral system and "create" a Turkish majority where none existed. In the end, the dispute over the Sanjak would hinge not on nationalities, but on France's own strategic needs as it weighed its obligations to its Syrian charges against the changing climate in late 1930s Europe. This book argues that it was European needs, not Middle Eastern identities, that determined the Sanjak's fate. In this way, the Sanjak question reflects broader European concerns of the period.

My account of the Sanjak question engages two of the urgent issues of the decades after World War I. If one of the most significant themes that defined the League of Nations and the international community at large during the 1930s was self-determination (and its shadow, the minorities question), the other was certainly appeasement. Appeasement became after the 1930s a term of opprobrium suggesting huge and dangerous compromise. Faced with the nationalist German leadership's insistence on claiming neighboring territory, European leaders agreed again and again to give Berlin what it demanded in order to avoid conflict.

In the Sanjak, too, the outcome was based on France's fear, this time her anxiety about the consequences of alienating Turkey. The Paris government was adamant about keeping the government of the new Turkish republic on its own side during the threatening European war, insistent that Atatürk not repeat the fatal mistake of his Ottoman predecessors. Many decision-makers in Paris and Geneva were convinced that Turkey's loyalty hinged on the outcome of the Sanjak question. In the face of the looming war, the government of France gave the Turkish government whatever it sought, hoping thereby to neutralize Turkey, and thus guarantee anti-German forces a nonhostile regime in the eastern Mediterranean and access to Turkey's Straits and the Black Sea.

In French calculations, consideration of the Syria mandate took second place to France's own strategic interests in the approaching war, an outcome hardly inconsistent with the nature and origin of the mandate system. After all, the League of Nations mandates had provided a novel compromise that allowed European powers to extend their control over other world areas while at the same time providing the facade of self-determination that Wilsonian ideology demanded. Colonialism had become unacceptable in the ideological aftermath of World War I, as articulated by Woodrow Wilson in his Fourteen Points speech to Congress in 1918, but Europe's Great Powers had been unwilling to relinquish their empires. The League's mandate system responded to these calls for self-determination, allowing European governments to reconfigure their former colonies in a way that could provide a facade of self-rule while continuing Great

Power hegemony over Asia and Africa. The mandates served European interests, under the guise of providing mentoring so that their former colonies, now mandates, could attain the maturity required for independence. Mandates in Africa were even more rigid than those in the Middle East, where the populations had been promised at least some semblance of self-rule. Nonetheless, the mandate system was quite flexible in permitting the continuation, even the expansion, of European control. For at least some in Paris, then, the Syria mandate was to benefit France; if it had to be altered to serve French interests, there could be little room for noble regrets.

Policy-makers in Paris, although cognizant of their responsibilities to the people of Syria that resulted from their mandate over the territory, made their decisions primarily on the basis of considerations of French diplomatic and military requirements. Having acquiesced in the League of Nations' politics of identity that insisted local populations would determine their own futures, French officials set in train a process of polarization in the Sanjak in which mutual regard gave way to violence as newly empowered identity groups consolidated their separateness and competed for adherents. As the process was turning violent, the French turned their back on the whole project, walking away from the League's insistence on identifying the national affiliations of the people in favor of a back-door deal with Turkey that ignored any semblance of self-determination or the consent of the governed.

Despite the sub-rosa process by which the Sanjak of Alexandretta became part of the Republic of Turkey, the ideology of self-determination has been seen as so essential to legitimate government that the fiction has been maintained for decades. Today's Turkish citizens "know" that the population of the Sanjak "voted" to join Turkey. Turkish narratives, interviews, and memoirs reverberate with nationalist pride over the Sanjak that was "returned" to Turkey through the wishes of the people.

Like any victory narrative, this tale eschews accuracy and nuance in favor of simplicity and parable. Although Turkey and Syria have begun the process of opening their borders to each other, Saydo's argument retains a broader significance. In the name of self-determination of peoples, communities were divided, neighbors became hostile, and exclusionary identities were the presumed new normalcy. The ambiguity so common in Saydo's world—where an individual could claim more than one collective or change affiliation as needed—continues to give way to violent conflict as outsiders insist that "peace" is dependent on the creation of ethnic, linguistic or religious homogeneity. The story of Saydo and his neighbors offers a glimpse into how animosities can be created and conflict fomented, challenging the notion that essential identities are unchanging and hence necessarily divisive.

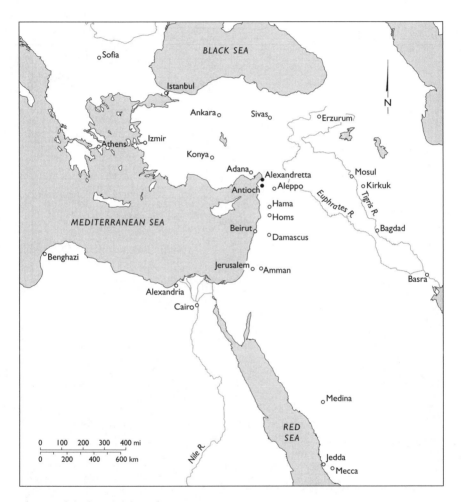

The Sanjak in the Eastern Mediterranean

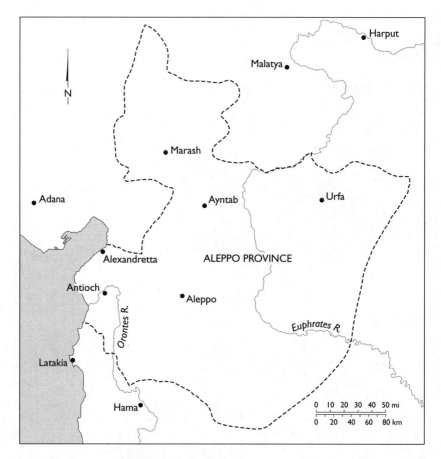

Ottoman Province of Aleppo, Nineteenth Century

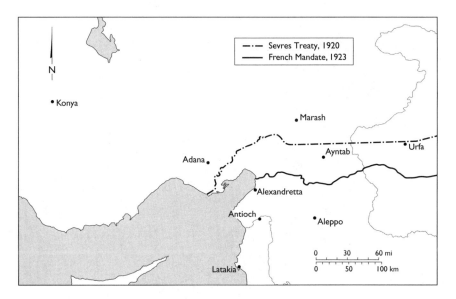

Treaty Borders

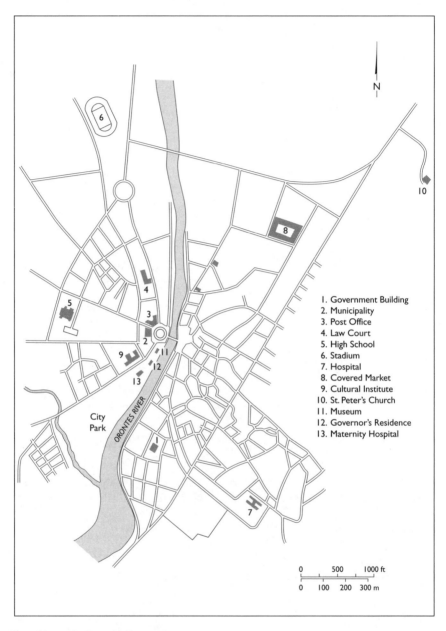

N

1. Government Building
2. Municipality
3. Post Office
4. Law Court
5. High School
6. Stadium
7. Hospital
8. Covered Market
9. Cultural Institute
10. St. Peter's Church
11. Museum
12. Governor's Residence
13. Maternity Hospital

City
Park

ORONTES RIVER

0   500   1000 ft
0   100   200   300 m

City of Antioch, Circa 1940

|| 1 ||

Fezzes and Hats

Antioch's markets pulsed with the hum and clatter of the craftsmen's instruments and the cries of its peddlers. From the shops and the streets wafted conversations and sales jingles in Arabic, in Turkish, and in various mixtures of the two languages, to which certain French words were added, "bizarrely pronounced." In the words of government official Pierre Bazantay, it could seem either an untranslatable music—or cacophony.[1]

These markets stretched for miles from their entrance just beyond the bridge over the Orontes (Asi) River, snaking their way in the direction of the mountains overlooking the Sanjak of Alexandretta's largest city. On any given day, the people of the city mixed with those who came in to sell or to shop. Muslims, Christians, and Jews, Turks, Arabs, and Kurds greeted and jostled each other in the market, which housed not only the shops where people purchased their produce and clothing but also the workshops where many of the area's goods were manufactured. People returned home along Antioch's narrow streets, which wound along the riverbank and up toward the hillside that was home to the ancient Cave of St. Peter, the cave in the mountains above Antioch that had served as the first Christian church. Indeed, Antioch had long been a city of enormous importance to Christians. St. Peter and St. Paul lived in Antioch in the early years after the death of Christ, and the city became home to a patriarchate and a center of Christian life.

But the Christians had not been the first to consider Antioch's site important. Long before the birth of Christ, its location on the Orontes River had drawn the attention of traders and emperors, who had built towns that meandered along the river's path. One of Alexander the Great's generals founded Antioch around 300 BCE. By the early Roman period, the city boasted a population of close to half a million people, making it the third largest city in the world (after Rome and Alexandria). It was controlled in succession by Persians, Byzantines, Arabs, Armenians, Seljuks, and Crusaders before becoming part of the Ottoman

Bridge over the Orontes River, downtown Antioch. Courtesy of: Mehmet Saplama.

Empire in 1516. From the Ottoman conquest on, Antioch was attached to its neighbor, Aleppo, and stood midway between that great international emporium and its port in Alexandretta.

Alexandretta, for which the Sanjak was named, is a coastal city, commanding a protected, accessible bay on the Mediterranean to its east and controlling the pass through the mountains by which invaders marched west and north toward Anatolia. Through the end of the nineteenth century, Alexandretta was the port for goods carried on donkeys' backs from northern Syria and by camel caravans from Iraq. It had functioned for centuries as Aleppo's outlet to the sea, and Aleppo's role as one of the largest European trading centers of the entire Ottoman Empire had reinforced Alexandretta's significance.

Most of the Sanjak's forty-seven hundred square kilometers, however, was rural—acres and acres of farmland scattered with small villages and the market towns to which the cultivators were drawn. Like most of the rest of northern Syria, the people of the Sanjak grew olives, wheat, and vegetables, raised animals, and manufactured many of the products needed by the regional population.[2]

That population was remarkably diverse, a legacy of those many groups who had crossed, conquered, and settled the region. By the early 1930s, five languages were heard commonly in the streets: Arabic, Turkish, Kurdish, Circassian, and Armenian. The city of Antioch boasted a number of places of worship: three Armenian institutions (Gregorian, Protestant, and Catholic), a variety of Catholic congregations (Chaldean, Syriac, Latin, Greek, and Maronite), and Jewish and Greek Orthodox groups—in addition to its many mosques.[3]

Although little has been written about how the local people responded to such remarkable variety, it is likely that Antioch's population shared the outlook of their neighbors in the regional hub city of Aleppo, a mere forty-five kilometers away. Aleppines thought of their great diversity as a positive sign, reflecting their role as a center of commerce: the city's human diversity reflected its importance.[4] In any case, linguistic diversity was so common that most people spoke more than two languages. Far from determining one's national identity, language was an instrument for commerce, prayer, and government—and often a different language would be used for each.[5]

The people of the Sanjak of Alexandretta had been under Ottoman rule since 1516. In the Ottoman world, group affinity had been based not on language but on religion. Muslims were the majority, and Islam the official religion of the empire. Under Ottoman rule, non-Muslim communities were officially recognized, even permitted to implement their own laws and allocate their own taxes. Censuses counted Muslims, varied Christian groups, and Jews. Although the Sanjak was home to two schismatic Muslim groups, the Alawis and the Druze, they were still counted as Muslim in the Ottoman census.

At the end of World War I, France occupied the Ottoman provinces south of the Taurus mountains. Although the Ottoman government had not been party to the Allies' secret wartime agreements that would dismember the empire, the sultan signed terms of surrender at Sèvres that divided his realms among the victorious European powers. Refusing to accept the Sèvres Treaty, Turkish nationalists began a struggle against invading Greek, French, British, and Italian forces that continued even as the Allied Supreme Council at San Remo, Italy, awarded France the mandate over Syria on April 28, 1920. Exhausted from World War I, and fearing that fighting just north of its new Syrian territories would continue, France broke ranks with its European allies and concluded a separate peace with the new Turkish leadership on October 20, 1921, the Ankara Treaty. The agreement ended hostilities between France and Turkey, ceded Cilicia to Turkish forces, created a boundary between France's zone in Syria and the nascent Turkish republic, provided for an exchange of prisoners, and confirmed the rights of minorities. During the treaty talks, Turkey insisted that a special status be provided for the Sanjak. As a result, article 7 of the treaty read: "A special administrative regime shall be established for the district of Alexandretta. The Turkish inhabitants of this district shall enjoy every facility for their cultural development. The Turkish language shall have official recognition."[6]

For the French authorities in Syria, Turkish leaders' demand for special recognition for a Turkish minority would have seemed neither peculiar nor unwelcome. French officials had themselves emphasized differences within the Syrian population, reflecting the fusion of their scientific fascination with human racial taxonomy and their long-term fixation with protecting "minorities." France, Great Britain, and Russia had all exploited the presence of religious minority groups since the early 1800s in the Ottoman Empire to justify their intervention in the Sultan's realms. Their claims that Muslim governments routinely persecuted non-Muslim minorities took no account of the long centuries of peaceful coexistence during periods of Muslim rule in Spain, the Balkans, and the Middle East. Clinging tightly to their own notions about Islam's violent intolerance, and conforming to a long tradition of accusations that dated back even before the Crusades, Europeans insisted that they were forced to intrude into Ottoman domains to defend the rights of non-Muslims. Their accusations led directly to increasing European military intervention and to control over parts of the Ottoman state. The Russian Empire initiated the Crimean War ostensibly over the rights of the Ottoman Empire's Christian Orthodox minority; the French used a similar argument to justify their occupation of Mount Lebanon in 1860. Britain insisted that its interventions in Lebanon were to support Druze rights; in Palestine Britain claimed to be needed to support the Jews.[7]

Mobilizing the old argument that the French presence would guarantee the rights of "minorities," the French divided Syria into enclaves as soon as

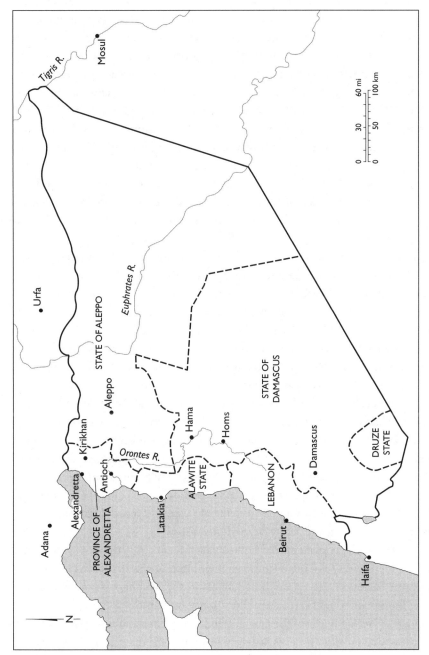

France Divides the Mandate, Circa 1922

France took control in 1920. They created a separate Alawi entity in Latakia and a special Druze one in the south, ostensibly to protect these nonorthodox Muslim groups from oppression by the majority. Mount Lebanon and the coastal strip to its west had already been set off as a separate state. To finish the project, the French divided the north from the south, separating Aleppo from Damascus. It is clear, however, that these "protective" measures were instead a central part of France's strategy in the face of widespread anti-occupation demonstrations of the 1920s and 1930s, anti-French activism that included many of these minorities. If the country could be divided and the populations separated and marked as different, unrelated, and mutually hostile, it would be more difficult for them to collaborate in their anti-imperial activism. In addition, it seems, the French feared an upsurge of Sunni anti-Western sentiment, and wished to reduce easy contact among the people of the mandate.[8] Separating off the Sanjak of Alexandretta created yet one more exclusive area, "protecting" Turkish residents from the oppression of their non-Turkish neighbors.

The French mandatory regime's wishful thinking about the inherent, essential, and irreconcilable differences among the Sanjak's people would be difficult to apply in practice. Bazantay, a local Armenian notable working with the colonial regime, was pessimistic about France's desire to demarcate ethnic categories in the Sanjak. It would not be possible, he said, to "establish a clear classification of the population, based solely on ethnic characteristics. The races have, over the course of the centuries, gone through so much mixing that it is difficult now to distinguish them." There was internal diversity even within religious and linguistic categories, he explained. For example, he pointed out, Sunni Muslims spoke Arabic, Turkish, Circassian, and Kurdish. If instead one began with the language group as the "differentiating character," one could see even greater heterogeneity: "Orthodox Christians, Catholics, Alawis, and Arab Muslim Sunnis use, in effect, Arabic as a common language."[9] As Bazantay pointed out, no cleavages cleanly divided either linguistic or religious groups in the Sanjak, making it quite difficult for the colonial regime to delineate clearly defined "minorities" who needed protection from clearly defined "majorities."

The Sanjak's special status did not insulate it from either the economic or the political ferment of the region surrounding it during the 1920s and 1930s. The interwar period saw the growth of schools in the Middle East; young people from the Sanjak sought secondary education at institutions in Syria, Egypt, Lebanon, and Turkey. Some of the Sanjak's students rubbed shoulders with activists whose anticolonial sentiments had been evident in the massive uprisings against British and French control; others lived in the Republic of Turkey, where they not only learned about a new style of government but also witnessed the elaboration of an extensive nationalist ideology. Members of an educated young elite brought new ways of understanding not only the politics of the Middle East but also the role of Europeans, and the nature of communities.[10] If anything, the Sanjak's special situation opened still further the floodgates of the ideological currents that swept over the interwar Middle East.

The Sanjak's ambiguous status as an autonomous province that was simultaneously part of Syria *and* committed to protecting the language and culture of its Turkish residents facilitated the spread of new ideologies, as advocates of Syrian independence and supporters of the new Turkish nationalism displayed their growing political allegiances in the streets and shops of the Sanjak's cities. Violence flared in Antioch during the summer of 1936 as local supporters of Turkey battled the city's security forces.

The incident began at a circus, over a hat. Mehmet, whom the French administrators of Syria would have labeled "chapiste" to indicate the brimmed hat he was wearing, was watching the spectacle in Antioch on July 3, 1936, when a drunken spectator—a soldier stationed in the local garrison—grabbed Mehmet's hat and threw it on the ground. As Mehmet became incensed, the soldier responded by crushing the hat under his foot. The drunken soldier's comrades intervened on behalf of the hat-smasher, while "civilians" (according to the French report) sided with Mehmet. Civilians and soldiers exchanged blows and rocks, and the crowd swelled as the adversaries left the circus to take their altercation to the streets outside.

The night watchman sounded the alarm, but the police patrol arriving on the scene was unable to stop the combatants, who by now were supported by a crowd of nearly five hundred people. Local commanders ordered the soldiers back to their barracks, which left an excited crowd on the streets. For some in the crowd, Mehmet's brimmed hat symbolized much more than a mere head covering. It had become a new symbol of group identity, which now lay—literally—trampled by the soldier: "We will die instead of going back. Until when are we going to bear this insult? Death is preferable!" Pursuing the soldiers toward the direction of the barracks, the swelling crowd wavered when confronted with a triumvirate: the provincial governor (Kaymakam), a leader of the local Turkish community, and an officer of the security services. Most of the crowd dispersed as the officials demanded, while one group pressed on, hurling stones at the soldiers when they reached the barracks. When the police brigadier and his agents turned them back, the crowd returned home singing the Turkish national anthem.[11]

The brimmed hat that set off the evening's events was the most potent and ubiquitous symbol of the new Turk. A new way of thinking about identity had emerged from the postwar struggle over Anatolia. The defeated Ottoman sultan had signed the Sèvres Treaty at the end of World War I giving much of western

Anatolia to Greece, creating an Armenian state in the east, signing over the Ottoman Arab provinces to Britain and France, and leaving open the possibility of a Kurdish state in the southeast. When Greek troops landed in 1919 to stake their claim to their assigned part of the peninsula, grassroots forces joined outlaw Ottoman military troops led by Mustafa Kemal to contest the Allies' plan to dismember the central Ottoman lands. A nascent anticolonial struggle consolidated its hold on the Anatolian population. Insisting that the Ottoman sultan's agreements were illegitimate because he had been forced to act under foreign occupation, Mustafa Kemal and his allies created a Grand National Assembly that claimed to be the repository of legitimate power as long as the foreign occupation compromised the sultan's authority. By the time these forces—acting on behalf of the "Turkish nation"—had defeated the Greeks, they had been accepted in their own right as the legitimate leaders of the state—under the sultan, of course. The Treaty of Lausanne, signed in 1923, officially ended hostilities and provided international recognition for the new Republic of Turkey.

During the years that followed, those victorious forces struggled to define the nation in whose name they now ruled. Would the new nation be restricted to all Turks? If so, how was "Turk" to be defined? During the last decades of the Ottoman Empire, the definition of "Turk" proved to be unstable—at times used narrowly to indicate backward rural people, at others used as a synonym for "Muslim" and, in the writings of nineteenth-century poet Namik Kemal, to suggest membership in a distinctive, ethnically specific collective. Would it include all Muslims, and Muslims only? Having won the struggle against Greek invaders, who had been partly supported by the indigenous Greek Orthodox population, this seemed to some like an appealing option.[12]

The new Turkish identity that emerged from this postwar anti-occupation struggle was delimited, codified, and advocated by the war hero Kemal. Taking sole power with the dissolution of the Sultanate in 1922, the new leader emphasized nationalism, secularism, and "modern" European practices, including the use of surnames. The nation was defined as "Turkish," a territorial designation that included all those who lived within the new borders—with the exception of those Orthodox Christians forced to emigrate to Greece.[13] Becoming president of the new Republic of Turkey the following year, Mustafa Kemal took the new surname Atatürk (Father Turk). He was photographed frequently wearing the brimmed European headgear he insisted was the only appropriate head covering for modern societies. Dispensing with the bygone era's fez, turban, and veil became de rigueur for anyone hoping to signify support for Turkey's new nationalist and secular regime.

At the same time, those who rejected Atatürk's secular, republican, and nationalist program also focused on the hat. Indeed, the first documented dispute in the Sanjak over hats took place *within* the Turkish community, a decade after Atatürk and his supporters established the new nation. At four o'clock in the afternoon on December 10, 1934, Hoca Kürd Muhammad Efendi, imam of Antioch's central mosque, began his theology lesson at Yeni Cami by weighing in on the new fashion, clearly linking the hat with secularism and the new government in Turkey: "If in Turkey the believers wear the hat, it is because they are forced by the government. Here, thanks to God, the government leaves us completely free. As a result, true Muslims should not wear this head covering." As grumbling began among some of those present, an incensed artisan sitting near the imam removed his brimmed hat and put it on the stool directly in front of the preacher. The imam flung it far across the room. In the ensuing clamor, the hat owner left the mosque and collected some of his friends to confront the imam. A group of anti-hat local Muslim notables gathered to protect the imam as he made his way home. That evening, local police, worried about retaliation against the imam by angry hat-wearers, stood guard at the Habib Neccar mosque as he led prayers. All was quiet. At ten the next morning, however, a dozen people were injured when "Turkish youth" (hat-wearers) fought against the partisans of the imam. One of those wounded, Selim Çelenk, was the editor of Antioch's daily Turkish-language journal *Yeni Gün*.[14]

The Turkish-speaking elite of Antioch found themselves divided over the incident. Members of the important Bereket and Kuseyri families led the anti-hat-wearing contingent. By contrast, prominent attorneys Vedi Munir and Abdulgani Türkmen (who would become leaders of the Sanjak's Kemalist movement) stepped in—as hat-wearers—to avert the violence that threatened.[15]

More than a decade after the creation of the Republic of Turkey, Antioch's Turkish leadership remained divided over the Atatürk projects that hat-wearing symbolized. Early in the 1930s, Antioch's highest ranking religious scholar—the mufti—had coordinated a Kemalist group of Antioch's old elites to support Atatürk's regime, but by early 1936, French officials believed that the struggle between the Kemalists and the traditionalists had been resolved in favor of the anti-hat-wearing (non-Kemalist) faction. Barely two months before the circus riot, in fact, one French official claimed that the outgoing provincial governor, Ibrahim Edhem Bey al Moumen, had managed to calm what he called the "Turkish political currents" during his term (1924 to April 1936). Because of Ibrahim Edhem Bey's courage, the official claimed, Turkish nationalist acts had ceased, and "if there exist still in the Sanjak Kemalist sympathizers, it [the movement] is made up only of isolated people, whose range of action does not exceed a very small and politically limited clientele."[16] The circus riot must have caught the French authorities in Antioch by surprise. Clearly, a large group was still willing to take to the streets—either simply in opposition to the French soldiers or over honor, hats, and Turkish identity.

The successful nationalist struggle that expelled foreign invaders from Anatolia and overturned the Treaty of Sèvres was not replicated in neighboring Syria. While Atatürk and his colleagues had struggled against the Allies' plans to dismember Anatolia, France had taken charge of Syria as a League of Nations Mandate. French troops faced down not only the supporters of Emir Faysal, who had worked with Great Britain to defeat the Ottomans during the war, but also defeated a loose popular coalition in rebellion against French rule.[17] Despite overwhelming antipathy against France and the notion of French control within the mandated territory, the wartime Sykes-Picot agreement between Paris and London had allocated Syria to the French, the San Remo Resolution of 1920 had confirmed it, and the newly formed League of Nations ratified the deal.[18] French forces brutally suppressed the revolt and created a French administration in Damascus; Britain would soon designate the ejected Faysal as their candidate to become king of Iraq.

The mandate institution administered by the League of Nations assigned the African and Asian territories of the defeated empires to the victorious Allies. According to the League of Nations, mandates were to be applied to "peoples not yet able to stand by themselves under the strenuous conditions of the modern world." The tutelage of such peoples was to be entrusted to advanced nations who could best undertake this responsibility by reason of their resources, their experience, or their geographical position. Mandates in Africa—known as type B or C mandates, almost a regency status—accorded the European mandatory powers extensive control with which to bring their immature charges to political maturity. The former Ottoman territories, acknowledged to be more advanced while still needing instruction and counsel, were assigned a type A mandate. This was a high-minded pursuit, according to the writers of the League of Nations Covenant that created the system: "The well-being and development of such peoples form a sacred trust of civilisation." Although the mandatory powers were expected to make annual reports to the League of Nations Permanent Mandates Commission, article 22 of the Covenant did not impose a mechanism by which the League could control the European mandatories.[19] Indeed, no provision was included to define when the inhabitants of these territories would be eligible for full membership in the modern world, or when the Europeans would be freed of their "sacred trust."

The people of Syria were hardly convinced of this need for tutelage and rebelled repeatedly against French rule. The French mandatory government implemented a range of colonial strategies to quell the violence and neutralize the opposition, from bombing and the destruction of large residential areas to intelligence surveillance and infiltration to the creation of representative institutions.[20] Finally, at the end of a long strike in 1936, the French agreed to negotiate an independence treaty, and the leaders of Syria's National Bloc government traveled to Paris to begin negotiations with France's Popular Front government.[21]

After sixteen years of chafing under French control, Syrian leaders returned triumphantly from Paris in September 1936, bringing with them a Franco-Syrian Treaty that promised Syria's independence. The Syrian delegation stopped in Istanbul before returning to Damascus, arriving on the Orient Express on September 23, 1936. They were met with the warm greetings of the French chargé d'affaires in Turkey, the lieutenant governor of Istanbul, and a great many resident Syrians. The next day, in a gesture that dramatized their acknowledgment of Turkey's national project, Syrian leaders left flowers at the foot of the monument to the new Turkish republic.

La République, Istanbul's French-language daily, printed the statement of Hashim al-Atasi, Syria's president and head of the visiting delegation. Thrilled by the new Franco-Syrian Treaty, the Syrian leader proclaimed his respect and friendship toward Turkey. "I am very happy to have the occasion to express my profound and eternal affection toward Atatürk and the Turkish nation." There was no doubt, he stated, that Turkey would be delighted with Syria's forthcoming independence. The ties uniting Turks and Arabs went back thirteen hundred years, he pointed out, and he was certain their "brotherly friendship" would extend into the future.

Outlining his National Bloc's dreams for Syria's independent future al-Atasi said he envisaged a democratic regime, "the most perfect form of government." He promised that as soon as his delegation arrived in Damascus, they would conduct legislative elections, constitute a Chamber of Deputies, form a cabinet, and elect a president of the republic. This new Chamber would ratify the Franco-Syrian treaty, organize an army, and begin the reforms needed to revive the country. Within three years, he predicted, Syria would be admitted to the League of Nations. He ended his speech with the promise that the rights and powers Antioch and Alexandretta enjoyed under their autonomous administration would be continued under the Syrian government.[22]

The Turks were initially bewildered. It soon became clear that the status of the Sanjak, which topped their list of concerns, had been largely ignored by the Syrian leaders. Hardly pausing over the Syrian nationalists' dreams for Syria's future, a reporter demanded, "Then no change for Antioch and Alexandretta? Before it was the French mandate . . . and now the Syrian mandate replaces it?" "Yes," replied al-Atasi. "There is no change in the situation. Antioch and Alexandretta will keep the same rights as during the French mandate."

La République seemed incredulous that Syria's leaders had not only neglected to draw up special provisions for the Sanjak in the Franco-Syrian Treaty, but had, indeed, apparently paid no attention at all to its special status. "We are obliged to declare that the speech of the Syrian delegates on the subject of Alexandretta and its hinterland are entirely unclear. Having opposed in principle the system of mandates, we are pleased with the current arrangements that seem to ensure deliverance for Syria. . . . But we do not accept that Syria's mandate would be applied to Alexandretta and its hinterland." *La République* demanded the application of the Ankara Treaty of 1921 in both letter and spirit and declared, "if that is difficult, it is a very short road to proclaiming the independence of Alexandretta and its hinterland."[23] Completely focused on their pursuit of independence from French control, the Syrian negotiators had spent little time considering the future of the special administrative unit. The Sanjak was, after all, simply part of the Syrian mandate; its only defining feature in their eyes was the promise to provide opportunities within it for the cultural and linguistic needs of Turkish-speakers. They were stunned by the Turkish fixation with the area, and tried to remedy the situation with another interview. Faced with growing anger in the Turkish press, President al-Atasi's secretary, Naim Antaki, claimed that al-Atasi's words had been misunderstood. Antaki, a thirty-three-year-old lawyer, backpedaled. "I note with regret that this question was made the object of a misunderstanding in today's Istanbul journals. There is still nothing definitive on this subject." Subsidiary questions would only be taken up in Syria after the elections and the treaty's ratification. The Turkish press was hardly satisfied.

"Doesn't the new treaty have special clauses concerning Alexandretta and Antioch?" a reporter asked.

"I don't know," Antaki responded. "We know nothing. The French have acted until now as they want. They have promulgated a heap of laws and decrees. We will study all of these acts separately."

The reporter continued, "The French concluded a treaty in 1921 [i.e., The Ankara Treaty] including the concession of autonomy to Alexandretta and Antioch. Will this treaty be examined by you?"

Again, "I don't know."

The reporter pressed: "That is to say that you would study the question of according autonomy to these two regions?"

Antaki responded, "Instead of saying something inaccurate, it is better to affirm one's ignorance. Thus, I would tell you once again, I know nothing."

Apparently unsatisfied, the reporter tried yet again. "But, by the new treaty that you have signed, haven't you recognized all the international engagements contracted by France in the name of Syria?"

"Yes, the treaty includes an article to that effect."

"In that case, you have accepted in principle to accord autonomy to the regions of Antioch and Alexandretta in conformity with the dispositions of the treaty signed in 1921 by M. Franklin-Bouillon [i.e., the Ankara Treaty]?"

Antaki evaded. "As I have observed all this hour, it is necessary first to complete the elections and the ratification of the treaty by the new Chamber."

"Could one admit the hypothesis that the new parliament rejects the treaty that you have signed?"

"All is possible in the world," Antaki responded.[24]

Instead of improving matters, Antaki's effort to stem the hostility in the Turkish press seems only to have exacerbated the situation. The interview ran under the title "The Syrian Delegation Doesn't Escape" and was followed by a furious editorial. The Syrian delegation seemed astonished by the public outcry castigating them for offering nothing to the Sanjak, for not even properly focusing on the issues. The delegation had been unprepared for the Turks' insistent interest in the fate of the Sanjak, was unable even to recall the treaty's provisions about the Sanjak, and was poorly informed about France's diplomatic commitments in Alexandretta.[25] Thrilled over their success in finally negotiating an independence treaty, they had paid little attention to the fate of the small border district. France's representative in Istanbul was cynical about the emphasis the story was receiving throughout the Turkish press, speculating that the Turkish government had ordered that the issue be given "maximum volume."[26]

Turkish journalists seemed shocked that neither al-Atasi nor Antaki could discuss the future of the district, pointing out that it had been the subject of only one of thirteen articles in the Ankara Treaty of 1921. Turkish foreign minister Rüştü Aras's official statement on the newly signed Franco-Syrian Treaty first lauded the new agreement creating an independent Syria. "We salute with satisfaction the constitution of autonomous governments based on the principle of nationalities in the parts of Syria detached from the Ottoman Empire." Moreover, he pointed out, Turkey had renounced its rights to sovereignty in Syria in the 1923 Lausanne Treaty that followed upon the success of the nationalist forces and provided international recognition for the new Turkish state. The Ankara government was optimistic that it would enjoy neighborly commercial relations with an independent Syria, similar to its recent relations with Iraq. Aras's only hesitation focused on Alexandretta: "We hope that by the treaty of union concluded between the Syrians and the French, with whom we enjoy the most friendly relations, a local and autonomous regime would be accepted for the regions of Alexandretta and Antioch, whose population of 280,000 souls is almost entirely composed of Turks."[27] Aras was proposing a wholly separate regime for the Sanjak, basing his political claim on a linguistic premise: its residents were "almost entirely" Turkish.

Both *La République*'s editor and Turkey's foreign minister were asserting new and interdependent claims to the Sanjak. The 1921 Ankara Treaty had, indeed, provided special status to the Sanjak's Turkish population, provisions requiring conduct of affairs in Turkish. It was quite a stretch, however, to claim, as the journalist had, that this treaty provided "autonomy" to the region. If *La République* was correct in its assertion that the Sanjak was legally autonomous, and if the foreign minister's claim that the population was overwhelmingly Turkish was accurate, then—according to the ideology of self-determination of peoples—the Sanjak *should not* have been included in the 1936 Franco-Syrian Treaty. If ethnic identity were to be the key to political destiny, a Turkish area could hardly be included within the soon-to-be-independent Syrian state. These interdependent assertions that the Sanjak was both autonomous and Turkish would lead inexorably to the demand that it should be disconnected from Syria. The issue would be no longer about the rights of a Turkish "minority" as provided in the 1921 Ankara Treaty, but instead about the need for a wholly different form of government.

In an effort to stem the growing hostility, France's representative met in Istanbul with Turkish officials to reassure them about the new treaty. But when the French consul emphasized that the rights of minorities would be respected in the Sanjak, the interim Turkish foreign minister exploded. "The Turks of the Sanjak . . . could not be counted as a minority in Syria; they constitute the whole of the people of a separate territory, benefiting from a special regime legally ordered!" He insisted that Turkey should have been consulted about the Sanjak's future and that before France withdrew from Syria, France's functions in the Sanjak would have to be taken over by others—not Syrians.[28] The contrast was stark: Syrian leaders' nonchalance about the Sanjak could hardly be more different from the position of the Turkish regime. The Turkish press began to clamor for a change in the Sanjak's status before the implementation of any independence for Syria, demanding an autonomous or, better, an independent Sanjak. Within days, Turkish journals in Adana in southern Anatolia were describing the Sanjak as a Turkish land mistakenly included in a country under French mandate.[29]

In the Sanjak itself, those opposed to Turkey's claim proposed three other alternatives. Sixteen of the Sanjak's high elected and appointed officials circulated a petition rejecting both independence from France and autonomy from Syria; they demanded instead the status quo and the continuation of French control, maintaining all the rights and privileges that existed in the Sanjak. "This region is, in effect, composed of minorities both ethnic and confessional who make administration especially complex and difficult." They asked that, in view of the very diversity of the population, the power of both the local governor and the French deputy be reinforced. This group was clearly worried, in light of recent events, that "each provocation between elements of different races could have the greatest consequences on the social and political order."[30] Clearly, one part of the local elite accepted France's colonial contention that only the strong control of the mandatory power could keep inherently incompatible groups at peace.

Rejecting French colonial domination, many in the Sanjak supported the independence promised in the still-unratified 1936 Franco-Turkish Treaty and advocated the Sanjak's continued attachment to independent Syria. Like those who led the influential Syrian National Bloc, numerous local officials had been encouraged by the Treaty and supported the National Bloc's policy of constructive engagement with the French to accomplish Syrian independence.

A third political ideology was gaining strength in the Sanjak. Adherents of the League of National Action, led by Zaki al-Arsuzi, castigated the National Bloc and the established Syrian nationalist leaders for their ineffectiveness. Syrian political parties, they insisted, were interested in their own political success and the continuation of their networks of influence. Instead, the League of National Action, established in 1933, worked to mobilize the grass roots. Their goal was to unify the broad range of Arabic speakers in the Sanjak regardless of their religious affiliation, hoping to inculcate a broad nationalist ideology among them. They had little interest in the political machinations of the parties in Damascus or any kind of engagement with the hated French occupiers.[31]

While the non-Turkish elites in the Sanjak scrambled to define their project, the Sanjak's Kemalists were laying the groundwork for a local Turkish response. The "Turkish party" in the Sanjak mobilized quickly, meeting continuously from the time of al-Atasi's interviews in Istanbul. Selim Çelenk, the owner of *Yeni Gün*, returned from Turkey on September 29, 1936, and the next evening met with some fifty others at the home of local leader Abdulgani Türkmen to compose a telegram in protest of the Franco-Syrian Treaty. "We note with regret that our cries and our pleas for fifteen years demanding a regime in the Autonomous Sanjak of Alexandretta that would assure the protection of our human rights and our national development have not been heard." Now, instead of respect for the rights of the Turks, they had learned that the Franco-Syrian treaty would annex the Sanjak to Syria.

> We protest with every fiber of our being against any order or any moves toward placing the Turks of Antioch and Alexandretta under the Syrian Administration like a flock of serfs. In light of its geographical situation, its historical tradition, and its ethnic particularity, our district has an independent existence, and we expect to enjoy the right to autonomy in the Sanjak, that we will be able to rule ourselves, and that our rights will be respected.[32]

The Turcophile group's telegram not only claims past discrimination, but also asserts the major elements by which any nation makes its claim: historical tradition and ethnic difference. According to the group, if the Sanjak's Turkish character did not elicit its separation from an independent Syria, its Turkish-speakers, now imagined as a separate nation, would be reduced to a status equivalent to serfdom.

Captain Refik Bey arrived from the Turkish city of Adana on September 30 to create an infrastructure for Turkish mobilization inside the Sanjak. An adviser to Adana's military security service, he spent a week pretending to be a correspondent while conducting extensive meetings with local Turkish leaders. By the time he returned to Turkey on October 6, he had created an eight-member executive committee for a "society for Annexation to Turkey," under the presidency of Antioch notable Abdullah Murselzade. Section committees, each with a president and three members, were formed in five major areas of the Sanjak: Alexandretta, Antioch, Reyhanlı, Kirikhan, and Beylan. According to local police, Refik's goal was nothing less than the creation of a movement.

In his effort to contrive a bloc in the Sanjak supportive of Kemalist principles and, ultimately, connection to Turkey, Refik set up clear guidelines. The executive committee and its sections would try by all peaceful means to attain the attachment of the Sanjak to Turkey. If these means did not succeed, as a last resort they would set loose an insurrection. However, the official leadership, the executive committee, would not take an active part in that insurrection. Citing Palestine as a model, Refik claimed that the executive committee would restrict itself to diplomacy, at the same time working to benefit from the actions of three newly created armed bands. Each band would have two hundred men; the first band would operate in the Hadjilar sector, the second in the Arda district, and the third in the Reyhanlı sector. According to Refik, the arms and munitions were ready, and the men who would participate in the bands had been designated. The revolt would be bloodless, Refik insisting that no injury was to be caused to the inhabitants; no offense or outrage would be carried out against anyone. These bands would not cut off travel routes, and brigandage would be forbidden, but all the people in contact with France and Syria, and all those hostile to the Kemalist regime, would have both their property and their lives threatened. The revolt was intended to prove politically threatening to both France and Syria. It would also employ economic tactics: Refik Bey insisted that debts and taxes due to the government or to institutions under its authority be withheld. This measure was also to be applied to debts held by certain merchants.[33] Refik Bey's activities managed not only to unify Antioch's Turcophiles but also to embolden them. Turcophile leaders Vedi Munir and Abdullah Murselzade claimed that the Sanjak would be reconnected with Turkey within two months; moreover, the neighboring Kürt Dağ region and part of Azaz would similarly be occupied.[34]

Indeed, the demands of the Turkish leaders inside the Sanjak ranged widely during these initial days. In the immediate aftermath of the announcement of the Franco-Syrian Treaty, officials in Turkey and in Antioch had demanded only the implementation of protections for Turks and a "continuation" of the Sanjak's autonomous status. While this group hoped for minimal change in the status quo, another group of Turcophiles telegraphed French high commissioner Damien de Martel demanding "the connection of our hearths to Turkey," claiming that their attachment to any other state would be inconceivable. Kemalist demands had escalated rapidly from protection for Turks to a new kind of autonomy and soon evolved into a demand for connection with the "motherland."[35]

To reinforce their claim to the Sanjak, the Turkish government created a new historical narrative that went beyond simply claiming the Sanjak as part of Turkey and insisted that it was the Turks' land of origin. Published on October 10, a statement entitled "A Page of History," by İsmail Müştak Mayakon, the deputy to the Turkish Grand National Assembly from Siirt, asserted that Turks had ruled the Sanjak for forty centuries. The Sanjak of Alexandretta, he declared, was the ancestral land of the Turks, from which they had spread into central Asia. According to Mayakon, the Turks were called "Hatay" when they reached the border of North China; Hatay, Hittite, Hata, Ata, and Etti, were all names for the ancestors of the Turks. Thus, the disputed Sanjak was nothing less than the Turkish homeland; the people in it should be called Hata, and the state they were to create should be named Hatay. The U.S. ambassador to Turkey claimed that "from then on all newspapers generally refer to the Sanjak, in accordance with Mayakon's suggestion, as 'Hatay.'"[36] High Commissioner Martel claimed that the Hittites had not been spoken of for three thousand years in this region. The speed with which this new formula became common among local Turcophile groups, he said, "attested to the discipline with which the organs of propaganda carry out the instructions they receive."[37] The new narrative portrayed Turks and Turkishness as victims within the Sanjak. Their rightful homeland had been taken from them; Turks were being oppressed in their very place of origin.

The Arab nationalist leadership in Damascus grew alarmed by this extraordinary campaign to mobilize Turkish sentiment.[38] The challenge these Arab leaders faced was quite different from the Turkish nationalists' project. While the Turcophiles had been moving quickly and effectively—creating an infrastructure, recruiting partisans, lobbying governments, planning events, planting news stories, and formulating new narratives—Syria's representatives had found themselves unprepared from the time they had first announced the new treaty in Turkey. Their appointees in the Sanjak, confronted with the new Turkish demands, fell back into a reactive stance that would harden into a posture as they were repeatedly called on to respond to steps taken by others. The Turcophile population had mobilized to force change; it was much more difficult to elicit activism among the people who were intent on maintaining the status quo, at least until their own situation became threatened.

A group of Antioch's leaders articulated their own Syrian nationalist ideology in an October 1936 petition to the ruling National Bloc in Damascus, which they copied to High Commissioner Martel based in Beirut, the French Ministry of Foreign Affairs in Paris, and the League of Nations headquartered in Geneva. The petition derided the "declarations of the Turkish Minister of Foreign Affairs, tendentious publications of the Turkish press, and the pretensions of a small number of Antioch pro-Turks." The petitioners objected to any change in the Sanjak's status "to please a handful of Turks whose numbers do not reach a quarter of the population," comparing the situation of the Sanjak's Turks favorably to that of the larger "oppressed" Arab people living in Turkish Cilicia.

"The Liwa [the Sanjak] is an integral part of Syria from the historic, geographic, and ethnic points of view and will remain eternally Syrian. Arabs compose the overwhelming majority of the population, 150,000 against 60,000 pro-Turks, and we reject all efforts to give the Liwa a special status independent of Syria; we protest against all actions of all natures and we consider it a matter of right and security."[39] Like their Kemalist counterparts, these leaders made their argument on the basis of linguistic affiliation, disputing the Turkishness of the Sanjak and asserting an Arab identity on the basis of Syrian history and ethnicity.

Stakes were high in this demographic debate. "Self-determination of peoples" suggested that the character of the population would decide the destiny of the territory. For both Syrian and Turkish nationalists, the immediate priority would be to prove that they were the most numerous in the Sanjak. The resolution would be determined not by simple counting, however; the challenge would be revising each resident's self-perception to embrace only one identity. As subjects of the multilingual, multiethnic Ottoman Empire, the Sanjak's residents had never been expected to claim a sole and exclusive identity. Now, with each "side" claiming a majority, it had become essential for the first time to define "Arabs" and "Turks" in order to count them. Two challenges arose immediately: if the categories that mattered were to be Arabs and Turks, what should be done with people who either claimed neither identity (Alawis, Kurds, Armenians) or with the people who claimed both (the results of centuries of fluid group boundaries)?

European imperial powers found little solace in the area's ambiguous group definitions, and even less in the region's long history of intermarriage and cohabitation. On the contrary, French claims to Syria and Lebanon in the interwar period rested largely on the notion that inhabitants of the region were unable to live peacefully together. This was not a new contention on Paris' part: as early as the 1860s, France had worked to "protect" Ottoman minority communities from the majority. One effect of European "protection" of specific Middle Eastern groups had been to sharpen the lines that distinguished ethnic and religious communities from each other. Insisting that Syria's different faith and ethnic groups would inevitably clash, the French divided their part of Syria into five different states, trying to keep Alawi, Druze, Maronite, and Muslim areas separate. The Syrian rising of 1925 had illustrated not only the danger that a common front might pose for the continuation of French occupation; the united resistance even suggested that France's legitimation for its continuing occupation had been rendered moot. If the varied groups could now band together, a major premise legitimating the French occupation would be exposed as invalid.[40] The ability of this diverse population to act collectively *against* French rule suggests other imperial interests at stake in keeping Syrians divided.[41]

In Turkey, a sense of common identity had emerged from the struggles against Allied occupation. The new Grand National Assembly meeting in Ankara had worked to define the character of the state they were in the process of creating. By the 1930s, Turkishness had triumphed over the alternatives. Kemal Atatürk jettisoned Islam, which some had seen as the glue that would bind the new nation, viewing it as incompatible with the Western-style state he sought to create. "Ne mütlü Türküm diyene," was the slogan: "How happy is one who can say 'I am a Turk.'" Atatürk presided over thoroughgoing efforts to re-imagine the history of the Turks, and to purify the Turkish language of "foreign" elements. Historians working with the newly created Turkish Historical Society explored the nation's past, giving primacy to ancient Turks, whom they claimed to prove were the forerunners of all other civilizations, the creators of the world's first language, and the earliest inhabitants of Mesopotamia and Anatolia.[42]

As Atatürk worked to fashion a Republic of Turkey from the central lands of the defeated Ottoman Empire, Westernization and secularism went hand in hand. His reforms were far-reaching: abolishing the Caliphate, the highest office in the Muslim world; rejecting the Muslim lunar calendar for the European version; and exchanging Arabic characters for Latin letters. For the new Turks, even the daily project of getting dressed was to be transformed. Atatürk prescribed a new code of fashion, one that would present the Turkish people to the world as a Western nation. Traveling the country in support of the new sartorial conventions, Atatürk rejected a revival of some "authentic" Turkish costume: "Internationally accepted civilized dress suits us too. . . . Shoes or boots on your feet, trousers on your legs, then shirt, collar and tie, waistcoat, jacket and, to complete it all, headgear with a sun-shield, which I want to call by its proper name: it's called a hat."[43] Despite reaching far back into a distant past for an authentic Turkish identity, Atatürk rejected a recreated folkloric dress in favor of "civilized" apparel. Robes, turbans, and fezzes were remnants of the years between ancient and modern glory, and must be jettisoned.

Turkish nationalists mobilized the carefully elaborated components of their new identity in the struggle to claim the Sanjak. New clothing was an important way Turkish activists could make Antioch appear to be Turkish. Hundreds of local young men began to wear brimmed hats, and some women began to abandon the veil. Kemalists distributed free hats to peasants in small villages throughout the Sanjak as well.[44] These hats would mark them as supporters of Kemal

Atatürk, setting them off against the non-Kemalists, who continued to wear fezzes. Soon, leaders of the newly formed Arab nationalist League of National Action sought their own marker, rejecting the Ottoman-era fez in favor of the sedara, a head covering created by Iraq's new King Faysal.[45] On the streets of the Sanjak, headgear was becoming the clearest way to symbolize the growing divisions among the people.

The Turkish press played a pivotal role in disseminating the characteristics of the new Turk: introducing the new script and calendar, disseminating the new narratives, and advertising modern apparel. The press was also instrumental in exacerbating tensions within the Sanjak. Newspapers from north of the border provided information about the Kemalist government's views; they also inflamed local sentiments by printing unsubstantiated reports about the Sanjak, reports that were read aloud in the city's cafes.

On October 4, 1936, Antioch's Kemalists closed their stores and garages in protest against the Syrian president's announcement of the Franco-Syrian Treaty. The city remained calm as hundreds of artisans gathered at the Uruk-Pinar Café, where they listened enthusiastically to Istanbul newspapers read aloud. At half past four in the afternoon, they left the café for the bridge over the Orontes River—the center of commerce, the location of police headquarters, and a favorite location for mass gatherings. When they arrived in front of the police station, police officers urged the protesters to disperse. As part of the crowd refused, crying "Vive!" and "We don't want to," the commander ordered his gendarmes to load their weapons. The provincial governor intervened, successfully dispersing the crowd without further opposition. The next morning, some 150 Turks paraded through town.[46] In the Café Yildiz three days later, a special issue of *Yeni Gün*, was read aloud. The journal asserted that France and Turkey were about to engage in negotiations over the independence of the Sanjak, news welcomed by an approving, applauding crowd of local Kemalists.[47]

The press became a crucial battleground in the contest over the Sanjak, and French officials struggled to balance some degree of press freedom with the need to prevent violence. Pierre Durieux, the highest ranking French administrator in the Sanjak, who held the title of delegate, claimed as early as October 5 that campaigns by both the Turkish press and the Syrian press were exacerbating tension between the Turks and the Arabs of the Sanjak. His boss, High Commissioner Martel, had already instructed the press of Syria and Lebanon to abstain from commenting on the Sanjak. Martel contrasted the government-enforced silence of the Arab press to "an entirely different attitude . . . adopted by the Turkish press, and articles of a very violent nature were published in the journals of Ankara and Istanbul, especially the official 'Ankara.'" The Turkish government, he claimed, was providing inaccurate and misleading information, which would endanger the negotiations recently begun between the French Foreign Ministry and its Turkish counterpart.[48] Refusing to permit the director of the Turkish daily *Tan* to send a correspondent to the Sanjak, Martel fumed, "The attitude taken by the Turkish press in the Sanjak affair makes it impossible to send a Turkish journalist to Alexandretta. I have given for my part necessary orders to the Arab press to avoid an inopportune polemic. I can only hope to see the Turkish government do the same."[49]

Martel's insistence on silence in the Syrian press worried the Arab nationalists, who anxiously telegraphed him on October 8. They expressed shock at *Yeni Gün's* reports describing upcoming French-Turkish negotiations about possible independence for the Sanjak. Such discussions, they claimed, would be contrary to the new relationship between France and Syria that had resulted from the recent treaty agreement. The telegram demanded that the French high commissioner "intervene in earnest to put a stop to this comedy that is played each day on the theater of this Arab Sanjak," and that he suspend *Yeni Gün*, "which, by its false publications, constitutes one of the most important elements of trouble and sedition."[50] Arab nationalists found themselves at a disadvantage, unable to publish their own version of events while both the local Turkish and foreign press were broadcasting an alternative perspective that advanced Turkish views.

Tensions continued to escalate, with public readings and rampant rumors. Still, the Sanjak's governor, Husni al-Barazi, a member of the Syrian nationalist National Bloc party, discounted the existence of real animosities, blaming outsiders for the apparent polarization of the local population. In a letter to Syria's interior minister, the governor pointed to newspaper editors as the culprits. Both the press inside Turkey and the Sanjak's own Turkish-language press "produced a great impression at Antioch . . . Encouraged, they displayed their hostility to Syria, to its respectable government and to its representatives in the city." According to al-Barazi, were it not for the wisdom and energy provided by the local government, there would have been serious incidents. The governor worried about agents surreptitiously fomenting trouble, almost to the point of bloodshed, in an effort to permit the Turkish government to claim vital necessity in detaching the Sanjak from Syria.[51]

French delegate Durieux disputed the Syrian governor's analysis, instead laying responsibility for the growing politicization between Turkish- and Arabic-speaking groups at the feet of the Arab press and the Turkish government. The Arab press blamed French officials for the situation, he claimed, aiming "at nothing less than to allow the public to believe that the Turkish problem has never existed and that it had been completely invented out of whole cloth by the successive deputies of the High Commissioner." At the same time, he argued, the Turkish government was responsible for intervening in the Sanjak through its advice to local leaders and special emissaries, especially the Turkish consul, stationed in neighboring Aleppo.[52] Echoing a widespread French belief in the inherent incompatibility of the varied local groups, Durieux claimed that it was only the French presence instituted in the region after 1921 that had allowed Turks and Arabs to live together peacefully. Ever since the Syrian delegation began treaty negotiations in Paris, he claimed, local Turks had taken every opportunity to make themselves visible. They had staged celebrations of Turkish fetes: the children's holiday, the holiday celebrating the capture of Izmir, the holiday of the flowers, the sporting holiday, and the memorial to the dead of the Great War. Through these spectacles, he claimed, local Turks had acquired a greater consciousness of their collective strength, finally coming to believe that Turks actually possessed a real majority in the Sanjak.

Durieux noted that not even French colonial education had been successful in turning these local Sanjak Kemalists away from the new Republic of Turkey. "Despite the sound methods of pedagogy adopted in the local educational institutions under the watch and control of French masters, the ideas of emancipation and modernism have not ceased fermenting in the imagination of the young, as Kemalist politics would achieve their most cherished wishes."[53] At the same time, Durieux was aware that the Sanjak's Turkish-speakers were not unified in their support of the Kemalist revolution in the new Republic of Turkey. Some were simply traditionalists; others were guided by personal interest. Durieux acknowledged that many of these Turks would join non-Turkish-speakers in the Sanjak in preferring the status quo. Nonetheless, he claimed, if forced to decide between unity with Syria or with Turkey, even the most tepid supporter of the new republic would choose to affiliate with Turkey. Durieux speculated that because of recent redistricting, Sunni Arabs made up barely a handful of the Sanjak's population and were spread throughout the area. He also noted that most of the Arabic-speaking Alawis and Sunnis were like serfs on the land and under the domination of the Turkish landowners. Durieux worried that "the political antagonism currently existing between Turks and Arabs appears full of consequences, especially if it is augmented by the press campaigns of Turkish and Syrian journals."[54]

The Syrian parliamentary elections stipulated in the Franco-Syrian Treaty would be a crucial first test of the Sanjak's future course, and both the Arab and Turkish nationalists understood what was at stake. Elections were the primary way popular sovereignty would be enacted, the most important determinant of whether a government was legitimate. If the people of the Sanjak participated in these elections, they would be engaging in the legitimizing process, thereby identifying themselves as part of Syria. Turkish activists, claiming that the Sanjak was autonomous, demanded that its residents refuse to participate in the voting. Participation or boycott became a visible measure of the Sanjak's affiliation; the outcome would be apparent to all at the polls on November 14.[55]

When they met in Antioch on October 4, Antioch's Turkish leaders took the boycott plan a step further, urging a broad program of nonrecognition and non-participation. No payment of taxes to the Syrian government from this day on, they insisted. They continued preparations for armed conflict, organizing and procuring weapons. The police chief described their spirits as "boiling," inflamed by the articles appearing in recent days in the Turkish press. These Kemalist leaders wanted the Sanjak to be incorporated into Turkey. One worried police official concluded ominously, "Judging from the spirits among the Turks and Arabs, it would not be pessimism to add that we find ourselves on the eve of tragic events."[56]

Syrian leaders divided over how to interpret Turkey's intentions. When High Commissioner Martel met with National Bloc government members in Damascus the day after this Kemalist meeting, he carried the news that Turkey was working at the League of Nations to prevent implementation of the Franco-Syrian Treaty. While some Damascus leaders hoped Turkey was simply trying to safeguard Turkish culture in the Sanjak, others worried that this step reflected Turkey's intent to meddle in Syrian and Arab affairs.[57]

A group of Turkish notables met daily in Antioch to discuss strategy during the following weeks, continuing their organizing around the November 14 election. They dispatched a series of telegrams protesting the situation in the Sanjak, missives that they hoped would reinforce the hopes of local Turcophiles while also framing the terms of the contest. "Twenty thousand Turks in the [neighboring] Bujak districts took a decision of solidarity, sending representatives to the local action committee to participate in a great cause," read one. Another announced, "Armenians in the Sanjak decide to sympathize with the Turkish cause." The telegrams also emphasized the economic crisis in the Sanjak, suggesting that continuing ties to France meant that devaluations of the franc would create increasing hardship in local markets.[58]

French officials tried to mitigate Kemalists' hostility to the Syrian parliamentary elections by offering them a guaranteed seat in the new Syrian assembly. With the agreement of the ruling group in Damascus, still worried about Turkish foreign minister Aras's efforts in Geneva, Durieux met with Mohammad Adali, the Sanjak's current parliamentary representative, to convince him of the necessity of giving up his seat to a representative of the Turkish group.[59] Within a few days the response was clear: Kemalist leaders in the Sanjak not only refused the effort to replace Muhammad Adali with a Turkish representative but also reiterated their insistence that Turks would neither take part in the upcoming elections nor present a candidate. Turkish leader and *Yeni Gün* publisher Şükrü Balcı made the Kemalists' motive explicit: sending a deputy from the Sanjak to Damascus would complicate the task of Turkish negotiators in Geneva by indicating that the local population actually recognized the Sanjak's dependence on Syria.[60]

French police reports trace a steady escalation of Turkish boycott organizing within the Sanjak, efforts that included propaganda in the press, personal lobbying, and the distribution of hats with brims. Their goal: "Strive for the elections being made by a minority and proclaim that the elected deputies do not represent the Sanjak."[61] For this to work, non-Kemalists would have to boycott the elections as well. Turkish leaders in the Sanjak and in Ankara argued that Alawis and Armenians were natural allies in the boycott, because these groups also opposed control from Damascus.

While plans to enlist Alawis and Armenians in the Turkish boycott may have seemed far-fetched in the wake of Turkey's oppression of the Alawis and the Ottoman persecution of the Armenians, Turkey's new nationalist ideology suggested that both groups were, in truth, Turkish. Reşit Galip, Turkey's minister of education, had told his Armenian colleagues in 1934 that "anthropological comparisons and ancient historical data leave no room for doubt . . . that the Armenians have the same ethnical origins as the Turks." The consequences, according to Galip, should be clear: Armenians should perform their duties as citizens of Turkey.[62] Turkish historians in the 1930s insisted that Alawis were the original Turks, and had simply forgotten their language over the centuries. The Sanjak's Kemalists trying to recruit Armenians, Alawis, and others argued that not only were they not Arab, they were, indeed, Turks.

Two leading Alawis from Turkey, a wealthy agriculturalist and a rich fish merchant, arrived on October 14 to try to convince local Alawis to align themselves with Turkey's claims on the Sanjak and boycott the coming Syrian legislative elections. They discussed Turkey's attitude toward Alawis, emphasizing Turkey's progress and the Ankara regime's sympathy for the Alawi community.[63] Around the same time, the Sanjak's main Kemalist leader, Abdulgani Türkmen, arranged to speak with Sadek Maruf, Alawi deputy from Antioch. Türkmen began by asserting that the Turkish population treated others well, deploring a recent well-known incident in which an Alawi was slapped by a Turk. He explained the Turkish election boycott to the Alawi leader, encouraging the Alawis to follow suit. Both had a common interest, he explained, because the presence of elected representatives in Damascus would mitigate the prospects for an independent Sanjak. When Maruf explained that he did not have the kind of authority necessary to induce the Alawis to take the Turkish position, Mr. Türkmen insisted that the Sanjak was Turkish and that the Alawis had everything to gain by supporting the Turks.[64]

French Special Service officers reported on a meeting with Armenian leaders on October 13 at the home of Turcophile Ali Riza Effendi.[65] The Kemalist leader of the Kirikhan district had been requesting the meeting for days, according to French intelligence, who believed the meeting had been instigated on direct instructions from Ankara. Turkish leaders told the assembled Armenian notables to forget the past. "Turkey has changed a lot and has made great steps toward progress. At this hour, order and justice reign. There is complete equality among Turkish citizens regardless of their religious ideas. Syria wants to obtain its independence. We also want to obtain ours under French or Franco-Turkish control. This regime can only be in your favor. We will live here on the best terms." The Turks encouraged Armenian leaders not to participate in the next elections, and to show their solidarity with the Turks, whose regime would treat them favorably.[66] According to the report, Armenian leader Katchadour Karabadjakian responded that he was pleased with the amicable relationships in the Sanjak between the two communities and hoped to see them continue. He thought it would be difficult to convince fellow Armenians to forget the past, particularly in light of the present situation near Sivas in northern Turkey, where Armenians were being treated badly to make room for Muslims immigrating from Bulgaria. Nonetheless, he promised to bring the proposal to the Council of the Armenian community. Despite his promise, French officials remained confident of the division between the Armenians and Turks continuing. "The Armenian population places little confidence in the Turkish element, the notables letting me know of the unanimity of their sentiments in this regard, and of the fact that it is not their intention to abstain from voting. They simply want to maintain a limited contact with the Turkish milieu to know exactly their thoughts and their goals."[67]

Turkish national celebrations at the end of October provided an immediate opportunity to display Turkishness, and it was seized by the local activists. Brimmed hats were sold everywhere; there was a run on red fabric to be used in sewing Turkish flags.[68] Despite warnings from the Service of Public Instruction, many schoolchildren engaged in small pro-Turkish demonstrations on the day of the celebrations, October 29. Angry officials recommended either suspension for those responsible or temporary closure of the Turkish section of the school for young girls, where many of the participants studied. Furious, the girls' parents (a Who's Who of Turkish leaders in Antioch) complained directly to High Commissioner Martel, "The Turkish girls school is being closed and the students dismissed for being absent the day of our national holiday. We call the attention of the representative of France to this fact, who promised respect for the national culture of the Turkish inhabitants of the Sanjak, and we demand that he respect our rights."[69]

Intelligence reports repeatedly asserted that Turkish activists were growing both more aggressive and more overt in their efforts. Continuing press attacks proved too much for the local Special Services chief, Gacon. He accused *Yeni Gün* of publishing articles "destitute of the most elementary correction, articles provoking an intense emotion among the moderate Turks, Arabs and Christians." The newspaper referred openly to the Republican People's Party, the ruling

Kemalist party in Turkey, and its local organization, the People's House, or Halkevi. As Gacon noted, both this Turkish political party and its organizing arm had been outlawed in the Sanjak. However, they were not even being treated as clandestine organizations. Gacon warned of the political consequences of such news stories, despite the apologies of publisher Şükrü Balcı, and asked that the journal be suspended and Balcı investigated. "It is important to make known to this person that he must submit to the laws of Damascus and not those of Ankara," he concluded.[70]

By the end of October, the press campaign, the Kemalists' efforts to create an appearance of Turkishness in the people's dress, and their insistence that non-Turks adhere to the electoral boycott became too much for both the French and the Syrian officials. They feared that Turks were exercising coercion in order to enforce the election boycott. "In the towns as well as in the remotest villages of the plain or of the mountain, all our subjects of Turkish language have been ordered to abstain. Others have been threatened with reprisals if they do not conform, or for having declared that they refuse to adopt the hat instead of the tarbush [fez]." Syrian officials suggested the program might even be treasonous: the Kemalist party had never been authorized in Syria, and those of its members who were Syrian nationals were engaged in relations with a foreign power that aimed at taking Syrian territory.[71]

At the same time, the Sanjak's Arab leaders were growing increasingly anxious about the evident paralysis, as neither the French mandatory government nor the Damascus National Bloc regime seemed able to counter Turkish efforts. Arab leaders from Alexandretta and Antioch wrote to the Damascus government complaining about the Turkish propaganda, which they viewed as leading toward the Sanjak's annexation to Turkey. However, Syrian National Bloc officials in their turn considered this an international dispute, and therefore the responsibility of France. Visiting from Damascus, national economy minister Mustafa Kuseyri castigated the head of French Special Services. He accused France of exhibiting "criminal indulgence" in not taking more radical steps against the Turkish press, and declared that the Turkish demonstrations had not been countered energetically enough. According to Kuseyri, the creation of a local affiliate of Turkey's Republican People's Party was tantamount to treason. He argued that France, the mandatory power, must not only oppose Turkish propaganda but also take positive steps on its own to support and encourage the elections. Kuseyri blamed the French for the situation, accusing them of defaulting because of external concerns. "If the local authorities do not act it is because the Turkish question in the Sanjak goes beyond the internal body and places it on the international map."[72]

At the same time, French authorities in Syria were exasperated by the lack of effort among the Syrian leadership. Gacon laid much of the blame on the inaction of the Arabs themselves.

The Turcophile party is now engaging in activities and propaganda using means of intolerable pressure, not provoking any reaction among
Arab Sunnis and Alawis. Only the apathy of these elements permit the
Turcophiles to elevate the tone. The articles of *Yeni-Gun*, the campaign
for the wearing of hats was crowned with success in the villages up to
then indifferent to the political movements of Antioch; political meetings where they talk openly of the Halkevi and of the Turkish People's
Party [Republican People's Party] have come to pass. The Turcophiles,
contrary to what they affirmed, exhort the Alawis and the Arab Sunnis
of the district to abstain from the elections. . . . The Turcophiles use
their force and cohesion in the face of the apathetic weakness and the
internal quarrels of their political adversaries.[73]

These elections were free, the French official insisted, and it was up to the candidates to organize their own campaigns. "To not confine the political destinies of
the Antioch district to an entrepreneurial Turkish minority, it is necessary that
the opponents group themselves and form a united front to fight against the Turcophiles." Gacon was furious at the turn of the contest, convinced that France
would be made the scapegoat. The Syrians reproached the French for interfering
in local issues but were now passively awaiting French intervention: "while the
boat takes water one reproaches it also more violently yet without intervening
with the least energy."[74] Durieux likewise warned that Damascus's representative
in the Sanjak would have to work to gain the support of the local Arabs instead
of trying to hide behind the authority of the French.[75]

High Commissioner Martel nervously considered the situation in which his
regime found itself, blaming Turkish propaganda for the intensity of the situation. He claimed that, although the Turks were behaving properly with the
mandatory authorities and proclaiming Franco-Turkish friendship, their behavior with the local population was quite different. He described the Syrian leadership as still reeling from their experience in Istanbul back in September. After
centuries of Ottoman rule, the local people "fear the Turks and have no illusion
of the capacities of Syrian resistance. But wanting at all cost to avoid compromise, they seek to discharge all responsibility by leaving it to France to settle the
legal dispute . . . it is France who will be held responsible for the concessions
imposed by the circumstances by declaring that France has sacrificed Syria to
the interests of her own politics in her dealings with Ankara."[76]

The Sanjak question took a dramatic turn on November 1, 1936, when Kemal
Atatürk addressed the Grand National Assembly in Ankara. "The great question
of the day, which at the present moment constantly preoccupies the Turkish
people, is the fate of the region of Antioch and Alexandretta which in reality
belongs to the purest Turkish element."[77] Turkey's 1920 National Pact had

released areas with Arab majorities from the control of the newly declared Republic of Turkey. But for Kemal Atatürk, the Sanjak was clearly Turkish. Turkish historian Yüçel Güçlü claims that Atatürk's commitment to the Sanjak was one of
the main reasons he resigned his military command at the end of World War I to
join those who fought against Allied plans for Anatolia. According to Güçlü,
those present in the chamber shared Atatürk's sentiments about the Sanjak:

> When the President talked, more outspokenly than had been generally
> expected, about Alexandretta and Antioch, the House rose to its feet
> and applauded almost frenziedly. This official and authoritative state-
> ment was indicative of the persistence and tenacity behind the rising
> temperatures of popular feeling among the Turkish inhabitants of the
> Sanjak. Moreover, Atatürk himself had measured the tempo of the
> Turkish thesis and rights and this pronouncement made it clear, not
> only that the demands would be pressed, but also that the Turkish na-
> tion discovered that the fate of its brothers across the frontier was in-
> spiring it with emotions it could hardly keep under control.[78]

Kemal Atatürk and the Grand National Assembly enthusiastically committed
themselves, on November 1, to revising the postwar borders and claiming territory outside their own state that, they claimed, was inhabited by Turks.

Atatürk's demand for the Sanjak was not only because of its Turkish population, however; the former military commander had strategic interests as well.
Throughout the 1920s and 1930s, he had been working to consolidate his revolutionary regime and to secure it from attack. The Republic of Turkey had been
born during a military struggle against a variety of European powers intent on
dismembering the whole region. In 1936, many in the new republic still perceived some of these countries as threats. Italy was often viewed as a potential
challenger; Alexandretta could be the Achilles' heel through which the country
could be invaded. When Italy began to fortify the Dodecanese Islands, close to
the Turkish coast, in 1934, Atatürk believed the bases could only be intended to
support an attack on Anatolia or to disrupt shipping in the eastern Mediterranean.[79] Italy's invasion of Ethiopia the following year appeared to the Turkish
leadership as confirmation of Italy's aggressive intentions, and Italy's presence in
Libya only exacerbated Turkish fear. Turkey's strategic anxieties were further
heightened with Italy's invasion of Ethiopia in October 1935, Germany's rearming of the Rhineland in March 1936, continuing apprehension over Bulgaria's
designs in Thrace, and the increasing division of Europe into armed camps.

The Ankara government reacted by seeking League of Nations approval to
remilitarize the straits connecting the Mediterranean to the Black Sea (the Bosphorus and the Dardenelles), demilitarized after World War I. U.S. observers

were quite impressed with the diplomatic initiative and the skill of Turkey's leadership, who had consulted widely and gained support for their project before proceeding to a conference at Montreux, Switzerland. This meeting had been an enormous success for Turkey. United States ambassador John Van A. MacMurray claimed that Turkey had "handled [the Straits question] with a maximum of correctness and in a short time secured an eminently satisfactory solution and a reputation for being 'the good boy' of Europe." Although characterizing Turkey's approach to the Sanjak dispute as "more aggressive," MacMurray was convinced that the Ankara regime would resolve the current dispute in a manner consistent with its conduct on the Straits question.[80]

Like other diplomats committed to multilateral dispute resolution, MacMurray feared Turkey's potential alienation from the League process with an anxiety born of Germany's recent defection. Berlin's claims to neighboring territory had exacerbated divisions between those who wished to revise World War I borders and those who refused to do so. Although Turkey's foreign minister, Rüştü Aras, had been instrumental in creating the 1934 Balkan Entente, an alliance whose goal was to create stability in the region by preventing the revision of the World War I borders, it now seemed that Turkey's Grand National Assembly was claiming part of the Syria mandate. Anxious over the possibility of alienating the Turkish regime in this charged atmosphere, French officials had tried to reassure Ankara with an exchange of notes between Suad Davaz, Turkish ambassador to the League of Nations, and French foreign minister Yvon Delbos, a communication that continued through December.[81] For French administrators in the Sanjak, a quick resolution to ongoing Franco-Turkish talks in Geneva would be crucial. Durieux contended that the inhabitants' uncertainty over the Sanjak's fate seemed to exacerbate the conflict. Until some resolution could be attained, people would continue to be uneasy and to choose sides. While France and Turkey were negotiating, French mandatory authorities did not dare take any steps that might either alienate the Turkish government or empower the local Syrian administration. Only with "the approval of the text that will establish a concrete modus vivendi decided by the Turkish and French governments" would it be possible to end the recent ban on demonstrations and public meetings.[82] In the meantime, mandatory authorities had to step lightly. When, on November 10, *Yeni Gün*'s publisher, Şükrü Balcı, asked local officials about information he claimed to have received from Beirut that the Sanjak would be receiving at least as much autonomy as the French were providing Syria and Lebanon, Durieux could respond only that there was nothing official on the subject, and asked that it not be printed.[83]

As French authorities equivocated, the population was subjected to a rising crescendo of rumors and reports. By early November, people heard regularly that Turkish troops were on the verge of invading. Reports indicated that residents were being ordered to abstain from elections. Sides were being chosen, and one's affiliation was evident by one's clothing. The local government found itself unable to act in the face of growing fear and intimidation. The situation in rural Amuk and Kirikhan, where many of the landowners were Turkish, was particularly fraught. "During the last weeks they preached holy war against anyone of Arab origin and [issued] formal orders that no one participate in the elections," Durieux warned Martel. But there was much at stake, he reminded his superior. "The government of Ankara will try without doubt to demonstrate that the whole region is entirely Turcophile and that an eventual referendum authorized by the League of Nations would give the Turkish Republic near unanimity of votes."[84]

On November 10, Pierre Durieux promulgated an "Official Declaration" simultaneously in Arabic, French, and Ottoman Turkish. "The Delegation has learned from various sources about partisan news stories being spread in all of northern Syria about the future status of the Sanjak of Alexandretta," it began. Durieux's office denied the rumors categorically, attributing them to the sick imaginations of individuals and calling on people to be skeptical of rumors and demoralization campaigns. He reassured the Sanjak's population that French negotiations with Turkey were being conducted in an atmosphere of respect within the parameters of the Ankara Treaty, and ordered local officials to bring those who threatened public order to the courts.[85] Nonetheless, the very next day Durieux wrote to his superior in alarm. "Recent events in the Sanjak make immediate repression necessary to counter disturbances in public order and propagation of false news." He demanded house arrest for any Syrian nationals openly advocating the Kemalists' call for a tax strike, supporting an election boycott, and distributing Turkish propaganda. According to Durieux, the Turkish consul at Aleppo seemed to be involved in the resurgent Turkish propaganda, and French officials anticipated major problems as a result. Intelligence reports claimed that the consul had arrived incognito in the Reyhanlı region on November 8 to encourage emissaries "known throughout the region to preach insubordination to Syrian rules, total abstention from elections, and a tax strike." The Turkish consul, according to the French delegate, was directly responsible for the "fermentation des esprits" in the area. The Turks' behavior, he feared, could have serious consequences during the elections.[86]

A strike by schoolchildren in Kirikhan began on November 10, in solidarity with those whose school had been suspended after the Antioch Turcophile celebrations of October 29. The school's staff was working with police to protect nonstriking students from attacks by striking students armed with sticks. On November 14, the strikers began throwing stones into the school during class time.[87]

On November 11, three days before the elections, Antioch's procurer general was attacked and seriously injured in what was clearly a political crime.[88] Martel responded to this personal assault and the escalation in press attacks by reminding Durieux to avoid any unnecessary sanctions, but to deal severely with anyone whose actions would be likely to create trouble during the elections. Six activists ("notorious Turcophiles") were exiled to Homs or Hama, and *Yeni Gün* was suspended for having transgressed the limits of moderation.[89]

On November 13, Istanbul's population viewed a motion picture said to have been smuggled out of Antioch by *Cumhuriyet* editor Yunus Nadi, one of Atatürk's close allies. The film portrayed a demonstration by the Sanjak's Turks, in which "an enormous crowd" had thrown their fezzes into the river. The audience had cheered wildly, working itself into an anti-French frenzy.

It was in this environment that the residents of the disputed Sanjak of Alexandretta faced the first elections under the 1936 Franco-Syrian Treaty.

2

The League Takes the Case

Turkish activism in the Sanjak had escalated dramatically during the first half of November 1936 as Turcophiles encouraged the population to boycott upcoming Syrian elections in order to demonstrate that they refused to consider themselves Syrian. The Turkish press claimed success: despite what it called "the rigor of the measures taken" to coerce men to vote, fewer than half of those eligible went to the polls in the Sanjak, a sharp drop from the 70 percent who had voted in elections just five years earlier. Still, participation in the Sanjak was higher than in Damascus.[1] It was not only the Turkish boycott that had limited participation: the anticolonial League of National Action had urged the Arabic-speaking Alawi and Syrian Orthodox communities to abstain as well. Moreover, the Sanjak's sitting deputies in the Syrian Parliament enjoyed little popularity, and had no support among the local people. Durieux, delegate of the French high commissioner, suggested that potential voters were intimidated by the presence of election watchers and nervous about the threatened return of Turkish forces. Instead of crediting the low turnout to successful Turkish activism, however, Durieux blamed it on the ineffective political action of the Damascus government.[2]

This first stage of elections had chosen electors who would, in the next stage, designate the new members of the Syrian Parliament on November 30. Turkish activists tried to make the second-stage electors and the candidates sign a statement promising that they would neither vote nor stand for election. A notable from Amuk claimed that the Turkish consul in nearby Aleppo had been pressuring him not only to boycott the elections but also to urge Armenians to join the boycott. Sitting Sanjak representative Mustafa Kuseyri decided to stay in Damascus after threats that Turkish nationalists would be targeting not only the electors who voted in this second stage but also their children. According to Kuseyri, Syrian leaders could hardly mobilize their supporters unless the French took immediate measures to reassure the electors and silence the threats, even advocating the deployment of French troops.[3]

Diplomatic efforts to resolve tensions succeeded only in exacerbating them. As it became public knowledge that the French and Turkish governments were trying to negotiate a resolution of the dispute, local Turcophiles spread rumors that the negotiations would soon lead to the Sanjak's independence, and that if they failed, the Turks would invade. Anxiety ran high: if Turkey was on the verge of taking over, it would be best to support their boycott. The possibility of a diplomatic resolution, combined with fear of alienating the Turkish government during delicate negotiations, exacerbated the reticence of local French officials, who became increasingly unwilling to take severe action against Turkish agitators.[4] Instead of cracking down on those making threats and advocating the boycott, Durieux asked permission to allow the return of six Turkish leaders exiled just before the first stage of elections and to reopen the girls' school that had long been the site of Turcophile protests.[5]

As the second stage of the elections approached, the situation continued to worsen. Durieux telegraphed Beirut seeking instructions for the "serious bordering on disturbing" situation in which he found himself. Turks continued to propagandize everyone, including Sunnis, Alawis, and Christians, he wrote. Electors for the next stage were receiving undisguised threats from both local partisans and outside messengers hoping to elicit large-scale abstentions. The Turcophiles were trying to obstruct access to polling stations, organizing a transport strike in Antioch on election day, and encouraging Turkish villagers to bar the routes. Panic rose in rural areas as rumors of an imminent Turkish invasion circulated.

In these conditions, Durieux was faced with a dilemma. If he insisted on protecting electors, securing routes, facilitating transport, and reinforcing the voting centers, he would be accused of coercing the electors into participating. At the same time, he worried that if the vote took place in the current environment, the external pressure would so completely distort the electoral results that they could wrongly be interpreted as an indirect plebiscite favoring the Turks.[6] High Commissioner Martel refused his request to delay the elections, claiming postponement would not only encourage Turkish claims but also compromise the French in the eyes of the National Bloc of Syria, with whom Paris had just negotiated a treaty. Instead, Martel told his delegate to take steps to ensure public order without making it appear that there was pressure on the electors forcing them to vote. If the electors abstained when faced with the threats of the Turks, the French would explain the situation to the Damascus government. Syrian leaders were already criticizing French inaction, he fretted, comparing their ambivalence in the Sanjak to the resolution with which Great Britain had countered the Turkish claim to Mosul. Syrian nationalists insisted that France could turn aside the threat to Alexandretta by taking an "energetic attitude." Martel complained that this position held France responsible for the Sanjak's fate.[7]

French officials were frustrated with the Damascus regime's passivity, and demanded that al-Barazi, Antioch's governor, make it clear to the electors that they were expected to carry out their civic duties. An official proclamation on November 24 insisted that order would be maintained, that electors should fear no pressure, and that Sanjak officials had arranged cars to transport electors to minimize the effects of the Turkish garage strike.[8] The voting on November 30 simply reaffirmed the status quo: the Sunni and Armenian deputies sent to Parliament in 1932 had been reelected; it took a runoff to send Alawi deputy Sadek Maruf back to Parliament. Convinced that the "operations would be completed without incident," Durieux left his office in Antioch.

As Durieux approached the bridge over the Orontes River on his way to Alexandretta he saw the first parade of children forming, carrying a Turkish flag and singing the Turkish national anthem, followed by a compact group of Turkish "artisans." Within minutes, the demonstrators reached the municipal building, cursing the just-elected delegates to the new Syrian Parliament. "Down with the traitors! We want the Turks!" The crowd moved on to the homes of the two reelected legislators. The police, caught while breaking the Ramadan fast, arrived quickly to disperse the demonstrators.[9]

Another group forming near the Great Mosque blocked the route as Gacon, chief of Special Services, drove home. Police officers plunged into the crowd but were powerless to disperse it. When Gacon called for Abdulgani Türkmen, leader of the local Turkish community, three others emerged from the crowd, claiming to be empowered to negotiate on its behalf. Gacon responded that he considered them to represent no one but themselves, and in any case would not accept any conditions. Abdulgani soon arrived, flanked by the "Turcophile general staff" of Selim Çelenk, Şükrü Balcı, Semih Azmi, Tecirli Mehmet, and Vedi Munir. Gacon ordered them to disperse the crowd immediately, making clear that the police would proceed without caution if they were unsuccessful. Within a few minutes, the crowd melted away into the markets.

Another group of demonstrators began congregating in front of the house of Haji Edhem, president of the Antioch municipality, shouting insults, throwing stones, and trying to force open the door of the house. The demonstrators, deterred by shots fired from inside the house, moved on to the home of Haji Muhammad Adali, the reelected deputy from Antioch and former Syrian minister of agriculture and commerce.[10] Standing on the street outside Adali's house, the crowd began to boo, insult, and abuse the residents. Some two thousand demonstrators were enraged when they heard shots from the house and responded by throwing stones and shooting their own revolvers. Two children and one police agent were wounded. Another group, estimated at three hundred, gathered at the home of Mustafa Kuseyri, who had previously reported intimidation, insults, abuse, and throwing of stones. Again, shots were fired from the house, to which the demonstrators responded with more shots. Police and gendarmes dispersed the various groups of demonstrators, and calm was restored throughout the city by eleven o'clock in the evening.

Gacon waited anxiously after quelling the riots, expecting that the Turcophiles would not tolerate such a defeat. The next day, opponents of the elections circulated among Christian and Alawi merchants, forcing them to close their shops by threatening to plunder those that remained open. In the fruit and vegetable market, Alawi merchants fled. Alawi peasants who had come to the market as usual to sell vegetables had been assaulted and their fezzes thrown into the Orontes River.

Although many of Antioch's notables were insulted and harassed in the streets on December 1, 1936, the morning after the elections, the most popular target was the home of Mustafa Kuseyri. By eight o'clock that morning, the growing crowd in front of the reelected legislator's house was estimated at fifteen hundred people. Within minutes, Antioch's mayor made a formal petition to French authorities: he was no longer master of the situation and requested military intervention. When the captain of the French Special Services arrived at the scene, he found a crowd of many thousands of people shouting insults, abuse, and threats at the mounted gendarmes. Military forces set themselves up behind the gendarmes, and delivered an ultimatum: if the crowd did not disperse, they would be cleared by force.[11] The warning seemed to inflame the mob, who responded by demanding the immediate arrest of Mustafa Kuseyri, claiming they were ready to die before leaving. After the cavalry cleared the way, the surrounding throng refused to give up. They began throwing stones at both the gendarmes and the cavalry, then escalated to firearms. The first shots fired at the house wounded Kuseyri's young son inside. When the mandatory forces responded with machine-gun fire, the crowd instantly dispersed, leaving behind one dead, Mustafa Mahli, a thirty-year-old shoemaker, and one severely wounded, a twenty-eight-year-old cobbler who died that afternoon.

As the crowd was regrouping, Abdulgani Türkmen arrived with Turcophile leaders, protesting against the injuries the children had suffered during the previous evening's demonstrations and condemning the use of firearms by the people inside Mustafa Kuseyri's home. Durieux responded sharply, calling his complaints a "rare impudence." He reported, "I informed him that if his intervention could lead to the dispersion of the demonstrators, the forces of order would wait. If not, the clearing of Herod Street would be accomplished by force." Türkmen succeeded in this only partially, and French forces began their assault. By noon, troops had cleared the main streets, protected the route to the mosque, reinforced the police, and set guards at the city's intersections and sensitive areas. Durieux established martial law and declared an overnight curfew; troops occupied the various quarters of the city. Police searched everyone moving around the city, arresting two people for carrying arms. Funerals for those killed proceeded without incident the next day, and outside the city people remained calm. Within a week, Antioch had resumed its usual functioning.

Antioch's prominent Kemalists presented the post-election incidents quite differently in their report to the Turkish consul at Aleppo. The events were simply a French-Syrian attack on innocent Turks. A group of young children had paraded in front of the homes of Haji Edhem, Muhammad Adali, and Mustafa Kuseyri, singing Turkish songs. Machine guns—which had been installed ahead of time by the French authorities in the houses of Kuseyri and Muhammad Adali—opened fire on the group of children. Revolver shots were fired from the house of Haji Edhem, and many children were seriously injured. French authorities had responded to calm demonstrations with brutal force. It was this version of events that the Turkish consul in Aleppo transmitted to Ankara and to Turkish journals.[12]

Both the Ankara government and the Turkish press were furious. Yunus Nadi, an editor close to the government, wrote a column in Istanbul's daily *Cumhuriyet* calling on Turkey to intervene if France could not keep the peace. The crimes should not go unpunished, and submitting the problem to the League of Nations hardly seemed adequate "after so much innocent blood has been spilled." "What is the good of going there, stepping over the bodies of innocent men?" The Turkish papers claimed that people in Antioch were "being subjected to a reign of terror," accompanying their stories with blood-soaked photographs. Turkish officials insisted that outrages were being perpetrated against the Turks of the Sanjak. By December 4, a tone of urgency marked the Turkish government's letter to France's minister of foreign affairs.

> The disturbances brought about by a direct infringement of the sovereign rights of the Turkish inhabitants of that district have had tragic consequences to which the Government of the Republic cannot remain indifferent. The fate of the Turks of Alexandretta and Antioch, the treatment to which they are subjected, and the deaths of several among them have produced the most painful impression on the inhabitants of the neighboring Turkish provinces. Your Excellency has no doubt been informed of the most recent proceedings in the Grand National Assembly, when the deep anxiety voiced by the members was merely a somewhat attenuated echo of that felt by the whole Turkish people.[13]

The Turkish government cited the recent riots as evidence that only Turkey was dedicated to the protection of the Sanjak's Turkish-speaking people.

Yvon Delbos, the French minister of foreign affairs, responded that "complete calm now reigns in the whole district." In a barely veiled accusation, he contended that the actions taken by the mandatory authorities "had become necessary owing to the activities of elements foreign to the Sanjak and to Syria, which were endeavoring to exercise pressure on the population, sometimes going so far as threats of death." Foreign elements were responsible for the violence, and the attitude of the Turkish press had made matters worse, according to Delbos. Moreover, despite the escalating situation and France's obligation to provide security, government forces had intervened only in one episode, on December 1 in Antioch, when police trying to protect a member of the Chamber of Deputies were attacked by stones and gunshots. By the time the armed forces restored order, there were a number of victims, including two dead. Mandatory authorities were working to calm sentiments within Syria and the Sanjak, Delbos concluded, but their work was made more difficult by the tone of the Turkish press and rumors that armed bands were forming at the border.[14]

Suad Davaz, the Turkish ambassador to France, refused all responsibility for the growing violence, which his government attributed to French policy: "The news that has reached my Government is extremely alarming, and the present situation of the Sanjak is such as to produce extremely regrettable consequences if a remedy is not speedily found." The Turkish government requested a discussion of the situation at the next meeting of the League of Nations Council.

News of the riots spread beyond the region. In Baghdad, political circles anxiously followed the news from the Sanjak, fearing that Turkey's demands there were merely the first phase of a more general Turkish irredentism that might even extend into Iraq. Moreover, the large Syrian community living in Iraq felt threatened, comparing this situation to the case of Palestine. The Arab nationalist stance of Iraq's government, French officials feared, might lead them to enlist other Arab rulers' intervention in the Sanjak crisis, but they doubted that the Bagdad government would go that far. Instead, France's ambassador to Iraq suggested that the Iraq government's Arab loyalism could lead its cabinet to busy itself at Ankara in diplomatic efforts.[15]

French officials were even more concerned when echoes of the Antioch riots reached as far as Germany. Gilbert Arvengas, France's consul general in Hamburg, reported that the Hamburg press had published a telegram from Ankara on the riots, attaching long commentaries on the history and special situation of the Sanjak of Alexandretta, especially its considerable Turkish population. The French consul quoted the *Hamburger Nachrichten*: "The new Turkey, for which Alexandretta and Antioch are not only important from the economic point of view (petroleum), but which also constitute incontestable parts of the national State, awaits a better solution and at least the realization of the promised autonomy." German commentaries focused on the injustice of Turkey's frontiers, imposed by outsiders, comparing them with the injustices suffered by Germany. "We know similar sketching out of borders, made at our expense after the war, and we also understand the sentiment of Turks regarding their lost territory." Another writer commiserated, "One understands that the attachment of the Turkish minority to its true homeland has not ceased, and we know by the bitter German experience, notably in the Germany of Sudetenland, that the administrative organs often attempt to realize by all means the separation of the minorities."[16] In the highly charged international climate at the end of 1936, German newspapers claimed the Turkish experience as their own, encouraging Turkish irredentist claims to neighboring territories. For Paris, the comparison was disturbing at best.

When the the League of Nations Council opened its session in Geneva on the morning of Friday, December 11, Turkish foreign minister Rüştü Aras asked the members to deliberate on measures to remedy the "painful situation of the Turkish inhabitants of the Sanjak," before turning to the "substance of the dispute," the future of the contested territory. Present that morning were thirteen Council members, representing Bolivia, the United Kingdom, Chile, China, France, Latvia, New Zealand, Poland, Romania, Spain, Sweden, Turkey, and the Soviet Union. The special session had been called to hear an appeal by the Spanish government, but the representatives agreed to hear the Turkish government's request as well. While asking the League to defer its decision on the "substance," Aras nonetheless proceeded to lay out Turkey's case, in order to justify the Turkish intervention.

Aras rejected the French government's claim that the Sanjak was part of France's Syria mandate by comparing it to Cilicia. In 1920, when the League of Nations assigned the mandate to France, French troops were also occupying Cilicia. Nonetheless, France relinquished that territory to Turkey the next year. What then, Aras asked rhetorically, was "Syria" in 1920? If the San Remo Resolution of 1920 had included Cilicia, then France as mandatory could not have ceded it to Turkey; Cilicia was therefore not part of the mandate, and France had not acted as mandatory. It followed, then, that other territories France occupied at the time of the San Remo Resolution were not included in the mandate either. He insisted that the Sanjak was similar to Cilicia, and could just as easily be given to Turkey.[17]

As far as Turkey was concerned, then, the fate of the Sanjak of Alexandretta had not yet been juridically determined in 1920. The line France and Turkey had drawn to demarcate Syria's northern boundary was "unconditional" over most of its distance, but became "conditional" when it reached the Sanjak "with a Turkish majority." "When, in 1923, those two countries made this line a political frontier without in any way modifying conditions that had previously been attached thereto, there was no French mandate over the Sanjak, and it was not as a mandatory Power that France entered into undertakings towards my country." For Turkey, the Sanjak was "conditionally abandoned," to be an autonomous province under French authority. Turkey had never intended that the Turkish population of the Sanjak would one day be placed "under the yoke of a non-Turkish community."

Aras argued that the French view "that the League is the depository of all rights in this matter" was erroneous. The disposition of the Sanjak had been between Turkey and France, but *not* in France's role as a mandatory power over Syria. "The mandate drawn up in 1922 and applied in September 1923 cannot extend to the territory of the Sanjak, which (after, as before, the adoption of that instrument) remains distinctly and conditionally under the sole authority of the Government of the French Republic."

Aras assured the Council of Turkey's continuing and perpetual ties to the Turkish population of the Sanjak, while simultaneously expressing Ankara's profound sympathy and support for Syria. Aras then addressed what, for Turkey, was the underlying issue. "The Turkish population of the Sanjak," he emphasized, "will always constitute a national element of the greatest importance for Turkey." It was a disarmed and independent Alexandretta that the Turkish ambassador demanded, a Sanjak that would provide significant advantages to France, Syria, Turkey, and all the surrounding areas, to be served by the port of Alexandretta. Once Syrians understood the potential benefits, they would forgo a "purely formal allegiance" in favor of "Franco-Turco-Syrian collaboration." However, the present Syrian oppression made it urgently necessary for the League of Nations to "take the destiny of the Sanjak into its hands." Aras demanded that troops hostile to Turkey be removed from the Sanjak in favor of neutral forces placed under the control of the League. The Council decided to appoint a rapporteur to meet with representatives of France and Turkey and try to work out some resolution. The Council president's nominee, Sweden's representative Rickard J. Sandler, was accepted by both countries.

After affirming France's strong ties of friendship with Turkey in his response to Aras's argument before the Council four days later, Pierre Viénot, French Undersecretary of State for the Middle East and North Africa, confessed his great surprise to learn that France had controlled the Sanjak for fifteen years solely on its own authority and not as any part of the mandate for Syria. On the contrary, he argued, France's role in the region had been clearly defined ever since the signing of the San Remo Resolution in 1920. France had not been sovereign in Syria or the Sanjak, he argued. "The mission of France was merely to take all appropriate steps to form the communities peopling those territories into States fit to exercise full sovereignty and enjoy complete independence." That would require both the creation of administrative institutions and the fixing of boundaries, he continued. It was in this context, according to Viénot, that France had engaged in the discussions with Turkey over its border with Syria, discussions that had resulted in the 1921 Ankara Treaty. The line created as part of France's mandatory duties clearly left the Sanjak on the southern, that is, the Syrian, side of the border. The Lausanne Treaty two years later reiterated this line as the boundary between the two countries.

Viénot claimed, moreover, that France's withdrawal from Cilicia carried no implications for the Sanjak or the mandate generally. It was, he said, "a de facto situation" only: the limits of military occupation do not establish territorial boundaries. Evacuating Cilicia indicated nothing about France's official role as mandatory power during the negotiations over the Ankara Treaty of 1921. "When France was negotiating with Turkey in 1921," Viénot told the League Council, "she was acting under her mandate. She had no other qualification to negotiate and no other motive for negotiating, apart from the mandate." The Sanjak of Alexandretta, despite its special administrative regime and recognition of Turkish language and culture, remained part of Syria, and "had no special claim to independence apart from the Syrian community to which it belonged." The Ankara Treaty never envisioned the Sanjak as an independent state, according to Viénot. Its provisions, created to protect the Sanjak's Turkish population, would remain in force under the new Franco-Syrian Treaty. All stipulations of the Ankara Treaty and Lausanne Treaty would be taken over by the new, sovereign Syrian government.

The French diplomat insisted that neither the Sanjak's Turks nor the Turkish government had complained about the way the Sanjak had been administered during the fifteen years of the mandate. Nonetheless, he emphasized that the recently negotiated Franco-Syrian Treaty was merely a draft, still unratified and conditional. The government of Turkey would be able to intervene during the long period required for ratification of the treaty and the three provisional years following ratification. Even then, both the League of Nations Mandates Commission and the League of Nations Council would have to evaluate the treaty before Syria would be considered for admission as a new state by the more inclusive League of Nations Assembly. At any time in this long process, Turkey's reservations could be addressed.

Viénot ended by emphasizing the illegality of the Turkish proposal to sever the Sanjak from Syria. Article 1 of the Mandate for Syria and Lebanon specified that only two states, Lebanon and Syria, would become independent. In addition, Article 4 indicated that the mandatory power (France) must prevent the loss of any territory. Since the Sanjak had been included in Syrian territory since Syria became a state in 1922, severing it now would result in a loss of Syrian territory in contravention of the mandate. As Viénot pointed out, France as mandatory power was responsible for protecting Syria from any loss of territory. Moreover, aside from what Viénot saw as a clear legal case for the Sanjak continuing to be part of Syria, he pointed out that the results of independence for the Sanjak would be serious:

Syrian opinion, and Arab opinion in general, would not fail to note that Syrian independence would entail as its corollary, not the achievement of Syrian unity, but the amputation of a territory attached to Syria ever since Syria has existed as a State—that is to say, during the last fourteen years. Need I say that such a decision might have very serious consequences? Its effect would be to nullify the efforts at conciliation and pacification pursued by the mandatory Power. It might even lead to the return to a state of disturbance the violent manifestations of which in certain parts of the Levant will be fresh in the memory of all of you and which might be aggravated as a result of the solidarity of the Arab peoples.[18]

Viénot contended that severing the Sanjak from Syria would have serious and possibly violent consequences, affecting not only the hopes of "Syrian public opinion" but also Arab opinion more generally and even the stability of the Sanjak itself.

When the League Council opened its deliberations to the public on December 16, the newly appointed Rapporteur Sandler announced that France and Turkey had agreed to postpone further League discussions and implement measures to calm public opinion within the Sanjak. However, France refused to allow the League to send its own gendarmes to Syria, asserting both French ability and its sole responsibility to keep the peace. Viénot countered that League observers should be sent to both sides of the border to gather information, promised that France would reduce its troop presence on their arrival, and offered to delay French ratification of the Franco-Syrian Treaty. Sandler then proposed that the League of Nations should send three observers to the Sanjak, while France and Turkey continued informal conversations. He carefully defined what the observers would *not* be engaged in. They would not explore the substance of the question, investigate the recent riots, or pacify the region. "Their duty will simply be to observe and to keep in touch with the facts in order to be able to inform the Council if necessary." The Turkish government refused to support this proposal. Alarmed by the "painful situation in which the populations of the Sanjak are placed," Turkey had asked the League for "the complete neutralization of the disputed zone, to enable a serious enquiry to be made on the spot concerning the events which have occurred, and to prevent the atmosphere being again disturbed by further forcible measures." France rejected Sandler's suggestion as well, not only because it diminished the mandatory's legitimate powers but also because, France claimed, the situation had not deteriorated as Turkey alleged. Aras, in his turn, maintained that the new proposal to send a committee of observers would be ineffective. He contended that the observers would be unable to gather information because they would be forced to rely for that information on local authorities "who, in our view, are responsible for the past events." Nonetheless, Aras promised to abstain from voting, because, although he did not support the proposed commission, he did not want to prevent the sending of the observers.[19]

As the International Mission of Observers to the Sanjak of Alexandretta prepared to leave for Geneva, news reports from Ankara sounded the alarm. As a result of rampant violence, the Sanjak remained in a state of siege, with armored cars patrolling the streets. High Commissioner Martel tried to correct the dispatches, emphasizing that civilian rule had been restored, borders remained open, no more than 250 additional soldiers had been transferred to the Sanjak, and twenty arrests had been made for carrying prohibited weapons.[20] Martel's efforts elicited the opposite effect: Ankara's Agence Anatolie dispatch on December 22 accused the French Agence Havas of publishing false information. The Turkish press agency insisted that the situation in Antioch had hardly returned to normal, with thirty-man military detachments carrying machine guns and fixed bayonets continuing to patrol the streets day and night and oppressing the population on the pretext of investigating passersby. Agence Anatolie put the number of arbitrary arrests at thirty-eight and claimed that people had been beaten and robbed as they were thrown into prison. The people of the Sanjak, Agence Anatolie claimed, were groaning under this oppression and were at the end of their patience. They did not celebrate the national holiday this year, and students walked around wearing black bows on their lapels to indicate their grieving for the two victims of the incidents of December 1. According to Agence Anatolie, the situation in the villages was even worse for the Turkish population, whose taxes during this recession were still calculated on their income in 1926. Although these sums were beyond the peasants' capacity in the current economy, mandatory agents persisted in collecting the taxes, even if it meant entering the stores with their Arab gendarmes and selling cheaply all they found there. At the same time, according to Agence Anatolie, the Syrian press was pursuing its pernicious propaganda on the people of the Sanjak, even claiming that the Council of the League of Nations had decided against the Turkish claims. Nevertheless, the Turkish news agency insisted, neither the misinformation nor all these oppressions could succeed in lowering the morale of the Sanjak's people.[21] The Turkish press escalated their rhetoric in the face of Martel's efforts to counter its claims, providing the Turks of the new republic with horrific images of the persecution of their own compatriots living in the Sanjak.

The International Mission of Observers to the Sanjak of Alexandretta traveled to Ankara at the end of 1936, arrived in Aleppo on New Year's Eve, and proceeded directly to Antioch. It was a party of five Europeans who greeted 1937 in the contested territory: three European observers and two staff members.

L. J. J. Caron of the Netherlands had previously served as governor of Bali, Hans Holstad from Norway had presided a decade earlier over the League of Nations commission for the Greek-Turkish population exchange, and Charles van Wattenwyl was a colonel from the Swiss army. League of Nations Secretariat members Peter Anker of Norway and Charles Mottier of Switzerland accompanied the observers.[22]

The International Mission had announced before leaving Geneva that they wanted to avoid everything that could suggest that they had been influenced by any of the parties. High Commissioner Martel insisted that neither French nor Syrian officials organize any kind of official reception for the arriving observers. Meeting with the Syrian National Bloc government, he argued that the best way to plead their case would be to allow the observers to travel freely, without intervention, so they could best appreciate the true situation in the Sanjak. Trying to make contacts and sway their opinion would only hurt Syria.[23] According to Martel, the Arab government in Damascus viewed the three League of Nations observers with a "lively satisfaction." Local opinion had become exasperated by a combination of the aggressive tone of the Turkish press and its daily dramas portraying the Sanjak as an area of fire and blood. Syrian frustration was especially acute because Martel had prohibited Arab journals from responding and engaging in polemic. Like Martel, the Syrian government hoped that the presence of impartial witnesses would permit the reestablishment of the facts after

League of Nations Commission. Courtesy of UNOG Library, League of Nations Archives.

all the false news spread by the Agence Anatolie.[24] They remained convinced of the justice of their case, and there seemed little reason to doubt that the status quo was, in any case, the most likely outcome.[25]

The government of Turkey, on the other hand, intended to make its case before the new International Mission of Observers to the Sanjak of Alexandretta directly. With the Sanjak still in French/Syrian hands, Turkey had to demonstrate the Turkishness of the Sanjak to the observers, staging performances on the streets of the Sanjak that would portray the Turkish affiliations and affections of its people. Turkish efforts began before the Mission even left Ankara, arranging for the observers to witness passionate protests along the route.[26] Turcophiles in many places within the Sanjak were creating new flags of the "independent territory of Hatay" to greet the arrival of the League observers. A new "Active Committee of the National Turkish Party" was created at Antioch, with Abdulgani Türkmen at its head. Their mission was to organize demonstrations, create petitions, and collect signatures to present to the observers. Although the group publicly demanded the Sanjak's independence—a status similar to both Lebanon and Syria, all still under French control—French officials believed that the new "Active Committee" had been charged by the Ankara government to work not toward independence, but instead toward the Sanjak's eventual attachment to Turkey.[27]

The imbalance between the two "sides" necessarily led to very different strategies. The Republic of Turkey was clearly a player in the Sanjak question: Turkey claimed the right to the Sanjak on the basis of demography and the desires of the population. Intervention within the contested Sanjak was completely consistent with Turkey's stated position, and the Turkish government's behavior was dramatic, insistent, and overt. Until the middle of 1937, the closest Turkish consulate had been in Syrian Aleppo, which had become the destination for frequent journeys by Sanjak Turks seeking advice and support; now Ankara set up a support infrastructure directly over the border in the Turkish town of Payas. Turkish officials intervened repeatedly with French mandatory authorities to complain about specific actions within the Sanjak, and lobbied the League of Nations observers actively. The Turkish government sent a representative to accompany the observers on their initial journey to Antioch, stationed a representative in their hotels, supplied translators, wrote complaints, organized demonstrations, and arranged petitions. This was Turkey's dispute, and Turkey's government could hardly have played a more direct role.[28]

France was, technically, the other party to the diplomatic negotiations in Geneva. But its interest in the outcome of the League of Nations process was far different, and that difference was reflected in Martel's tactics. France controlled the Sanjak as a result of the 1920 San Remo Resolution and the 1922 Mandate for Syria and Lebanon, and if the League chose to revise the mandate, the consequences in Paris would be minimal. Should the League actually alter the Sanjak's status, it would be the Syrian nationalists and the Syrian government who would feel the repercussions. Those who would be hurt were the same people who had rebelled against French occupation in the bloody events of 1936.

The National Bloc government, which had come to power in opposition to French control, had adopted a position of constructive engagement with French mandatory authorities while awaiting ratification of the Franco-Syrian Treaty which Paris had promised Syria. The attitude of the collaborationist government in Damascus was clear from the Ministerial Declaration presented to the Syrian Parliament on December 22 defining the Syrian government's response to the situation in the Sanjak. The declaration expressed optimism about the outcome of ongoing negotiations, reiterated that the Sanjak was "indispensable for her [Syria's] existence," and reaffirmed Syria's rightful claims to the Sanjak according to international law. After emphasizing their continuing hope for close relations with Turkey, and expressing optimism that the current impasse would be resolved, the declaration lauded France:

> We cannot consider this question without giving homage to our grand and noble ally, France, who has warmly taken the defense of the rights of Syria confided in her by the League of Nations, at the same time that M. Viénot was making elegant speeches in our favor; these speeches had the greatest echo in the Arab countries.
>
> The evolution of this affair and the close and confident collaboration established between France and Syria is a magnificent proof of the advantages of all types that we will achieve in the Franco-Syrian treaty of alliance.[29]

The legislature approved the declaration unanimously, and was especially noisy in acclaiming provisions of it that promised an amnesty and French aid. This overwhelming support for such an effusive statement of French actions, the "homage" to Syria's "grand and noble ally, France" reflected, ironically, the ruling party's hopes for imminent independence from that very power. The compromises made by the ruling parties in Damascus alienated many of the nationalists who had fought with them against French hegemony.

The declaration called for patience among the population, and trust in the French to resolve the dispute over the Sanjak. According to the declaration, the theater of activity would be diplomatic offices in Geneva, not the streets of the Sanjak. While Turkey and local Kemalists were working to perform the Turkish nature of the region, French officials and the Syrian government seemed to be calling on the Sanjak's Arabs to simply remain off the stage. Although this absence might compromise the eventual outcome of the dispute in favor of the

other party, the mandatory regime was unwilling to support Arab or Syrian nationalist activism. If French officials encouraged Syrian nationalists to organize
in the Sanjak to counter Turkish claims, they feared it would let the nationalist
genie out of the bottle again. The French commitment was to the League and to
their European allies; they were loathe to encourage any local activism that
might compromise their control within Syria, their dominance in Geneva, or
their alliances within Europe. The Syrian government, not even independent,
was unable to stand up against this French posture, especially since the National
Bloc's greatest goal was the implementation of a treaty—*with France*—for its
own independence. Until then, it would not even have representation within the
League of Nations. In the face of both French and Syrian passivity, then, efforts
to show the International Mission of Observers that the Sanjak was not Turkish
would have to be organized by opposition groups, chiefly the League of National
Action.

On the Turkish side, the most effective organization for mobilization was the
Halkevi, or People's House, of Antioch, where Kemalist leaders met and strate-
gized. The Halkevi embodied local Turcophiles' connection with the Republican People's Party, which had created these institutions throughout Turkey to
consolidate its revolutionary regime, which appeared still fragile a decade after
the new Turkish regime had taken power. By the end of the 1920s, as part of his
attempt to create a Western-style culture and government in Turkey, Atatürk had
declared himself ready to introduce a multiparty state. The short experiment
with multiparty politics was a disaster, and the Kemalists concluded that they
had more work to do to create a modern Turkish population appropriate to the
new, modern Turkey.

The Halkevleri (plural) were to be a large part of the answer. Fourteen of
them opened in Turkey in February 1932, with dozens to be inaugurated in
Turkey's major cities over the next decade. The Halkevleri were to be controlled
by Turkey's only remaining political party, the Republican People's Party. They
had the dual role of disseminating the new values of the Kemalist state among
the population while simultaneously discovering, preserving, and glorifying
"authentic" Turkish language and culture. The authenticity project was famously
advanced when Béla Bartók used the Halkevleri in his efforts to collect genuine
Anatolian folk music. Historians emphasize instead the importance of the
Halkevleri as a means for propagating Kemalist values and ideologies. Throughout most of Turkey, the Halkevleri organized civic festivals on state holidays,
taught Turkish anthems, staged patriotic plays, organized sports teams, and
functioned as an important center of adult education. In the Sanjak, especially in
Antioch city, the Halkevleri went a step further. They not only educated the population into what constituted "Turkishness"; the Antioch Halkevi also served as
the official disseminator of Turkish goals and strategies in the struggle over the

Sanjak's future.[30] Now, the Halkevleri in the Sanjak had an urgent task: to propagate the appearance of Turkishness throughout the disputed province. If the League was to assign the Sanjak on the basis of the identity of the local population, the Halkevleri would be central in the struggle to demonstrate to the observers that the residents of the Sanjak were Turks.

By the time the International Mission of Observers arrived, Turkish and Arab nationalists alike sought ways to display their own dominance in the Sanjak. While French and Syrian authorities had the advantage of being visibly present (officially, culturally, and linguistically), the Kemalists had to find ways to make Turkishness similarly visible to the eyes of the international observers. The dramatic events that nationalists produced in their campaigns to win hearts and minds were anathema to French colonial forces, who were committed to the familiar role of colonial policing, which emphasized maintaining order and discouraging or suppressing impassioned demonstrations.

Turks enlisted headgear as the most visible symbol of Turkishness. Atatürk himself had emphasized the importance of Western-style dress in fashioning the New Turk, and brims were an essential element of the new style. Kemalists hoped that the observers would see Western-style—that is, Turkish-style—hats everywhere they went, convincing them that the region was truly Turkish. To that end, hats flooded into the Sanjak and were distributed free of charge in an effort to make a visual statement to the observers.[31] The French Security Services office for the Azaz and Kürt Dağ districts reported that one local notable returned from Turkey on January 6 bringing back with him a thousand hats and caps.[32] Packages of hats were sent to the village of Bik Obassi in Kürt Dağ by two unknown Turkish emissaries and immediately distributed among the inhabitants.[33]

The observers were greeted on their arrival in Alexandretta on January 4 with two days of dueling demonstrations. As they met with Durieux at the municipal building, one hundred Turcophiles demonstrated outside. Two hours later, an estimated five hundred pro-Syrian demonstrators followed, and the next morning, the same number of Turkish villagers descended on Alexandretta. The observers seemed less concerned with the protesters than with technical questions, however: the economics of Alexandretta's port, and statistical summaries of Turkey's imports and exports during the previous years were the first subjects to which they turned their attention.[34]

Nonetheless, interviews with the Sanjak's people were an important part of their research, and the observers received delegations throughout their stay. French Security Services had eyes and ears everywhere during the visit of the International Mission of Observers, and their summaries of the interviews emphasize Turkish claims of victimization. "We present you first our thanks for coming because it is your arrival that saves us from the perpetual threat of bayonets," Turcophile leaders asserted on January 5. "For fear of being beaten, mistreated or imprisoned, we seclude ourselves and we will be prevented from breathing, even deprived of the right to walk freely. From now on, it is impossible for us to continue this life of slavery and the atrocities committed against us . . . etc. [*sic*]." Another group of Turcophiles complained of the unbearable municipal taxes and the local government's injustices against Turkish merchants and owners.[35] Omar Numan, the Turkish official accompanying the observers, wrote for *Tan* that even despite the partiality of the French-controlled process, the International Mission recognized the existence of the Turkish majority.[36]

With the International Mission of Observers in place in the Sanjak, the governments of Turkey and France continued negotiations in Geneva in an effort to reach a bilateral agreement. Two "White Books" circulated in the Sanjak summarizing relevant sections from official agreements on the status of the Sanjak, while the French and Turkish governments exchanged official notes through the month. The positions of France and Turkey remained essentially irreconcilable. Each government claimed that its position was based on Ankara Treaty of 1921; they continued to disagree on the capacity in which France had made that agreement. If, as France claimed, it was acting as the mandatory power for Syria at the time of the agreement, then the Sanjak was part of the mandate. Turkey, on the other hand, insisted that it had never recognized the mandate or France as mandatory and had concluded the Ankara Treaty outside the confines of the mandate system. When Turkey demanded that the Sanjak be given its independence on the same basis as Lebanon and Syria, France refused, claiming that the mandate precluded its ceding territory and explicitly promised the eventual independence of only two states, Syria and Lebanon. France insisted that the Sanjak of Alexandretta's separate administrative status had never been intended to lead to a separate political status. Turkey responded that, since the Sanjak had never been part of the mandate, this was all irrelevant. Moreover, since Turkey had ceded the Sanjak to France qua France, not as a mandatory power, Turkey refused to consider the possibility that it would become part of or under the control of any other country.[37] For France, the Sanjak was part of Syria; Turkey claimed it had always been a separate entity.

In December meetings, Turkey proposed a settlement making the Sanjak a demilitarized, independent state in confederation with Syria and Lebanon; its security would be guaranteed jointly by France and Turkey. In a long letter to Henri Ponsot, the French ambassador to Turkey, Foreign Minister Viénot set forth the reasons for France's rejection of this proposal as a basis of discussion. First, the precedent it would set in the current European context would be completely unacceptable. After quoting at length from the German *Westfälische Landes Zeitung* of December 28, Viénot warned of the larger issues raised by Turkey's claims for the debates then raging across Europe over the mandate system, irredentism, and the desirability of revising the boundaries established at the end of World War I:

> The position of the Turkish Minister of Foreign Affairs could be considered as a precedent in the issue of revision that is now becoming reality and lead to a discussion of the value of the mandates. . . . If one begins to consider the territories under mandate in the Near East, one cannot see why the question of the mandates in Africa could not be posed as well. The negotiation in Paris of the Turkish Foreign Minister merits great attention because it does not simply reflect the possession of a territory in the North of Syria, it raises the questions that go much further and that it will be necessary to speak of one day or another.

Moreover, the proposal that France and Turkey jointly guarantee the security of the Sanjak was unacceptable because it would give Turkey political rights "in a foreign territory without any basis except the interests of the Turkish population inhabiting that territory: one sees certain states, notably Hungary, who could use this precedent to reclaim a right of intervention in the affairs of its neighboring countries." If Paris agreed with Turkey's proposal, Viénot feared that France not only would undermine the validity of the mandate system but also that it would be setting a dangerous precedent by supporting territorial claims on the basis of language.

France also worried that the tripartite confederation Turkey proposed would be fraught with serious problems. The state would have two hundred thousand people, including an activist Turkish population, and would no longer be attached to Syria. Instead, the independent Sanjak's economic life would be tied to Turkey and Turkey's use of the port, and would grow to be very dependent on its neighbor to the north, "fatally escaping from our influence to become a satellite of Ankara." In addition, if the confederation actually pursued an independent foreign policy, France's dominance in Lebanon ("the bastion of our position in the Levant") would be threatened. Essentially, a tripartite confederation that included Turkish guarantees for one of its members would allow Turkey to return to its former influence in the Levant, "the reestablishment to our detriment" of the situation before World War I. The French government insisted that any formula to resolve the situation must be compatible with the Syrian territorial character of the region, and must not result in the liquidation of the French mandate. Turkey's suggestion for a tripartite confederation met neither of these conditions.[38]

As negotiations dragged on, the Ankara government became increasingly frustrated. Turkey refused France's proposal that the two governments leave aside the juridical issues and instead discuss practical matters that would redefine the administrative, military, and economic regimes of the Sanjak, creating a demilitarized area with a free port. The U.S. ambassador in Turkey noted that, by the beginning of January, the Turks were "greatly exasperated" with the state of negotiations, and "the propaganda of the local press has since taken on a new virulence, even proclaiming Turkey's readiness to face the world in arms rather than suffer humiliation in this question." Viénot fumed that Turkey was trying to take advantage of the difficult international situation. Pointing out that Turkey's location had proved to be of great importance during the recent war, he fretted that "the position that Turkey would adopt in case of conflict is a subject of serious preoccupations for the French government." The government in Paris was growing increasingly worried that France's behavior toward the Sanjak would be crucial in Turkey's decision about its loyalties in the event of another war.[39]

Each government turned to Great Britain, looking for support for its own position. Turkey proposed that the Sanjak become a demilitarized, independent state, whose open port would encourage trade throughout the region. The French argued that independence would lead inevitably to a Turkish takeover of the Sanjak, and that neither France nor England wanted to risk Arab good will over the loss of the Sanjak. Britain feared the Sanjak question would bring the realization of Britain's own nightmares: conflict between Britain's two friends France and Turkey, instability in the eastern Mediterranean where Britain still hoped to achieve an agreement with Italy, and encouragement of Turkish claims on other former Ottoman provinces (like British-controlled Mosul in northern Iraq).

With France's refusal to consider a resolution based on Turkey's demand for an independent Sanjak, there could be no further bilateral movement. The French Foreign Ministry informed the Syrian government that the talks had ended in failure. French prime minister Leon Blum had promised Turkish Foreign Minister Aras that France would take a new position, but French ambassador Ponsot returned to Ankara on January 3 with no new proposals. On January 5, Aras spoke to the Republican People's Party, reporting to a clearly disappointed audience that no progress had been made during the negotiations.[40]

The same day, Kemal Atatürk decided to take matters into his own hands, in what American observers called a "theatrical and mystifying" move. As early as November 1, 1936, Atatürk had insisted before the Grand National Assembly that the Sanjak question was the important topic of the day. His government had accused French authorities in the Sanjak of forcing Turks to vote in the Syrian elections, and of harassing those who refused. By the time the League of Nations discussions had formally begun in Geneva on December 14, his government was expressing public outrage at the situation in the Sanjak. When he learned not only that the bilateral talks had failed, but also that the French ambassador had returned to Ankara with no new instructions from Paris, Atatürk abruptly, on January 5, boarded a train in Istanbul that was bound for Konya, headquarters of the Turkish army's Southern Command. At Eskişehir, his chief advisers boarded the train: İsmet İnönü, Turkey's prime minister; Foreign Minister Aras; Şükrü Kaya, the interior minister; and Fevzi Çakmak, chief of the General Staff. They talked in the president's train car well into the night. The ongoing virulent press attacks on French obstruction, along with Atatürk's public engagement in the crisis, led to fears that the president's sudden journey south was a prelude to a military invasion of the Sanjak.

By morning, however, the other officials were heading back to Ankara, while Atatürk continued on toward Konya, the crisis temporarily averted. Nonetheless, Atatürk threatened to resign and lead the army into the Sanjak himself if its fate could not be resolved in a manner consistent with Turkey's honor. *Cumhuriyet* quoted the Turkish president's statement on January 7:

> Turkey is prepared to defy the whole world when it is faced with a principle affecting its honor. Hatay is a personal matter for me and I made this very clear to the French ambassador right from the beginning. It is absolutely unthinkable that in the present state of the world such a matter should be allowed to become a cause for armed conflict. But I have taken this into my calculations and I have made my decision. If even one chance in a thousand of such a trend should appear on the horizon, I shall resign from the Presidency of the Turkish Republic and as a private citizen, with a few comrades, I shall carry on the struggle.[41]

France's ambassador to Vienna, Gabriel Puaux, illustrated the international interest in the Sanjak situation, warning that he had heard confidentially from an Austrian government source that Atatürk "had decided on 5 January to leave the League of Nations and seize Alexandretta." His confidant had explained that the intervention of İsmet İnönü and the head of the military had convinced Atatürk not to proceed. Foreign Minister Aras reassured the Balkan Entente that Turkey would remain within the Geneva process.[42]

High Commissioner Martel predicted dramatic results if Turkey "abandoned the terrain of right for that of intimidation." Nervously citing threats in the Turkish press that Ankara would quit the League of Nations and claim the Sanjak by force if necessary, he insisted that Turkey would pay a steep price in the currency of its hard-fought status in the international arena.[43] Carrying out these threats, he argued, would alienate both the Soviet Union and England. Martel feared this claim on the Sanjak elicited European fears that Turkey would return to the "politics of the Sultans," trying to recreate Ottoman expansion. Such suspicions would complicate the already difficult diplomatic conditions in Europe, exacerbating Italy's worries about Turkish intentions toward Rhodes and the Dodecanese Islands and threatening Great Britain's own hegemony in the region, since Alexandretta controlled not only the Syrian hinterland but also the Mosul region in Iraq. Martel claimed that France, too, must be concerned about the outcome of Turkey's demands. Kemalist ambitions would threaten France directly, he argued, by encouraging Syria's leaders to question their reliance on France, proving the bankruptcy of the "politics of the treaty." Syrian leaders might instead seek the protection of another foreign power, or engage in direct negotiations with Turkey. "Our interests in the eastern basin of the Mediterranean would be compromised and our failure would have inevitable repercussions in the Arab world."[44] Atatürk's threat to ignore the League's process and take the territory by force evoked another set of demons. The Turkish president's insistence that the Sanjak's Turks should be connected with Turkey seemed to parallel the German government's growing claims of entitlement to neighboring territory on the basis of the large number of German-speaking residents. Like Germany, Turkey was now threatening to abandon the League of Nations if its demands remained unmet. President Atatürk's speech seemed to threaten Europe's ever more tenuous stability on three fronts: insisting on revising the borders created at the end of World War I, making irredentist claims to territory on the basis of language, and challenging the authority of the beleaguered League of Nations.

U.S. ambassador MacMurray remained convinced, however, that Atatürk would not follow the German path. Citing the Turkish president's realism, his hitherto "scrupulous observance of international engagements," and his unwillingness to alienate Turkey's French, British, and Balkan allies, MacMurray insisted that Atatürk would postpone any military force at least until after the League Council met in January. MacMurray suggested that this dramatic episode might have been intended to demonstrate to France how serious Turkey was about the Sanjak.[45] Certain of Atatürk's restraint, MacMurray claimed that Turkey would continue to renounce revisionism in favor of working through established international channels.[46]

The shadow cast by Atatürk's train journey spread over the Sanjak as well. Rumors were rampant that Turkish forces were on the border, and indeed, the Turkish government established new military posts at Payas, directly over the line. French police claimed to have reliable information that the goal of these new bases was not only to reinforce soldiers who might be necessary to occupy the Sanjak but also to "raise the morale of the Syrians living near the border, to encourage them to claim autonomy for the Sanjak, and to participate, if needed, in demonstrations organized by the Turks."[47] Incursions had been increasing since the middle of December as tribal groups and armed bands from Turkey crossed into the Sanjak and the neighboring Kürt Dağ region. The cross-border raids combined with Atatürk's night journey to create a growing sense of insecurity and instability in the region, as rumors swirled about the impending invasion of Turkish troops.[48]

Against the backdrop of local insecurity, diplomatic impasse, and threatening global conflict, the International Mission of Observers continued its work on the streets of the Sanjak. Believing that collective self-determination would be playing a pivotal role, the various claimants worked to display the identity of the collective "self" for the eyes of the League's observers. Competing demonstrations escalated by the second week of their visit, as each "side" struggled to produce convincing displays of strength in an attempt to influence what the observers would report. To carry out their demonstrations, each group recruited villagers from an ever-growing region.

The first in a series of demonstrations began with rumors on January 9 that the Turkish students of a mixed Antioch lycée planned a strike. In anticipation, an estimated five hundred Arab students walked out of their classes to demonstrate in front of the government building, shouting "Vive Syria," carrying the Syrian flag, and chanting the Syrian national anthem as they passed in front of the Tourism Hotel, where the League's representatives were staying. Local Alawis followed with their own demonstrations.[49] Turkish leaders responded with a "Salute" to the International Mission of Observers the same afternoon, as an estimated two to two and a half thousand supporters, including many women and children, arrived at the hotel. Although there were no flags, some of the children carried ribbons with Turkish colors, and demonstrators carried seven placards, written in Latin characters, with slogans calling for independence and equality. In front of the hotel, they all doffed their hats and caps to salute the League observers, who were standing on the steps. The same evening, the observers received a number of Turkish groups seeking to air their complaints, which were largely economic, and to express their desire for the independence of the Sanjak. Rumors circulated about an Arab counterdemonstration planned for January 11.[50]

The numerous demonstrations, not only in Antioch and Alexandretta but also at Kirikhan, resulted in some arrests but few injuries.[51] By contrast, the observers' visit to Reyhanlı on January 10 was calamitous. Turkish activists had been notified of the observers' visit to Reyhanlı and the previous day had begun bringing villagers into the city from the surrounding area. As the observers' cars turned north at Yenişehir, they were greeted by Kemalist men and women crying "Vive Hatay!" "Vive Independence!" "Vive Atatürk!" By half past three that afternoon, the observers arrived at the Reyhanlı mayor's office to begin their interviews with the municipal council and Turcophile groups. When the Turks' interviews had been finished and the observers were preparing to speak with Arab representatives, one of the Turkish interpreters objected, claiming that these Arabs were not qualified to speak on behalf of the Reyhanlı population because many of the Arabs favored Turkey.

The cries from the street brought the League observers to the balcony overlooking the market. Hundreds of Turcophiles dressed in European clothing stopped a group almost as large whose members were dressed in local costume. The two groups exchanged blows, and the non-Kemalist crowd backed away, throwing stones to protect their retreat. Gunshots rang out as the observers saw their own guards joining local gendarmes to break up the conflict. Guards were thrown on the ground, molested, hit, beaten, and disarmed by the Turkish crowd, who took their weapons and ammunition. The observers watched in horror as a man fired his rifle, and they saw the man withdraw, hit. The same gunman fired many times. On the street in front of the mayor's office a man dressed as an Arab lay on the ground, dying. The municipal doctor examined him and found a fracture at the base of his skull from a rifle bullet. Two people with leg injuries showed their wounds to the League observers to verify their injuries. The events produced twenty-five casualties: on the basis of their dress, officials identified eighteen Arabs, at least four Turks, and one Armenian wounded by gunshots or blows. One of the injured gendarmes, an Armenian, was hospitalized in Antioch with a fractured arm and numerous bruises on his back, four injured Arabs went to the hospital at Aleppo for treatment, and a man injured by a pistol blow to the head died during the night. Kirikhan's justice of the peace came to Reyhanlı to begin an inquiry and arrested seven people, including the son of the president of the municipality of Reyhanlı, a Turk who had fired his gun.[52]

That evening, seven of Antioch's most prominent Turks wrote to Gacon, the commander of Antioch's special services, expressing their outrage at the events. Their version of the day's incident was entirely different from the descriptions provided by the League observers, local police, and French officials. According to the Turkish letter, armed Arabs from neighboring Harim had been brought to Reyhanlı by their village head. These Arabs "spontaneously opened fire on the Turkish inhabitants who had met at Reyhanlı hoping to welcome the observers." The attack had caused the deaths and injuries of Turks; according to the Antioch Kemalist leaders, the Turkish population had been the "object of an armed aggression when claiming her rights in a peaceful manner." The letter-writers held the district governor largely responsible, claiming he had been known to encourage Arab elements and to decorate his own home with Syrian flags and was suspected of threatening neighboring village heads. As far as these Kemalist leaders were concerned, the Turks in this incident had been innocently trying to attain their rights and were victimized by a district governor trying to provoke incidents "under the eyes of the observers."[53]

Arabic-speakers of all religions gathered the next day, an estimated twenty to twenty-five thousand people, some arriving from the neighboring villages. Fifteen hundred to two thousand Armenians from Musa Dağ, of whom many were former soldiers, paraded with the French and Syrian flags at their head. In a procession that lasted almost two hours, marchers carried Syrian and French flags and fifteen different signs with inscriptions in French and in Arabic calling for respect for France, the Franco-Syrian Treaty, the League of Nations, and "Syrian Unity." Some of the slogans challenged the Kemalist program directly. Aleppo's nationalists sent a band for the occasion, which set up opposite the Tourism Hotel and played during the parade. Thirty Arab nationalist youth from the paramilitary Steel Shirts participated. On arriving at the entrance to the observers' hotel, the crowd heard speeches by four young men from the Arab nationalist League of National Action. Each of the speakers focused on his attachment to France and to Syria, and claimed that the Sanjak was Syrian in spite of the propaganda, which, in any case, did not reflect local sentiments.[54] These young men from the League of National Action presented their own patriotic passions as the equivalent of French nationalism and equalitarianism.

> On the occasion of our peaceful demonstration, we, Syrian citizens, are pleased to inform you that our national conception is inspired by the French nation, a nationalism in which religions and races harmonize in a noble synthesis for the realization of the human ideal. As a result, our Turkish citizens remain brothers for us, and the tendencies of separatism that have recently appeared are only a natural consequence of the intensive propaganda made by the Turkish government in our neighboring zone.

Demonstrators applauded League observers repeatedly as they stood on the balcony of the hotel. The speeches finished with a request that the International Mission of Observers receive League of National Action leader Zaki al-Arsuzi; in the afternoon, the observers received a delegation from the Syrian League of National Action.[55]

One of Antioch's Kemalist leaders left immediately to report on the events to the Turkish consul in Aleppo, and returned to Antioch carrying directions: "The Turks must make a counterdemonstration on the 12th more imposing than that of the Arabs; they must turn out very energetically and not fall back on being mishandled."[56] Antioch's Turcophiles moved into high gear. That evening, they distributed one hundred tins of gasoline among the Turkish garage owners and chauffeurs to enable them to bring all the Turkish villagers between seven and seventy years old to Antioch. Seventy trucks brought thousands of people from Alexandretta, Kirikhan, Beylan, Reyhanlı, and neighboring Turkish villages.[57] In the increasingly polarized atmosphere that accompanied the dueling demonstrations, local authorities invited International Mission of Observers to Durieux's official residence, bringing the focus of the march outside the city, to the other side of the river.

In a driving rain that Tuesday morning, thousands of demonstrators paraded in front of the French residence, where the League observers were standing.

Instead of focusing on the signs they carried calling for rights, independence, justice, and a long life for Atatürk, however, League official Anker's attention remained on the bad weather and his sympathy for the poor peasants and city-dwellers, men, women, and children, assembled for hours in open air badly protected from the rain. Toward the end of the procession, Kemalist leader Vedi Munir greeted League observers: "Despite the bad times and the rain, the population is demonstrating to reclaim their rights before the eyes of the delegates of the League of Nations."[58] As the procession ended, ten young men on bicycles wearing cockades with Turkish colors rode into the predominantly Alawi Affan quarter of the city. The patrol stationed in the quarter to guard against any trouble tried to intervene as local Alawis converged on the young men, carrying sticks to obstruct their passage. In what local officials called an "incident of little importance," thousands of Alawis who gathered at the scene were soon dispersed by police.[59] Porous neighborhood boundaries were hardening as Antioch's people began to demonstrate their affiliations in the streets.

The activists' goal seems to have been achieved: the League observers were spectators at massive displays of Arabness and Turkishness in the Sanjak. Writing of the January 12 events, Anker reflected, "What impressed us most was the extreme excitement, indeed ecstasy, of certain groups of demonstrators, and, on the other hand, the miserable state of the participants drenched by the rain, especially the children and babies in the arms of their mothers during the deluge." Nonetheless, he wrote that the observers did not attach much importance to the crowd estimates or even to the demonstrations, which, he wrote, proved nothing. "I will not hide from you that we will be very happy when the last demonstration was finished, after having passed an hour in the rain."[60] Concerned about the future consequences of the escalating demonstrations, Martel ordered that these spectacles cease.[61]

The League observers tried to understand the Sanjak's demography beyond the representations in the streets. They considered French statistics, which classified the population by language, which illustrated, with self-interested assurance, that 80 percent of the people preferred the status quo. The French characterized the Sanjak as a hodgepodge of minorities ("macédoine de minorités") in which 38 percent were actually Turkish; of those, one-third (13 percent) were primarily urban Kemalists, and two-thirds (25 percent) were peasants, "traditionalists, partisans of the Caliphate." "All the other groups, on the contrary, generally express pro-Syrian sentiments and demand the attachment of the Sanjak to Syria." According to French officials, while the Kemalists wanted union with Turkey, the rest of the Turks preferred maintaining the status quo, with its low taxes, lack of military service obligations, freedom to practice religion, and freedom of dress. Arab "extremists," very few in number, hoped to "Arabize" the region "by fair means and foul." Nonetheless, the French insisted that the people of the Sanjak wanted to be absorbed neither by Syria nor by Turkey, but instead to have the rights of all minorities respected.[62]

In a January 15 letter to Edouard de Haller at the League of Nations Secretariat in Geneva, League official Anker, still accompanying the observers in the Sanjak, began with the French population figures before presenting his analysis of the motives of each activist group. Those who spoke Turkish, he claimed, were estimated to be around ninety-one thousand people, including some of the Kurds and all of the Circassians, who spoke Turkish along with their "mother tongue." Arabic-speakers could be estimated at around ninety-nine thousand, including Sunni Arabs, Alawis, Arab Christians (primarily Greek Orthodox), and some of the Kurds. Armenian-speakers numbered some thirty thousand. As Anker pointed out, there was disagreement over which group the Alawis belonged to. Turks claimed that Alawis were actually Turks, but according to Anker, all the Alawis observers had spoken with contested that claim, "declaring without hesitation that they consider themselves Arabs."[63]

Rejecting the French assessment of the activists as simply extremists, Anker tried to make sense of their motivations. Although many of the "chapistes" (the hat-wearers supporting Kemalist goals in the Sanjak) explained to Anker that they hoped their personal debts would be reduced by a change in regime, Anker believed this to be only part of a bigger set of issues, psychological, political, and economic. He cited Turkish national pride, as the Turcophiles, recalling their earlier rule over the Arabs, now refused to be dominated by them. Moreover, local Kemalists looked with pride at the progress of their neighbor to the north; many had firsthand knowledge of conditions in Turkey as a result of their studies there, on scholarships furnished by the Ankara government. Anker also listed the aspirations of young people to be liberated from their parents, and the desire of young women to "obtain the same liberties as their sisters of Kemalist Turkey." These, he claimed, were all quite abstract effects of Turkey's propaganda. For the Kemalists in the Sanjak, independence would be only the first step on the way to attachment to Turkey.

Arab activists were motivated by their desire for a unified Syria as well as by their broader, pan-Arab sentiments. Although Anker had heard from many Alawis of their opposition to independence or attachment to Turkey, he did not believe them to be entirely supportive of the idea of a unified Syria; he thought they wanted French protection from both Ankara and Damascus. Armenians were quite fearful of Turkish domination, and preferred to remain tied to Syria, though many wished the French mandate to continue. Those Armenians who had taken refuge in Syria after World War I were clear about their intention to leave the Sanjak if it came under Turkish control. Despite their fears of Turkish domination, Anker noted, Arabs, Alawis, and Armenians referred to their "Brother Turks" and their "Turkish compatriots," expressing respect for the

Turks. Anker claimed that the Turkish partisans of "Hatay" did not express the same sentiments toward the non-Turkish groups.[64]

Indeed, local Turkish leaders worked to discredit their adversaries in the eyes of the League Commission. Seeking to challenge the impression that the pro-Syrian demonstrations represented the attitudes of the population, the Kemalists claimed the events had been orchestrated by partisan government officials. "The demonstrations organized by a small group of minority elements today against the independence of the Sanjak, on the insinuation and instigation of the Mayor of Antioch, the Gendarmerie Commandant and other Syrian functionaries, has led the Turkish Majority of the Sanjak to respond. The markets of Antioch, Beylan and Reyhanlı have remained closed today to protest against the recent demonstrations," telegraphed Antioch's Kemalist leaders.[65] A group of Turcophiles from Reyhanlı wrote to the International Mission of Observers on January 9 trying to diminish the import of Arab demonstrations. "Responsible government agents encourage and oblige minorities in Hatay to carry the Syrian flag, provoking thereby an imaginary movement." The people of Reyhanlı, they continued, were showing their solidarity with their (Turkish) Antioch brothers by also closing their shops in compliance with the Kemalist strike.[66]

The argument that this pro-Syrian movement was "imaginary," that it was coerced by local officials, and that it did not represent any real political impulse was extremely important to the Turkish narrative. Turkey's 1920 National Pact states that the new republic would be comprised of all remaining Ottoman territories not populated by Arabs. For the Sanjak to be part of Turkey, according to Turkey's own ideology it had to have a non-Arab majority. If "Turk" could be defined to include all non-Arabs, Turks would be a majority. The existence of large demonstrations might suggest that local people preferred to be connected with Syria, and imply that non-Arabs could hardly be considered "Turks" for Ankara's purposes.

The Turkish government's demographic argument for the Sanjak was treated with great skepticism by High Commissioner Martel, who was convinced that Turkey's demand on the Sanjak had ulterior motives. He denied the salience of the demographic argument, pointing out that Turkey had made no claims to part of Bulgaria despite the eight hundred thousand Turks who ended up in that country when the borders were drawn. Instead, Atatürk's government was claiming the Sanjak, with one-fourth that many Turks, because its real goal was to become a major world power. Recognizing that they could make no demands on the Balkans, Martel surmised, Turkey nonetheless understood that great states need colonies and sources of raw materials. Its Arab neighbors offered both great potential for economic development and significant petroleum reserves. Bulgaria was untouchable, but the Arabs had neither political stability nor the ability to resist. Turkey's goal was nothing less than the retaking of all of the former

Arab provinces under French mandate, Martel argued. The theory of Hittite origins, he feared, could easily be extended to the Arabs. Indeed, one of Atatürk's recent linguistic claims had suggested that Arabic words could remain within the Turkish language, since both had originated from the same place. "One could also claim one day that the Arab peoples descended from the Hittite and that their blood brothers have the duty to deliver them and unite with them." Recent Turkish allusions to Mosul and claims to Kürt Dağ (which the Turks had begun calling Turk Dağ) only reinforced Martel's anxiety.[67] His fears were shared broadly among intelligence agents in Syria, who believed Sunni Muslims—like the Turks—were inherently anti-Western, and specifically opposed to France.[68]

While the High Commissioner fretted about Turkey's hidden agenda and the population created spectacles to call attention to their collective identities, France's deputy chief of mission in Berlin, Pierre Arnal, warned that the Sanjak affair could provide the kind of encouragement to Germany that might menace world peace. He heard in Berlin a "particular and persistent resonance" in Turkey's claims to the Sanjak, and cautioned that France's whole diplomatic posture could be undermined by this issue. Turkey's claim to the Sanjak, he argued, was dangerously revisionist, challenging not only the postwar treaties but also the institution of the mandates, and even the League of Nations itself. Ominously, it raised the "ethnic minorities question," and put France in a very awkward situation. Arnal viewed with horror the German Ministry of Propaganda's use of the Sanjak question as a precedent: "If Turkey obtains satisfaction in some way, what encouragement for the Reich!" As Arnal pointed out, the German government counted huge German populations outside its territory, "1.4 million in Poland, .4 million in Danzig, 3.5 millions in Czechoslovakia, 6.3 millions in Austria, not counting those in the Baltics, Hungary, Romania and Alsace," many millions more than Turkey was claiming. Moreover, couldn't Germany itself hope to reclaim its former colonies? Germans accused France and Britain of employing an unacceptable double standard: when Atatürk first made his claims to the Sanjak in the Grand National Assembly, "no one cried scandal, no one . . . accused the Gazi [Atatürk] of threatening the peace of the world." France had been attentive to Ankara, a far different response than her outright denial of German claims. "If one admitted that Turkey could demand a revision to her borders, why not acknowledge it for other countries?" Arnal accused Germany of encouraging Turkish intransigence, throwing fuel on the fire of an emerging Franco-Turkish dispute from which Germany hoped to benefit. For this French diplomat, the Sanjak question could have serious and unfavorable repercussions "on our interests and our prestige vis à vis the Muslim world, not only in the Near East, but also in all of North Africa." French interests could also suffer in all of Danubian and eastern Europe, as far as Romania, "where the Reich had not given up on superseding France." Pointing to both recent economic negotiations

between Germany and Turkey and Germany's decades-long commercial relations with the Ottomans, Arnal speculated that Germany was partly responsible
for Turkey's tone in this dispute. If Turkey's ultimatum worked, Germany would
then "benefit from the international circumstances" to carry out its own fait
accompli. France and England's failure to respond to either the Italian conquest
of Abyssinia or Germany's remilitarization of the Rhineland could only provide
encouragement, he argued.[69]

Balkan leaders were likewise following developments in the Sanjak, worried
both about compromising their good relations with France and the precedent
that Turkish claims could provide. The Balkan Entente, which Turkey's foreign
minister had helped to create, was devoted to maintaining the postwar borders
without revision. Turkey's Foreign Minister Aras reassured members of the
Balkan Entente that the only problem was France's "politics of evasion." Romanian
Foreign Minister Victor Antonescu seemed agitated by Turkey's position, "in
which he claimed to see an inspiration for Germany." At the same time,
Antonescu seemed doubtful that Atatürk would carry through his apparent
threats.[70] American observers agreed. United States ambassador MacMurray
seemed fascinated with Atatürk, convinced that, despite his threats, he would
continue to work within the framework of the League of Nations as he had over
his plans to remilitarize the straits connecting the Mediterranean and the Black
Sea.[71] For Britain, the Franco-Turkish dispute was a "first rate nuisance."
Although not of any direct concern, it did bring up questions of mandates and
colonies.[72]

For France, the stakes were high: Giving in to the Ankara government on the
Sanjak question would stoke international disputes over revisionism, irredentism, ethnic minorities, and the efficacy of the League of Nations. Rejecting
Turkey's claim increased the likelihood of alienating an important ally in the
eastern Mediterranean as war loomed closer. On the ground, the situation was
becoming increasingly polarized and dangerous. On January 18, 1937, days after
the tragic murder in Reyhanlı and while the observers were still in the Sanjak
gathering information, France's prime minister Leon Blum wrote to the Turkish
ambassador in Paris, offering a new formula. While reiterating the validity of the
French legal position and its responsibilities to the Sanjak, Blum opened the
possibility for a political solution that might provide the Sanjak with a special
status once Syria attained its independence. He also suggested that a transitional
regime could be established that would treat the Sanjak as a distinct entity, still
under French mandatory rule.[73] To ensure that the Ankara Treaty would remain
in force, France proposed a long-term mandate for the Sanjak, with a high commissioner of French nationality to be appointed by the League of Nations. The
transitional regime would make the Sanjak a separate entity, "while giving satisfaction to the Turkish demands concerning administrative and cultural questions";

it would demilitarize the territory, and it would assure Turkey use of the port at Alexandretta.

The new French proposal seemed to comply with both of Martel's essential demands, preserving the French mandate and the Sanjak's connection to Syria. At the same time, it met Ankara's insistence on separation, and allowed the two disputants to reach quick agreement on "fundamental principles" that would guide the future of the Sanjak. The Sanjak would become a separate entity, independent in domestic affairs, and tied to Syria in foreign affairs, customs duties, and monetary issues. Turkish would be the official language; another might be added in the future. Syria and the Sanjak would each have legislative assemblies and executive authorities; a French official would be appointed by the Council of the League of Nations to administer the Sanjak. There would be no army in the Sanjak; France and Turkey together would guarantee its territorial integrity. The League of Nations Council would set up a committee to study the situation and create a Statute and a Fundamental Law for the Sanjak; the observers already in place should remain to provide the committee with all necessary information.

The League of Nations Council adopted the Sandler Report on January 27, 1937. Known by the name of the rapporteur who had brokered the final negotiations, the Sandler Report provided the outlines of a settlement within the framework suggested by the French. The Council dissolved into congratulations: to Sandler, Anthony Eden, and the representatives of both Turkey and France. Turkish foreign minister Aras called it "an international understanding based upon justice and equality." According to French foreign minister Delbos, "the understanding we have reached will result in a stabilization of the situation in the Eastern Mediterranean." In this process, Delbos claimed, "the closest attention has been paid to the vital interests of Syria as well as those of the Sanjak of Alexandretta." The new Syrian state "will only secure tranquility if her relations with her neighbors are friendly. Between Turkey and Syria, only confident and cordial feelings can and should prevail."[74] Many who spoke emphasized that this resolution illustrated the tremendous importance of diplomacy in resolving conflict, and stressed the role of the League of Nations in its peaceful outcome.

That outcome, the result of diplomacy between two member states of the League of Nations, guaranteed a separate status to the Sanjak, privileged Turkey in its administration and protection, and elevated the Turkish language to preeminence. While local activists struggled to stage their claims for the political future of the Sanjak, that future seemed to have been decided without taking into account either the desires of the local population or the observations of the League's own commission. In the Sanjak and in Damascus, the response was immediate.

3

The League Decides

Turkish efforts to secure their claim to the Sanjak had spilled onto the streets, as activists aggressively demonstrated their opposition to the disputed territory's participation in Syria's November 1936 elections. The arrival of the observers sent by the League of Nations provided an opportunity for both Syrian and Turkish nationalists to perform their identities. Taking seriously the assumptions of the interwar politics of self-determination, each group tried to convince the Europeans that it represented the majority in the Sanjak. French diplomats, in turn, stepped up their negotiations through the League of Nations, working to maintain their mandate to govern the Sanjak while putting an end to the escalating unrest that threatened French control. The Sandler Report, adopted in January 1937 and hailed by the League's members as a triumph of reconciliation, preserved the French mandate and the Sanjak's connection to Syria while also establishing the region as a separate, independent entity in domestic affairs, with Turkish as the official language. But as this chapter will illustrate, the consequences of Turkish activism and French diplomatic maneuvering could not be simply put to rest by a carefully worded document created by authorities in Geneva. The demonstrations, activism, and street violence fomented by the diplomatic dispute had mobilized the local population, producing new divisions along sectarian lines that would have long-lasting repercussions for the region. What looked like a peaceful resolution, therefore, actually served to split the population into distinct cultural groups, ironically producing lines of fracture within the newly "unified" region.

Rumors of the Sandler Report circulated wildly around the Sanjak, confirmed by radio broadcasts about renewed negotiations in Geneva. While the diplomats in Geneva cheered the compromise making the Sanjak independent, angry Syrians poured into the streets without even waiting for an official announcement. Merchants all over the country, in Aleppo, Damascus, Dayr al-Zur, Homs, Hama, Latakia, Antioch, and Alexandretta, closed their shops on

January 24,[1] while Damascus medical and law students walked out of their classes, crying "Alexandretta is Arab" and "Alexandretta or Death." The students advanced down the main streets of Damascus to the city's major lycées, including the Greek Orthodox and Catholic schools; French police claimed that they resorted to violence as they sought to persuade other students to follow them.[2] As a leader of the ruling National Bloc tried to calm the angry students, they responded in fury. "Forget the talk, let's move on, leave the joker." The enraged official cried out after them, "Go find arms that we could fight the Turks!"

Though simply a prelude to the angry protests that followed, student demonstrations in front of Syria's government offices, the Orient Palace Hotel, and the British Embassy reflected a transformed discourse. The new analysis articulated a more comprehensive set of concerns, with speakers accusing the Ankara regime of behaving like Europeans trying to colonize others, and spoke to a broader Arab nationalism. An Iraqi student cried, "I am an Iraqi Arab and ready to give my blood for Alexandretta!" With their fury focusing on French betrayal, five hundred students entered the Christian Bab Tuma quarter on the eastern edge of Damascus's old city, shouting with excitement. Their target was the Lazarist school, which they surrounded, scaling the walls and forcing the doors, despite the efforts of the staff to keep them out.

Although France and Turkey evoked the greatest condemnation, the students' rage soon turned to the Syrian government. They broke dozens of windows trying to force their way into the College des Frères Maristes, a structure embodying the direct connection between the French and the Syrian regime: the French school had been built on land owned by the family of Syrian prime minister Jamil Mardam. Stopped by a police barricade as they approached the Turkish Consulate, the students redirected their steps to the offices of Syria's government. Prime Minister Jamil Mardam climbed onto the hood of his car to make himself heard in an effort to assuage their anger. "The government works day and night for Alexandretta, the Sanjak is Syrian Arab and will remain always," he exhorted the crowd. "The government will defend the rights of Syria. Let everyone return to his work."

"What else can the government do? The agreement has been concluded," challenged the demonstrators.

"The government cannot only accept what is imposed on it. Your patriotism is not superior to ours, we will show you that. Among you, some are seeking to plot against the government. It is strong!"

The demonstrators cried out, "The people are above the government, and right surpasses force!"

Sadallah al-Jabiri, who held portfolios as minister of both foreign and internal affairs, took his turn next, trying to reassure the demonstrators and asking them to leave quietly. Unsatisfied with the government's efforts to quiet them, the students decided to meet the next morning at the Faculty of Law and dispersed. Damascus's shops remained closed.

At the same time that the demonstrators held the Syrian government responsible for the League of Nations betrayal, mandatory authorities were holding Jamil Mardam's government culpable for the riots. Fain, Martel's delegate in Damascus, met with Mardam soon after the events, demanding to know what his government proposed to do about the "violation" of the educational establishments and aggression against the French faculty. Fain emphasized the gravity of the situation, and Mardam assured him that the Syrian government would "respect the lives and the goods of foreigners, especially the French."[3]

Mardam's National Bloc government and its policy of constructive engagement could be severely compromised by the alienation of the Sanjak. The Bloc had ridden the wave of the successful general strike to power in 1936 as a nationalist party committed to Syrian independence. Tactically, however, they were committed to a policy of cooperation with French authorities, eschewing armed struggle since witnessing the devastating consequences of the Great Revolt that ended in 1926. The 1936 Franco-Syrian Treaty promising their independence still had to be ratified in Paris, and the National Bloc government acquiesced to all France's demands to prove Syria qualified and civilized enough to merit that sovereignty. Their policy of collaboration would now be completely discredited by France's apparent treachery: instead of achieving their goals, Syria's compliance was resulting in the loss of their territory. The fury of the population was being manifested on every street-corner.

French High Commissioner Martel provided talking points to press outlets and to French officials throughout Syria, trying to put the best possible face on an agreement he knew would elicit angry accusations. "The Sanjak remains Syrian," he insisted. The Sandler Report had set aside the "Turkish thesis" that would have made the Sanjak an independent state. Moreover, since the Sanjak would be demilitarized, the threat of a Turkish military occupation had been averted. An added benefit, according to the High Commissioner, would be the creation of an Alexandretta free-trade zone that would help in the economic development of the whole region. This agreement, Martel contended, would provide a "solid basis for the future relations of Syria with the large neighbor to the north." The best outcome had thus been achieved, but only through the support of Britain and Russia. Martel instructed French officials to take special care to point out to Syrian officials that Syrian opposition to this international decision would have serious consequences, and that the kind of opposition and bad faith that had been displayed in the Damascus demonstrations could not prevail against the "solemn decision of the Council of Geneva." In fact, he claimed, if the Syrian government rejected this agreement, they would risk compromising its most important outcome, Turkey's formal recognition of Syrian territorial integrity.[4]

Although Fain tried to comply with these instructions when Prime Minister Mardam and President al-Atasi returned to Fain's office the next day as promised, he found the Syrian leaders had a much darker understanding of the Geneva decision. In a telegram they sent to both the French government and the League of Nations, they argued that the proposed change to the Sanjak's status was "inimical to the stipulations of the Franco-Syrian Treaty, far exceeds the provisions of the former accords between France and Turkey, and sacrifices the legitimate rights and the vital interests of Syria." They predicted unfortunate consequences not only in Syria, but throughout the Arab world, and hoped that France and the League of Nations would respect international obligations and assure the integrity of Syria.[5] Mardam insisted that the Sandler Report contradicted the 1921 Ankara Treaty, and the Franco-Syrian Treaty just concluded. Moreover, the Syrian leaders were distraught that France, having just signed a treaty of independence with Syria, had so quickly proceeded to sacrifice part of that state. For Mardam, the Sandler Report marked the newest example of the continuing division of Syria, which had already resulted in parts of the country being spun off to create Palestine, Lebanon, and Transjordan.

Fain tried to proceed with Martel's talking points and urged patience, but the Syrian leaders insisted that they could not wait for the forthcoming Statute and Fundamental Law for the Sanjak, explained that they could not prepare public opinion, and pointed out that the opposition parties had taken an active role in the previous day's demonstrations. The Syrian leaders found little of comfort in the Sandler Report, despite Martel's optimism, calling the decision to make Turkish the Sanjak's official language "a catastrophe that risked compromising everything," and worrying about Turkey's agreement to protect the frontier. During the demonstrations, rumors that the National Bloc had resigned were widespread, and government officials trying to calm demonstrators had been received badly. Moreover, members of the Syrian government were not only surprised by the Geneva decision, they were stunned by the rumors suggesting even worse things to come: one claimed that the Sanjak was being given to the Turks, another implicated the Syrian government in having taken part in the decision, a third predicted that the Turkish presence in the soon-to-be independent Sanjak was preparation for an occupation of Syrian territory. Syria's leaders protested that they had been seriously compromised not only by the news coming out of Geneva but also by the way it was being disseminated. They were receiving even the gravest of news only after it had already been published widely.

The recently elected Syrian government would have to navigate carefully. On one side, the French government, the real power in Syria, insisted not only that the Syrian government respect the League's decision, but that its failure to quell growing popular opposition would show it to be unready for the independence promised by the still unratified Franco-Syrian Treaty. On the other side, the

Geneva agreement to which they were expected to acquiesce promised the further dismemberment of Syria, a prospect no nationalist government would tolerate. The loss of the Sanjak would directly threaten the Syrian government's
hold on power by compromising it in the eyes of the Syrian population.

As they had in the 1936 general strike, the National Bloc leaders led from
behind, supporting demonstrations when it was clear that they had little choice.[6]
The massive opposition that spilled into Syria's streets was organized by other
groups, including all of the forces arrayed against the ruling party: the League of
National Action, the United Front, the Syrian Popular Party, and the Communist Party.[7] These antigovernment groups argued that the Sandler Report provided clear evidence that the National Bloc's collaboration with the French
colonizers was not to Syria's benefit. While the demonstrators loudly denounced
Turks, France, and Leon Blum, the Syrian government was, without question,
among those the protesters blamed for the debacle.[8]

Over the next days, the Syrian government vied with "the youth" for the
attention of the country. The "young nationalists" vehemently opposed the
patience counseled by the Syrian government, demanding its immediate resignation. "The government took power and received the confidence of the
Chamber only in order to apply the treaty guaranteeing the integrity of Syrian
territory; if this will not be respected, the cabinet must resign." Some even
accused the government of complicity with the Turks.[9] The student group that
met on January 26 was not impressed with the reassurances of the Syrian interior
minister, who repeated assurances of the government's intent to protect the
Sanjak of Alexandretta. Their telegram was short and direct: "The special student congress meeting at Damascus to examine the question of Alexandretta
declares to the Powers who decide the fate of the weak that it disapproves and
will never recognize any solution which makes Arab Alexandretta a region that is
not Arab in its culture and its politics." The group not only decided to continue
their strike but also refused to participate in demonstrations sponsored by the
government they scorned, keeping their own actions separate. The distance
between the two groups seemed unbridgeable on the morning of January 27,
when the students urged stores to close in protest over the Geneva agreement,
and the government-sponsored Steel Shirts paramilitary youth organization
responded by circulating around Damascus's markets in uniform, carrying sticks
and opposing the closures.[10]

Mardam's government sought some sort of middle course between alienating
its French patrons and enforcing the disastrous League of Nations settlement.
While promising the French that it would instruct police to take rigorous
measures, the government used the demonstrations to display its own nationalist credentials, vowing in fiery speeches to work to overturn the Geneva
agreement, promising to personally take Syrians' grievances to Geneva, even

suggesting it would take up arms to avoid losing the Sanjak. At the same time, however, government leaders began looking beyond the loss of the Sanjak, telling Fain that if they had to swallow the bitter pill of losing the Sanjak, they would demand compensation in improvements to the Franco-Syrian Treaty, especially on the question of Lebanon. Still, some National Bloc leaders resisted, implicitly questioning the continuation of their policy of collaboration, insisting that they could not accept the Sandler Report and would prefer to negotiate directly with the Turks after independence. For some in the Syrian government, the National Bloc's continuing commitment to working with France was tied to the recently concluded Franco-Syrian Treaty; they would respect that treaty only if France would guarantee that it would be executed.[11]

Fain warned Martel that Syrian leaders had become discouraged, leaving agitation in the hands of the youth of all the parties, "with all the dangers that this implies."[12] Martel had anticipated that it would be difficult to change the Syrian government's hostile position, encouraged as it was "not only by their anxiety to maintain their own popularity, threatened by the outbidding of the extremists, but even by the force of nationalist opinion."[13] The National Bloc was now facing not only the long-term disapproval of the opposition parties, especially the Syrian Popular Party and the League of National Action; now they would have to face down their own members, in whose eyes their policies of collaboration had been discredited.

When French undersecretary of state Viénot officially informed Martel of the terms of the agreement three days after the demonstrations had begun, he presented the Sanjak's new status as the price of Syria's security. The French government had been motivated by Syria's need for secure borders, which were being threatened by Turkey's larger designs. In signing the agreement, France sought to prevent the dismemberment of Syrian territory, to preclude any Turkish pretensions to interfere in Syrian affairs through the Sanjak, and to secure a final settlement of the problem. In the absence of a final resolution, Viénot warned, Turkey would have renewed its demands as soon as the mandate was over, and the French could not be certain that the Turks would then limit themselves to demanding only one province. The Sandler Report, on the contrary, would commit Turkey to recognizing and enforcing the entire Syrian-Turkish border. "I understand," Viénot wrote, "that the concessions included in the Council's resolution could be painful for Syrian patriotism, but this is the price of Syrian security." He claimed that the Turks had agreed to Arabic being the second official language, to be formally confirmed at the May meeting of the League. Viénot urged Arab leaders in Mecca, Beirut, and Baghdad to try to convince Syrian leaders "of the necessity to not compromise the results obtained with such trouble by an inopportune intransigence." His final warning: the Syrian government's rejection of this decision on the Sanjak's future would be exploited by the

Turkish government to justify additional demands.[14] Damascus students were hardly convinced, rejecting not only the Sandler Report but also the National Bloc officials who had been unable to protect Syria's territory. In an effort to prove their independence and their refusal to be manipulated by the Damascus regime, they explicitly rejected the government's efforts to participate in officially sponsored demonstrations.[15] Their first order of business was passing three resolutions: to maintain their strike, to abstain from participating in any demonstration not organized by themselves, and to protest the government's closure of a school in Aleppo. They clearly looked with disdain on the government-sponsored youth organization, taunting the National Bloc's Steel Shirts as "Tin Shirts."

The students' demonstration underscored their contempt for the Syrian regime. Four thousand people walked past the Parliament chanting "Repeat o plains, Say o hills, that Alexandretta will not disappear before the Youth disappear." As they passed its offices, the students lauded the newspaper *Al-Ayam* and its publisher, "persecuted by the despots" in the National Bloc government, who had suspended the paper for one day. By contrast, they had nothing but insults and derision on arriving at the offices of the Bloc's newspaper, *Al-Qabas*. By noon, the students dispersed in order to avoid being associated with the subsequent official program.[16]

The official demonstration had been called by National Bloc leader Fakhri al-Barudi, who promised a speech on the Alexandretta situation. At 12:30, local people and the paramilitary Steel Shirts armed with sticks collected at the

Arabness Above All. Courtesy of Mihrac Ural.

Umayyad mosque, as al-Barudi exhorted the crowd. "We would never abandon Alexandretta, we must prepare ourselves to defend our territory, we have a government that we could overthrow if it fails in its duty." He claimed to have just created a regulation for military service that even included women. "Are you ready to defend your country?"

"Yes! Yes!" his nearly two-thousand-person audience responded. They followed forty students in uniform through the center of Damascus with signs reading "Our blood for Alexandretta," and "We will die for Alexandretta." In front of the government building, al-Barudi demanded that the council president and other officials, who had just emerged onto the balcony, reassure Syrians. Mardam's words were less fiery. "We are of the people and work for the people. . . . The Alexandretta question that preoccupies you demands all of our attention and we will fight for her as we have always fought to demolish the bastions of despotism." He told the crowd that notes had already been sent expressing Syria's point of view, explained that the situation would not be reviewed in Geneva until March, and promised to defend Syrian rights. "Return to your occupations. If we do not succeed in obtaining our rights, we will have a new attitude on your account regarding our ally France and the League of Nations," he promised. Al-Barudi ended the demonstration: "We must have confidence in this government which does not resemble the previous governments." The crowd of National Bloc supporters calmly dispersed.[17]

The National Bloc had a difficult task ahead, convincing the population of Syria to continue supporting their policy of constructive engagement in the face of the double insult: the League of Nations decision compromised both the territorial integrity of Syria and the nationalists' fundamental anticolonial goals. Not only would the Geneva agreement detach the Sanjak from Syria but also it would leave a French high commissioner in the Sanjak even after Syrian independence.[18] Colonial officials feared that the situation in the streets had begun to mirror the February 1936 uprisings, with students leading the movement. Although the French had been frustrated with the Damascus regime, they were becoming even more concerned about the growing power of the opposition. Fain believed that opposition groups, especially the League of National Action and the Syrian Popular Party, were actively infiltrating local schools, instigating student anger, and encouraging Greek Orthodox students to behave as if Jamil Mardam were a traitor. The National Bloc government was appearing powerless. "Its Steel Shirts becoming Tin Shirts was badly received, its orators like Barudi and Bayruti were paid little attention."[19]

In the Sanjak itself, news about the acceptance of the Sandler Report in Geneva was broadcast by Istanbul Radio and the Turkish press, eliciting joyful celebrations among the Kemalists.[20] Boats ferrying jubilant Turks to Alexandretta only exacerbated the fears of National Bloc leaders Jamil Mardam and Shukri al-Quwwatli, who warned French authorities of the strong response in Syria. France's ambassador in Ankara intervened, discouraging Turkish tourism to the Sanjak.[21] The Turks' enthusiasm was in sharp contrast to the disappointment of local Arabs and Armenians, whose chagrin mounted with the declaration that Turkish would be the area's official language. Shops in non-Turkish areas of Antioch remained closed for three days. On the eve of reopening the shops, two Arab nationalists visited the League observers, still in the region, to convey their disappointment and to clarify that resumption of business should not be interpreted as any change of attitude.

League official Anker had not been privy to the full terms of the agreement, but confidently expected that the release of complete information would change local attitudes. Before reading the Sandler Report, Anker was reporting optimistically that further information about its provisions would moderate the early responses as pro-Syrian groups recognized that the situation was not all bad, and Turcophiles began to realize that their victory had hardly been complete.[22] On receiving the full text, however, Anker's attitude changed, and he grew increasingly uncomfortable with his own continuing role. "We have the impression, after reading the Council decisions, that they are actually more unfavorable to Syria than one might imagine from the communiqués of Agence Havas. Also, I fear that the malaise elicited among the Syrians and in Arab and Christian circles of the Sanjak could only be increased when they know here the exact terms of the adopted text." Anker and the observers refused to accept the thanks of an Antioch Turkish delegation, reminding them that the International Mission of Observers had served only as observers and had not been responsible for the Geneva agreement.[23] Arriving in Süveydiye on February 2, the League observers were welcomed warmly by the local population gathered in the streets. In their meetings, Alawi, Armenian, and other Christian leaders each expressed disquiet about the Geneva decisions and articulated a desire to remain within Syria. One elderly Orthodox priest, tears falling, spoke of his fear that Turks would once again dominate the area. With the arrival of people from the neighboring villages, the throng on the streets grew, and "despite the displeasure and anxiety manifested regarding the Geneva result, we were the object of acclamations and an enthusiasm that was a bit surprising and embarrassing."[24]

The observers had been in the Sanjak for almost one month, aware everywhere of the respect for their mission and the confidence placed in them by the local people. Without regard for their experience, without waiting for the observers to produce a report, an agreement had been reached between the Turkish and French governments, and a binding resolution had been taken in Geneva that was but little informed by the conditions within the Sanjak. The "satisfaction vive" that Martel had noted among the Syrian elites, their confidence in the League of Nations process, had been betrayed. The International

Mission of Observers' charge to observe and report back, the observers had presumed, would have some influence on the League's decisions about the future of
the Sanjak. Demonstrations, petitions, delegations, and letters had all been
intended to influence what the League observers saw in the Sanjak. When,
instead, the French and Turkish leaders came to an agreement among themselves completely disregarding the International Mission of Observers' project,
it appeared that all local efforts—and all of the observers' work—had been
irrelevant.

"The profound disappointment caused by the solution announced for the
Sanjak Question," began the Damascus police report, "the discontent that, for
various reasons, grows against the Government and the National Bloc, the news
that circulates about the autonomist and separatist movements in various
regions . . . creates a state of emotions without precedent. It is generally believed
that Syria is close to dismemberment."[25] As Martel and others had anticipated, a
decision on the Sanjak that was unfavorable to the Syrian government severely
compromised the National Bloc regime in Damascus. Martel was sympathetic in
his condescension:

> That the decision taken at Geneva is of a nature to rouse Syrian opinion,
> no one could doubt. Accustomed to judging things on the national
> plane, the Syrians cannot yet understand the need to accept, on the
> international plane, compromise solutions. After having become intox-
> icated for many months with dreams of independence, unity and
> Pan-Arabism, they have awakened suddenly to see that the best mari-
> time province is to be detached from the territory. The blow, without
> doubt, is hard.[26]

The Sandler Report on Alexandretta gave the National Bloc government
nowhere to hide, caught between its anticolonial base of supporters who had
brought it to power in the recent elections and the French, to whom it believed
it must behave "responsibly" in order to get the Franco-Syrian Treaty ratified.
France was committed to the process of the League of Nations, whose members
had decided to sever the Sanjak from the rest of Syria. The National Bloc was
committed to the government of France, which it saw as providing (and promising) Syria's route to eventual independence. What Martel called "Syrian opinion," on the other hand, was swayed by neither France's compelling international
process nor by the National Bloc's consuming dream, but instead by the immediate loss of an important and productive province and the dispossession of
their families and neighbors living there.

The mood in Turkey was quite different, as local radio broadcasts and newspaper stories celebrated victory. As Izmir's people took to the streets, the local

French representative could only express relief at the lack of anti-French sentiment. The January 31 demonstration celebrating the "liberation" of the Sanjak's
Turks and the "victory of Geneva" was, he claimed, orchestrated by the government, whose police agents had encouraged residents to decorate their homes
with Turkish flags and participate in the celebration.[27]

The Turkish central government was already looking beyond the January 27
League of Nations decision accepting the Sandler Report that made the Sanjak
independent. The government refocused its attention on the next stage, when a
League committee would draft the Statute and Fundamental Law that would
provide the crucial definitions of how the Sanjak's new status would be implemented. Hoping to consolidate Turkey's gains, Selim Çelenk returned from
Turkey to debrief the Turkish consul in Aleppo. Atatürk himself had approved
the new Hatay flag, according to Çelenk, and the Turkish interior minister would
become honorary president of the new Hatay Party, which would also include
such luminaries as two Turkish colonels and Atatürk's special secretary. In addition to working on a new constitution for the Sanjak, the group had already
begun identifying the officials who would administer Turkish affairs in the
Sanjak, and making plans to include the disputed villages of Bayir and Bujak as
an integral part of the Sanjak.[28]

Hoping to define the Sanjak as a strictly Turkish area, the Ankara regime
resisted identifying another still-unnamed language, as recommended by the
Sandler Commission. An Arabic-language radio broadcast from Istanbul on
February 3 explained the demographic argument that Turkish delegates to the
League were using to insist on the exclusive use of Turkish in the Sanjak. Basing
their argument on statistics taken from *Petit Parisien*, combined with an innova-
tive definition of "Turkish," the Turcophiles insisted that non-Turkish groups
would be injured if Arabic were accepted as an official language. According to
the Kemalists, the Sanjak's sixty-four thousand (Arabic-speaking) Alawis were
"Turks of race and language." Neither the twenty-five thousand Armenians nor
the Sanjak's five thousand Kurds spoke Arabic. Thus, the use of Arabic as an official language would compromise the rights of ninety-five thousand people in
order to satisfy the rights of some forty thousand Arabs. Those who did not use
Turkish, the sole official language, could take advantage of translators in Arabic,
Armenian, Hebrew, or Kurdish for internal affairs. As for relations with the rest
of Syria, the broadcast recommended the use of French, the universal language.[29]

Turkey's claim that recognizing Arabic as an official language would infringe
on Alawis' rights must have sounded strange to the Arabic-speaking Alawis.
Nonetheless, defining the Alawis as Turks was an essential part of Ankara's
strategy: its claim to a majority in the Sanjak was based on a count of Turks in
which Alawis were included. As the new Turkish narrative had evolved during
1936, the assertion that the Sanjak was actually the homeland of the Turks now

featured an avowal that some of those earliest Turks had never left the Sanjak. The original Turks, who remained while the rest of the group moved on to Central Asia around the time of the Hittites, had lost their original language and taken on the languages of their neighbors and conquerors. Turkish officials began to encourage the use of the term "Hittite" to refer to these people, the Alawis, who had merely adopted Arabic, they claimed, as a result of centuries of historical accident.

The Ankara government was only the most recent of many who had attempted to define the Alawis. Druze, Sunni, and Christian polemicists had variously portrayed them as an ancient Canaanite group, an offshoot of the medieval Ismaili Muslims, Muslim-like heretics who worshiped Ali, and offshoots of the Shiites found today throughout Iran. They are described in eleventh-century Druze theological writing, in Crusader chronicles, in the work of the famous fourteenth-century Sunni theologian ibn Taymiyya, and in nineteenth-century missionary accounts and translations.[30]

Long concentrated in the area around Latakia and living in the Sanjak for as long as people remembered, the Alawis by World War I had come to be mostly poor peasant farmers. They had been subjected to Ottoman efforts to make them religiously orthodox, and to the whims of the local landowners and officials whose fields they worked and whose wealth they produced.[31] Alawis had played an important role in the resistance to the French occupation of Syria after World War I as allies of other anticolonial forces.[32] Recognizing the dangers that could ensue if Syria's Alawis continued to coordinate their anti-French struggles with their neighbors, French colonial authorities created separate states for the "compact minorities," working to keep Alawis (and Druze, also a major force in the resistance) from working together with the rest of Syria's people.[33] Like the Turks, the French had defined the Alawis as not-Arab, in an effort to keep them divided from an increasingly anticolonial "Arab" nationalist Syria. Also like the Turks, the French had argued that their separation of the Alawis was necessary to "protect" them from their neighbors. Now, the Ankara regime was arguing against an official status for the Arab language using the premises of the French colonial argument: the Alawis did not belong with the Arabs, and keeping them apart would somehow protect their rights. Designating Arabic as an official language in the Sanjak would therefore infringe on the rights of Alawis as one of the Sanjak's minorities.

The Turkish government's presumptions about the Alawis' identity, like the French treatment of his coreligionists, infuriated Zaki al-Arsuzi. The Sanjak leader of the League of National Action had grown up in a well-known Alawi religious family. After his early education, he had studied philosophy at the Sorbonne before returning to teach school in the Sanjak, a committed believer in European ideals and national liberation. He was stunned to encounter French efforts to thwart Syria's independence and divide the local population, and horrified by the French treatment of Alawi students. He claimed that his experiences in the colonial classroom led to his political projects.

> When the school principal was called away during a French exam in 1930, Alawi students came thronging to take their exam as I was ignorant of the identity of the students, just as I was ignorant that there was an established policy concerning the various sects . . .
>
> Another Frenchman, one of the prep-school language teachers, entered the room where I was conducting the exam. He glanced at the list of grades then bellowed in amazement: "How did you give such grades? Are you not aware that these students are Alawis?"

Al-Arsuzi was surprised that Antioch's classrooms were segregated by religion, a policy he refused to implement. He recounted the story of a student, who claimed that when Christian students made mistakes, the French teacher demanded, "Are you an Alawi? . . . Are you a dumb beast?" and wrote on the board "Alawis are on the same level as dumb beasts."

According to al-Arsuzi, Alawis were recruited in large numbers to serve in the army under the French, but the colonial regime feared that if they became really educated, Alawis would "join their voice to the voice of the sons of their race, the Arabs." Such unity, after all, would exacerbate France's nightmare.[34]

Faced with the apparent dissonance between the political ideals he had espoused while studying European political thought and the behavior of French officials in Syria, al-Arsuzi set to work to create a youth movement devoted to realizing an Arab nation. He used his position in Antioch's schools to recruit adherents to his ideology and to the new League of National Action. Created only in 1933, the League of National Action was the answer of a group of young nationalists to the "honorable cooperation" policy of Syria's National Bloc. Their demands went beyond the achievement of an independent, secular, and democratic Syria to advocate the liberation of the entire Arab world, to be achieved without collaboration with either France or other imperial forces. Moreover, the League of National Action's anticolonial agenda was combined with an economic justice project, seeking agrarian reform and an end to the oppression of the rural underclass.

Al-Arsuzi reshaped the League of National Action in Antioch into a force dedicated to countering Turkish designs on the Sanjak. Until he was fired by the French, al-Arsuzi taught a unified Arab history and philosophy in his courses, and mobilized his students to create an extensive Arab nationalist infrastructure, including the kind of sporting and culture youth clubs that were ubiquitous in Europe and the Mediterranean during the 1930s. Under his leadership, inclusive

Arab institutions came into being, incorporating even the poorest Sanjak residents and explicitly breaking down barriers the French had been trying to consolidate between groups. His students integrated the previously Christian Fine Arts Club with the Alawi Renaissance Office, which was transformed to become the Arab Renaissance Office. The League of National Action in Antioch was consistent in attacking the French mandate, demanding Syrian independence as one step toward the creation of an Arab nation. Not surprisingly, al-Arsuzi's League of National Action received little support from Antioch's Arab elite, who maintained "a grave social antagonism" toward him. He intended his newspaper, *al-Uruba* (Arabism) to provide an alternative to the French and Turkish dailies, especially *Yeni Gün*.[35] The League of National Action focused its energies on countering the claims of the Sanjak's Kemalists, even introducing its own set of "Arab" symbols in opposition to those of local Turcophiles. It answered the Turks' brimmed hat with the headgear Faysal had adopted: the sedara. In response to the Turks' focus on "the New Turkey and the Great Leader," al-Arsuzi's Leaguers emphasized an Arab empire stretching from Egypt through Iraq. They attached green and white cockades to their jackets to counter the Turks' red and white, and they organized demonstrations in response to each one staged by the Halkevleri. Like the Turks, al-Arsuzi urged his followers to boycott the 1936 elections, although not as a supporter of the Turkish boycott effort. Instead, the League of National Action boycott was to register opposition to the continuing French occupation and to the French mandatory rulers' refusal to allow al-Arsuzi to stand for election.[36]

As al-Arsuzi and the League of National Action struggled to confront the new situation in the wake of the Sandler Report separating the Sanjak from Syria, a newly formed Hatay Committee joined the Republican Peoples Party, working inside the Sanjak to mobilize and coordinate written propaganda, face-to-face contact, radio broadcasts, and economic inducements. Information and propaganda flowed in both directions across the northern border. *Yeni Gün* owner Selim Çelenk returned from Turkey on April 5 carrying pamphlets with the title "The Turco-Arab Conflict," printed in both Arabic and Turkish (in Arabic characters) and ostensibly published in Cairo by the Society of the Turco-Arab Conflict. The pamphlets claimed that most of the Sanjak's people wanted autonomy, with the exception of Armenian Dashnags and a few Sunni Arabs who were attached to the Syrian nationalists. By mid-April, the People's Houses were distributing an Arabic translation of İnönü's lecture on Hatay and a bilingual brochure, "Arab-Turkish Friendship."[37] At the same time, the local Hatay Committee provided material to external audiences; when a military group marched in the city, for example, Hatay Committee members photographed the parade and sent the photographs into Turkey, where the government would exploit the images to explain the need to send reinforcements to the frontiers.[38]

Hats continued to proliferate in the Sanjak, but not without consistent and continuing effort. Abdulgani Türkmen had distributed four hundred hats to supporters in the winter, but by April some of his partisans had reverted to their fezzes, "tired of the promises made by the Turks, especially the promises of independence not yet realized."[39] French police reported that Turkish agents in Kilis had worked on the Bekliye tribal leaders camping on the border, first threatening them, then inviting them to wear brimmed hats and yield to Turkish views. Tribal leaders agreed, and sent one of their number to speak with the part of their tribe still further south in Syria. But their tribal chiefs refused, according to French sources, claiming that they were Syrian, that they had property in Syria, and that they did not want to do anything against their government.[40]

The Kemalists moved beyond staging Turkish identity to constructing an economic component to their propaganda. Mehmet Sait Koray, a director of one of Turkey's largest banks, İş Bankası, arrived in the Sanjak on May 3 for an extended business trip. As far as the French could determine, Koray's mission was to parlay the difficult economic conditions of the Sanjak into political advantage by promising the people relief. "Under the pretext of an economic mission toward creating branches of his bank in the Sanjak of Alexandretta, he gathered the demands of all the insolvent clients of the French Land Bank and the Agricultural Bank, suggesting that the Turks would soon lower their discount rate to 3 percent without a mortgage, against a simple guarantee of two signatures," Durieux reported. "Various private meetings took place in which were gathered the notables and merchants of the city. It is evidently a new form of Turkish propaganda." Within his first week in the Sanjak, Koray had met in Antioch with a Greek Orthodox banker, a famous merchant family, the former mayor of Kirikhan, oil and cereal merchants in the market, and all of Antioch's Turcophile leaders. During the following two weeks, he visited Alexandretta, Kirikhan, Reyhanlı, and Süveydiye. Koray took care to notify his future competitors about the advantages he would be bringing into the market, informing the head of the Antioch branch of the Syrian Bank that Turkey's İş Bankası had already decided to open two branches, one in Antioch and one in Alexandretta. Koray added that, with İş Bankası intervention, the Turkish government had agreed to purchase the Sanjak's silk cocoons for use by Bursa's silk weavers at one-third more than the current price and send it duty-free to Turkey. Moreover, Koray added that he would have the backing of the director of the Rome Bank at Aleppo.[41] To display the effects of their promised assistance, officials sent issues of a Turkish magazine featuring various Sumer Bank projects within Turkey to a number of Antioch's Greek Orthodox and Alawi notables and to some of Alexandretta's Armenian merchants.[42]

Having promoted the Sandler Report as a guarantee of secure borders and cordial Syrian-Turkish relations, French officials grew alarmed at Turkey's direct intervention along a lengthening span until it appeared that the entire Syrian-Turkish border was being contested. French officials intercepted letters to Syrian refugees in Turkey and to chiefs of the Kürt Dağ region just east of the Sanjak, inciting them to organize a revolt within Syria.[43] Moreover, talk of a Turkish military incursion abounded during the spring of 1937, with reports of a Turkish army of forty-five thousand mobilizing along the entire line from the Mediterranean all the way east to Maraş; some even claimed that high-ranking but out-of-uniform Turkish officers were being sent to circulate inside Syria's cities, from Latakia on the coast, to Qamishli at the Iraqi border, to Dayr al-Zur in the very center of the country.[44]

Martel was forced to admit that the situation had proved him wrong. Instead of limiting Turkish ambitions, he admitted, the Geneva settlement had actually emboldened them. They were now seeking to extend their sphere to include "all of northern Syria." "Active propaganda" had been introduced into neighboring Kürt Dağ, to promote the creation of a separatist movement there that would allow that region to be included in the Sanjak. Further east, in Syrian Jazirah, Turkish agents were actively seeking the allegiance of Kurdish leaders. It was the Turkish consulate at Aleppo that coordinated the "incessant propaganda that, sometimes by promises and sometimes by threats, seeks . . . to intimidate the populations." For Martel, this Turkish effort was nothing short of an imperial program. He viewed the Turkish press with its "violent tone" as "overtly preparing the way for this nascent imperialism," in which "the whole future of Syria and of French politics in the Levant States are found in play."

> It is not possible to close one's eyes any longer, nor to have illusions about the projects of Mustafa Kemal [Atatürk]: he thinks that the new ruling about the Sanjak, far from resolving in a definitive manner the questions hanging between Syria and Turkey, marks the debut of a new stage that, for the Kemalist regime, inheritor of the Ottoman Empire, must be a glorious stage. . . . If the Turks are not stopped in their course in a very firm and possibly brutal manner, in order that they understand that France, so liberal in its negotiations about the Sanjak, will not tolerate unjustifiable encroachments on the rest of Syrian territory, we must count on the rapid development of a politics that tends to provoke the parceling out of Syria.[45]

Like France', Viénot, the high commissioner had been convinced that Turkey's goal was the Sanjak and that the Ankara regime had agreed to recognize Arabic and the rights of the "minorities." Now, he was having second thoughts and reconsidering French willingness to appease Turkey's demands.

Martel's fears of Ankara's imperial interest in Syria were exacerbated by events on the border not only because of the immediate consequences of cross-border raiding but also because Turkey might cite the border insecurity in demanding even more territory during discussions in Geneva.[46] Within the space of a few nights in March, armed bandits looted a shop at the far eastern end of the border, others engaged in a firefight in the west, and uniformed Turkish soldiers plundered sheep from a Syrian village just across the line.[47] Raiding from Syria into Turkey also escalated. Fifteen bandits raided a town sixty miles inside Turkey on the night of March 15, cutting the road between the Turkish cities of Mardin and Diyarbakır, stopping sixteen cars and robbing their occupants. Chased by Turkish gendarmes and villagers, thirteen of the looters managed to reenter Syria. Two Turks had been killed in the skirmish and another three wounded. Turkish officials claimed that during the first seven weeks of 1937, 1,025 animals had been stolen in some twenty attacks out of Syria; only seventy-two had been returned. Turkish officials were quite frustrated. Governors of border provinces appealed to local Syrian officials, and, finding no success, turned to the French high commissioner.

Nonetheless, Martel remained much more focused on Turkey's policy and propaganda, discounting the importance of the cross-border raiding in itself.[48] When challenged by the Turkish ambassador in Beirut, he insisted that interactions along the border were fine, with good relations and cooperation between the border officials of both countries. He confronted the Turkish official in turn, claiming that the recent arrival of activists Omar Numan and Kör Ruşdi had brought increased political propaganda and clandestine meetings, and that Turkey was harboring Syrian bandits whose extradition was being sought by French authorities. Martel complained that Turkish radio news broadcasts in Arabic criticizing the French government in Syria constituted meddling in its internal affairs, described the tone of the Turkish press as "astonishing," and protested about their rude insults of high-ranking French officials. Moreover, their publication of "falsehoods" did not help to calm public opinion. Martel recounted how surprised he had been to learn from La République on April 2 that three Turks in the Sanjak had been killed and their goods pillaged. He pointed out that if this news were true, he would hope to receive details of the incident from his Turkish counterpart, including the names of the three victims so that justice could immediately be pursued. If the news were false, it would be fitting for La République to publish a retraction. Martel insisted that, while both governments were working to preserve their relationships, the cross-border incidents that had outraged the Turkish government were not a matter for his concern.[49]

For the Turkish government, the border incidents called for immediate action. Turkey's interior minister spoke to the Grand National Assembly in Ankara on April 7, confirming that at least ten Turkish soldiers had been killed in attacks over the previous weeks by armed bands that had formed in Syria and had returned to Syria. Faced with this situation, the interior minister told Turkey's parliament, the government would mobilize a military force, calling up reservists to provide security at the frontier. France's military attaché in Turkey, alarmed by the declaration, warned the minister of defense in Paris that France would be able to demand suppression of this mobilization ("which constitutes an act of threat and intimidation to our side") only if the French could propose an acceptable alternative, perhaps an international commission acting on both sides of the border.[50]

For Syrian prime minister Jamil Mardam, already alarmed at the incursions taking place into Syria, the troop buildup on the northern side of the border made French intervention even more urgent. Mardam produced a list of eleven recent incidents in which armed men crossed from Turkey into Syria, stealing gold, currency, animals, carpets, and other property; sometimes they injured local residents. The perpetrators, he claimed, were Turkish bandits and Syrian criminals taking refuge in Turkey. Pointing out that Syrian officials did not have enough troops to prevent the incursions, Mardam asked the French to intercede with the Turks to prevent the raids "in the interest of good neighborly relations."[51]

French authorities had been nursing concerns about northern Syria, where many residents had become increasingly alienated by the growing power and attention garnered by Damascus. Activists in Damascus had considered exploiting the northerners' resentment of the loss of Aleppo's status as Syria's first city, hoping to make common cause with the northerners and the Turks against the French occupation. French intelligence reports revealed that some Syrians, both Muslim and Christian, were sympathetic toward Turkey. Many Syrians had attended the Izmir Fair, and had returned home impressed with the legal and economic reforms of their northern neighbor. Merchants spoke favorably of the protection the Turkish government accorded industry and agriculture, and remembered wistfully the large markets that had been available to their own businesses in the vast Ottoman Empire. Although Turkey remained a Muslim country, many of those interviewed by French agents believed that secularization had tempered religious rivalries. Moreover, according to a French report, Turkish propaganda found a particularly favorable reception among some higher officials whose status could be compromised by the National Bloc's recent accession to power. These potential Syrian allies of the Kemalist regime included officers retired from the Ottoman army, chiefs of clans established on the northern frontier who were continually in contact with Turkish agents, and some of the heads of the communities.[52]

Mardam's National Bloc government began trying to understand and catch up with Turkey's efforts to win support among Arabic-speakers in northern

Syria and the Sanjak, sending Maruf al-Dawalibi, a twenty-nine-year old Paris-trained lawyer from Aleppo, to teach Arabic in the Antioch lycée. Previously a leader of the National Guard youth organization in Aleppo, al-Dawalibi would be paid by the Damascus government not only to teach, but also to provide special lectures for the Arabic program. Special Services officer Gacon was outright suspicious, noting that the appointment had not gone through proper channels, inferring that the new teacher had actually been sent from Damascus to direct Arab agitation and to keep the National Bloc apprised of what was taking place within the Sanjak's schools.

Indeed, it appears that al-Dawalibi was in contact with the opposition League of National Action in the Sanjak, and one of his jobs was to prevent antigovernment agitation. On March 17 he told the League's leaders, "Currently, the Geneva negotiations are going in our favor. The Syrian delegation let us know that it wants us to remain calm. If we do not obtain the anticipated results, the government will resign and a rebellion will break out all over Syria. We will not forget the Arab inhabitants of the Sanjak and we will support them financially and with weapons." Al-Dawalibi added that he had come to Antioch to keep Damascus current on what was happening among the Arabs and the Turks, but his title of functionary precluded his compromising himself very overtly. He advised the group not to hold any demonstrations, send any telegrams, publish any journal articles, or carry out any strikes, emphasizing that all directions would be coming exclusively from Damascus.

Despite his rejection of outright rebellion, French officials were angry about the new teacher. As they saw it, the Syrian government had introduced into Antioch Lycée "a disturbing element charged with animating the Pan-Arab flame." They suspected Husni al-Barazi of having played an "unfortunate role" behind the scenes, trying to "trouble the atmosphere of relative calm in which we live, and making himself the agent of Arab propaganda in the Sanjak." The new situation could lead to stirrings of pan-Arab nationalism, "of which the consequences could be incalculable."[53]

Although the French had previously blamed the National Bloc government for its inaction in the face of Turkish mobilization against the elections, they now insisted that the Bloc remain passive, suppress all opposition to the Geneva decisions, and refrain from anything that might alienate the Turks. Martel was furious to find out that the Syrian government had been returning all mail addressed to "Hatay." When Turkish postal officials began expunging "Syria" and "Alexandretta" on envelopes and replacing them with "Hatay," Syrian officials instructed the post office to return these letters with the comment "Territory does not exist in Syria."[54] Martel insisted that the local government had no power over the mail, which was the responsibility of the high commissioner. More important, he fumed, such gestures would make an impact in Turkey, and because international postal conventions indicated that France managed the postal system, the Ankara government would think that the mandatory administration had ordered the return of the letters.[55] Officials in Paris were intent on reaching an agreement with the Republic of Turkey, and the French colonial regime in Syria insisted that the Damascus government do nothing to compromise its success.

While refusing to permit the Syrian government to make independent decisions on such issues as the mail, Martel was counting on the National Bloc to enforce order and keep pan-Arab sentiment under control. The League of National Action remained at the forefront of opposition to the Sanjak's separate independence, and its growing success seemed to compromise the nationalist credentials of the National Bloc government. As promised, Jamil Mardam was permitted to travel to Paris to try to make Syria's case for retaining the Sanjak—and to shore up the appearance that his government was making serious efforts. Here was an opportunity to legitimize the Bloc's policy of honorable collaboration.

Jamil Mardam came away with little from his April meeting with Leon Blum in Paris. The French prime minister claimed that he had only Syria's best interest at heart when agreeing to the Sandler Report. The French had focused on practical politics instead of legalistic rights, he insisted, in the hope of preventing disagreements with Turkey that "would become dangerous" if the French were no longer protecting Syria. Blum acknowledged that his thinking had already become "obsolete," but the best he would offer was a promise to follow the Sanjak affair closely, to attend the League of Nations Council meeting in May, and to remain "watchful that your essential rights will be respected."

Counting on France's role and Blum's declared support for the Sanjak, Mardam planned to go to Geneva for the next Council session, and hoped that Henri Ponsot, French ambassador to Turkey, would go as well. Mardam placed great confidence in Ponsot, Martel's predecessor as high commissioner, claiming that he had been concerned in this affair since the beginning and that he "understood our point of view." Pursuing the Bloc's policy of collaboration, Mardam continued to throw in his lot with the French government. At every opportunity, he emphasized his government's compliance with French expectations, approving the Franco-Syrian Treaty, exercising restraint around the Sanjak affair, and refusing to compromise with the opposition. "We will finish the Alexandretta affair without [the opposition], counting on the loyal support of France, with whom we remain allies and friends." Undaunted by developments in Europe or Damascus, Mardam continued to believe that collaboration would yield the best outcome.

When he was informed of Turkey's proposal for a forty-member parliament and twenty-five-hundred-member police force for the Sanjak's two hundred thousand people, Mardam found it both unacceptable and impractical. He was particularly outraged by the plan to introduce the "fundamental principles of the [Republican] People's Party," objecting specifically to giving women the right to vote by pointing out that women's suffrage was not even accepted by "the great European countries." The Syrian prime minister claimed that the Turkish government's proposal was trying to get away with a maximalist understanding of the January 1937 agreement, and asked the Mandates Commission of the League of Nations to "resist these unjustified pretensions. Contrary to our interests as it is, the Sandler Report at least implicitly recognizes that the Sanjak continues to be part of Syria. The Turks pretend not to know that." Having thrown in his lot with the French, Mardam could only hope that French diplomats would be wary in the continuing discussions over the new Statute and Fundamental Law that would define the basic institutions of the independent Sanjak.

Nonetheless, Mardam's historical and strategic appraisal suggested that French policy had been misguided since 1921, when France gave Turkey the Arabic-speaking region of Cilicia. Syria's natural frontier, he argued, was the Taurus mountains, which meant that Cilicia was part of his country. Moreover, despite Turkey's declarations of liberalism, Turkey had already begun circumscribing the religious freedom of the Arabic-speaking Alawis of Cilicia. By giving Payas to the Turks, the French had allowed them to control the whole strategic Gulf of Alexandretta; now they were claiming not only the Sanjak but also three additional cantons under the pretense that they, too, had Turkish majorities. Mardam lamented that it was no longer inconceivable for Turkey to lay claim to Aleppo, and despite the hostility of the Alawis, Ankara seemed interested even in Latakia. Turkey's attitude, according to Mardam, was creating disquiet among all the Arab countries. For Mardam, pan-Arabism remained a dream, but one increasingly under the formidable shadow of an organized and strengthening Turkey. Cilicia had opened the door to Turkey's claims south of the Taurus, and Syria's prime minister worried that the Sanjak question might just be a prelude to future disputes. The French had taken the wrong tack in trying to appease Ankara; Britain's firmness had successfully fought off Turkey's claims to Mosul, and Mardam continued to hope that the French would exhibit similar resolve.[56]

While Mardam's government needed the French to stand firm, however, the Blum government seemed ready to bend to all of Turkey's demands. In part, France was motivated by a desire to avoid direct conflict with Turkey simply because France was still rearming and not ready to engage in confrontation, especially with hostilities looming closer to home. More important, though, France was eager to find in Turkey an ally against those who seemed to encircle France's home territory. The previous few months had been quite traumatic for Leon Blum's Popular Front government in Paris. When Hitler began rearming in the Rhineland right on its eastern border, France had been unable (or unwilling) to resist. Just a few months later, the Spanish Civil War had created instability on its southern border. During that same year, 1936, Mussolini's Italy was working to create alliances among those Balkan states not already aligned with France. Uncertain of the outcome in Spain, and with Italy (and more recently Bulgaria) hostile in the eastern Mediterranean, it seemed essential for France to create some sort of alliance system to protect its interests in the eastern Mediterranean, and Turkey would be a necessary partner. For France, then, the Sanjak was hardly worth the cost of alienating Turkey.

Turkey's urgent interest in the Sanjak arose partly from the same set of events. Although Turkey had rebuilt its navy in the 1920s largely through Italy's financial assistance and the purchase of Italian vessels, this relationship had cooled as Turkey's fear of Italy's designs grew. Italy's interest in southern Anatolia had been evident before World War I, and had been rewarded with a "zone of influence" in the Sèvres Treaty at the end of World War I. Now Mussolini's repeated statements about Italy's need for room to grow, its illegal arming of the Dodecanese Islands off the Turkish coast, and its recent invasions of Ethiopia and Libya combined to set off alarms in the Ankara government. It seemed clear after the spring of 1936 that France was unwilling to protect its own borders; Turkish strategists surmised Paris would be even less likely to protect Turkey's. For the government of the new Republic of Turkey, the port of Alexandretta was the obvious route for an Italian invasion from the Mediterranean.[57]

France's own Marine Department's analysis was similar, illustrating the strategic significance of the Sanjak by pointing out that Britain's preeminent strategist Horatio Herbert Kitchener had advanced Alexandretta as a better target than the Dardanelles for attacking the Ottoman Empire in 1915; the Germans at Mersin had displayed their own interest in the city. Alexandretta controlled not only a large hinterland but also an easy passage straight into Anatolia between two mountain ranges, along with the railroad lines necessary to move troops and materiel. "In the hands of a nation of the first rank with considerable interests in the eastern Mediterranean, Alexandretta could thus become a permanent menace for the other states (especially for Syria)," the French report warned. "One imagines that England (with Cyprus and Palestine) or Italy (with the Dodecanese Islands) would find there very precious elements of power, preponderance and defense in this region, whose economic and military importance could become very great." It would be essential for France to retain control over the port, not only as the terminus of the Iraqi oil pipeline but also as "an indispensable cover for all naval establishments destined to protect our interests in Syria." Nonetheless, the report continued, France had no desire to expand in the eastern Mediterranean, and already had a naval base at Tripoli; on the contrary, since leaving Cilicia, most of the Bay of Alexandretta was no longer under French control. The Turkish government, on the other hand, had readily available sea,

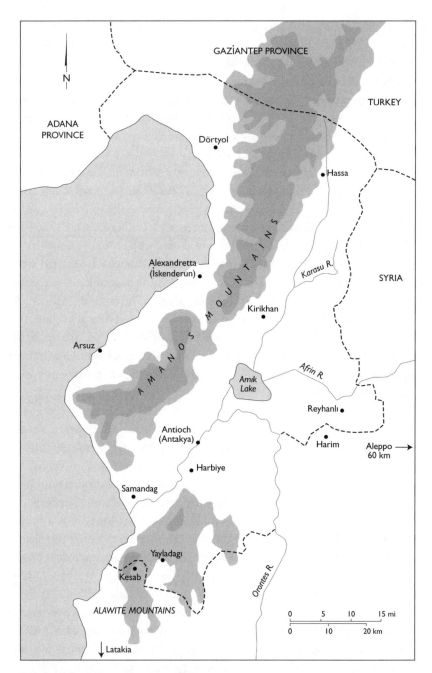

Sanjak of Alexandretta/Province of Hatay

ground, and air forces in the immediate vicinity. Thus, France's own interests required that it maintain friendly relations with Turkey, and that no other power gain control over Alexandretta. Neither an international convention nor League of Nations–guaranteed neutrality would be adequate. The French Marine report recommended instead that France develop the port commercially, keep it out of the hands of any third party, and implement a situation similar to Yugoslavia's use of Macedonia's port.[58] Turkish control over the port at Alexandretta would be better than any other alternative to French control, and France's friendship with Turkey was worth a very high price.

While French strategic priorities placed Alexandretta into Turkish hands, Syria's prime minister continued to entrust his hopes to French advocacy at the League of Nations. Mardam recognized that the Sandler Report could be interpreted in a variety of ways, ranging from the reinforcement of the Sanjak's distinctive character and autonomy as part of a strong confederation with Syria to the creation of a nearly independent Turkish Sanjak whose connection with Syria was merely formal. After approving the Sandler Report, the League of Nations Council had appointed a Committee of Experts to draft a new Statute and Fundamental Law for the Sanjak of Alexandretta. The Committee of Experts was to be assisted by the League's observers, who remained in the Sanjak. Six experts accepted appointments to the Committee of Experts, chaired by Maurice Bourquin, of Belgium, professor at the University of Geneva. The others had long histories in diplomacy or colonial administration. After earning a degree in law and pursuing a career in journalism, Robert de Caix had become secretary-general of the French high commissioner's office in Syria and from 1925 to 1938 had served as France's representative to the League of Nations Mandates Commission. Sir James MacDonald Dunnett had recently been reforms commissioner for the government of British India. Dr. R. A. Kollewyn (Netherlands) was professor at the University of Groningen and had recently served as a judge in the Dutch Indies. Numan Menemencioğlu was secretary-general of the Turkish Ministry of Foreign Affairs. Karl Ivan Westman, Sweden's representative to the League of Nations, would represent Rapporteur Sandler.[59]

Turkey was ready when the Committee of Experts met for the first time on February 25, offering a complete draft of both a Statute and Fundamental Law for the new, independent Sanjak. Menemencioğlu, Ankara's representative, suggested that since time was short, these could serve as a basis for discussion, facilitating the work of the group. The group could discuss the draft Statute while doing the background study necessary to consider the Fundamental Law. Unwilling to be rushed into considering Turkey's proposal, the Committee of Experts demurred, beginning instead by examining the report produced by Rapporteur Sandler.[60] They proceeded with background to the current situation, posing questions to which French representative Caix responded with information about the organization, sources of power, and means of funding for the current administration in the Sanjak, especially the justice system. Although the Turkish representative expressed reservations about the French answers, he did not elaborate.

As the Committee of Experts turned to the Sandler Report, it immediately tied itself up in trying to define the term "entité distincte." Why had the previous committee referred to the Sanjak as an "entity" instead of using a more commonly accepted definition of a political unit, and from what was it intended to be distinct? This fundamental question led to significant debate as members tried to define the most basic nature of the Sanjak's status. For example, if the Sanjak was to be simultaneously independent and tied in confederation with Syria, what would be the limit of each domain? In what areas would the Sanjak have complete freedom? In case of discrepancy, which set of laws would prevail? If Syria were to conclude a foreign policy agreement that conflicted with the Sanjak's Statute, would the treaty be relevant in the Sanjak because its foreign policy was to be consonant with Syria's, or would the Sanjak's own internal law override the supposedly dependent foreign policy? Menemencioğlu argued that any foreign policy legislated by Syria was to be limited by the absolute internal independence of the Sanjak. Kollewyn disagreed, pointing out that if foreign policy was to be Syria's responsibility, then Syria had responsibility to make decisions; the Sanjak could not impose limits.[61]

As the Committee of Experts met from February 25 to March 17, and again from April 22 to May 15, its members produced varied drafts of a Fundamental Law and Statute and wrote numerous reports. By the end, they had scrutinized not only Menemencioğlu's draft Statute and Fundamental Law, but also the French representative's analysis of the bases for the Statute and Fundamental Law, a second draft Fundamental Law, a memorandum on demilitarization, and reports on the protection of minorities, currency, the port of Alexandretta, customs, and postal services. The League observers returned from the Sanjak to provide their assessments as the Committee of Experts deliberated.[62]

High Commissioner Martel left Beirut on May 15 to be present when the Committee of Experts presented its draft of the Statute and Fundamental Law for the League of Nations Council's discussion. He was accompanied not by Jamil Mardam, but by Count Stanislas Ostrorog, a veteran French diplomat who had long been involved with Syrian issues.[63] Despite Ostrorog's optimism, rumors within the Sanjak were predicting the worst. On May 19, leaders of the League of National Action in Alexandretta sent a telegram to Jamil Mardam, Syria's Chamber of Deputies, Syrian opposition leader Abd al-Rahman Shahbandar, and youth leader Fahmi al-Mahayri to offer the ultimate sacrifice on behalf of the Sanjak. "The Geneva news excites spirits. Moral state abnormal. We await precise declarations. Arab sons of the liwa [sanjak] are ready to spill their blood for its defense." A group of women sent their own telegram to Syrian leaders the next day, "Geneva news disturbs us. We request precise declarations to end our uneasiness. The Arabism of the liwa is sacred for which the Arab women of the liwa would sacrifice their souls."[64] Opponents of the National Bloc government had little confidence in France's ability to save the Sanjak.

Martel's delegate, Durieux, accused Alexandretta's governor, Husni al-Barazi, and Antioch's mayor, Abd al-Qadir, of instigating the rumors and anxiety in the Sanjak. French officials claimed that al-Barazi had visited Aleppo on May 19 in order to meet with nationalist groups to decide on a course of action if the new League of Nations Statute severed the Sanjak from Syria. According to Durieux, the Antioch mayor was spreading the word that Syria's Fifth Battalion would "join their cause," assuring the nationalists that they would have the support of Arab gendarmes and officers. French security officials warned that the League of National Action was planning an anti-French protest, and arranging to import Arab villagers "at the instigation of Arab functionaries." It was especially troubling to the colonial administrators that the Sanjak's Arab government would collaborate with the League of National Action and other "extremists."[65] French fears of a wide insurrection seemed confirmed when they learned that the League of National Action had met with the Communist Party and other nationalist groups and decided to form the Arab Popular Front. Its General Staff, to include one person from the League of National Action and three Communist Party members, planned to meet nightly and would receive instructions directly from Aleppo; members would then transmit the orders of the General Staff to the Arab population. According to French intelligence, the new Arab Popular Front was armed, and could count on clandestine support from Syrian government officials, including Minister of the Interior Sadallah al-Jabiri. In addition to dispatching letters of protest to all of the foreign consulates, the group began planning for a mass strike.[66]

Fearing that the situation would escalate, Durieux demanded the removal of the Sanjak's "high functionaries of authority who are at the head of this movement with an insurrectional character." To maintain order, agitators should be transported to the interior of the Sanjak and kept under surveillance. He proposed alerting the police and army, and advocated the prohibition of all demonstrations. Durieux met on May 21 with Governor al-Barazi, whom French officials suspected of complicity with the "extremists" opposing the Geneva resolution, to remind him that he represented the forces of order, and to reiterate that the army would only intervene if the police were unable to maintain the peace. Durieux reported that al-Barazi had "confirmed the interdiction of all demonstrations on the public roads taken during the previous agitation and thus found himself under obligation to intervene personally this morning to reestablish order."[67]

Even as local National Bloc officials agreed to keep the people in line, opposition groups stepped up their efforts to resist the Sandler Report. The call from a new Arab nationalist organization, the Committee of the Defense of the Liwa of Alexandretta and Antioch, was distributed in pamphlets on May 21. Addressed to the "Sons of the Arab Liwa of Alexandretta, Arab brothers in the distress and misfortune," these pamphlets disseminated an emotionally charged call to action.

> On this day where the sun shines on a stricken Liwa, her Arab towns and villages rise in insurrection before the universe, by their general strike, by protesting against the criminal and tyrannical hands that have been set upon us, upon our land, upon our nationality, without regard to the treaties concluded or legitimate rights. The telegrams from Geneva have been publishing for a week the news of the Statute of the Liwa, and from their tenor, which unveiled the mysteries and put the truth of the day, one can no longer doubt the existence of a plot against the Liwa, against us, the Arabs. All these different commissions were . . . to deceive and disguise the truth. To you sons of the Arab Liwa, friends of the Arabs in distress and misfortune, the Committee of the Defense of the Liwa addresses its appeal and invites you to learn to face boldly the tyranny and to resist falsehood. . . . To you, sons of Arab Syria, lions of Iraq, heroes of Nadj and the Hijaz, lions of Yemen, men of Egypt, sons of the Arab Maghreb, we address our appeal to let you know that if the Liwa, which the Powers bargain over, escapes us, it is because of the distraction of the Arabs of the Liwa, but also of your own distraction and your silence for its defense. The Arabs are resolute to the death without hesitation for the Arabism of the Liwa and therefore they will do their duty. If they triumph, it will be a triumph for the Arabs and if they fail, God forbid, it is you who will suffer the consequences of the disillusion before God and before history. To you especially men of the nationalist regime in Syria and Leaders of the Nation, we address our cry of distress and charge you with the responsibility of the loss of the Liwa. We address our appeal to all the Arabs, demanding of every Arab city, even more, of every Arab village, to play its part in the defense in organizing a local committee of the defense of the Liwa of Alexandretta so that your men cooperate with their brothers in the action and the sacred struggle. This is our first cry that we address to you and we await the echo in your actions and in the very bottom of our hearts. Antioch, 21 May 1937, the Committee of the Defense of the Liwa of Alexandretta.[68]

Demonstrations began the same day, stores remained closed, and the predominantly Arab students of the Protestant schools stayed away from classes in protest.[69]

Abdulgani Türkmen was furious when he saw the pamphlets. He fired off a telegram to the high commissioner warning of the dangers of disseminating the pamphlets and implicating Syrian officials directly in the bloodshed he feared would follow. The Sanjak's Alawi and Greek Orthodox citizens, he alleged, had been "seduced by certain suggestions and excitations" and were now set against the Geneva program. The Syrian press had that very day published telegrams intended to set one group of citizens against another, and public pronouncements that implementing the Sanjak's new status would be "welcomed by blood" had aroused "just indignation in public opinion." Türkmen insisted that Syrian officials were participating in this campaign, and warned that "the responsibility for whatever deplorable incident might be produced as a result of these continuing incitements will be the unique and exclusive responsibility of the functionaries of the Syrian government."[70]

Demonstrations resumed in Antioch at six o'clock on the morning of May 22, as the League of Nations prepared to discuss the Statute and Fundamental Law. Youth patrolled the market, threatening shopkeepers who opened their stores. Police called for reinforcements to control the hundreds of demonstrators who had begun throwing stones. The arrest of one "known agitator" made the mob furious; they began stoning symbols of French control, attacking officials at Telephone Central and the Bureau of the General Security, and throwing themselves on the police station in an effort to free their comrade. Police chief Zannardi fired his revolver into the air and his assistant fired two musket shots, which "calmed the demonstrators, who stopped throwing rocks but did not stop circulating."[71]

It was Governor al-Barazi's arrival that defused the situation. The demonstrators welcomed him warmly as he arrived at the Place Gouraud; soon after he had conferred with the demonstration's leaders, most of the crowd withdrew. Al-Barazi managed to get the prisoner released from police custody, and most shops reopened in the afternoon. There had been no injuries among the demonstrators, though four officials had been struck and injured slightly by the stones.[72] Two days later, a strike in Alexandretta closed shops and schools, apparently with the support of the National Bloc.[73]

The clandestine role of local Syrian officials in these demonstrations reflected these functionaries' irreconcilable positions. French officials insisted that the Syrian National Bloc government maintain order, while the National Bloc party's constituency was furious at the loss of another part of their land. Southern Syria had been set apart immediately after World War I as the Palestine mandate; the new state of Lebanon had been carved out at the same time and had just received a separate treaty of independence from France. Now the League of Nations was taking away the Sanjak of Alexandretta, and French colonial authorities insisted that Syrian officials maintain order in the face of growing public

Barazi Harangues the Crowd. Alexandretta Demonstration, May 31, 1937. Courtesy of
Archives du ministre des Affaires étrangères et européennes, Nantes (Archives of the
Minister of Foreign and European Affairs, Nantes).

anger. Although Antioch's Syrian nationalist governor, Husni al-Barazi, had prohibited public demonstrations, French colonial rulers blamed him for the public
spectacles, claiming that he had been colluding with the anti-French League of
National Action. According to the interim high commissioner al-Barazi had played
an active role, even previewing the speeches, which made him partly responsible for inflaming emotions and allowing the defamation of French officials.

Damascus officials held a much less conflicted position. For the ruling
National Bloc, Syria's independence was the most urgent goal, and the ratification of the Franco-Syrian Treaty was the necessary next step. French prime minister Leon Blum had still not submitted the recently signed Franco-Syrian Treaty
to the French Parliament,[74] and French mandatory authorities used the delay to
compel the submission of the Damascus government. When interim high commissioner Meyrier pressed Syrian prime minister Jamil Mardam to intervene
against demonstrations, Mardam hastened to comply.[75]

With National Bloc leaders forced to acquiesce to French demands (whatever
local administrators may have wished), the Syrian regime became an obvious
target for anticolonial resistance. Speakers at the joint Communist Party and
League of National Action rally portrayed the Syrian government as aligned
with fascist forces gathering strength across Europe. An estimated one thousand

people from all classes participated in the protest at the Roxy Theater on the evening of May 26. Representatives of both parties blamed France for the growing animosity within the Sanjak, insisting that Paris was working together with Ankara against the needs of the Syrians. Likening France to Paris's fascist enemies and calling on all workers and peasants to struggle against the colonizer, one speaker accused the colonial regime of "braiding the strands of intrigue in this region and, in secret, encouraging the Turks in their anti-Arab propaganda in order then to feign sympathy for us." Another claimed that the "French fascists" and Syrian officials were together driving the demands of the Sanjak's Turks. "The detachment of the Sanjak from Syria would signify the end of Arabs, Armenians and Turks," according to one speaker, because it would mean the triumph of the French fascist colonizers and the Turkish fascists. The conflict was ideological and class driven, not ethnic. The secretary-general of the Damascus Communist Party called on all of the Syrian parties to work with the French Communist Party, "the most powerful party in France," to get the Franco-Syrian Treaty signed in Paris. "It is not only the French fascists who are the enemies of democracy, but also the Italians and the Germans," he insisted, painting the Sanjak conflict on a broader canvas and urging his audience to defend even to death the rights of the Syrians and the Sanjak. Their fight was for bigger goals: the people needed to rid the Sanjak of the fascist French functionaries, who were betraying the Syrians and their compatriots for their own interests and must be expelled from the country. "We address the speech to M. [Leon] Blum, and inform him that France cannot become a sincere friend of Syria unless she accords her a complete and total independence; that the Franco-Syrian Treaty does not shut off independence but, if it is applied with complete sincerity, this independence will be nearly complete." To illustrate French treachery, the speaker claimed that French officials had, just the previous Monday, caused armed Turks "to come from neighboring villages in order to drive them to action against the Arabs and to make this region a field of national carnage."[76] For the League of National Action and its Communist allies, unpatriotic fascist French colonizers were behind Turkish claims. They appealed to Socialist Leon Blum to respect French promises against those who worked against both the French prime minister and the Syrians: the French fascists who had fomented all the trouble.

In Geneva on May 24, the League of Nations prepared to deliberate on the Sanjak's future. Rapporteur Sandler provided a written copy of the Committee of Experts' report to the League of Nations Council and described the continuing disagreements over the status of the Arabic language and the inclusion of neighboring territories in the newly independent Sanjak that was to be created. Five days later, with the outstanding issues resolved, the League of Nations Council approved the report of the Committee of Experts, accepting the new

Statute and Fundamental Law of the Sanjak of Alexandretta. The Statute of the Sanjak defined the nature of the Sanjak's independence reflecting Turkey's more expansive definition: a "separate entity, enjoying full independence in its internal affairs," dependent on Syria for its foreign affairs, and sharing with Syria a customs and monetary administration. When it came into force on November 29, 1937, the Sanjak would take over all the assets and liabilities of the French mandatory administration, including its concessions, laws, and appointments, until the newly elected authorities voted to change them. In order to facilitate the connections between the Syrian and Sanjak governments, each would appoint a commissioner; the legislative assemblies of each entity would create a liaison system. The customs regime would be determined by a joint commission of four representatives from Syria and two from the Sanjak; while the regimes would be identical, customs administration would be separate. According to the Statute, citizenship would include those currently living in the Sanjak, those who had previously been in the Sanjak, and those whose fathers were of the Sanjak. Although Sanjak citizenship brought Syrian citizenship, the reverse was not to be true. Syria's diplomatic corps would protect the interest of the Sanjak's citizens and issue their passports. There would be two equal official languages, Turkish and Arabic.

Still unsure of whether the Sanjak's complete internal independence trumped Syria's ability to make foreign policy or vice versa, the Committee of Experts decided to make the League of Nations the arbiter. "No international agreement concluded by the State of Syria which is likely to affect in any way whatever the independence and sovereignty of that state, and no international decision having the same effects, shall apply to the Sanjak without the express consent in advance of the Council of the League of Nations." On the other hand, if the Sanjak's government wished to make international agreements related solely to the Sanjak, it must inform the Syrian government. If that government did not respond, the Sanjak could ask that the League delegate submit the question to the League of Nations Council.

The new Fundamental Law of the Sanjak created a balance of power between three branches of government. The Sanjak Assembly, a single chamber of forty members, would be the legislative branch "in the name of the people of the Sanjak." Elections for the four-year seats would take place in two stages, both by secret ballot, in a process that was sketched out in the Fundamental Law but would be elaborated and supervised by a League of Nations commission. The executive power would be in the hands of the president and an Executive Council (of no more than five members) responsible to the Assembly. The Assembly would elect the president for a five-year term to represent the Sanjak at official ceremonies, promulgate laws passed by the Assembly, and draft an annual budget and finance law. The Assembly would have responsibility for levying taxes and contracting loans, as well as approving the credits for expenses included in the executives' draft budget and finance law. The president, on advice of the Executive Council, would have the power to dissolve the Assembly and order fresh elections. He would appoint judges to the Sanjak's Supreme Court. The Executive Council would be required to enforce that court's judgments, which could not be reversed by either of the other branches of government. However, none of the courts would be permitted to question the constitutionality of laws passed by the Assembly. The Assembly could add to the Fundamental Law by two majority votes of the new Assembly three months apart. Amendments to the Fundamental Law, using the same process, could only be entertained beginning five years after independence. There was no provision for amending the new Statute.

The Sanjak would guarantee its citizens basic rights, including the right to be free from search and arrest except as provided by law; also to be protected were freedom of conscience, the press, association, and religion (there was to be no official religion in the Sanjak); compulsory elementary education was provided by the law; and no one was to be deprived of property without judicial proceedings. On the other hand, these individual liberties could be restricted by the Assembly "in the event of serious disorder or insurrection" and by the president "in urgent cases." Demilitarization of the Sanjak would prohibit the creation of armed forces, introduction of conscription, and manufacture or maintenance of weapons or ammunition designed for warfare. The police and gendarme forces would be limited to fifteen hundred men, and their arms and ammunition would be permitted.

The Statute created a Turkish Free Zone in the port of Alexandretta, which the Sanjak government would lease to Turkey for fifty years. All employees in this zone would be appointed by Turkey and responsible to Turkey. Except fees for common services, like towing and pilotage, all revenues from the Turkish Free Zone would go to Turkey. "Every facility shall be afforded to the Turkish Government for ensuring connection between the Turkish Free Zone and the railway linking Alexandretta to Turkish territory."

The Committee of Experts codified three different and potentially incompatible methods to enforce the new protocols. According to article 5 of the Statute, the League of Nations would appoint a French delegate who would live within the Sanjak and would have the power to suspend any legislation or administrative action contrary to the new Statute or Fundamental Law for up to four months, during which time the League of Nations Council would consider the matter and make the final decision. At the same time, article 7 provided France and Turkey with enforcement responsibility for the Sanjak. "The French Government and the Turkish Government shall give effect to the recommendations which the Council of the League of Nations may make to them to ensure that the decisions taken by the Council are respected. If, in virtue of the Council's decision, the two Governments have to take joint action, they shall previously consult one another regarding the details of such action." Yet article 55 of the Statute provides that "during such time as the mandate remains in operation, they [the Statute and Fundamental Law] shall be applied to the fullest extent compatible with the exercise of the said mandate." The Statute made the League of Nations, France, and a Franco-Turkish condominium each separately responsible for enforcement of the new laws of the independent Sanjak.[77]

In the League of Nations Council that day, League members congratulated each other on a job well done. As many of the diplomats noted with relief, this multilateral, peaceful resolution of the Sanjak question did more than simply resolve the fate of the Sanjak; it did more even than consolidate the bonds between France and Turkey. In this agreement, French foreign minister Delbos exclaimed, his country had "made a positive contribution to the great work of peace which the League of Nations tirelessly pursues." Others emphasized the efficacy and enormous significance of the League itself as a power for peaceful diplomacy. The Soviet Union's Foreign Commisar Maxim Litvinov described the resolution of the Sanjak's status as "a great success for the League of Nations, the strengthening of which is an important element of the policy of my Government. It is a great satisfaction to note that the friendship between the two nations has been strengthened; such a strengthening of the ties between two countries which are carrying out a policy of loyalty to the League of Nations and the principles for which it stands, and to the organization of peace and collective security, is certainly a great success for the cause of peace itself."[78]

Delbos also emphasized the bigger geostrategic prize in resolving the Sanjak question: the Ankara regime had reassured Europe of its desire to protect the stability of the region:

> The scope of the agreements just reached extends beyond the limited problem of which they are the solution. In receiving Egypt into the League of Nations, the Turkish Minister for Foreign Affairs reminded us the other day of the importance his country attached to the *status quo* in the Eastern Mediterranean. The settlement of the affair of the Sanjak of Alexandretta unites France and Turkey for the maintenance of peace in the Near East and thus supplements the work undertaken by the French Government at the time of the signature of the Franco-Syrian and Franco-Lebanese treaties.[79]

Having given in to Turkish demands, France was convinced that Turkey would remain a loyal member of the League of Nations and refrain from undermining the League's increasingly contested consensus. Anthony Eden, representing Great

Britain, took a different tack, extolling the ways this settlement accommodated all parties' needs. "The fullest protection is accorded to all the local interests concerned, of whatever race or creed. Not only are Turkish interests protected, but the interests of the Arab population and those of the various minorities in the Sanjak are no less fully safeguarded. I trust, therefore, that this settlement will find a ready acceptance, not only in the Sanjak itself, but in all the neighboring countries." Delbos rejoiced that this agreement helped to reconcile the interests of both Turkey and Syria, stating that France had "effectively safeguarded the interests of the country still under her tutelage."[80]

The League of Nations had validated the division of Ottoman lands and the creation of new states after World War I; now it had peacefully resolved to remove part of the territory it had allotted to Syria and make it yet another new state. British and French claims that this division would somehow safeguard the Sanjak's population beggared the imagination. In any case, the very people whose interests France was claiming to safeguard quickly challenged France's assertion.

|| 4 ||

Transition to Independence

Turkey's government was jubilant about the Sanjak's new Statute and Fundamental Law. They had lost the battle to make Turkish the only official language, but they had succeeded in the main project: the Sanjak was to become an independent country, despite its continuing ties to Syria. Moreover, the new Fundamental Law acknowledged a Turkish plurality in the area. Istanbul's semiofficial newspaper *La République* emphasized the bigger international issues at stake in its headline story, "A New Victory for the League of Nations and for Peace." Menemencioğlu, who had been closely involved with the negotiations, insisted that the peaceful resolution would be a boon not only to all residents of the Sanjak but also to all people concerned about world peace. Not only had his government successfully protected the future of the Turks living in the Sanjak; the outcome had proved to the world that "the Turkish Republic has no designs on this territory." He was convinced that the tiny new country would have a "happy future" and insisted that it would be a shining example of the potential for successful international collaboration. All the agreements between France and Turkey would ensure its security, and "from now on it is certain that the independence of the Hatay will mark a new era in the friendship between Turkey and Syria."[1] In Menemencioğlu's eyes, Turkey had successfully safeguarded a threatened population and at the same time ensured cooperation with its neighbors and set a precedent for preserving world peace. In Ankara, the Grand National Assembly quickly ratified the new Franco-Turkish Agreements signed by their governments in Geneva on May 29, 1937, alongside the League of Nations Council resolution accepting the Sanjak's new Statute and Fundamental Law.[2]

On June 5, Kemal Atatürk entered Istanbul triumphant. He had made the Sanjak a cornerstone for his regime and a test of his prestige, even threatening to resign in order to conquer it militarily, if necessary. He had won international recognition of the Sanjak as not only independent, but as home to a Turkish majority. In recognition, military and civilian leaders met him at the train station on the Asian side of the city; Jordan's King Abdullah, on a state visit to Turkey, was on deck as the presidential yacht crossed the Bosphorus, saluted by a line of warships and escorted by planes flying overhead. That evening, illuminated ships passed in review in front of Dolmabahçe Palace. The Counselor of the United States Embassy in Turkey, G. Howland Shaw, was a bit cynical about the display: "Full advantage was taken of the opportunity for impressing an Arab ruler with Turkish might and convincing him of the support enjoyed by the Turkish Government in its stand on the Hatay question."[3]

In Syria, the Sanjak's new Statute and Fundamental Law brought widespread opposition. A motion that the Syrian Chamber of Deputies approved on May 31 was forwarded to French authorities and to the League of Nations: "All efforts to alienate Syrian sovereignty and to amputate a part of the territory constitute a flagrant blow against the Franco-Syrian Treaty recently voted. The Syrian nation, having placed all her hope in international justice, does not recognize any solution which destroys her unity and compromises her renaissance, and intends to struggle against the blow with all her faith and the force of her right."

The same day, Syria's population poured into the streets to register their opposition. Aleppo's merchants closed their shops at noon, and by midafternoon some seven thousand people, including the Steel Shirts, processed from the courtyard of the city's major mosque crying "Alexandretta is Arab." "Dignified speeches" were presented in front of the French delegation, and four nationalist leaders (one Syrian Catholic, one Greek Orthodox, and two Muslim) presented an official letter asking the French Parliament to ratify the Franco-Syrian Treaty quickly. The League of National Action joined the National Bloc and Communists in closing the markets of Antioch and Alexandretta the same day.[4]

The big demonstrations took place on June 3, as opponents of the new Statute and Fundamental Law took to the streets in Idlib, Jableh, Latakia, even Amman. Suqs were closed throughout Syria, in Antioch and Alexandretta, in Dayr al-Zur, Damascus, Homs, and Hama. Husni al-Barazi's prohibition of all demonstrations was effective within the Sanjak, which saw no street protest while five thousand people demonstrated in Damascus. Even though the National Bloc was being subjected to withering criticism, its leaders could readily agree with the opposition on the unacceptability of the League of Nations' program for the Sanjak. Prime Minister Mardam reassured the protesters that their sentiments would be sent to the delegation at Paris. Fakhri al-Barudi reasserted the Arab nature of the Sanjak and went further, criticizing Ankara's attitude toward Syria, claiming that the Ottoman regime had been oppressive, and accusing the Kemalists of ingratitude for the aid Syria's government had provided them during the campaign for Cilicia. Opposition leaders urged popular unity and joint struggle to defend the Sanjak and threw their support behind the new Committee for the Defense of the Sanjak that would bring together all the parties under the leadership of opposition leader Shahbandar.[5] The new Committee for the Defense of the Sanjak met the same day in Damascus, composing a protest that "condemns the amputation of the Sanjak and the misreading of the sacred rights of Syria recognized by the League of Nations; protests energetically against the formal blow given to the Franco-Syrian Treaty; allies itself with the motion of the Chamber and declares with all its force that the Nation consecrates itself to combat all unjust solutions. . . . The Committee calls on the international conscience to respect the rights of the people who are victims of the predominance of Force over Right."[6]

Despite French reassurances about the Sanjak's continuing ties to Syria, the new Statute and Fundamental Law transferred most of the attributes of sovereignty out of the hands of the Damascus regime. Under the new rules, the Sanjak would have its own postal system; Alexandretta would become a Turkish free port; international agreements affecting the Sanjak would have to be approved by the League of Nations Council; and the president and elected assembly would be able to conclude treaties and participate in foreign representation without approval from Damascus. The common customs regime between Syria and the Sanjak would actually require a mixed commission, implicitly creating two separate systems. This new government would be quite expensive, as the U.S. Consul General in Beirut, J. Theodore Marriner, pointed out. The population of 250,000 would be forced to pay the salaries of the president, a cabinet, police, forty deputies, customs and postal services, and other officials. The assembly itself, Marriner observed, would encourage Turkish dominance; although the minimum representation for each group had been set at eight Turks, six Alawis, two Arabs, two Armenians, and one Greek Orthodox member, he predicted that the proportion of Turks would increase as people recognized the advantages to be gained through connections with the most powerful group.[7]

With the new Statute and Fundamental Law interpreting the Sanjak's independence to the benefit of Turkey, National Bloc leaders in Damascus seemed unable to do more than struggle to channel Syrians' anger. According to Marriner, recent widespread strikes confirmed that the National Bloc's anxiety over losing popular support in the wake of the Sanjak question had been justified. Parades in front of the Parliament building in Damascus exposed a public furious at the loss of the Sanjak. Even the U.S. consuls were receiving letters opposing the Sanjak's new status, claiming that it "seriously jeopardizes the interest of Syria and . . . is of a nature to violate the material as well as moral rights of the Syrian people. . . ." Nonetheless, Damascus officials suggested no alternatives to the recent decision in Geneva; even the parliamentary resolution expressing opposition to the Geneva decision recommended no process that would make nonacceptance legally binding.[8]

In the Sanjak, however, the behavior of activist government officials infuriated Abdulgani Türkmen. In a telegram to Durieux on June 3, he complained that the Sanjak's Syrian administrators, especially Governor al-Barazi, were actually inciting some of the people of the Sanjak against the Turks. He quoted al-Barazi's June 1 speech, which had been published in Aleppo's *Al-Shabab*: "If it is necessary, 70 million Arabs will shed their blood for you. Neither the League of Nations nor anyone is capable of abasing this quadricolor flag floating over your heads that you are prepared to die for." Turks in the Sanjak were responding anxiously to the speech, according to Türkmen, who demanded action by the French: "If an administrator who occupies the highest post publicly pronounces in favor of one and to the detriment of the others, if he tries to threaten those who do not think as he does with 70 million Arabs, what will become of the public he is addressing? How can a functionary be left at the head of an administration after a declaration so serious and so enraged?"[9]

French officials were likewise disturbed by local reactions to the Geneva decision, laying responsibility at the feet of small groups of agitators. Communists in Alexandretta were "always appearing at the head of groups of children charged with throwing stones at our police and with breaking our windows," wrote Mentque, the interim French delegate, while Zaki al-Arsuzi played the activist role in Antioch. Nonetheless, Mentque insisted, it was not these "mental defectives" who were behind the agitation, but those remaining in the shadows who played the role of agents provocateurs. Abdulgani Türkmen's letter illustrated the need to neutralize these forces. In any case, Mentque claimed, the results of the Sanjak question were hardly significant to most of the people living in the region. "One could be convinced," he wrote, "that the inhabitants of the Sanjak, both Arabs and Turks, are, in overwhelming majority, clearly satisfied with the verdict of Geneva, that they are solely preoccupied with freely devoting themselves to their affairs and are exasperated with seeing their shops periodically closed, under threat of theft, for political reasons of which they do not approve." All that needed to happen, Mentque opined, was for Governor al-Barazi to act authoritatively to ensure "the most absolute calm." The French official seemed optimistic that al-Barazi understood that his partisan behavior must end and forbid all demonstrations in public spaces.[10] For this French official, the Geneva vote was final. It entirely changed the situation, transforming those who continued to oppose the Sanjak's independence into outlaws; in contrast, Kemalist leader Abdulgani Türkmen, was now on the side of the law.

Jamil Mardam telegraphed France and the League of Nations expressing his objection to the notion that the Sanjak's new status was just and Turkey on the side of right. According to Syria's government, the new Geneva statute "detaches from Syrian control a province whose history, ethnography, predominant language, religious events, circumstances, treaties since the World War, and even

the claims of Turkey's official representatives in the Ankara Accord [1921] ...
the Lausanne Treaty and the Ankara Accord [1926] has never ceased until the
present being part of strictly Syrian territory." Important connections linked
Syria to the province of Alexandretta, and its port served the entire nation. For
Mardam, Syria and the Sanjak "constituted an indivisible whole" that had been
recognized since World War I by the Great Powers as well as Ankara.

Mardam's insistence that Syrians cared deeply about the Sanjak did not jibe
with French notions that the population was disinterested. For the Syrian prime
minister, the Sanjak's new status was unnecessary, it destroyed Syrian unity, and
it did not correspond to the desires of the people. The 1921 Ankara Treaty had
already provided all necessary facilities for development of Turkish language
and culture within Syria. Moreover, the new Statute had been created without
consulting the interested population, who would have been clear about their
desire to remain part of Syria. Mardam cited İsmet İnönü, Turkey's chief negoti-
ator during the postwar discussions at Lausanne, who had insisted on "the right
of peoples to dispose themselves." Now, the Syrian prime minister argued, Turkey and the League of Nations were turning their backs on their own ideals.
These decisions were not consonant with the League's own procedures and had
been made in great haste, without even awaiting the report of the International
Mission of Observers who had been still in the Sanjak collecting information.[11]

The Syrian government contested each section of the Statute, claiming that it
infringed the rights of a nation to determine external relations in all of its territory, that its military clauses threatened the Sanjak's security, and that its customs regime compromised Syria's interests. Syria could not consent to this
elimination of its internal sovereignty over one of the most important regions of
its land, Mardam insisted. "In addition to her honor, her vital interests forbid
her." Moreover, Mardam challenged the notion that Syria would continue to play
a decisive role in the Sanjak under the new status. When France had signed the
Franco-Turkish Agreements on May 29, 1937, to guarantee the territorial integrity of the Sanjak, Syria had not been included as a coguarantor. If the Sanjak
were to be really tied to Syria, why was Damascus left out of the documents
guaranteeing its protection?[12] Countering Turkish, French, British, and League
of Nations gratification in the positive consequences for all parties, it seemed to
Mardam that the Sanjak's ties to Syria were being severed without cause and
with apparent indifference to the wishes of the local population, the huge economic cost to his country, and the high political price for his own party.

Violence accelerated in the Sanjak during the first days of June, as small incidents escalated, mobilizing angry crowds and resulting in injuries. In Antioch,
two men singing Turkish songs insulted Arab inhabitants; the next day, a Turk
attacked an Alawi; the third, Turkish officials were stoned as they walked to
work. Over and over, troops were called out to establish order.[13] The *New York*

Times wrote on June 8, 1937, that martial law had been declared as a result of riots between Turks and Arabs, and that fifteen people had been injured. Calling the international press "alarmist," French officials in Ankara insisted that rumors of martial law were groundless.[14] Both the Syrian and Turkish governments attributed nefarious intentions to the increasing attacks. Syrian officials laid blame at the feet of both the Turks and the French, claiming that the Turks were trying to compromise the efficacy of Syrian officials, and accusing the French of further exacerbating tensions by ordering the troops out of Alexandretta after the recent incidents. When Syrian officials requested that the French take urgent measures, French administrators accused the Damascus regime of abdicating responsibility. "Does the Syrian government consider that the Syrian authorities in the Sanjak of Alexandretta are without the power to assure public order and to calm sentiments? As a result, does the Syrian Government ask that the mandatory authorities become exclusively responsible for assuring public order?"[15] To the Syrians, it appeared that the French were colluding with the Turks to discredit the Damascus regime.

Turkish leaders in the Sanjak, in turn, held Arab officials responsible, even though some of the incidents had been instigated by Turks. Calling the Antioch incidents "regrettable" and their consequences "disastrous," the Turcophiles went on to analyze the causes of the "deplorable" situation, laying all blame on the government in Damascus and its functionaries in the Sanjak. First, the local Kemalists claimed, Syria's government had rejected the League of Nations Council decision to make the Sanjak independent, and Syrian officials had declared publicly that they would work to prevent the Sanjak's detachment from Syria. At the same time, Syrian nationalist Fakhri al-Barudi's Committee for the Defense of the Sanjak called students to arms and published manifestos with "fantastic" titles like "Our bayonets will make pieces of the League of Nations decision about the Sanjak" and "We will prove the Arabism of the Sanjak by letting our blood flow." It was al-Barudi's work that had pushed a group of Alawi and Greek Orthodox youth (in affiliation with the League of National Action) to "create incidents," according to the Turcophiles' narrative, actions consistent with Syria's encouragement of resistance as the only way to deliver the Sanjak. Incendiary speeches and propaganda had been published in the local press in an effort to create enough violence that outsiders would recognize the disastrous consequences of detaching the Sanjak from Syria. According to the Kemalists, Arab leaders were trying to prove that the Sanjak's new status would be inimical to the cause of peace. That is why Syrian functionaries, including the highest-ranking one, Governor al-Barazi, were tolerating violence. "In one word, the Syrian government does not want to recognize the Geneva accord on the Sanjak. Its representatives in the country are of the view that the Accord could be taken back if they create troubles in the Sanjak. They could thus prove that calm could not return in the Sanjak unless the administrative mechanism and the public force are directed by representatives of the Syrian government." Indeed, the Kemalists alleged, the very authorities being asked to preserve the peace were among those intentionally fomenting discord in order to discredit, then overturn, the Sanjak's new status.

Local Turkish leaders recommended radical steps to transform the situation. The League of National Action in the Sanjak should be "recalled," the governor of the Sanjak and the mayor of Antioch must be dismissed, and local government should be restructured as a transitional regime in accordance with the principles of the Sanjak's new Statute and Fundamental Law. Since the principles and even the date of the application of the new situation had been determined at Geneva, they argued, there was no reason to maintain Syrian authority in the Sanjak; such authority could only be dangerous to both the Sanjak's future and its security.[16]

French authorities seemed reluctant to go that far. Instead, interim French delegate Mentque decided to bring together leaders of all the political groups active in the Sanjak for a two-day meeting, which the convener himself described as "difficult and arduous." After long discussion, the meeting's ultimate product, what the French called a "pact of reconciliation," was a letter asking High Commissioner Martel to come to the Sanjak to calm the people, give advice, and help bring an end to the current tension. Although the joint letter referred to the various parties' desire for reconciliation, each group blamed the others present for the recent violent incidents. Many thought sufficient armed force indispensable for maintaining order in the Sanjak. Claiming they were powerless to stop perpetrators of individual crimes, they demanded that the French continue to assume the responsibility of maintaining public order.[17]

France's role in the Sanjak had grown more ambiguous with each succeeding international agreement. The San Remo Resolution of 1920 had designated France as the mandatory power for Syria, obliged to provide security and tutelage. The 1936 Franco-Syrian Treaty provided Paris direct control but required it to work with a new Syrian administration during the transition period to independence. With the new 1937 Statute and Fundamental Law and its concurrent Franco-Turkish Agreements, Paris had become co-guarantor with Turkey of the Sanjak's security and the rights of its inhabitants. France was thus simultaneously the mandatory power exercising complete control, a co-governing power with the Syrian regime in Damascus, and co-guarantor of the Sanjak. Article 55 of the new Statute for the Sanjak muddied the situation at the same time as it tried to prioritize these roles, insisting that France must apply the Statute's provisions "to the fullest extent compatible with the exercise of the said mandate." Indeed, the Statute stipulated that the Sanjak would remain under French mandatory control until the Syrian mandate ended.[18] During the transition period before the new regime came into force on November 27, 1937, the French insisted that the Sanjak's Syrian administration would continue, and local police and government responsibilities were to remain unchanged. As the high commissioner's office interpreted his complex sets of directives, French officials could intervene in the Sanjak's affairs only to maintain public order, and then only if there were actual disturbances that the local authority was unable to handle, if there were imminent danger of trouble that only French authorities could prevent, or on the request of local officials. Even in these situations, however, the French would have to work together with local Sanjak authorities who had been part of the Syrian regime. If Martel's delegate in the Sanjak found it necessary to take charge, he must officially requisition the military authority. "Our intervention must of course have an essentially provisional character and end as soon as the situation permits. Our preoccupation in the matter must be obviously to avoid anti-Turkish troubles likely to be exploited by Ankara, but we must also in the measure possible safeguard the authority of the local administration and maintain the situation springing from the application of the treaty."[19] To mollify Turkey's demands that Syrian officials be removed, French officials called those local leaders aside to impress on them the tenuous nature of Syrian rule. Martel was trying to balance obligations under the Franco-Syrian Treaty with commitments under the new Franco-Turkish Agreements, while Viénot, the French undersecretary of state for the Middle East and North Africa, considered France's goal in the Sanjak to be primarily the maintenance of order to prepare for the application of the Sanjak's new regime.[20]

For French officials in both Paris and Syria, the Statute and Fundamental Law had become the only recognized future course for the Sanjak; it was "a decided thing and there would be no question of going back on these international engagements."[21] They repeatedly warned the Syrian government that Damascus would lose all its remaining authority in the Sanjak by refusing to cooperate in their implementation. Discussions about the Sanjak's future status were no longer relevant; protests were counterproductive and would threaten not only the peace but also the Syrian regime's credibility in Europe. The only pressing requirements had become a peaceful transition, and avoiding Turkish anger. The late riots had resulted in a threat by Turkey to use its own force. Anxious French officials demanded not only that local authorities maintain order: if the Damascus regime was unable to appease Turkey, French officials said, France would step in directly and do it itself.[22] By June 8, there had been no further incidents, stores had reopened, and Zaki al-Arsuzi of the League of National Action was working on calming local tensions.[23]

For military officials in Paris, France's continuing long-term presence in the region was a welcome consequence of the new Sanjak agreements. Instead of severely limiting their role in Syria, as the still-unapproved Franco-Syrian Treaty of independence provided, the French Ministry of Defense insisted that French commitments to guaranteeing the Sanjak's territorial integrity would require both a continuing military presence on the Syrian coast and the willingness of the Syrian and Turkish troops to function under French control.[24] France's foreign minister agreed, adding that the new Statute and Fundamental Law for the Sanjak "thus give us a new argument to win acceptance for a solution that interests us for many reasons." The resolution of the Sanjak question by the Statute and Fundamental Law, which made France co-guarantor of the security of the Sanjak with Turkey, could be used by France to effectively extend its occupation of Syria indefinitely, regardless of the provisions under the 1936 Franco-Syrian Treaty that had promised Syria's independence.[25]

Although the Syrian government appeared to acquiesce to the Sanjak's new status, Sanjak officials continued organizing opposition. Governor Husni al-Barazi, Antioch's Mayor Abd al-Qadir, and other Syrian functionaries organized a congress at Antioch to decide what to do next. Working through the League of National Action, al-Barazi ordered each Arab village to send a representative. The meeting on June 30 included some three hundred men. French informants reported that the delegates soon split, as important Arab notables walked out and created an alternative conference. According to French officials, the meeting ended with the two groups failing to reach any agreement and the dissident notables refusing to participate in opposing the Sanjak's new status.[26]

The demonstrations that took place on July 6 were only partly focused on the politics of the Sanjak's future. It was mostly women who gathered at Alexandretta and at Homs, protesting against price increases in basic necessities that accompanied a year of severe economic hardship. Crops were expected to be bad, months of drought had led to hoarding and speculation in the cities, and the condition of local livestock was critical. The incursions of hungry nomads into the towns seemed to exacerbate the growing fear of Turkish invasion. To make the situation even worse, Paris had revalued French currency, which created tremendous instability within Syria and resulted in merchants demanding gold instead of the usual coins. Moreover, worldwide depression continued to linger. For many in the Sanjak, the economy was a much more urgent concern, overshadowing the struggles over which foreign capital would have the opportunity to preside over their misery. Police intervened to keep the women from pillaging the marketplace, and at Alexandretta, one police officer was wounded. French authorities remained skeptical about the real reasons for the demonstration, behind which they perceived the collaboration of the Communist Party with a Damascus government seeking to assert its own influence on "Syrian elements in the Sanjak."[27]

When the high commissioner returned from his leave in France, he traveled to the Sanjak as requested by the notables who had met with his delegate in early

June. French officials made extensive preparations, hoping that the high-profile visit would help calm the situation on the ground while simultaneously bolstering the military and police presence. Turks prepared their new Hatay flag, ready in case anyone displayed a Syrian flag. The Turkish consul at Aleppo, worried about violence in the streets, asked French authorities to ban all demonstrations. The colonial administration compromised, prohibiting all parades with flags.[28]

Martel arrived in the Sanjak on July 12, visited Kirikhan, Reyhanlı, Alexandretta, and Antioch and came away assured of the people's love for France and their satisfaction with the status quo. In Antioch, he addressed heads of all the communities in a speech simultaneously translated into both Turkish and Arabic, urging calm and good relations among the various groups as the Statute and Fundamental Law were implemented. He was received at Alexandretta by a delegation of National Bloc and Communist Party leaders.[29] *L'Orient* quoted his Alexandretta speech at length, in which he claimed that the League of Nations Council had been inspired by "the diversity of the populations who live in the Sanjak, the variety of rites, the linguistic differences." He urged his audience to provide proof that "the diverse elements of the population of the Sanjak already have enough political maturity to collaborate harmoniously for the realization of a new state of things.... Between Syria, with whose destinies it will remain associated, and neighboring Turkey, the Sanjak is called upon to become not a reason of discord, but, much to the contrary, an element destined to facilitate relations between the two peoples, Syrian and Turkish, the means to draw their friendship closer." Martel promised that France would impartially and unfailingly assume its mission to maintain order, and said he was pleased to be able to reassure the Turks that they should expect friendly relations with their neighbors. "I count on the understanding of all the inhabitants of the Sanjak that, by respecting their reciprocal rights, they cooperate in what concerns them, in this politics of understanding and peace-making."[30]

The political diversity of Martel's audience was evident during the banquet that followed. Martel noted the Kemalists wearing morning coats and bowler hats and the overwhelmingly young "Arab extremists" led by the young Zaki al-Arsuzi wearing the sedara made famous by Faysal. "Between the two," Martel noted the fez and an anything-goes style of dress that marked the "moderate notables of all shades: Turks, Armenians, Greek Orthodox, Alawis." Characterizing the atmosphere as "simple and cordial," Martel was pleased with the "unanimous applause [that] greeted the speech by which I praised M. Durieux, announcing his departure for the important post of Naples."[31]

The high commissioner claimed that he heard no dissident notes during any of his stops around the Sanjak to mar the vast chorus of accolades. At Reyhanlı, the site of bloody events during the visit of the International Mission of

Observers, Martel encountered a varied crowd of Turks, Kurds, and Circassians who demonstrated noisy joy at the passage of his cortège. Armenian notables at Kirikhan, "whose population had risen under French occupation, claimed to owe everything to France and that they would rely on French support to assure their future peace and security in the Sanjak." In Alexandretta, Martel claimed he preempted any criticism by a mixed delegation of young men representing three parties, the National Bloc, the League of National Action, and the Communist Party. "They addressed some friendly phrases of welcome at me, and I responded that some substantial words were more valuable than a long discourse, which deprived them of the courage to pronounce the diatribe they had prepared against the Geneva accords." Martel basked in the favorable attention he observed everywhere else, concluding: "Respect for France is above antagonisms."[32]

For the Damascus government, Martel's visit was embarrassing. Having passed resolutions and agitated against the the Sanjak's new status, they could hardly be associated with the French high commissioner's trip to the Sanjak, and he did not pass though Damascus on his way. Martel claimed that the Syrian government had tacitly approved the trip and seemed willing to have the Sanjak's new Statute put into force without ever explicitly sanctioning it. Reassured by the people's apparent love for France, the high commissioner offered his advice to both Governor al-Barazi and Prime Minister Mardam. Martel believed the Syrian government to have "too openly relied on organizations of young men in whom the Syrian government perceived the essential element of an activist Arabism." These men had been tactless and had made errors that had led to results antithetical to French wishes. If the Syrian government continued to be represented in the Sanjak by "some fanatics," he warned, Turkish propaganda would succeed in attracting members of other communities who only wanted to coexist in peace. Martel was confident that the Syrian prime minister "understood these things very well," and would try to end the Sanjak's National Bloc activism that had "compromised the Syrian cause while defending it badly. We hope that he will convince his immediate collaborators and above all that he will succeed little by little in pacifying that which remains of the virulence among the lower echelons of the National Bloc."[33]

While Martel was reveling in his warm reception and lecturing Syria's leaders, Ambassador Ponsot summarized the response in Ankara, where the press reported Martel's speech and joined in the celebrations that marked the visit. "The whole Sanjak is making merry, noted Istanbul daily *Cumhuriyet*." Yunus Nadi editorialized in *La République* that the Sanjak remaining attached to Syria, in an arrangement that would make "Hatay" similar to a Swiss canton, would "bring security and prosperity to all the inhabitants without exception."[34]

French officials, hopeful that the high commissioner's visit would encourage people to accept the Sanjak's new status with calm resignation, were surprised to note growing polarization instead. Less than two weeks after Martel returned home, his delegate wrote that the opposition was increasingly "under the control and even under the threat of political groups who, devoid of moderate notables among their directors, have become law in the country and persist in feeding the conflict separating the two races." The responsible groups, the (Arab) League of National Action and the (Turkish) People's Houses had come to form states within the state, each doing its own policing and sending propaganda agents into the villages, each even providing its own schools. New People's Houses had been established at Reyhanlı, Kırıkhan, and Beylan, and Kemalist leaders had sent an estimated 140 people, officially as teachers, to disseminate propaganda in the villages. French officials insisted that this activity stop immediately.

Interim Delegate Mentque was especially interested in proscribing the League of National Action, headed by Zaki al-Arsuzi. "I do not need to remind you of his curriculum vitae and his chronically inappropriate actions and words," Mentque wrote, his words pulsing with French imperial disdain for Syria's Arab "extremists." "This individual, encouraged by impunity and brazenness, finally brought over the Governor, the Mayor of Antioch, and the Gendarmerie Captain, and, at the head of some rabble wearing Iraqi hats, he dictates law in the Alawi and Christian quarters of Antioch, organizing patrols in the streets and thrashing all those among the Arabs who do not want to adhere willingly to the 'League of National Action.'"

Mentque warned that if the French did not quickly put an end to both groups' illegal activities, these agitators could prevent the smooth transition to the new regime. Fearing that their continued activism would create grave conflicts, he proposed immediate measures to reestablish the prestige of the local and mandatory authorities, "which is steadily declining and held in check by the schemings of certain leaders." In order to ensure that the law was respected, to create balance between the two groups, and to reinforce French power, Mentque asked permission to immediately close both the Halkevleri and the League of National Action as well as the Communist Party cells. French officials hoped that closing down the "extremist" groups would also encourage moderate leaders to step up by restoring "some virility to the notables whose prudence has stood them aside, and who ardently hope, whether Turks or Arabs, that these riots in the streets and artificial agitations come to a rapid end." Mentque was especially optimistic that his plan could work after receiving a conciliatory letter from Governor al-Barazi, who had previously provided quiet support for the League of National Action. The French representative believed that he would not be accused "of partiality if we treat on the same footing the friends of the League of National Action and the adversaries of the Halkevi."[35]

Agreeing that a "certain effervescence" continued within the Sanjak among "extremist Arabs" in the League of National Action, and that the Kemalist Halkevi "parried blow for blow," Martel ordered that each group be required to adhere to a 1909 Ottoman-era law still in force that required political organizations to provide information about their actions and membership. French officials would dissolve any organizations that refused to support the Sanjak's new status. In addition, Mentque would give instructions to his military commanders to maintain order in the streets if the local authorities, police, and security services were unable to do so.[36] Mentque's confidence in his evenhandedness meant little to Abdulgani Türkmen, who lost no time in telegraphing Martel to complain about the infringement on the rights of the Sanjak's Turks. According to Türkmen, his group had received verbal authorization allowing them to open schools in the villages for the instruction of Turkish peasants, providing "a service to civilization and humanity." Closing the schools took away the possibility of "intellectual progress, which is a natural right for all who are human." The young, he wrote, saw this action as aggression against the liberty and individual rights recognized in the new Statute and Fundamental Law, and asked that the French authorities convey their opposition to the League of Nations. "Mr. High Commissioner, could the desire to learn to read and to write in one's maternal language be a subject of reproach?"[37]

Both Türkmen's appeal and the discourse of the League of National Action mobilized the language of the French Republic's basic values, each group emphasizing its adherence to the ideals of liberty and democracy, presenting itself as struggling for "liberty" and "individual rights" in the face of oppression. Ironically, the two groups that the French delegate identified as most threatening to French plans for the Sanjak were those whose rhetoric explicitly tied their own political program to France.

The League of National Action and the Republican People's Party each recognized the importance of continuing their activism, even after the League of Nations had decided to make the Sanjak independent, determined its form of government, and assigned the languages to be spoken. According to the Fundamental Law, the parliament would reflect the population in the Sanjak: each identity group would be represented in proportion to its presence in the population. Voters would register by community, and seats would be assigned by community based on the relative numbers of voters; mobilizing their adherents to register would be the route to each group's power and representation in the government.

A devastating division among Alawis resulted from the new system of representation. Ankara's insistence that Turks comprised the Sanjak's majority was predicated in part on the assertion that the Alawis were really lapsed Turkish-speakers and, indeed, the original Turks. The Sanjak's Kemalists worked tirelessly to educate local Alawis about their inherent Turkish identity. The project pitted the French delegate's two "extremist" groups against each other: while the Halkevi tried to recruit Alawis to register as Turks, Alawi Zaki al-Arsuzi organized the members of his community to support the pan-Arab cause. Having been oppressed for as long as they could remember by their own landowners, French schoolteachers, colonial officials, and Sunni elites (both Turkish- and Arabic-speaking), they were now sought after as possible "swing voters."

Alawi-on-Alawi violence resulted directly from the representational system put into place by the League of Nations Committee of Experts. Assuming that members of a specific identity group would share the same political goals, they expected proportional representation to allow the majority group's agenda to become dominant while still ensuring that minorities could be heard. Ironically, the system based on the assumption that identity determines political goals resulted in the scissure of the Alawis between two opposing political ideologies. The results were division, destruction, and death.

Violence flared on August 9, when an unplanned procession of eight Alawi supporters of the Turcophile Shaykh Maruf approached the office of Antioch's examining magistrate to give depositions in the case of a fight that had taken place in neighboring Süveydiye six months earlier. Shaykh Maruf was the Turcophiles' greatest asset in their efforts to "convert" the Alawis to Turkishness; indeed, two of his sons had traveled to Turkey the same morning, apparently to import weapons.[38] As the Kemalist-Alawi visitors passed, supporters of the League of National Action booed them, crowding behind them as they made their way to the government building. Some Turks nearby noticed the verbal abuse being hurled at their Alawi allies and in turn joined the procession behind the members of the League of National Action. Sensing trouble, the police dispersed the lot of them.

A short time later, a group of Turcophiles, still angry at the earlier taunts, encountered two leaders of the League of National Action. Sticks, stones, and pistols were the weapons of choice as Turks, Alawis, and Arabs fought. When a policeman arrested a Turcophile stone-thrower, the officer was attacked by dozens of Turcophiles, allowing the prisoner to escape as the policeman fell to the ground. The violence spilled over into the market, where Kemalists attacked a fez-wearer. As French officials tried to control an angry mob, Captain Queru, inspector of special services, heard gunshots and turned in time to see a man throw a black gun onto the roof of the neighboring barbershop. The weapon was a 9mm Mauser automatic pistol recovered by the driver, who had climbed a nearby telegraph pole to get to the roof; police experts claimed that the pin had broken, preventing it from firing again. The target was the French officials' car, whose radiator was pierced.

By late morning troops had restored order, but the market remained closed. In addition to the property damage from stone-throwers, there had been many injuries on both sides; men as young as eighteen and as old as fifty-seven were wounded by knives, sticks, guns, and stones. One of those wounded, a twenty-five-year-old Alawi grocer, died in the hospital the next day from stab wounds to the abdomen. Funeral speeches by members of the League of National Action hardly pacified the situation, according to French reports.[39] Sabet ben Hasan Şarbatcı, called Kör Sabet, was accused of the shooting. Thirty years old, a café owner in the yarn bazaar, Kör Sabet had spent five years in prison for shooting and wounding a police officer in 1928. The suspect claimed he was not the perpetrator; in fact, he asserted, he hadn't even participated in the demonstration. He had been on his way home from a wedding in Kirikhan when he saw another man throw his gun on the ground. Picking it up, he noticed that it was loaded and threw it onto the neighboring roof. During interrogation, French officials concluded that Kör Sabet was part of a "terrorist arm" connected with the Republican People's Party, based in Antioch's Halkevi.[40] Mentque wrote the same day that the great tension in the city was becoming particularly dangerous because of the prevalence of firearms among the population, and he requested instructions.[41]

Still enraged, Alawis in the Dört Ayak quarter attacked an Alawi Turcophile the next morning. Authorities heard gunshots as they arrived, and called for a patrol of gendarmes to enforce peace. Despite their efforts, the events in Dört Ayak threatened to re-create the previous day's turmoil. An "Arab Turcophile (chapiste)" driver from Süveydiye, alarmed by the situation, ran toward the bridge; when Arabs threw stones at him, he replied with gunfire. Despite the presence of military patrols, tensions continued to rise, exacerbated by the morning's events and by the funeral services for the man fatally injured the previous day. Turks attacked Alawis in the market; an eighty-year-old grain vendor was injured when a Turk struck his arm with a stick; three others were hit in the head and the back with sticks.[42] French officials called in the leaders of all political activist groups and threatened serious repercussions if they did not control their adherents.

Alawi-on-Alawi violence spilled over into the countryside, as some fifty people from Jedida village arrived at the home of Shaykh Maruf, armed with sticks. Agitated, the local merchants closed their shops. The village head and the police worked to calm people, and met the men from Jedida as they left Shaykh Maruf's home, escorting them to the edge of town in an effort to prevent conflict with the shaykh's men. Nonetheless, while on the road the group encountered sixty armed men from the village of Kürt Deresi. The two groups engaged in a firefight, Shaykh Maruf's pro-Turkish Alawis against Jedida village's pro-Syrian Alawis. The government sent gendarmes to help restore order.[43]

Having reassured Ankara that they could maintain security in the Sanjak, French mandatory authorities urged the French ambassador to Turkey to contradict the rumors of recent violence that he anticipated would be circulating in Ankara. The incidents were not serious, they claimed; they had begun between "moderate and extremist Arabs" and only later involved Turks; some shots had been fired and some injuries sustained, but order had been restored easily and the French were the "perfect masters" of the situation. The high commissioner's office asked the Foreign Ministry to intervene with Turkish authorities to tone down attacks by the Turkish press, whose polemics might force them to implicate Turkey's own "agents of propaganda" in the recent violence, which had threatened French officials directly.[44] Although they recognized the role of Turkish activists in instigating the split among Alawis and fomenting the recent troubles, the mandatory administration remained unwilling to confront the Ankara regime on its responsibility. Indeed, Turkish ambassador Suad Davaz visited the French Foreign Ministry in Paris to emphasize the importance of maintaining order in the Sanjak. The conversation was described as cordial, as the Foreign Ministry officials reassured him that the violence was actually among Alawis and there was no need for Ankara to be concerned. The discussions turned to other topics, as Davaz mentioned the positive impact that Martel's visit to the Sanjak had produced, and French officials updated him on the situation along other parts of the border.[45]

Despite reassurances that the situation was under control, police were uneasy when morning dawned on August 11, convinced that any small incident could spark a riot. When a fifteen-year-old Alawi apprentice accidentally wounded a twenty-year-old Turkish café employee's arm with a butcher's knife, the police chief reported that this "incident, of little importance itself, seriously aggravated the situation." Mobs around the city threatened communications in Antioch, keeping officials from getting to their offices. "Excitement reigns in the city," the police chief wrote. "The mob, whether Turk or Arab, was no longer rational and was behaving without judgment."[46] Insisting that the measures to date had been insufficient, Mentque ordered Antioch's army commander to "take all measures to reestablish order in the streets and reestablish calm." Mentque specified what measures he thought necessary: inspecting for illegal weapons, closing places where agitators meet, and imposing a curfew.[47]

Within half an hour, the army, gendarmerie, and general security forces had begun searching the headquarters of local political organizations. Inspections turned up nothing at the headquarters of the League of National Action, but police seized many revolvers in the Antioch Halkevi. They also found "very compromising" secret correspondence from Tayfur Sökmen, who was stationed immediately over the border in Turkey's Dörtyol, letters with instructions for carrying out political agitation in the Sanjak. In the north of the city, police arrested eight people (including one woman); authorities confiscated two pistols, one automatic pistol, five revolvers, three daggers, one knife, and five shotguns. In the afternoon, police searching the Dört Ayak and Affan quarters found seven automatic pistols, nine revolvers, fifteen daggers, sixty-five German cartridges, five shotguns, eight rifles, and five knives. The shotguns and rifles seized not only lacked permits but also were classified as weapons of war (large caliber bullets). Authorities arrested twelve people, one of whom possessed the equipment to make large caliber cartridges, for keeping prohibited weapons. Colonel Mesney ordered that both the League of National Action and the Halkevleri be provisionally closed beginning at noon the same day.[48]

Shortly after midnight following the raids, two dark-colored cars drove at high speed past the police post on Antioch's bridge in the direction of the Turkish frontier. Neither driver responded as police shouted to halt. When they arrived in Alexandretta at half past three in the morning, the drivers again refused to stop, despite efforts by both police and customs agents. The cars sped on into the night as officials fired on them. One of the cars was found later; the other crossed into Turkey with its passengers, Antioch's Turcophile leaders who had disappeared earlier in the day, Abdulgani Türkmen, Selim Çelenk, Şükrü Balcı, Vedi Munir, and Fevzi Şemsettin.

The telegram explaining their flight summoned the rhetoric of liberty and freedom. "The representatives of the Turkish Democratic [Republican People's] Party were obliged to leave for the frontier of the Sanjak of Antioch. The unfortunate Sanjak of Antioch is deprived of all communication with the whole world following the [regime] of fire and blood provoked by the bayonets of the soldiers of the French military cordon." The Halkevi leaders had fled to Turkey to raise the call to those who would help them resist the Sanjak's Syrian and French officials who, they claimed, saw the Sanjak's independence as inconsistent with their own interests. The Kemalist leaders accused these officials of fomenting divisions among the Sanjak's groups, hoping to demonstrate the impracticability of the Sanjak's new regime. Indeed, the Turcophile leadership accused mandatory officials of a direct hand in the recent violence, having formed, directed, and agitated these groups so that they could use their crimes "as a pretext to attack the Turks of the Sanjak as well as other groups who have accepted the agreement."

> Night and day houses are attacked, doors forced open, women and children imprisoned, the cruelties that are committed against young innocent people have achieved such an insupportable degree that one is led to forget the epoch where the unfortunate innocents were thrown in the basement of barracks. There is no longer any personal liberty, nor liberty of residence. They attack without fear of national acrimony. Liberty of conscience is judged a crime; the power of government, the laws

have become the instrument of death and the courts of justice the slaughter-houses.

The telegram continued with a complaint against the "illegal" attack by armed Syrian soldiers against the "Central Bureau of the Party formed legally." Both personal and civil liberties were being sacrificed, they claimed, as not only Turkish peasants but also Arab and Alawi villagers who were not hostile to Turkey had come "under the blow of an aggression of bandits armed with French rifles." The telegram ended with a protest against the inaction of the League of Nations and the governments of France and Turkey, who had been charged with the security of the Sanjak and its people.[49] In leaflets distributed after their departure on August 12, Kemalist leaders sounded similar themes, explaining that military authorities had taken over and closed political organizations, including the Halkevi. "Malevolent enemies of the country" were trying to divide "those committed to national unity and to use them as instruments for their ambition. We beg that our public take special guard against these ambitions."[50] It was opponents of the Sanjak's independence who were creating animosity, they insisted, with the assistance of Syrian officials; French representatives were complicit.

Antioch's police chief described a city divided on the morning of August 13. Arab and Alawi shops were open, and people circulated freely; Turkish shops were closed that morning. Arabs tried to prevent Turks from buying food and produce in their shops.[51] Small incidents became serious, as Antioch's population took sides in the increasingly polarized city. Young Arabs taunted a Turkish café worker as he walked to the Christian quarter to buy some arak from a tavern keeper. As he threw his empty bottle to the ground, shots rang out. A young Arab was the perpetrator, angry that Turks were provisioning themselves in the Christian quarter of Antioch.[52] Soon after, two Alawi drivers arrived at the city's east entrance, their car full of tomatoes. While unloading the vehicle, they were set upon by Turkish drivers with sticks. Three of the Turkish drivers were arrested, three others were pursued; one Turk was lightly injured, as were the two Alawi drivers. Alawi gardeners working near the tannery heard news of the attack on their fellow Alawis and fired their shotguns at the Turkish-owned tannery.[53] Antioch's police chief Garabed feared that the events would further polarize the city, as one of the bullets grazed a young Armenian man. Armenian neutrality had already been tested in the Sanjak, and now Greek Orthodox leaders were exaggerating the recent incidents, according to Garabed, to "sow panic in the Armenian Community to drag them into a conflict against the Turks."[54]

French authorities claimed that the Halkevi leaders who returned to Syria on August 13 after their late-night flight had met with the disapproval of the Turkish regime for alienating so many. Relying on the testimony of a Kemalist informer whom they claimed had been present, French intelligence reported that the fugitives met in Ankara with Turkey's interior minister, Şükrü Kaya. The interior minister insisted that their campaign in the Sanjak, quite costly at 25,000 Turkish lira, had achieved nothing more than the Turks could have achieved at Geneva, where the League Council would have given them the Sanjak as part of their country within a few years. He accused them of overestimating their own strength and of so badly mishandling the situation that they had alienated all the other groups, thereby compromising Turkey's position.

> You have always claimed that in the Sanjak you would have the majority, a large part of the Alawis and all of the Armenians would be in agreement with you. But we have established that this is not true and that in the Sanjak all of the non-Turkish elements are against you. You seek to constantly compromise Turkey who incurs the risk to give you satisfaction. It is not possible to create an uneasy atmosphere with France for Alexandretta. If we had an interest, we would enter into war not for the Sanjak but for all of Syria. We cannot put ourselves on poor terms with the Europeans to please you. Despite all the advice given, you provoke incidents there instead of living in good harmony with the other groups. You are responsible . . . for the current situation. Turkey has been your dupe.

Şükrü Kaya held the leaders responsible for miscalculations so serious that they could threaten not only Turkey's claim to the Sanjak, but even its relations with France. He demanded that they stop creating incidents that alienated the other parties. On their return, the Turcophile leaders distributed flour among the poor, who were still reeling from the local violence that had exacerbated the after-effects of the worldwide depression. French officials suggested that the gesture hardly mollified their followers, who remained furious that their leaders fled when tension was at its height.[55]

The months that had passed since the creation of the Sanjak's new Statute and Fundamental Law had witnessed increasing polarization within the Sanjak's population as Kemalists and Arab nationalists struggled for the hearts and minds—and voter registrations—of the population. French officials had responded with a military crackdown, a curfew, and surveillance, all in the hope of proving to the Turks that France was capable of keeping the peace. Nonetheless, rumors began circulating on August 13 that a Turkish battalion was marching on the Sanjak to restore order "in accordance with the Geneva agreement." At the same time, Dubecq, chief of general security for the Sanjak, reported rumors of a smaller scale intervention: the Turks would send forty partisans over the border, who would then split into four groups, each armed with rifles and ammunition. The first would remain around Payas, the second would move into the Beylan mountains, and the remaining two would be located in the mountains between the Alawi territories and the Sanjak. Their goal: "to kill leaders of the Arabophile groups and attack their villages and their partisans." They were to be directed by Turkish officers, and the local Turcophile leaders had received instructions to support them.[56] Local officials seemed to give some credence to the rumors. Already on August 9, security forces had battled a group of Turks and fugitive Syrians who crossed the border north of Hajilar. These men seemed to be part of a larger group of ten or twenty who routinely raided border villages at nightfall. Police chief Houel claimed that the goal of the incursions was to oblige the villagers, "who remained loyal to their old costumes, to adopt Kemalist principles, especially hat-wearing." In this case, it seems, the village head and his brother had been collaborating with the band, and both were arrested.[57]

Rumors of an imminent Turkish invasion were at least partly behind the Turks' unwillingness to reopen their shops, according to Special Services captain Queru. When he called local Turkish leaders together at his office, they claimed they were powerless to stop the rumors. On the other hand, they suggested, if administrative leaves could be arranged for Syrian appointees Governor al-Barazi, Mayor Abd al-Qadir, and financial officer Hassan Jabara, all could be arranged.[58] Insisting that the French and Syrian officials were inadequate to provide security, the Sanjak's Kemalist leaders wrote to the League of Nations asking for a neutral commission to investigate the political situation in the Sanjak.

The continuing market closure threw a wedge into the growing division among the Sanjak's Turks. "Moderate" Turks circulated a petition in Alexandretta echoing the official French explanation that blamed "extremist" Turkish notables for thwarting the efforts of the "moderates" to reopen the markets. These "moderates" had collected more than one hundred signatures, including those of some Armenians and Arabs in support of a statement that called for a delay in the implementation of the Sanjak's independence.

> No one is unaware that all the inhabitants of the Sanjak of Alexandretta, without distinction of race or religion, have lived in tranquility during the mandate. The initiative to endow this region with an independent regime has sowed the seeds of discord among the diverse groups who have lived for centuries in good harmony. The spirit of rivalry has taken birth and it appears a little more each day that the current situation can only have bloodshed as its outcome in the country. Already we have witnessed indications of these fears: the incidents that have arisen for some days at Antioch. We undersigned, representing the majority of the inhabitants of the Sanjak of Alexandretta, come respectfully to expose this situation, asking for a direct French administration of the

country until the country shows the maturity for independence. This is the only way to avoid a catastrophe and put an end to the misery of the population of the country.[59]

It was the League of Nation's program for independence that had brought about the animosity now witnessed in the Sanjak, according to the people the French identified as "moderates." The signers sought to end the escalating conflict by postponing the new status of the Sanjak in favor of continuing direct French control.

The Turkish press, on the other hand, blamed French officials in the Sanjak for the growing violence. Turkey's *La République* published an article describing renewed clashes, accompanied by a photograph of Turks assassinated at Antioch. Frustrated mandatory officials grumbled that they had already explained to the Turkish consul general at Beirut that the situation had been caused by political action of both the Halkevi and the League of National Action, and had been brought under control. Moreover, when French officials had reassured the Turkish consul that the Syrian newspapers would not be permitted to exploit local conditions, the Turkish representative had indicated that the Turkish government would make similar directives to the press.[60] Ponsot was sarcastic about the continuing Turkish press campaign. "To take an expression which is dear to them, 'the sensibilities of the Turks' in the Sanjak Question is always on display, and the recent incidents at Antioch provided a substantial meal." On the other hand, the editors were being more judicious than previously, and not blaming France. Instead, for *La République* and the rest of the Turkish press, Ponsot wrote, the people behind the violence were some Arab extremists. Turkey bore no responsibility, and its ally France was on its side in supporting the new status for the Sanjak. Although Ponsot saw this new tone as an improvement, he complained that the Turkish "news" was hardly accurate. One Adana paper reported that a thousand Syrian Steel Shirts were traveling to the Sanjak "to intensify the politics of terror," while another quoted a local Arab official as boasting "No force can stop us. If it is necessary, we will set our hands on the government." Turkish commentators disagreed over whether the Syrian regime was behind the violence or simply incompetent: "We claim that in spite of their good will, the elements that control Syria do not possess a will that will let them control the riots, and the capacities that will permit them to see from afar." The paper continued, "There are today incendiaries of all kinds in the world. Their essential task is to reinforce all extremist movements, to trouble the waters in order to advance their own small boat."[61] The Turkish press, according to Ponsot, was continuing to stir up feelings with inaccurate reporting; at the same time, their ire was no longer directed at France, which was now commonly presented as Turkey's ally in the Sanjak.

When Turkish foreign minister Aras repeated the press allegations, Ponsot reassured him that there had been no Steel Shirts entering the Sanjak. At Antioch, only the Turkish shops had remained closed, despite efforts of local officials to open them; moreover, they were closed as a result of an order given by a source Aras himself knew well. There was no list of forty Turks to be arrested; the Antioch delegate had simply informed Turkish and Arab leaders that if incidents were provoked, the instigators as well as the perpetrators would be punished. The abuse being cited in villages in Kuseyr had been directed against people wearing both fezzes and hats. For Ponsot, concerned with the Turkish government's role in exacerbating division, "these discussions were so far from reality they could not lead in a useful time to the establishment of facts and the fixing of responsibilities."[62]

Ponsot had a different agenda: he wanted to press the Turkish foreign minister on two issues of crucial importance to the French mandatory regime: Tayfur Sökmen's activities and Turkish efforts to propagandize the Alawis. The documents and arms confiscated from Antioch's Halkevi provided clear proof that Tayfur Sökmen had been relaying instructions from his headquarters just inside the Turkish border to Kemalists in the Sanjak. Sökmen claimed that his actions were warranted by the concurrent activity of the "Syrian Party," but French officials maintained that he exceeded the limits permitted by the Franco-Turkish Agreements. The high commissioner's office described the issue as straightforward: "There has been an act of terrorism perpetrated by a paid agent of the Halkevi who received his orders and his funds from Ankara through Tayfur [Sökmen] Bey."[63]

A week later, Ponsot confronted Aras on Turkey's intervention with the Sanjak's Alawis.[64] Conveying French intelligence about the Antioch events of August 9, 10, and 11, Ponsot told Turkey's foreign minister that the violence resulted largely from Turkey's propaganda efforts. Interior minister Şükrü Kaya had insisted that Alawis and Turks were brothers, and the Ankara regime had pursued this line as propaganda, working to convince the Sanjak's Alawis that they should commit themselves to the Turkish cause. Their efforts had resulted in July's intracommunal conflict, when Shaykh Maruf's sons returned from visiting Adana and Ankara. Ponsot pointed out that the incidents beginning on August 9 were simply a continuation of that earlier riot, "the direct consequence of the politics of division conducted by the Turks of the Sanjak."

Aras denied Ponsot's accusations, positioning himself in the role the European Great Powers used to play—as the representative of a liberal regime intervening in another country to "protect" the "minorities." The Turkish foreign minister insisted that the trouble among the Alawis resulted from the Syrian government's policies of religious exclusion, policies they had learned from their Ottoman past. He acknowledged that the Turks were spreading propaganda among the Alawis, but located responsibility for the violence with the Damascus regime's "religious politics, pursued among all the minorities with fanaticism, [that] could not but alienate their sympathies." Aras insisted that the men ruling Syria, former Ottoman functionaries, were "continuing in Syria the reactionary and fanatical politics of the Ottoman Empire, politics that by its intransigence could only make the Alawis and the Christians nervous." As a result, both Alawis and Greek Orthodox Christians were beginning to side with Turkey. "As for the Armenians, we are not in a hostile state with them. Do nothing to end their neutrality, I tell you. We understand they want to be cautious, but they will come to us, and will be the principle beneficiaries of the new regime and we expect that they will be, by interest, sincerely Sanjakistes." For the Turkish regime, the growing hostility was the result of the Syrian government's efforts to "Arabize the minorities of the Sanjak," and Damascus's insistence on a politics of exclusion that was alienating all of the local minorities and would, in the end, benefit Turkey.[65] While claiming that the Syrian government persisted in the "reactionary" policies of the Ottoman past that Ankara had rejected, the Republic of Turkey portrayed itself as liberal, democratic, and inclusive.

Continuing violent episodes reflected growing polarization. Arabs threw stones at two Turks; Greek Orthodox residents protected the victims. The next day, three Turks stabbed an Alawi near the Habib Neccar mosque; that same evening an Alawi stabbed a Turk. Three Turks attacked an Arab from Latakia, stealing two gold livres and destroying his fez. Alawis found one of their large irrigation waterwheels vandalized and blamed it on Turks. When Turks threw stones at four Alawis, the soldier accompanying them was hit by a stone in the leg. He fired into the air to alert the neighboring police, whose arrival dispersed the assailants. That same week saw a number of apparently political incidents in the Sanjak countryside. The fact that police reported "the Sanjak was quiet. . . . But people remained anxious" is an indication of what "quiet" had come to mean after the previous week's riots.[66]

The Halkevi's newest manifesto, distributed August 17, called Antioch in recent days the "theater of regrettable incidents that we had wanted to avoid." According to the manifesto, recent events were the work of those who hoped to overturn the new Statute and Fundamental Law by fomenting animosity between groups. Echoing the words of the League of National Action flyers, the Kemalists insisted that the varied communities had lived together on this soil for centuries, "as brothers and in peace," and the Republican People's Party was convinced they would continue in that way, despite the "vile ambitions" of some people and recent efforts to create divisions. The manifesto vowed that these efforts would not succeed. Fifty-two countries had signed an agreement guaranteeing the independence of the Sanjak, and the two Great Powers Turkey and France would guarantee its independence. Alawi notables understood this and were working to create concord, efforts notably evident recently in Süveydiye and Harbiye, "where our Alawi brothers maintained their calm and equilibrium in the recent incidents."[67] The manifesto insisted that it was the Kemalists who were allowing the Sanjak's people to continue to live together peacefully under the new regime, despite the connivance of the opposition.

Zihni Akdur, Turkey's new consul general at Beirut, informed French authorities on August 19 that he would travel to Antioch to investigate the recent incidents. That same night he arrived at the Tourism Hotel with his wife and children. Mentque was pleased: the Tourism Hotel, located in a predominantly Arab district, would allow Akdur to see that a Turk could live safely in an area that "public rumors persisted in presenting as dangerous." Mentque described the Turkish consul as very courteous and congenial, and reported Akdur's mission to be to analyze the seriousness of the recent incidents that the Republican People's Party "fugitives" had "grossly exaggerated." Mentque became concerned, however, when Akdur claimed that he had been assigned to make contact with the French authorities to collaborate in restoring calm. If Akdur was not confined to regular consular functions, he could rapidly become a spokesman for one part of the Sanjak's population, interfere in the exercise of the mandate, and threaten France's status as sole mandatory power. For example, he noted, local Turcophiles having difficulty resolving their issues could appeal to the consul instead of maintaining their confidence in "the impartiality and the protection of French agents." Akdur drove through the Sanjak flying Turkey's banner, met with Turcophile leaders, and walked through Antioch's Turkish neighborhoods followed by a mob of supporters. French officials complained that he was meddling in local affairs. The cancellation of his planned visit to the Armenian town of Bytias had narrowly avoided an international incident when the population, "seriously displeased at the announcement of this visit," had prepared to welcome him by throwing stones.[68]

Security Services worried about escalating Kemalist mobilization in the Sanjak, claiming that eight attendees at Alexandretta's Halkevi meeting on August 21 brought revolvers. Five other revolvers, sent by Shaykh Maruf's sons, were distributed among people attending. Security officials warned of the dangers that could result from the nightly meetings at the Alexandretta Halkevi, especially if they were to be attended by armed men. Alexandretta's security chief recommended that the government prohibit these meetings, explaining that the smallest unexpected incident could degenerate into a general battle that the local police would be incapable of repressing.[69]

At the same time, French officials worked to shut down the projects of the League of National Action. Conflict was ongoing between Alawis supporting Shaykh Maruf and those who followed Zaki al-Arsuzi. Following an incident between the two groups at Süveydiye, al-Arsuzi had tried to call a strike, but the messenger who was to implement the closure of the Arab shops at Antioch and Alexandretta was arrested and incarcerated before he could begin. French officials threatened al-Arsuzi with the same treatment, and the suqs remained open. Nonetheless, Arab efforts were having some success in the countryside as villagers again began wearing the fez and resisting Turkish propaganda.[70]

Mentque waited a week to return the Turkish consul's official visit, "to leave Akdur the time to reveal his true intentions." During their second conversation, Mentque inferred that Akdur had come to the Sanjak not only to investigate recent events, but actually to establish a consular post in Antioch. The Turkish consul told Mentque that Antioch's Turcophiles refused to reopen their shops because they were "profoundly frightened." He recognized that this fear was excessive, especially in light of the impartial attitude of the French officials; Colonel Mesny had reassured him that the army's only goal was to keep order and that it was not involved in politics. Akdur was similarly reassured that French officers would be taking over command of the Fifth Levant Battalion, of whom the Turcophiles were quite suspicious because its exclusively Arab officers supervised Alawi and Christian troops. Nonetheless, Akdur complained about local Syrian-appointed officials, including Husni al-Barazi, Abd al-Qadir, and Hassan Jabara, claiming they represented a government that continued to oppose the new status for the Sanjak in both word and deed. Mentque responded that the Statute and Fundamental Law stipulated that the status quo would be maintained until November 29, and refused to dismiss the officials. Mentque asked Akdur to be careful as he traveled through the Sanjak, concerned that the consular flag could provoke "intemperate enthusiasm" among Turcophiles or "spontaneous exasperations" among Sunni Arabs, Armenians, and Alawis. As Mentque pointed out, it was very regrettable "that the least incident could threaten the safety of this foreign representative and trouble the serenity of our friendly relations with our neighbors to the north."

Akdur offered to intervene with Antioch's Turks to reopen the suqs, closed since the August 11 raid on the Halkevi.[71] Turkish artisans were suffering from lack of work. The Turkish consul suggested that reopening the shops would "make the unease hovering over the city disappear and appease the apprehensions stirred up when seeing the shutters closed." He let it be known that he would be more inspired to intervene if some of the Turks recently arrested were freed, which would produce a perceptible calming, both with the population and with President Atatürk. But when Akdur handed Mentque a list of eight people, including Kör Sabet, the gunman who had shot at Mentque's car two weeks earlier, the French official balked. It would be impossible to release Kör Sabet, he explained, because it would seem a sign of weakness that French authorities could not tolerate if they were to retain the support of the population. On reviewing the rest of the cases, he found that three suspects had inadequate evidence against them and ordered their release. The next morning, August 24, Turkish shops reopened. Mentque was disturbed by the timing. "One cannot fail to attribute all the credit to the role of mediator played by the Turkish Consul, and this is an interpretation that must not be spread around too much if we do not want it thought that the future regime of the Sanjak will be, in fact, a Franco-Turkish condominium." In reality, he wrote, reopening the suqs was mostly the result of the fatigue felt by the "moderate" elements, "worn out by being dragged along by the extremists," and mostly concerned not to have their commerce be the victim of "political caprices."[72]

Fall brought a change in personnel in the Sanjak. Roger Garreau, the new delegate, was welcomed with a solemn ceremony in early September. He met with local notables and Syrian-appointed authorities and exchanged visits with Consul Akdur, still resident in the Sanjak.[73] The promised appointment of Turkish consuls-general, scheduled to take place soon afterward, renewed the question of Turkey's official role in the Sanjak during the extended transition period. The new status of the Sanjak would not come into force for nearly two months, and even when it did, Turkey's only official role would be to guarantee the security of the Sanjak. French mandatory authorities were adamant that Turkey should have no role in the Sanjak's internal affairs, and would resist any effort by the new consuls general to portray themselves as leaders of the local Turkish community in much the same way that Mentque had refused to consider Akdur as having any standing as a representative of local Turks and their supporters within the Sanjak.[74]

Kemalists in the Sanjak, still in disarray following the search and closing of Antioch's Halkevi, hoped to reinvigorate the movement with a strong welcome on October 5 for the Sanjak's new Turkish consuls. Women with bouquets arrived at the Alexandretta railroad station to cheer their arrival. The crowd was disappointed when the consuls failed to arrive, and when Aleppo's Turkish consul Firuz actually arrived in Antioch four days later, he took himself to the Tourism Hotel.[75] It seemed that no Turkish consuls would be appointed for the Sanjak immediately.

Consul Firuz seemed displeased with the situation he found in the Sanjak; "stormy" was the way France's "reliable source" described his meeting with Turkish leaders. Local Kemalist leaders "were obliged to admit that the Turks were a minority, that power rested in the hands of non-Turks, that at the time of the proclamation of the election results, the Turks would be put to shame in the opinion of the world, and the leaders in the opinion of Ankara." The consul told them that the Turkish government was not aware of the situation in the center of the Sanjak, "because if they had known it, they would not have attached so much importance to this question, that he himself would not have accepted the consulate of Aleppo. We will remain a minority to our embarrassment in front of the whole world." Aleppo's Turkish consul instructed local Kemalist leaders to try to get the support of the Alawis and non-Turkish Sunnis, hoping that the international commission envisaged in the Fundamental Law to supervise Sanjak elections would not distinguish between Arab and Turkish Sunnis. This strategy seemed to be the "only chance" that the Turks could make a respectable showing in the elections. The consul refused to provide local leaders with more funds, pointing out that they had already received more than 150,000 Turkish lira.[76]

Nonetheless, the Sanjak question continued to preoccupy the Ankara regime at the highest level. When Atatürk spoke with the French ambassador during celebrations of the fourteenth anniversary of the Republic of Turkey on October 29, he reminded Ponsot of his personal attachment to the Sanjak. More than three thousand people attended the ceremonies, including dignitaries from Iran and the Balkans. Always a night owl, Atatürk afterward met "until dawn" with a group that included French ambassador Ponsot, the British ambassador, and Romanian prime minister Gheorghe Tătărescu. As usual, Atatürk spoke mostly in French with the diplomats, and focused largely on foreign issues, emphasizing Turkey's friendship with England, which was itself tied to France, which would provide a solid foundation for Turkey's eastern and Balkan politics. Atatürk conveyed his hope that the Sanjak affair, "in which he had personally engaged his honor," would be resolved quickly, within a month and a half. Ponsot responded that the Statute and Fundamental Law would not come into force for another month, and the elections would not take place until April, so the resolution was likely to take much longer. The Turkish president reiterated that his honor was "in play. I have never suffered a defeat and I will not suffer one." According to Ponsot, "He spoke with the evident effect that it would be heard by men of allied and friendly states as well as by his collaborators, then the day dawned, Kemal Atatürk rose and held out his hand."[77]

As he read Ponsot's description of the conversation, Martel worried about the implications of Atatürk's remarks. He speculated that the Turkish government, which had "long deluded itself with the illusion of obtaining a parliamentary majority in the next elections" comprised of the Sanjak's Turks and their allied Alawis and Arab Sunnis, had just begun to reconsider its prediction. Despite Turkish propaganda and the funds they had distributed within the Sanjak, "the expected good will has disappeared." Martel described new organization and cohesion among the other communities, who were increasingly resisting Turkish "infiltration." Moreover, the international commission that would be overseeing the elections was in the process of producing lists and electoral procedures that would make fraud "practically impossible." According to Martel, Atatürk's comments reflected his government's increasing concern that an anti-Turkish majority might preclude Turkish participation in the new Sanjak government. "It is no doubt this perspective that inspired Atatürk when he said his honor was engaged and that he would never accept defeat."

Martel, convinced—as was Turkish consul Firuz—that the Turks were not a majority in the Sanjak, considered ways to make Turkish preeminence a reality in order to appease the Ankara regime. Perhaps Kemalist candidates could hold high offices.

> Now if it is impossible to transform a minority into a majority in fact, we could by contrast give here and now all appeasements to Ankara, and let the Turkish government understand that, in any case, we will exert ourselves to assure to the Turkish element an effective participation in the government of the Sanjak and in conformity with the importance that this element represents in local life. All the non-Turkish communities, the Alawis, the Armenians, the Sunni Arabs, the Greek-Orthodox, the Kurds and the Circassians, are ready to follow our directives.

The French high commissioner proposed appointing a neutral non-Turk to be chief of state, and appointing a Kemalist leader like Abdulgani Türkmen president of the Executive Council. "Acting in this way, we could provide service to the Turkish government itself, to whom positive assurances given in good time would remove the tendency to maintain, by a politics of intimidation, unreasonable demands likely to destroy the arrangements of the statute." With such reassurance, subverting the democratic process by appointing Turks to the most important positions before the elections had even begun, Turkey's anxieties could be assuaged and the Sanjak's peace and security assured.[78]

The League of Nations Electoral Commission for the Organization and Supervision of the First Elections in the Sanjak of Alexandretta (electoral commission) visited the Sanjak in the middle of November 1937. Its members included men with extensive experience in previous contested territories. Jacques Lagrange of Belgium had served as secretary-general of the Mixed Committee on Greco-Bulgarian Emigration. H. Ch. G. J. Van der Mandere of the Netherlands, director of the People's University at The Hague, had been a district inspector during the Saar Plebiscite. Herman Reimers of Norway was a barrister at the Norwegian Supreme Court, and had served as a judge at the Supreme Court of the Saar Plebiscite. T. Reid had helped write Ceylon's new constitution. Roger Secretan of Switzerland was a law professor at the University of Lausanne.[79] They arrived in Ankara on October 17.

Reid, president of the League of Nations electoral commission, made a speech in each city they visited. After first explaining that the League of Nations had a plan to give independence to the people of the Sanjak of Alexandretta to enable their prosperity, welfare, and peaceful development, he introduced the members of his commission. They had been chosen not to administer the Sanjak, but to "organize and verify the first elections of your future deputies to the Assembly of the Sanjak." He promised, "With your help, we will leave no stone unturned so the elections will take place in an atmosphere of calm, of liberty, and of impartiality. You will thus show to your many foreign friends who follow your evolution with interest, that the populations of the Sanjak know how to conduct their public affairs with dignity, self-respect, and respect for the opinions of others. We are convinced that all the electors will come without hesitation or fear to present themselves before the commission or its delegates, to register in the community to which they belong." Reid pointed out that local representatives of the various communities would be assisting them, and closed by thanking them for their warm welcome.[80]

Yeni Gün's description of the electoral commission's visit to Beylan emphasized the cordial reception they received from the population, especially the students. The paper outlined Reid's speech and his request that the population designate a Turkish and an Armenian representative. According to the paper, the commissioners then took the two chosen delegates into the office of the local administrator. The Turkish correspondent covering the story reported that, although the mayor had tried to prevent the Turkish representative from complaining about the difficulties Syrian functionaries were inflicting on the population, the president of the electoral commission heard his complaints and promised to take steps with French officials.[81]

Two days later, the president of the electoral commission wrote to French delegate Roger Garreau, asking French officials to provide extra personnel to assist the judges in regularizing the legal standing of those whose claims to voting rights had been clouded by nonpayment of taxes or other issues.[82] However, the problems that appeared with the early registrations were not those that the electoral commission had anticipated. The proportional representation that had been approved for the Sanjak's parliament had weighted electoral registrations with high stakes. Each "community" named in the Fundamental Law would be represented in the new Sanjak Assembly in proportion to the number of men who had registered in that group. Captain Gacon reported that Turkish landowners in the Amık region were trying to coerce Arab peasants to inscribe themselves as Turks in the registration rolls. The local delegation of three Arab notables visiting him claimed that in the Amık region, the landowners and superintendents were Turks while the cultivators were Arab. In one of Amık's villages, Ayranji Sharki, the delegation complained that landowners had been pressuring their Arab peasants for the previous three months, demanding that they inscribe themselves as Turks. For the preceding ten days, owners had exerted financial pressure on their cultivators, locking the doors of the fodder depots necessary to feed the peasants' draft animals. On November 15, two of the owners called together all of the Arab peasants of the village and made them register on the spot. The plaintiffs claimed that peasants were forced to take an oath on the Qur'an committing themselves to inscribe as Turks within twenty-four hours; those who refused would be immediately driven from the village. The gendarmerie chief's inquiry found the complaint accurate. Gacon included in his report an extract from *Yeni Gün* claiming that the Fundamental Law did not restrict each voter to vote only for his own community. Instead, each elector could register for any community of his choice.[83]

The election commissioners seemed pessimistic as they passed through Beirut on their return to Geneva, according to Martel. He reported their fear that Turkish vengeance during the electoral period would prove dangerous; he had reassured the commissioners that the mandatory regime would take all necessary steps to keep people safe. "The members of the Commission were impressed by the bitterness of the Turkish propaganda and the desire it revealed to assure Ankara a docile majority in the future Assembly of the Sanjak at any cost." The commissioners feared an outcome where sixteen Turcophile Assembly representatives might form a group and rally some representatives from the other communities to vote for what they feared would be "inconvenient" decisions. "All will thus depend on the cohesion of these minorities knowing how to meet this danger." Like Martel, it was clear to the commissioners that the Turkish population would not reach a majority of the registered voters and that they, too, worried about the results.

The commissioners were concerned about the officials who would be responsible for maintaining order during the transitional period. The Damascus government wanted to maintain its own appointee as governor after the end of the transitional period when the Sanjak became independent, hoping to form a Syrian counterweight to the two new Turkish consuls who were expected to be named to Antioch and Alexandretta. Martel had refused. The Damascus government, for its part, still declined to name the liaison called for in the Statute, because it was unwilling to provide the implicit recognition the appointment would give to the Sanjak's new status. Martel had suggested a compromise, in which Damascus would name an official representative (chargé de mission), but the National Bloc government had not complied. Martel himself had decided to give all powers to his own delegate, Roger Garreau, who would travel to the Sanjak on the transition date to inform the population. This seemed to reassure the members of the electoral commission.[84]

Both the French and Turkish governments were anticipating significant changes on November 29, 1937, when the Sanjak officially became independent. They disagreed, however, on what that independence meant about their own roles. In the eyes of the French, the Statute and Fundamental Law made it clear that France would remain the sole administrator for the Sanjak until the end of France's mandate over Syria. The Turkish government believed that

Ankara would be joint guarantors for the Sanjak's security as soon as its independence began. Two days before independence, the Turkish consul's visit exposed the deep chasm between their perceptions. "I am charged by my government to call your attention in a friendly manner to this point," the Turkish representative began. "If the day when the new regime comes into being French and Syrian flags are alone unfurled, it would be absolutely contrary to the sense of the Geneva accords. In unfurling these flags the day of the proclamation of the new regime, Syria and France would be signifying the annexation of the Sanjak by these two countries. In these conditions, the Sanjakians would be obliged to also hoist their flag." When Garreau inquired whether he meant by the Sanjakians those who spoke Turkish, the consul responded that "he made no distinction among all the inhabitants of a Turkish majority region." Garreau responded that the consul was interfering in internal affairs, and the Consul answered that from November 29 his government would consider itself charged with watching over the Sanjak jointly with the French delegate.[85] It was to be a continuing disagreement.

|| 5 ||

Independence

"The Turks of Antioch began celebrating at 5:00 p.m. on November 28," begins the police report. "Large quantities of fireworks were launched in the Turkish quarters. All of the shops of Uzun Çarşı were decorated and illuminated. At 8:00 a tambour [stringed instrument] concert at the Halkevi. At 9:00 a Turkish crowd processed around the various Turkish quarters with the tambour at its head. The celebrations continued at the Halkevi until 11:00."

The next morning, the day of the Sanjak's official independence, the celebrations began again. "Arcs de triomphe" had been set up, illuminated, and decorated with ribbons, flowers, and greenery around the city.[1] Trucks hired by the Halkevi and decorated with greenery brought peasants from the villages to Antioch for a parade. The program was extensive, lasting all day and incorporating the various groups the Halkevi had worked to mobilize. At eleven o'clock, young Turkish girls, some dressed in black and wearing white ribbons in their hair and others wearing red and white, left the Halkevi and paraded into the Turkish quarter singing the Republic of Turkey's national anthem, to popular applause. Turkish villagers danced to the music of the tambour in front of the Turkish Consulate. At the reception, the speeches of local Kemalist notables— exhortations emphasizing that their new independence was for all the people of the Sanjak, to live happily on "the land to which they belonged"—were met with furious applause. The Halkevi had sent many invitations to local notables of every group and, although none of the invited Armenians or Greek Orthodox leaders chose to attend, some Turcophile Alawis were among the celebrants.[2] Aleppo's Turkish consul Firuz arrived, to applause, in time to admire a group of boys and girls aged eight to sixteen, dressed all in white with red buttons, return to the Halkevi singing the Turkish national anthem. At the Consulate, the day was celebrated with the hoisting of a Turkish flag, to the consternation of the local non-Turks. At four o'clock, peasants were invited for a free meal at the Halkevi. The evening kicked off with the Turkish Sports Circle processing with their torches, their group flag and their music in the lead, clapping and crying "Vive Atatürk, Vive Hatay." Celebrations with music had been organized in the various Turkish shops. Although the crowds gradually dispersed, intermittent celebratory gunshots were heard in the Turkish quarters until one o'clock in the morning.

Although the local Turcophiles marked the Sanjak's independence with joyful demonstrations, Arab residents—still insisting that the Sanjak was an integral part of Syria—made little effort to mark the day they had been resisting for the six months since the League of Nations had voted to establish it as an independent entity. A crowd of nearly one thousand people, including many Alawi women and children, resisted police efforts to remove the Syrian flags that the League of National Action had unfurled in contravention of the mandatory regime's injunctions again flying any flags except the French. Troops were called and managed to remove the flags without major problems. Arabs were pleased to see the government also remove Turkish red and white banners from one of the celebratory arches that the Halkevi had erected. French officials closed the

Demonstration in Antioch, November 1937. Courtesy of Archives du ministre des Affaires étrangères et européennes, Nantes (Archives of the Minister of Foreign and European Affairs, Nantes).

League of National Action for two days for having violated Garreau's orders forbidding the showing of flags, and suspended *Yeni Gün* for "publishing untrue information," but there were no serious incidents and no injuries in the Sanjak.[3]

Arab nationalists across Syria protested the Sanjak's independence and the colonial regime. In Aleppo, the Committee of Nationalist Youth and Students distributed flyers calling for a meeting to organize a demonstration against the Sanjak's independence, and to protest the mandatory government's removal of Syrian flags in Antioch. Worried about the lack of adequate police resources after a group attacked a school run by the Maristes, and fearing other incidents, all of Aleppo's Christian schools dismissed their students early. The protest at noon drew only twenty students and a dozen leaders of the national guards, dressed in civilian clothes. After midday prayers at the mosque, in the presence of some two hundred people, Shaykh Maruf al-Dawalibi read a petition protesting the Sanjak's new status, to be sent in their name; the shaykh presented the protest to the government following prayers. No other protests took place in Aleppo; Syrian officials claimed to have prevented them.[4] The forty-eight-hour student

Women Sew the New Hatay Flags. From: *La Republique*, November 28, 1937, courtesy of Archives du ministre des Affaires étrangères et européennes, Nantes (Archives of the Minister of Foreign and European Affairs, Nantes).

strike at Dayr al-Zur's Lycée Tajhiz ended the morning of November 29 after the school director threatened parents that the students continuing to strike would be dismissed from school.[5] Alexandretta's Communist Party sent Martel a telegram on December 2 protesting the removal of the Syrian flag "and the intervention of the Kemalist government in the interior affairs of the Sanjak." "The people," they claimed, "are in effervescence."[6] Most of those few Syrians who protested the Sanjak's new independence on November 29 focused on the Antioch incident: the French removal of the Syrian flag.

Turkish leaders, in contrast, were furious during the first week of independence, castigating French authorities on the basis of rumors that Martel had declined to read the proclamation of the Sanjak's independence, chiding Garreau for removing Turkish banners from one of the arcs de triomphe, and objecting to the French refusal to allow the display of the new "Hatay" flag. The Turkish press saw nefarious intentions in French behavior during the first days of the Sanjak's independence, accusing mandatory officials of working to undermine the Statute and Fundamental Law and the Franco-Turkish Agreements. The headlines were menacing: "If Treaties Prove Useless the Turkish Nation Will Act," read one. Ankara's *Ulus* published an article, which was reprinted, according to the U.S. representative, in "every newspaper in Turkey," and which he believed to have been "inspired by Atatürk."

> We wish that the language of the French Government at Paris and at Beirut be the same. We wish that Beirut appreciate as much as does Paris the necessity for, and the usefulness and exigencies of, Turco-French friendship. We wish that the mandatory administration renounce its partisan attitude in regard to the Hatay; that it abandon its interest as to whether such or such element obtains greater representation; that it not seek to divide the elements of such or such a race under the pretense of defending and safeguarding the rights of those concerned.[7]

The article insinuated that mandatory authorities were not carrying out their instructions properly but were instead continuing to divide the local communities.

The press's accusation that French colonial authorities were working to thwart the new Statute and Fundamental Law was unleashed at the highest levels of the Ankara government. Turkey's ambassador to France, Suad Davaz, sent a long letter to French foreign minister Delbos on December 2, accusing the French government of bad faith and claiming the French had essentially created a colonial administration in the Sanjak. Davaz pointed out that Turkey had agreed to a six-month transitional period before implementing the Sanjak's independence in hopes of protecting Turkey's good relations with France. The Ankara government had expected that "under the impartial and beneficial tutelage of the

mandatory power an appeasement could be realized in the Sanjak," helping prepare the population to assume responsibilities for its own government. Davaz
insisted that such an appeasement depended on the adoption of policies completely consistent with the spirit of the Statute and Fundamental Law and the
Franco-Turkish Agreements. The spirit of these agreements insisted that the
rights of the populations of the Sanjak be respected, as well as the rights of
Turkey, "a power doubly interested as both a guarantor of the integrity of the
Sanjak and as designated executor of the eventual recommendations of the
League of Nations." Moreover, Turkey had stood ready to assist France and work
together in "the most loyal and friendly sense." However, Davaz continued, the
mandatory power had acted in a way that could not be considered benevolent,
especially since the arrival of Garreau as delegate.

The Ankara regime and the Turkish press had opposed Garreau from the time
he was first appointed French delegate in the Sanjak, mitigating their opposition
temporarily when Atatürk invited him to participate in Turkish independence
celebrations. Now, the Turkish government accused Garreau of working to
create continuing French domination by fostering conflict within the Sanjak. He
had made his intention clear in the speech he had given on receiving his new
position, in which he asserted that French authority would continue even after
the new Sanjak government was set up, a claim that, Davaz argued, amounted to
psychological pressure exerted on the Turkish population. Garreau had used all
the means at his disposal, including the military, police, judiciary, finance, and
administrative services. Davaz saw proof of the anti-Turkish hostility of Syrian
appointees in the economic pressures they brought to bear against "the Turkish
element alone," in their recruitment of "minority" gendarmes, their use of
officers hostile to Turks, their arming of non-Turkish villages, Garreau's assistance to non-Turkish groups preparing for elections, and "the vexing requisitions of which the Turks were the object and which produced only poor spoils of
some jammed revolvers." In addition, Garreau had not responded to repeated
offers of collaboration from the Turkish consul general at Antioch. According to
the Turkish note, Garreau had blamed the Syrian government for incidents, and
refused to accept the consul's role in presenting the grievances of the people of
the Sanjak; together, these would result either in setting the Turkish and Syrian
governments against each other or in preventing any collaboration between the
mandatory regime and the Turkish government. For example, Davaz continued,
Turkey's consul general had suggested that all flags be suppressed on public
buildings and homes, a recommendation ignored by Garreau, though it could
have prevented much of the ensuing strife. Instead, this very suggestion had been
"judged sufficient by Monsieur the Delegate of the High Commissioner to end
not only all collaboration with the Consul General of Turkey but soon after,
all relations." The behavior of the Sanjak administration had led to chaos, the

Turkish foreign minister claimed. Only by his government's "extreme moderation" and its hope of convincing the French government of the potential consequences had undesirable consequences been avoided.

The letter concluded with a threat. In these conditions, Davaz wrote, the Turkish government found itself unable to establish collaboration with France, as the co-guaranteeing power specified in the Statute. The Turkish government was therefore unable to share any responsibility for "that which will occur in the Sanjak before and after the elections." As a result, the government of Turkey was making "very express reservations on the conditions in which the elections soon to take place would be conducted, by a guardian authority not occupied at all with the demands of impartiality required for a popular consultation destined to show the sense of the will of the people."[8] Dissatisfied with the behavior of French officials in the Sanjak, who continued to support non-Turkish groups and refused the collaboration of the Turkish consul, Turkey's Foreign Ministry was henceforth refusing to take any responsibility for the outcome of the Statute's and Fundamental Law's implementation.

High Commissioner Martel focused on the implicit threat contained in both Davaz's warnings and the telegram that Aras despatched to his Antioch consul; both seemed to be directly connected with the forthcoming elections. He saw the position in Aras's telegram as a form of blackmail, its tone and orientation a means by which Turkey could reject the outcome of the elections if they did not show a Turkish majority: "if the elections give a Turkish majority, Ankara would be satisfied. If not, the results were contested from here and now." Aras's accusations against Garreau sought to prove French bias, claiming that the delegate had deliberately advocated for non-Turkish minorities by exerting pressure on their behalf and continuing to employ non-Turkish officials while generally refusing to collaborate with the Turkish consul. In Martel's eyes, the Ankara government was responsible for precisely the same misdeed of which they unjustly accused Garreau. "From the beginning, the Turkish Consuls deliberately abandoned their role as discreet observers; they became leaders of the partisans." Their support for the Sanjak's Turks combined with their accusations against French actions indicated a coordinated plan to discredit the election results if necessary. The high commissioner proposed that French officials in the Sanjak "associate themselves with the international electoral commission's work of great impartiality and not with those propagandists whose mission it is to coerce into declaring themselves to be Turks those elements of the population who are not."[9]

Aras's telegram reflected the major elements of disagreement between French and Turkish views of the Sanjak's new status. France believed that it remained the colonial administrator until the end of the Syria mandate, according to article 55 of the Statute. French delegates Durieux and now Garreau had consistently refused any power-sharing with a Turkish representative, fearing it would open the door to Turkish influence over the Sanjak's government. Garreau and the mandatory government took seriously their responsibility to "protect" the Sanjak's minorities by making sure all groups were able to participate in the upcoming elections. Moreover, they had insisted that Turcophile residents comply with their obligations under Syrian laws. Davaz had objected to precisely these issues, protesting that Garreau's administration had summoned the Turks to pay their tax arrears within ten days; Garreau had insisted that all of the non-Turks had already paid their back taxes and that expenses during the transition would be significant.[10] The Turkish ambassador accused Garreau and the mandatory regime of setting itself up as chief of the "minorities," administering the Sanjak as a colony, working to crush the Turkish population, and refusing to collaborate with the Turkish consul general; confiscation of illegal weapons from the Halkevi was just an extreme example of French anti-Turkish behavior. For mandatory officials, these acts were simply enforcing the obligations of their continuing rule.[11]

The central issue of contention was the role of Turkey in the new regime. Martel rejected both Turkey's contention that it had been designated to execute the eventual recommendations of the League of Nations and Turkey's insistence that France collaborate with Turkey's representatives. "This tendentious interpretation of the treaty of guarantee and territorial integrity is indefensible," Martel wrote to the French Foreign Ministry. The high commissioner thought it essential that the French Foreign Office take a very clear position immediately, demanding that the Turkish government remind its consuls of the nature of their job. He pointed out that the new Statute specified that the mandatory power's rights and its obligations to maintain order would continue until *Syrian* independence, not just for a period of six months. Moreover, the French high commissioner contrasted Aras's telegram with his recent conversation with Numan Menemencioğlu in Beirut, who "definitively told me that he hoped to see France take the administration of the Sanjak completely in hand from 29 November."[12]

The French Foreign Office insisted that the Statute set November 29, 1937, as the end of Syrian authority over the Sanjak, but it did not in any way mark the end of French control. "From this date until the constitution of the legislative and executive powers anticipated in the Fundamental Law, all the responsibilities of the government devolve upon the authority represented by the Delegate of the High Commissioner." Once elections were finished and the new government constituted, most governmental responsibilities and decision would be carried out by the government of the independent Sanjak; until then, there could be no new names or symbols for the Sanjak. Still, even after the new government was constituted, the French would continue to be responsible for the

Sanjak until the end of their mandate for Syria, that is, until three years after the French Parliament ratified the new Franco-Syrian Treaty. If the Ankara regime persisted in claiming authority in the Sanjak and accusing the mandatory government of manipulating the Statute and Fundamental Laws, they would have to submit their opposition to the League of Nations.[13]

Turkish foreign minister Aras interpreted the League's intent quite differently. The international body had planned to give Turkey "a role more or less extensive in the application of the new regime," he argued, and had shown that intention by insisting that the treaties between France and Turkey enter into force at the Sanjak's independence, not on some date in the future when the Syria mandate would end. Aras accused the French of violating both letter and spirit of the Statute and Fundamental Laws in their behavior in the Sanjak. The Turkish government demanded that the mandatory administration inform the people of the Sanjak that its presence was actually temporary, terminate the power of some Sanjak officials, and end its partisanship. Aras insisted that "neither article 55 of the Statute, nor even the direct, if temporary exercise of authority by the mandatory power, justified interference by the agents of the provisional government in electoral struggles and in the moral preparation for the elections."[14] The exchange of notes did little to settle the question of Turkey's role and the extent of French authority during the transitional period leading up to the elections.

Both agreed, however, that the elections would play the pivotal role in determining the character of the Sanjak's government. The system of proportional representation guaranteed predominance to whichever linguistic group was able to register the most people. Creating a majority became the central project for both the Halkevi and the League of National Action. Turkish activists in Aleppo and the Sanjak set out to repair their strained relations with those Sanjak Turks who had refused to support the new Kemalist ideology. Like the imam who had derisively thrown the hat across the room some years earlier, many of the Turkish-speakers living in the Sanjak disapproved of Atatürk's reforms and the actions of the local Halkevi. Turkish activists spent hours with leaders like [Sufi] Mevlevi Shaykh Mustafa Şaho in an effort to reconcile with these voters and claim their registrations.[15] Martel also accused Turkish leaders of engaging in politics by bringing in two physicians who began providing care around the Sanjak despite their lack of official authorization. "Their propagandist character is attested by the fact that they provide free care and penetrate in this manner into the most diverse milieus." Martel suggested expelling them.[16]

The League of National Action also worked to consolidate its presence in the Sanjak, trying to raise morale among discouraged Arabs. Nearly every night during the first week of December, members of the League of National Action met with local communists, trying to create a new organization with a new name.

Those present disagreed fundamentally about the role of the French, some arguing that, in the present circumstances, they could not separate themselves from French support, while the majority insisted that it was impossible to come to an agreement with the mandatory authorities. Hassan Jabara, director of the Sanjak's Financial Service, promised to seek authorization for the group's new headquarters, where they would publish their journal, *al-Uruba*.

The League of National Action's commitment to a broad-based Arab nationalism did not rely on Muslim elites. Leaguers were working among Christians and taking to the streets to enlist workers to their cause. One of the leaders, Muhammad Ali Zarka of Antioch, spent days at Alexandretta making the rounds of the fishmongers and the cafés frequented by the city's fishermen and boatmen. On December 8, he made them an offer. "My dear comrades, I was sent here by Zaki al-Arsuzi. From today, we will form an organization that we will call the Union of Arabs. Our goal is to give courses to the illiterate of our community. We have with us Christians and Armenians who are literate. We will give lessons two hours a day, because we cannot be defeated by the Turks."[17]

Whether because their campaigns met with success or some of the Sanjak's residents were simply tiring of the Halkevi's actions, many artisans took back their fezzes, rejecting their new brimmed hats. In early December, a group of Turkish villagers came to Antioch wearing fezzes as a challenge to the Kemalists; within a few days, twenty Turkish-speakers paraded around a Turkish-majority neighborhood at midday wearing fezzes. Al-Arsuzi's group proved itself similarly unable to gain as much traction as they had hoped. Some of the Sanjak's most prominent Alawis refused their support, including Shaykh Abdullah al-Ghali, who went to the Halkevi on November 29 to show his loyalty to the Sanjak's Turcophile leaders.[18] Each time "Turks" rejected Kemalism or "Arabs" wore brimmed hats, French authorities tried to find an explanation, unwilling to accept that people were making their *political affiliation* in Antioch on the basis of *political concerns* and not on language, even during this period of increasing polarization.

There was one thing on which both the Republican People's Party and the Arab activists could agree. Neither group trusted the French. Arab nationalists feared that France intended to continue its occupation indefinitely. Turks feared that French interference with the Armenians, Alawis, and Circassians would preclude a Turkish majority in voter registrations. Turkish news outlets accused the French of behaving in a way that would guarantee their own continuing power in the Sanjak without regard for the new Statute. Their accusations echoed official complaints from the Turkish government that focused on Garreau's assistance to non-Turks and his persecution of Turks, even charging him with arresting and torturing two Turks simply for having sung the Turkish national anthem. They claimed that all of these incidents, along with Garreau's speech on taking office, indicated that France would never leave the Sanjak.

The Halkevi planned a meeting in Antioch to seize on their common concerns, inviting "all the politicians of the Sanjak," including people who had
thrown their support to either the League of National Action or to the "moderates" who had refused to be connected with either group: prominent families the
Kuseyris, the Adalis, the Arsuzis, and the family of Subhi Barakat.[19] They seem to
have had little apparent success. Next, it was the Arabs' turn to try to find
common ground against the French. They proposed a Sanjak Union to enforce
the new Statute and struggle against those who were trying to sabotage the Sanjak's new status. Zaki al-Arsuzi's speech polarized the 150 notables assembled,
however. Moreover, discussion of the rumors that Italy would declare war on
Turkey if France relinquished the Sanjak led to an investigation and the League
of National Action's indefinite closure.

Arresting Zaki al-Arsuzi produced turmoil in the Sanjak. Supporters congre-
gated in front of the police station all afternoon, and police efforts to disperse
them met opposition. When a group attacked the police station, the police fired
on the crowd; some in the group fired back. By the time Zaki al-Arsuzi's brother
Nassib helped to disperse the mob, one demonstrator had been mortally
wounded, three others had been shot, and four police officers had been injured
by stones and sticks. In Antioch, Leaguers tried to close the markets. Gunshots
that evening induced local police to isolate the Affan quarter, where the agitation
had begun. Telegrams protesting al-Arsuzi's incarceration flowed into the delegate's office and the offices of the Damascus government.[20] On December 18, the
League of National Action leader was sent into exile at Kesab.[21]

The long-awaited high-level talks between French and Turkish military commanders revealed the continuing discrepancy between their interpretations of
who would wield power and responsibility in the newly independent Sanjak.
General Charles Huntziger, commander–in–chief of the French troops in the
Middle East, arrived in Ankara on December 16 at the head of a French military
delegation to take the first steps toward cooperating with Turkey to guarantee
the security of the demilitarized Sanjak in accordance with the Franco-Turkish
Agreements. An infantry company welcomed him, along with a military band
playing the Marseillaise and the Turkish national anthem. After an official welcome celebration, the military delegations got down to work. The Turks had
created the agenda, and began with contingency planning.

Although their first hypothetical case brought the central disagreement into
sharp focus, the sides grew more cordial as they considered opportunities for
joint action. What would happen if one of the two guarantor powers attacked
the Sanjak? France's ambassador to Turkey reported his version of the events:
"The Turks claimed, it is true, that they by no means ascribe to France the intention of taking possession of the Sanjak, but they underlined that if we would, for
any reason, introduce troops into the Sanjak, the Turkish populations of this

territory and those neighboring it would not fail to be so roused that, in this case, the Turkish Government would consider sending the same number of troops there." Ambassador Ponsot pointed out that the Turkish officers were framing the "exercise of one of the obligations which our mandatory power requires of us" as, instead, an aggressive act. For Ponsot, this first hypothetical case showed "in the clearest way" the Turkish government's insistence that its involvement in the Sanjak be, from the start, "on a footing of complete equality." Huntziger queried the Turkish officers: Would Turkey consider it aggression if France brought some troops into the Sanjak as reinforcements to help local police restore order? Fevzi Çakmak, chief of the Turkish general staff, responded that this would depend on the number of forces. Both sides agreed that eight hundred or one thousand reinforcements should usually suffice to maintain public order in the Sanjak. To calm Turkish anxieties, Huntziger conceded that if calm were not restored with so many troops, he could imagine the Turks sending the same number of forces into the Sanjak after an agreement between the two governments. Discussions adjourned after two tense hours, and began again in the afternoon on the same note as the two sides tried to edit the summary of their earlier conversation. When the two delegations contemplated an invasion by Syria, however, the two groups closed ranks, the Turks emphasizing "the value that the Turkish government attached to the envisaged collaboration and the possibility of closer rapprochement between France and Turkey in the eastern Mediterranean." Subsequent sessions were even friendlier, despite the French delegation's introduction of a hypothetical case in which Turkey were to invade the Sanjak. The final conversations, about demilitarization, descended into confusion over the differences between demilitarization of the territory and the disarming of its population. In the end, the two sides agreed that the French supreme commander of troops in the Levant would communicate a report about demilitarization twice yearly to the Turkish general staff, and the problem of disarming the population was postponed while each delegation consulted its government. The sessions ended "in an atmosphere infinitely better and calmer than that with which it had begun."[22]

At the conclusion of the talks, Huntziger issued a statement for the press telling of his "pleasure at having been able to effect a friendly contact with the Turkish General Staff" and asserting that he was "sure that he and his Turkish colleagues had arrived at decisions which would strengthen the bond of friendship uniting France and Turkey."[23] Most important for France's minister of war and national defense, as hostilities grew in Europe, the French navy would benefit from "certain facilities," and Turkey would permit its ships to pass through the Bosphorus and the Dardenelles.[24]

As the Huntziger contingent was leaving, Jamil Mardam arrived in Turkey on his return from Paris, where he had engaged in difficult discussions with the new

French government. Mardam had staked his own and the National Bloc's for-
tunes on ratification of the Franco-Syrian Treaty that they had negotiated with
Leon Blum's government in 1936. Opposition to Syria's independence had
proved so strong even under the left-wing Blum that he had refused to send the
document to Parliament for ratification; the new government of Édouard
Daladier included members of the colonial lobby who resolutely opposed loos-
ening France's hold on its overseas possessions. As a result of the new atmosphere
prevailing in Paris, the Foreign Ministry warned Martel that the Franco-Syrian
Treaty would never be ratified as long as the French Parliament "continued to
question the good will and sincerity of Syria's government."[25] Trying to mollify
those who doubted the wisdom of Syrian independence at the very time that
France might well need Syria's eastern Mediterranean bases, Mardam had agreed
to more concessions, which angered many nationalists at home. Before Mardam
even left France, his promises were loudly and publicly condemned by Syrian
nationalists, who warned that they would reject the revised treaty, even threatening to "resort to violence if it compromised Syria's national aspirations."

Mardam's arrival in Turkey had little in common with the September 1936
visit of the Syrian delegates freshly returned from successfully contracting that
Franco-Syrian Treaty. Instead of being greeted by hostile questions about the
role of the Sanjak, the Turkish government seemed intent on reassuring Mardam and the Syrian government. Mardam was met by Foreign Office officials,
municipal officers, and guards of honor at both Istanbul and at Ankara. In
reporting on his visit, the Turkish daily *Cumhuriyet* stressed Turkey's wish for
friendship with an independent Syria, and Turkey's confidence that outstanding problems between the two countries would soon be resolved. Editor
Yunus Nadi reassured Syrians that Turkey harbored no aspirations to annex
Hatay, and stated that the Sanjak's independence "was as much desired by
Turkey as was the independence of Syria." He placed the official relationship
between Atatürk and the Syrian prime minister in a historical light. "The
sincerity of the cordiality manifested between the two Chiefs of State was
undoubtedly due to the fact that Syria is a country which for centuries was a
part of the Ottoman Empire, and which therefore enjoys the sympathy and
understanding of Turkey, which takes a special interest in its well-being and
eventual independence."

Mardam's meetings with Turkey's prime minister, foreign minister, and others
in the Foreign Office proved reassuring. When he met President Atatürk, the
Turkish leader insisted that "the Sanjak is the strategic key to Cilicia, but Turkey
didn't need the key in her hands." According to Mardam's report, Atatürk told
him that Turkey would not even accept the Sanjak if Syria offered it. What Turkey wanted was only a "radius for Turkish populations of the Sanjak to develop
freely within the boundaries of the Syrian state, in the terms of the Geneva

settlement."[26] Before departing, Mardam spoke of "the brilliant future assured to Turkish-Syrian relations," clearly delighted with the discussions he had with Turkish officials.[27] The warm reception may have been partly responsible for Mardam apparently having a change of heart when he got home. The British ambassador was with Turkey's foreign minister when word came that Syria had decided to agree to "portions of Geneva settlement which they have hitherto refused to recognize." "As regards the Syrian visit, Turks made it a Turco-Syrian flirtation," the British ambassador telegraphed. "French wisely let them flirt and took no steps. No harm has been done and may be quite a lot of good."[28] Atatürk had signaled that he had no designs on the Sanjak, the Syrian government decided to recognize more of the Sanjak's new Statute and Fundamental Law, and Mardam's visit set the stage for the beginning of a rapprochement.

After Mardam left Turkey, he arrived in Aleppo on December 23 to a "tremendous welcome" from an enthusiastic crowd of townspeople and representatives of surrounding rural areas and desert tribes. In his short speech at the train station, at a lunch that the municipality of Aleppo gave in his honor the next day, and at the "monster tea-party" that the National Bloc had organized that evening, Mardam thanked the people of Aleppo for their welcome. Without providing details about either his negotiations in Paris or his conversations in Ankara, the Syrian prime minister declared that the Franco-Syrian Treaty would soon be ratified by the French, and expressed his hope that Syria would collaborate with Turkey and France over the Sanjak.[29]

Five days later, Mardam's chief adversary over the Sanjak, Zaki al-Arsuzi, and two of his collaborators returned from exile to an exuberant crowd estimated at nearly one thousand who cheered as the three emerged from their car and processed through Antioch's Affan quarter. Muhammad Ali Zarka gave a short speech in front of Café Abdu Husni, thanking the people in the name of Zaki al-Arsuzi, and then encouraged the crowd to disperse quietly. French police were reassured to note no other prominent men among those present.[30]

Davis, British consul in Aleppo, provided his government with a broad perspective on the political situation one month after the Sanjak had become officially independent. The Sanjak's new status had been a compromise in which neither the Turkish nor the Syrian government had gotten all they had hoped. The Damascus regime had always seen it as "a base betrayal of their interest by the French," and were forced to accept it because of "their complete lack of the means of forcible resistance." Turkey had accepted the Sanjak's new status "only with the mental reservation that the new regime was by hook or by crook to be applied in such a way that the Turkish element in the Sanjak would from the outset have complete dominance and would later consolidate their ascendancy to an extent that would render the Sanjak, in cold fact if not immediately in name, a mere province of the Turkish Republic."

While both the Syrians and the Turks had been forced to compromise, the real winners were French officials. Among the colonial rulers, Davis detected "a distinct undercurrent of satisfaction that in the Geneva negotiations the Syrian Nationalist government had been made to realise the exact measure of its own unimportance and negligibility and the true degree of its dependence on France." France, in turn, could not be expected to be a strong advocate for its mandatory protégés. "Unfortunately," Davis wrote,

> It is not generally believed here that the Geneva settlement is in any sense final; the Turks hope, the Arabs fear that the Sanjak will one day again become Turkish territory, and no-one is prepared to subscribe to the opinion that France would in the last resort use armed force to resist the Turks should they make an attempt to occupy the Sanjak. The fact that responsible Frenchmen here are apt to say quite publicly that their country would never fight for the Syrians, a pack of troublesome ingrates, does not tend to dissipate this fear. The lukewarmness, real or supposed, of France gives the Turks every reason to persist in an attitude of truculence from which they have much to gain and nothing to lose.[31]

As Mardam had recognized in his Paris talks, honorable cooperation had rendered his National Bloc regime completely dependent on French honor.

The Sanjak population at large did not share these larger political passions, Davis asserted, claiming that at least 75 percent of the population would be glad to live peacefully under the new regime. Outside forces continued to polarize them because of the central importance of community-based registration. "Neither Damascus nor Angora [Ankara] . . . have any intention of allowing the new statute to be applied impartially." In the ongoing struggle, he claimed that the Turks had the advantage. Syria's organization and resources could not match Turkey's, and its leaders had not managed to create a coherent front among the various non-Turkish groups in the Sanjak. Their calls for Sanjak natives living in Syria to return to register for the elections had been largely unsuccessful, and efforts to organize Arab clubs and youth movements to balance the Halkevi and Turkish youth organizations had been hardly more effective. Syrian appointees like Governor Husni al-Barazi had lost their positions when the Sanjak became independent, and the popular protests that had broken out in Syria's main cities had not compensated for the lack of mobilization within the Sanjak. The Turks had the benefit of "a more compact, disciplined and better educated body of supporters," and, combined with the advocacy of their newly appointed consuls, their well-organized clubs and youth organizations, and the availability of funding, they had so far been much more successful in mobilizing their supporters. Although few Syrians eligible for Sanjak citizenship were traveling to their birthplaces to register, some three thousand eligible citizens living in Turkey were now in route to the Sanjak with the assistance of the free transportation and expense funds being provided by the Ankara government.[32] In addition, local Kemalists were resorting to intimidation in an effort to get Arabs to register as Turks. Regardless of their organizational success, however, Davis was convinced that "most of the Turks and all of the Arabs would hate to witness the introduction into the Sanjak of many of the typical features of the Turkish republican regime, particularly the unveiling of women and the laicization of the state."

The effective Turkish organization was making things more difficult for French officials, Davis continued. In addition to their efforts to prevent the intimidation of non-Turks, mandatory officials persisted in trying to restrict the role of the local Turkish consuls. Garreau had reminded Antioch's Turkish consul that Turks in the Sanjak were Syrian nationals, and as a result, the Turkish official had no standing to represent them. A bigger and recurring problem was Turkish insistence that the Statute of the Sanjak had created a Franco-Turkish condominium, "an error which appears to persist ineradicably in Turkish circles." Davis saw the local Turkish consul's frequent interventions as an effort to make up for the disappointment of the local Turkish population. Having "helped to mislead" the Sanjak's Turks to expect that the Turkish flag would be unfurled on November 29 when the Sanjak became independent, they encountered "considerable dissatisfaction" when the Syrian flags were replaced by French flags.

Turkey's continuing insistence on equal power in the Sanjak exploded into fury as the League of Nations electoral commission prepared its report. Ankara's objection to the content of the report was grave; the Turkish government reserved its greatest outrage, however, for the process by which it claimed the report had been drafted. Turkish newspapers accused the electoral commission of visiting the Sanjak without consulting either the Ankara government or the Sanjak's Kemalists. Accusing French officials of introducing the commissioners only to pro-French and anti-Turkish elements, *Cumhuriyet* demanded that "the League not permit itself to be used as the tool of France and thus prejudice the success which it has obtained in bringing the Hatay question to a solution."[33] In his telegraph to the League of Nations' secretary-general, Turkish foreign secretary Aras expressed his "surprise at the procedure adopted by the organs of the League," claiming that the League was trying "to confront Turkey with a *fait accompli*." Aras accused the new electoral commission of disregarding Ankara's ideas and creating a set of election regulations that would be wholly unfavorable to the Turkish element in the Sanjak. Moreover, after completing the draft regulations, the electoral commission had officially communicated them to the French authorities in the Sanjak, and only unofficially forwarded them to the

Turkish government. According to Aras, French authorities in the Sanjak had behaved "not as benevolent and impartial authorities but as a party to the case, continually intervening in such a manner as to influence very considerably the result of the elections to the detriment of the Turkish element, which is predominant in the territory." Despite his vociferous complaint about the disadvantage under which his government would be suffering as a result of the new election regulations, the Turkish foreign minister could not provide specific examples because he had not yet seen the document.[34]

Reid, president of the electoral commission, denied collaborating with French authorities; the commissioners had communicated with local government officials as necessary to obtain the detailed information needed to organize the first Sanjak elections. The French officials, he wrote, "never attempted to influence the electoral commission's decisions, nor to ascertain what these decisions were, nor to share unofficially in the electoral commission's task." After the electoral commission's information-gathering visit to the Sanjak in October 1937, the commissioners had returned to Geneva to draw up the actual text of the electoral law "without interference from, or consultation with, any Government or any person connected with any Government." Moreover, the draft electoral law had been communicated to the mandatory authorities "not for approval or for criticism," but solely so that they could prepare for the elections; they had sent it to the Turkish government as a courtesy.[35]

The Turkish government, unmollified, insisted that the electoral regulations were the "keystone" of the compromise Statute and Fundamental Law. Turkish representatives had participated on the League of Nations Committee of Experts that had produced those new documents on which the electoral regulations were supposed to have been based; the Turkish government had also expected to collaborate with the electoral commission in its preparatory work. Aras understood that the electoral commission's work would be in two parts, one that would prepare the regulations, the other responsible for supervising the elections. His government recognized that neither French nor Turkish participation would be permitted in that second responsibility, but had fully expected that both French and Turkish assistance would have been necessary in the preparatory stage, "in order that the texts to be drawn up should not depart from the spirit of the compromise reached on May 29th, and should not lead to a resurgence of the dispute." Instead, Aras claimed, the electoral commission had relied solely on the French authorities, and as a result, "it had been unable fully to deploy its good will in the direction of just findings and of an equitable, impartial decision." Having been thus misled by their unbalanced procedure, the electoral commissioners had then neglected to officially inform the Turkish government of the new regulations. Aras argued that these procedural issues had led to electoral regulations that justified Turkish fears.

The Turkish foreign minister's greatest objection was to the process of voter registration. These regulations had "reduced" the registration process to a "census," a way to count the members of the various communities in order to determine the proportion of the legislators that would represent each community in the new parliament. Aras argued that registration must be seen—and carried out—not as a tally of community membership, but instead as the first stage in "the expression of the people's will." According to Aras, the people's will might not correspond directly to the people's membership in a particular identity group, but might diverge from that group: religious or linguistic affiliation might not determine political will. Aras argued that the Committee of Experts had explicitly rejected the use of this registration stage as "the mere taking of a census." The electoral commission had subsequently turned this understanding on its head by insisting that each person must be required to register in his own community. In Ankara's view, this first registration stage should require no League of Nations supervision, except to prevent duplicate registrations. "No indirect influence was to be exercised over the free expression of the people's will." By unjustly claiming the right to verify the "race" of each voter, Aras insisted, the electoral commission would distort "the expression of the people's will." He argued that the impact of the new regulations on staffing the polls, on penalties for infractions, and on allocating electors at the second stage would be to disadvantage the Turks. According to Aras, the regulations had been "designed to facilitate the formation of a coalition and its accession to power," and would not produce the sort of government that had been intended by the parties who had approved the Statute and Fundamental Law.

Turkey's demand that the electoral regulations be revised elicited consternation in Geneva. The commissioners who had produced them were very disturbed when the League of Nations Council agreed to discuss revisions, and they refused to participate in negotiations to change the electoral law, claiming it would "impair the honesty of the elections." Electoral commission president Reid offered to provide only "clarifications or information" to the Council if requested.[36] While League officials worried about whether to implement the electoral regulations over Turkey's objections, French diplomats seemed unconcerned, anticipating "an early disappearance of this stumbling-block in the development of friendly relations between France and Turkey."[37]

Ernest Lagarde, head of the Africa and Levant Department of the French Foreign Ministry, sounded the dissonant note. Insisting that Syrians looked to the French to defend their interests, Lagarde claimed that if France were to acquiesce to Turkey's claims, the French position in Syria and North Africa would be "very severely shaken," with troubles and disorders sure to follow. Moreover, he told his counterpart George William Rendel of the Eastern Department of the British Foreign Office, if the Turks were allowed to take the

Sanjak, it would be only a matter of time before they took neighboring Aleppo and laid claim to Mosul and its oilfields, "which might be most inconvenient for His Majesty's government."

In Lagarde's eyes, his own government's inclination to give in to all of Turkey's demands was based on the inaccurate notion that Turkey would allow "herself to be drawn toward the Rome-Berlin axis" if its plans in Syria were thwarted. According to Lagarde, however, the Turkish government's fears of Italian power in the Mediterranean would force it instead to continue looking toward France and Great Britain. At the same time, Lagarde was convinced that there was a danger that the Turkish government, if frustrated with the League of Nations, might take military action to gain the Sanjak; France would be unable to resist a Turkish occupation, and the Turks could insist that the League recognize the fait accompli.

Rendel met next with League of Nations officials Karl Ivan Westman and Édouard de Haller, whom he found to be very depressed. Westman was Sweden's representative to the League of Nations; Haller, a Swiss attorney, was a member of the League Secretariat and director of its Mandates Section. Both insisted that Turkey had no valid case in its objections to the electoral regulations and claimed that the Turkish government was demanding changes in the regulations in order to "create an artificial majority in the Sanjak, which would then be able to press for a plebiscite, which could easily be organized in such a way as to lead to the eventual union of the Sanjak with Turkey." Like Lagarde, these two officials saw a much greater danger: an expansionist Turkey intent on "the absorption of Aleppo and ultimately of Mosul." More immediately, they worried that "if the Turks succeeded in bringing about the alteration of the draft electoral law in the sense they desired, there would almost inevitably be rioting and bloodshed in the Sanjak, which would bring further discredit on the League." Westman blamed the French government for the current predicament, claiming that its original capitulation to Turkey in December 1936 had created the precedent for Turkish interference in the affairs of the Sanjak.

Rendel's conclusions were stark. Although everyone he had spoken with feared that Turkey's intentions were to revise the electoral regulations to create the illusion of a majority, Rendel saw no other alternative. "It emerged from all this that there was little hope of the question being considered on its merits. The Turks would only want the alteration of those parts of the electoral law which might prevent them from creating an artificial majority. It seems clear that their wishes will have to be met, and the precise method to be adopted in giving way to them is a minor technical matter, which the League will no doubt be able to arrange."[38] Turkey was ready to take matters into its own hands, and neither France nor the League was interested in preventing that. It would be better to change the regulations than to discredit the League or reveal French impotence.

Foreign diplomats in Turkey registered growing alarm about Atatürk's intentions, especially after the Turkish press employed the epithet used by the countries most hostile to the League of Nations: the "international organ of Geneva." On January 25, the Nazi Party newspaper *Völkischer Beobachter* published a front-page story on the Sanjak issue, claiming that the government of Turkey was going to protest the behavior of the French mandatory authorities in the Sanjak and the procedure the electoral commission had executed for drawing up electoral regulations. "Turkey should have known from past experience that the Geneva institution is an instrument which may be played from London or Paris at will," the German paper asserted. "To arraign France at Geneva means to indict her at Paris, the only difference being that whereas an accusation made at Geneva is refuted by others, in Paris the French themselves have to take the trouble." The German paper expressed sympathy for the Turks: "The activities of M. Garreau in the Sanjak remind us of the 'work' of certain foreign Plebiscite commissioners of post-war days in Germany. As we see, the methods of the French, where they have the power, have not changed."[39] At the same time, diplomats in Turkey who were opposed to German irredentism, unilateral actions, and allegations against the League of Nations found Atatürk's attitude quite troubling. United States officials remained unconvinced, however, pointing out that Turkey had not "seriously contemplated" withdrawing from the League. Such a step would not only be completely inconsistent with all of Turkey's recent international behavior but also would alienate Turkey from Great Britain, on whom Turkey had been growing increasingly dependent. Instead, the Ankara government was consciously encouraging this anxiety in the hope that its behavior would frighten France into becoming more receptive to Turkish demands.[40]

In Geneva, League of Nations officials huddled with Turkey's allies to create a strategy for dealing with Turkey's objections, which seemed all too threatening in light of recent attacks on the credibility of the League. Britain's close relationship with Turkey put Rendel in a central position. Should the League Council scrap the decision reached on January 27, 1937, to make the Sanjak independent, and instead partition the Sanjak and give the northern part to Turkey? Rendel was dubious that this would work, because it would leave Antioch, the city with the largest Turkish population, within the Syrian sphere; in any case, others preferred to resolve the impasse within the parameters of the Statute and Fundamental Law accepted on May 29, 1937.[41] Inviting the Turkish government to submit its own set of draft electoral regulations would be unacceptable, however, because the League had insisted that the electoral law be independent of either party to the dispute.

The League's director of mandates, Édouard de Haller, was agitated when he arrived to speak with Rendel shortly before the League Council meeting scheduled for January 27, 1938. He had just seen the draft of the speech that Turkish foreign minister Aras planned to give that afternoon. Rendel, too, feared that it would create significant problems, describing it as "extremely controversial," and containing "unfounded accusations, supported by untenable arguments." Since the Council meeting had already begun, there was no time to talk with Aras. The session dragged on so long that discussion of the electoral regulations for the Sanjak was delayed until the next day.

When Rendel took the draft Turkish speech to Anthony Eden the next morning, the British foreign minister instructed him to persuade Aras to change those parts that seemed to reopen the questions already resolved in May. Lagarde doubted that Aras would be willing to budge: the version that had so alarmed the diplomats had already been modified from a previous, even angrier, draft. Rendel described his hour-long effort to intervene with the Turkish foreign minister:

> [Aras] talked ceaselessly on a variety of subjects, but his main point appeared to be that the essential nature of all the agreements about the Sanjak from the Franklin-Bouillon Treaty of 1921 [Ankara Treaty] onwards had been based on the "condition" that there should be a Turkish majority in the Sanjak. His argument was that there had been an over-whelming Turkish majority in 1921, which had been illegally reduced by the French action in filling the Sanjak with refugees and other non-Turkish elements, though as a matter of fact most of these refugees have been driven out of Turkey by the action of the Turkish Govt [sic]. It was a condition of the Turkish agreement to all the arrangements about the Sanjak that there should now be a Turkish majority. The elections were merely a formality intended to give the Turkish majority a concrete expression. He could not take seriously any assertion that H.M.G. wished the elections to be free. Mr. Aras quite understood our loyalty to the French, but he could not accept anything which might have the effect of producing a non-Turkish majority.

Rendel responded that Britain's position did not come from blind loyalty to France but a commitment to a just settlement guaranteeing the rights of all, and insisted that the electoral law had been written by the neutral Commission for the Organization and Supervision of the First Elections in the Sanjak of Alexandretta and offered the best chance of having free and fair elections. If the Turkish government was correct, and the Turks were truly a large majority, he continued, they had nothing to fear. Foreign Minister Aras reiterated his contention that the elections "were a mere formality. What was essential was to secure a Turkish majority, but he did not mind how this was done." Aras was angry about "everything that had been done" in regard to the Sanjak, and was considering repudiating the May agreements. Rendel did manage to convince Aras to change the passages the British considered most objectionable.[42]

When Turkey's representative, Necmettin Sadak, appeared before the League of Nations Council on January 28, he summarized Turkey's objections to the electoral regulations, insisting that they included elements that had been rejected by the earlier League of Nations Committee of Experts, who had included all the requisite electoral regulations within the Fundamental Law. The electoral commission's additions to the election protocol in the Fundamental Law were unnecessary and unwelcome. Sadak repeated Aras's message: from the 1921 Ankara Treaty until the present, autonomy had been for the purpose of "conserving" the Sanjak's "Turkish majority and Turkish culture." The new Statute and Fundamental Law could "in no way conflict with this essential condition, either in conception or in application."[43]

League officials struggled to find a formula that could revise the electoral law in a way that would show the actual proportions of the various groups in the Sanjak as they had intended, while still meeting the demands of the Turkish government to recognize the existence of a Turkish majority. Complicating the problem, the Turkish government refused to accept any committee on which it was not represented, and insisted on unanimity in all decisions. According to Rendel, the French were unwilling to "stand up to" the Turks, so that any committee that might be formed to revise the regulations would be forced to accept whatever regulations the Turkish government wanted. While claiming that the French "readiness to accept practically any demands from the Turks was the real root of the trouble," Rendel pointed out that a new committee to revise the electoral regulations would absolve the French of responsibility, placing it instead on the League of Nations. While the French would avoid direct responsibility, the League would be compromised by the outcome. The British diplomat preferred that, if the French were willing to concede everything to Turkey, they take responsibility for their decisions, even make a bilateral agreement, and not compromise the League in the process. For Rendel, the proposed Turkish procedure would set an unacceptable precedent by putting the parties to the dispute on the same level as the arbiter, in this case the rapporteur.

League officials proposed a Committee of Three to revise the electoral regulations, but they were unable to induce the Turkish foreign minister to accept the new plan. Aras appeared to be quite agitated, perhaps remembering the process by which Turkey had lost the contested province of Mosul in 1925, and kept repeating that Turkey would not be misled. According to Aras, France and Turkey were in agreement on everything, and the resolution of the dispute was being held up by the rapporteur's intransigence. Aras eagerly accepted the suggestion that the two countries negotiate a resolution directly, even including the Syrian government in the discussions. When League officials drafted a formula by

which Turkey and France would negotiate their differences on the electoral regulations directly and refer the result to the rapporteur, however, the French government absolutely refused. French officials admitted that "the Turkish claims
were quite outrageous," that Ankara's proposed Committee of Five "was open to
grave objections from the League point of view," and that "the results of yielding
to the Turks in the Sanjak would be likely to prove unfortunate locally." France
could not risk quarreling with Turkey at the moment, "for reasons of major politics," but if Paris took full responsibility for giving in to Turkey on the Sanjak,
France's "position in Syria would become untenable." Delbos wanted France's
"capitulation" to Turkey to be made "on the responsibility of the League as a
whole, and not on that of France alone." French diplomats, pleading for a Committee of Five (the proposed Committee of Three with the addition of Turkish
and French representatives), "admitted that the Turks were resorting to blackmail." Recent events in the Mediterranean seemed so dangerous that the French
government was insisting on doing nothing "which might endanger the friendship of Turkey at this juncture."[44]

Great Britain agreed to the creation of a new and explicitly ad hoc Committee
of the Council to revise the electoral regulations (to include representatives
from Sweden, Britain, Belgium, France, and Turkey) whose decisions would be
taken unanimously. Rendel made it clear to his superiors in the Foreign Office
that he found this resolution "fundamentally unsatisfactory." Recalling his conversation with the Turkish foreign minister three days earlier, Rendel claimed
that Aras's goal was to ensure that the elections showed a Turkish majority. Rendel's analysis was that the Turks had come to fear that free, fair elections would
not produce that sought-after Turkish majority. "Indeed," Rendel wrote,

> we have very good reason to believe that the Turks are in fact no more
> than about 40 percent of the total population of the Sanjak, as the
> French and the local authorities have always contended. What the
> Turks want is that the electoral law should be amended in such a way as
> to ensure that, whatever the true proportions of the population may be,
> there shall be at least a 60 percent Turkish majority. The work of the
> Committee will therefore consist in altering those provisions of the
> electoral law which are intended to secure a free expression of the wish-
> es of the inhabitants of the Sanjak, so as to ensure a Turkish majority in
> any circumstances.

Rendel was concerned that, if the French government was hiding behind the
League of Nations in order to make concessions to Turkey without getting the
blame from the Syrians, this new solution would allow them to go even further
in appeasing Turkey's demands. Rendel anticipated that the non-Turkish

communities would respond violently to the betrayal of the League's promise of a fair election.[45] The new Committee of Five was approved by the League of Nations Council at its meeting early Monday evening, January 31.[46]

While the diplomats were wrangling in Geneva over electoral regulations, activists inside the Sanjak mobilized to take advantage of the opportunities the elections would present—and to avoid the consequences of a failure that would make them powerless in the new Sanjak Assembly. Two opposing tendencies were emerging. On the one hand, with the new Parliament's seats to be allocated by "community," Turkish and Arab nationalists sought to maximize their own numbers, increasing polarization. On the other, the "moderates" continued their efforts to bridge the growing chasm and reverse the polarization. On the last day of 1937, some five hundred leaders of the various political parties met in Antioch to create a unified organization devoted to the well-being of the newly independent Sanjak. The organization they created, the "National Union," articulated its goal: "to unify the efforts of all the population of the Sanjak within the framework of Syria and, consistent with the regulations in force, to work for its prosperity and deter the occurrence of disorder in the country." The National Union planned to encourage solidarity among all people in the Sanjak regardless of race or creed, to respect the rights of all, to improve education and public services, to stimulate agriculture, to strengthen, protect and encourage export, to foster industrial and agricultural sciences, to impose and collect taxes fairly. No interference in foreign politics would be allowed in the National Union's activities, which would remain confined to the internal affairs of the Sanjak. The National Union would welcome participation by every citizen, and would establish branch offices.[47]

The League of National Action did not support the new National Union. By early February, Antioch's predominantly Alawi Affan quarter had become a site of continuous conflict between supporters of the League of National Action and the National Unionists. Small incidents led to street brawls between the groups, as occurred late at night on February 4, when a member of the League stopped Jema Kafa on the street, asking for a cigarette. As Kafa extended his hand, the Leaguer threw the cigarette back at him, hurling along with it a varied set of insults against the members of the National Union. On cue, many Leaguers at a nearby café appeared (one holding a revolver), and supporters of the League of National Action exchanged blows with those of the National Union. Further violence was prevented when one of the local police, standing near the café, intervened, along with members of the "moderate party," to reestablish calm.[48] Two days later, three drunken adherents of the National Union and two drunken supporters of the League of National Action exchanged abusive remarks during an evening at an Antioch cabaret. When the men left the establishment, members of both groups intervened in the argument, which quickly degenerated into a brawl, soon dispersed by the police and gendarmerie. The next morning, more than a dozen supporters of the League of National Action attacked the house of National Union leader Albert Beyluni with stones and insults; one even fired at Beyluni. Police arrested Sahid al-Arsuzi (Zaki's brother) at the offices of *al-Uruba*. Antioch's police chief saw the hand of Zaki al-Arsuzi behind the attacks. "The Leaguers, elements of disorder, had received in recent days the directives of Zaki al-Arsuzi through Nedim Ward, to attack ceaselessly the National Union and its members in order to stand firm and make their attitude of opposition felt."[49] The French suspended the League's *al-Uruba* on February 8 for publishing inaccurate information "of a nature to trouble public order"; the paper's director and editor were arrested.[50]

Although the League of Nations Committee of Experts had assumed that people's political goals were determined by their linguistic or religious preferences, escalating violence in the Sanjak no longer respected these delineations. The Syrian government, motivated by French insistence and by Mardam's urgent political need to have the Franco-Syrian Treaty approved in Paris, overcame its resistance to the Statute and Fundamental Law and named Nabih al-Azma Syria's representative to the independent Sanjak.[51] At the same time, French intelligence reported that Arabic-speaking leaders of the League of National Action had been frequenting Antioch's Turcophile Halkevi.[52] Meanwhile, Turkish-speaking artisans had begun resisting the Kemalists, creating "a bloc of opposition against the directives of the Halkevi."[53] Politics seemed to be increasingly polarized, but the fault lines seemed to be associated with political goals instead of issues of identity.

Halkevi leaders stepped up their efforts to woo non-Turkish-speakers with pamphlets that simultaneously promised paradise to those who adhered to their philosophy and threatened retribution against those who refused. Their pamphlet "Appeal to the Sons of the Sanjak" accused the colonial regime of responsibility for the region's current misery. "How can there exist among you rich and wealthy people, well dressed, defended against the rigors of the cold and the heat of the summer at a moment when insufficient food and the terrors of hunger produce in your body, in your mind, in your eyes, in your hearts, and in your souls the mortal maladies that ravage among you, your fathers and your children, while the bodies of your survivors today appear to be silhouettes and ghosts?" Claiming that the Sanjak's people lived in the world's most fertile soil, the pamphet accused the mandate government of preventing the people from reaching the independence, tranquility, and liberty they hoped for, having "put all its moral, material, and political force toward sabotaging your desires and putting an obstacle between you and your hopes." This government would leave the Sanjak "willingly or unwillingly" as soon as the mandate expired, and any claims to the contrary were simply illusions. The pamphlet counseled solidarity among the various people of the Sanjak—"entente and union with the Turks, whether Alawis or Sunnis, who constitute the overwhelming majority in the territory. Be sure that the final word will rest with the Turks."

The call to unity devolved into a threat in the second pamphlet, which addressed the Sanjak's Greek Orthodox community. The pamphlet warned that if the members of that community did not denounce their leader, who was refusing to support the demands of the Turks, they would all be held responsible for his actions. "When the hour of reckoning sounds, we will not content ourselves with settling the account with him alone, but we will clear the account with all the children of the Orthodox community with no distinction among them." Instead, the pamphlet suggested an alternative course.

> You have with your own eyes verified the majesty and the dignity of the Turks, from the first centuries of their occupation of this region and other countries. You recall, in addition, without doubt, the era of their reign, of their domination, of their force. Despite this force, this domination and this power, the Turks treated you as brothers, you were respected and you were cherished. No evil came to you despite troubled conditions. We do not know as a result the reasons and the factors that make you today do what you do in acting against our justified national cause.

The authors promised respect for Greek Orthodox residents as in the past, in return for their support of the Kemalist project.

The third pamphlet targeted Hassan Jabara, the highest financial official in the Sanjak, accusing him of profiting handsomely from his collaboration with France. The authors pointed out that he had lately been quite poor. Now, on the contrary, he was extremely wealthy, in possession of many lands and buildings, "vast and immense." It was the French who were responsible for his change of fortune, choosing him partly because they believed him to be a leader of the Alawis. The pamphlet, in addition to vilifying Jabara and the French government he worked for, emphasized the Turcophile nature of the Alawis. "Pure Turkish blood, our glorious past, and the unity of our race would dissolve all conflict which could have or which will be produced between the two religions, Alawi and Sunni. Moreover, this unity guarantees against any schism that the ignorant, vile, fanatical and interested people whom we have cursed and who have cursed us would want to introduce. We, the Alawis and the Sunnis, of a single voice, always and eternally."[54] Alawis and Turks, the authors decreed, were one people distinguishable only by worship, unless, like Jabara, they had collaborated with the hated French.

The pamphlets were printed and distributed surreptitiously through the extensive infrastructure that the Sanjak's Turcophile leadership had created by the winter of 1937–38. The new Kemalist institutions had been designed not only to disseminate propaganda in favor of the Turkish party in the forthcoming elections but also to construct an alternative set of institutions for independence. The preparations were somehow simultaneously both unconcealed and clandestine, assisted by the Ankara regime. In early December 1937, for example, Garreau suspended Alexandretta's new Turkish journal *Vahdet* for eight days for having published a description of new commissions created by the Halkevi to substitute for the machinery of French mandatory government.[55] According to French intelligence, this shadow establishment encompassed all aspects of government, including security, courts, finance, and propaganda. A registrar (état civil) was headed by men of the judicial corps who delivered identity cards, marriage certificates and birth certificates and accompanied people on their official interactions with the mandatory government's état civil and general security administrations. Their "Police of the People," according to French sources, were "a secret for no one." In addition to a supreme chief of police and his assistant, the force included a chief of general security and an estimated one hundred men and women who patrolled the Turkish-majority quarters every night. This alternative government also kept a well-organized intelligence service, with agents among the Sanjak's administration. A Halkevi tribunal made up of numerous judges assigned to the various cities sat daily as an alternative to the mandatory courts. The French report complained that the so-called Popular Police were preventing Turkish plaintiffs from going to the regular government building to make their complaints. Instead, the Halkevi litigations, decided by their own tribunal, made judgments that were then endorsed at Ankara. The alternative government even included a sanitary corps, composed of at least three physicians and two military colonels. In addition, the French believed that some of the reserve officers living in the Sanjak were officers on furlough who responded to the orders of a secret military staff that was already in place and ready to be raised in a short time. An informant affirmed that a meticulous plan for mobilization was hidden outside the Halkevi and Consulate, and that the group kept lists for the distribution of arms among trusted men.

According to French officials, this elaborate system had been installed by Ankara. The Halkevleri "could accurately be styled 'Prefecture' or 'Sub-Prefecture'; they received their funds and their instructions directly from Ankara by the intermediary of the Consuls." Ankara remained the "strategic and administrative center," with various "annexes" throughout the Sanjak. Turkey's consul general in Antioch and Abdurrahman Melek in Alexandretta were the "supreme chiefs," while Abdulgani Türkmen served as president of Antioch's Halkevi. All of the annexes were in such "close connection with Antioch" that French intelligence considered them "an administration of a state within another state, ready to function immediately if a change of regime would take place." Liaisons were carried out by "meticulously chosen" agents.

The existence of this alternative government worried French mandatory officials not only because Turkey already claimed the right to intervene in the affairs of the Sanjak but also because of the continuing rumors threatening a Turkish invasion. Two men had only recently been sentenced to two months in prison and fines of 5 Turkish lira plus court expenses for having traveled among the villages telling the inhabitants to refuse to submit to the mandatory authorities. The judgment against them summarized their message: "The Sanjak has no connection with Syria. Turkey will immediately occupy the Sanjak and punish with pain of death each person who did not inscribe as a Turkish citizen at the Halkevi." According to the court, the two men had spread the word that recent arrivals from Turkey were actually partisans, soldiers, even armed officers whose uniforms would be sent along with the soldiers who would be attacking the Sanjak. According to French officials, the accused had instructed the villagers to wear hats because these Turkish forces would be brutal even with non-Turkish children and pregnant women whose husbands were not Turks.

French officials recognized not only the dangers inherent in the presence of an extensive propaganda apparatus and an alternative governmental structure apart from their own institutions, but also noted that some of the accused men's claims were too believable in the present circumstances. The borders were easily permeable, as many were returning for the elections, claiming to be Sanjak natives. "Once past the frontier, he is free to not present himself either to the General Security or to the municipal authorities, having only the chance of being discovered."[56] A combination of lax security and open borders for "Sanjak" Turks was leading to a dangerous influx of unregulated activists, while the extensive shadow government provided opportunities for organizing on behalf of Ankara's goals and threatening French control.

In Geneva, however, the French and Turkish governments continued to work together to find an acceptable formula for the Sanjak elections. The draft Turkey circulated to the new ad-hoc Committee of the Council charged with revising the electoral regulations repudiated efforts to count the various Sanjak groups, claiming that the Committee of Experts that had drafted the Fundamental Law had explicitly rejected a census. Casting its goals in the liberal language of freedom and self-determination, the Turkish government argued that the elections should reflect the will of the people, which must be allowed to be freely expressed regardless of the community in which each voter had been registered in the past. Any voter should be able to opt for any community, they insisted, claiming their approach would "democratize and humanize the electoral system by allowing the would-be voters freedom to choose their community."[57] Community affiliation was neither timeless nor essential, according to the Turkish government.

Therefore, verifying a voter's historic community would infringe on his freedom to adopt the identity he chose.

The League of Nations' proportional representation system, however, was based on the assumption that each person's community affiliation was inherent and unchanging. When registration had been completed, "the relative proportions in the Chamber of Turks, Alawis, Arabs, &c. will be permanently decided and all the elaborate machinery for the election of particular individuals will be of little importance." If anyone could declare himself a member of any community, Rendel warned, the well-organized Turkish community could use intimidation to produce a large majority in the Sanjak disproportionate to their real numbers, and the League would be unable to protect voters from this kind of coercion. The French delegation seemed unphased by the implications of Turkey's revised definition of community membership, responding that this was a political issue, to be resolved politically. The international situation now required them to accept Turkish demands. The decision had been made in January 1937 to make the Sanjak independent, they pointed out, and it would be impossible to go back now. In any case, they claimed, Turks were 40 percent of the Sanjak population, Armenians were 15 percent, and each would assuredly register in his own community. The others, French diplomats insisted, were more difficult to define, and the Turks would in any case achieve a majority in the registrations as a result. This would do no real harm to Syria, and the French government was ready to accept these electoral regulations, which would, no doubt, secure the majority for the Turks.

Rendel objected that these regulations, if implemented, would not only provide a basic majority, but would produce an overwhelming majority giving 70–80 percent of registered voters to the "Turkish community," allowing them to then demand a plebiscite for union with Turkey. Rendel suspected that he was watching a new political technique; after their victory in the Sanjak, it would then follow that the Ankara regime would use the same techniques to "get control of other areas" and ultimately to claim Mosul. "The French themselves might be affected by this, since they had a nearly 24 per cent share in Mosul oil and these developments might therefore cause a good deal of inconvenience and disturbance all round. Was it wise then to yield so readily and so completely to the Turks, and should we not by giving in to what was admitted by everyone concerned to be nothing more than blackmail, be starting a process which it might be extremely difficult to arrest?" While they were committed to following the Turkish proposal, French representatives suggested nonetheless that a procedure could be created to avoid the Turks' receiving such a large majority.

League of Nations secretary-general Joseph Avenol, recognizing the broader international implications of Turkey's program, feared that it would lead to a future disaster. He saw the Sanjak situation as even more dangerous than the situation in the Free City of Danzig, which the League of Nations had created by severing an overwhelmingly German-speaking population from Germany in order to provide a port for Poland. "It would certainly do no good to the League if it were now to give its blessing to an entirely fraudulent electoral law." Rendel agreed that it would be an "exceedingly anomalous and peculiar proceeding to decide first on who was to have a majority and of what size and then to arrange the electoral law afterwards." Avenol was willing to take the whole dispute back to the League Council and "drastically" revise the May 1937 settlement because it seemed impossible to reconcile the intention behind the Statute and Fundamental Law with the new Turkish demands.[58] The Sanjak's parallels to other European crises were clear to the League's secretary-general, who as a result was unwilling to simply comply with France's desire to appease Turkey.

When official discussions began on March 7, 1938, Rendel focused on the paramount issue: if the number of deputies in the assembly were to be fixed according to the number of voters who registered in each community, "the question of registration by communities was really the vital point of the whole elections." The registration part of the law had been designed to "establish existing facts on which to decide to what communities voters belonged." The Turkish draft took the opposite position, allowing each voter to choose his community regardless of his previous affiliations and irrespective of contrary evidence. Turkish delegate Menemencioğlu responded by denying the reality of mutually exclusive groups. Only the Turkish and Armenian communities were demarcated by a fine line, he insisted; the old Ottoman categories were no longer applicable, and language would not be admissible as evidence in distinguishing among the other communities because so many of the Sanjak's residents were bilingual. The Turks refused to permit the electoral commission any role in assessing an inhabitant's identity, which they claimed would necessarily be on the basis of the evidence of the local French or Syrian authorities.

Reid, president of the electoral commission, disagreed with the Turkish assessment of the nature of separate identities in the Sanjak. He insisted that the electoral commission's investigations in the Sanjak suggested that there would be few difficulties in determining to which community each resident belonged. Any election must rely on accurate voter registers, he argued, which should be based on "existing facts." The League's electoral commission was convinced that its original draft provided "the only way of establishing the communities accurately and objectively." In addition, it would be necessary to protect the Sanjak's people from "intimidation or undue pressure."

The discussion changed when the Belgian representative, who had presided over the Committee of Experts, agreed with Menemencioğlu. The Committee of Experts had indeed intended to allow each voter freedom to choose his own community.[59] With the French representative acquiescing to Turkish demands, the Belgian and Swiss representatives agreeing that the Fundamental Law was intended to provide flexibility to voters, and Secretary-General Avenol taking no action, Rendel found himself isolated, discouraged, and pessimistic. "It is now clear that if this point is conceded there will be no hope of obtaining any sort of fair representation for the non-Turkish communities, and that the elections will be nothing but a farce. We have considered urging that, if a plebiscite is to be held, it should be a genuine one with adequate precautions including secret ballot, but this would mean alteration of Fundamental Law and reference back to Council, and would probably not make much difference in the end." A plebiscite in which the residents of the Sanjak would have voted for their choice among varied political options would have required different preparations and provisions.[60]

Convinced that a fair election was no longer possible, the British diplomat suggested that France and Turkey could negotiate a compromise and settle on the number of deputies to be allotted to each community, thus avoiding "all the elaborate, expensive and dangerous pretense of the so-called 'registration by communities.'" If, as the Turkish government was claiming, it was impossible for even the voters themselves to decide to which community they belonged, there did not seem to be any purpose in pursuing the registration process. Turkey was insisting on registration on the basis of what they called "'volonté raciale,' i.e., the wish of the electors to see a particular race in control," instead of any kind of process that would "establish the facts." If there was now general agreement about which community should have a majority of votes, Rendel suggested that the ad-hoc Committee of of the Council could recommend an alteration in the Fundamental Law allowing them to set the total number of deputies to be allocated to each community. The Turkish delegation rejected his proposal, claiming this proposal had already been discussed and rejected by the Committee of Experts when they drafted the Statute and Fundamental Law. Next, Rendel proposed that each voter would have free choice, but his choice could be challenged by the official observer from his own community who would be present at the registration bureau; the electoral commission would have the final word in deciding to which community a voter "belonged." Menemencioğlu absolutely refused to allow the electoral commission power to decide the allegiance of a voter. Rendel suggested instead that the electoral commissioner might summon the registrant and explain that he was free to change his community but that "a formal act of change of allegiance would be required of him," including "exchange of the rights and obligations of one community for those of another." This would allow the freedom of choice the Turks desired, but would make it more difficult for people to inscribe themselves in a new community solely for the purposes of the election. In refusing this option, the Turks insisted that "there was in fact no distinction between the Moslem communities except a rather vague distinction of race, that the formal change of community would in fact be meaningless, but that the solemnity of the act would be tantamount to severe pressure on the electors against the free expression of their aspirations." Characterizing this as a "novel theory," Rendel was increasingly certain that the Turkish government's goal was to create an "overwhelming," artificial majority by inducing Alawis and Arabs to register as Turks. In the end, Menemencioğlu proposed a compromise that voters changing their communities make "a solemn declaration" that they were under no pressure to do so. In this as in most of the other points of disagreement between the drafts, the other members of the Committee of the Council supported Turkey.

As Rendel left to prepare for his new posting to Sofia, his frustration led to dark pessimism about the implications of the Sanjak situation for Europe. "If one may compare a small matter with a great one, the course of events is probably likely to follow closely that of recent events in Austria. Possibly an even closer parallel may be found in the case of the German minority in Czechoslovakia." Rendel's comparison came many months before the major European powers acquiesced to Germany's claims over the Sudetenland.[61] He agreed with his French counterpart Lagarde that this compromising situation resulted from France's misapprehension and mishandling of the international situation. "The French, who are inclined to look on all international problems as part of the military problem of defeating Germany in the 'impending war,' are extremely anxious to keep Turkey sweet in order to be able to count on her military support when the time comes."[62] Although Turkey did have significant economic ties with Germany, neither man thought it likely that Turkey would join its chief foe, Italy, against the Allies.[63]

French military planners projected a direct correlation between Turkey's likely participation in an upcoming war and French compliance with Turkey's demands in the Sanjak. Two weeks after Germany seized Austria, the French military attaché in Ankara wrote to Defense Minister Daladier emphasizing the need to appease the Turkish government. None of Turkey's defense agreements required any but the most limited provisions for military engagements, and Turkey's military agreement with the Soviet Union was unlikely to come into play, as relations between the two countries were "extremely guarded." There had not even been a Soviet ambassador in Turkey for ten months. The military attaché concluded that Turkey's alliances would not automatically draw Ankara into a European conflict. At the same time, he noted, Germany enjoyed a great deal of prestige in Turkey, as well as important commercial and intellectual ties; a German military mission, including professors of strategy and of tactics, contributed to Germany's strong influence on Turkey's army. Nonetheless, he doubted that Turkey was actually within Germany's political sphere, "and the Anschluss had not been welcomed favorably among the leaders whom the press faithfully echoed." Germany's enlargement, he pointed out, was viewed with alarm by Turkey's allies Yugoslavia and Romania. On the other hand, England's influence on Ankara had grown steadily since the Ethiopian crisis, and the two countries had concluded a number of military agreements allowing the British fleet to use naval assets belonging to Turkey.

Balancing all these factors, France's military attaché concluded that the Sanjak crisis could well play a role in determining Turkey's ultimate allegiance. France currently enjoyed little support in Turkey, he claimed, largely as a result of the Sanjak situation, which had "literally, during two years, poisoned relations between our two countries. As long as it is not resolved, and to the satisfaction of the Turks, we can be under no great illusion on the dispositions of the Turks vis-à-vis France in case of a general conflict. Nevertheless, as many Turks have told me, if France is allied with England, Turkey could not be against her." While concluding that Turkey would begin a conflict observing a "benevolent neutrality" for England—from which France would benefit—he nonetheless warned that the Sanjak issue remained crucial. Would French action "on such a limited issue as the Sanjak compensate for the eventual support which Turkey's military and geographical position could give us in case of war?"[64]

General Huntziger, France's supreme commander of forces in the Levant, had explained the importance of this "benevolent neutrality" in an official note the previous month. France's needs in the region in the event of an upcoming war were many: to access the Bosphorus and the Dardenelles connecting the Mediterranean with the Black Sea, to intercept Italian shipping in the eastern Mediterranean, to permit destruction of Italian bases in the Dodecanese, to have free access to France's established Levantine bases, and to permit the four million tons of petrol arriving annually in the eastern Mediterranean to pass through the Suez Canal. Huntziger argued that these would only be attainable if France was assured the "grand prize": Turkey's benevolent neutrality. He had come away from his conversations with Turkey's General Staff optimistic about the possibilities of more extensive military collaboration. According to Huntziger, Turkish foreign minister Aras had told him in Ankara, "If France and Turkey come to an understanding about the Sanjak, our collaboration will not stop at its borders; they could reach to the eastern Mediterranean and even elsewhere. We are ready there in large degree and you will see, to your profit, that we know how to be loyal to our friendships and to our alliances. France could not be anything for us militarily in case of war. It is geography that will decide it. But do you deny that the cooperation of Turkey could be useful to France in this case?" For Huntziger the answer was clear: he urged French officials to demand Turkish requital for French concessions in the Sanjak.[65]

The first staff members attached to the League of Nations Commission for the Organization and Supervision of the First Elections in the Sanjak of Alexandretta arrived in the region to begin preparations on April 9, 1938. This was the third group the League of Nations had dispatched to the Sanjak during the dispute. The first, the International Mission of Observers to the Sanjak of Alexandretta, had come in 1936 to observe the situation and make recommendations for its resolution; this group's presence had proven both reassuring and divisive to the local population. In the end, its mission had been preempted by the League of Nations Council agreeing to the Sandler Report on January 27, 1937, that made the Sanjak independent, a resolution that relied on none of the International Mission's observations. The second group was an earlier version of electoral commission that had traveled through the Sanjak in November of 1937 to gather the information it would need to write the electoral regulations for the newly independent Sanjak. Their recommendations had been extensively modified by the ad-hoc Committee the Council as a result of Turkish pressure. Now, the Commission for the Organization and Supervision of the First Elections in the Sanjak of Alexandretta had returned, this time to administer voter registration and elections to the Sanjak's first Parliament. President Reid had resigned, and was replaced as president by Reimers. British diplomat A.P. Nicol was appointed as the new member; like many of the others, he had experience in contested post-war territories, having served on commissions in the Rhineland and Bulgaria.

As they passed through Turkey, two electoral commission members and their secretary met with Foreign Minister Aras in Ankara. The Turkish foreign minister emphasized the political importance of the upcoming Sanjak elections and the potential repercussions of a Turkish disappointment, not only for relations between France and Turkey but also for the "prospect of peace in the Near East, which depended on the issue of the elections." When Aras threatened that unexpected results might lead to a Turkish response, the commissioners responded that they were committed to carrying out their duties "in a spirit of complete impartiality." Aras reassured them of his complete confidence, suggesting that if the outcome did not meet Turkey's expectations, the fault would be with others. On April 21, 1938, the League of Nations Commission for the Organization and Supervision of the First Elections in the Sanjak of Alexandretta arrived to begin work.[66]

|| 6 ||

Registrations Begin

While French diplomats in Geneva were making every effort to meet Turkish demands with the hope of gaining their alliance in the eastern Mediterranean, Turkey continued to blame colonial officials for actively working to subvert their aspirations for a Turkish majority in the Sanjak's forthcoming elections. Roger Garreau, the French high commissioner's delegate, traveled to Ankara at the beginning of May 1938 to work out a closer collaboration. Numan Menemencioğlu, the secretary-general of Turkey's Foreign Ministry, was optimistic, convinced that the Turkish community would obtain a very strong majority with the participation of nearly one-third of the Alawi population, a group he was certain would be registering "as Turks." Nonetheless, he insisted that Garreau take a series of steps to assure this outcome: all political prisoners must be amnestied in order to participate, anti-Turkish propaganda must cease, anti-Turkish officials must be fired, and non-Kemalist Turkish-speakers must be induced to register. Garreau quickly consented to a general amnesty and agreed to transfer those officials whom the Turks accused of activism against Ankara's interests. Although these steps might neutralize impediments to registration, Turkish officials worried that many Turks might simply stay home. Many of the Turks living in the Sanjak were not sympathetic to the Kemalist republic, opposing Atatürk's revolutionary measures, which had radically reformed many of their familiar institutions; if these Turks refrained from registering, they could compromise the likelihood of a Turkish majority. The People's Houses had been built in all of the Sanjak's important cities to cultivate favorable impressions of Turkey's new government, coordinate national festivals, provide information to the press, and organize sentiment in favor of Turkey during the upcoming elections, and Menemencioğlu hoped that all the Turks would follow their lead. Garreau countered that many of the Sanjak's rural people remained so attached to Muslim traditions that it would be difficult for them to adhere to the secular principles propagated in the new Turkey. "The obligation to change their turbans to hats evoked significant opposition among these old Turks who otherwise would willingly rally to their compatriots," Garreau pointed out. Although Menemencioğlu recognized their hesitation, he demanded that French authorities provide no support to the dissident Turks opposing the Kemalist goals for the Sanjak.[1]

Menemencioğlu was clearly delighted with the results of the meeting. France had agreed to rein in anti-Turkish forces in the Sanjak and to appoint new officials more amenable to Turkish control. He thanked Garreau for his loyal and broad-minded attitude. Garreau told the press that the discussions had taken place "in an atmosphere of sincere friendship and of mutual understanding, and they resulted in a complete understanding with regard to all the points touched upon." French officials would make "certain readjustments in the local administration . . . to ensure the strict neutrality of the native officials during the elections." Finally, Garreau announced a general amnesty for those who had committed political misdemeanors since the date of the Sanjak's independence.[2] Most encouraging of all, however, was Garreau's statement to the press on leaving Ankara in which he identified himself as a Turk.

> Before all else, I wish to tell you that I am a friend of the Turks and that moreover Turkish blood flows in my veins. How could this be? you ask. Some of my ancestors were Turks whom the Gallic King Troya brought from the Crimea and settled in the southern part of Vendee. These Turks long maintained their racial characteristics. It is therefore quite natural that I, more than anyone else, am a friend of the Turks. . . . We will do our best to see that the elections take place without disturbances and according to law.
>
> The population of the Hatay, with its Turkish majority, will realize its desire. . . . I should add that I have learned that the Turks in the Hatay constitute the element which has most respect for the laws and the regulations.[3]

The Turkish government clearly anticipated that Garreau would return to Antioch and work to ensure the Turkish majority he had predicted on leaving Ankara.[4]

The League of Nations electoral commission had been supplemented by seventeen men from eight countries, who were to act as presidents of the electoral bureaus that would be established in various districts around the Sanjak. The men were military officials, lawyers, judges, and professors. They were to be assisted by a cadre of interpreters, and by the representatives each community had chosen to witness the registration proceedings. The president of each bureau would instruct the local mayor which quarters or dependent villages to call for each succeeding day; the villagers would be required to bring their identity cards. Village heads and local elders would accompany the villagers to corroborate each voter's identity. Operations were to begin on May 3; each resident male more than twenty years old would arrive at the local election bureau to register himself in one of the seven communities specified in the Fundamental Law (Turk, Arab, Kurd, Alawi, Greek Orthodox, Armenian, Other) so that he would be able to vote in the forthcoming elections. His choice of community would be his most important decision as a voter, determining the number of representatives each group would have in the new Assembly.

Pamphlets produced by the Halkevi in both Turkish and Arabic appeared in Alexandretta the night before the first registrations. In a last-minute effort to draw more voters to register "as Turks," the authors appealed to popular desires for respect, power, and equality.

> Respectable Citizen, Careful, do not let yourself be swayed by the propaganda of those who want to make you and your family slaves. Inscribe on the Turkish list that wants to make the Hatay an independent government and you a Monsieur. After having inscribed on the Turkish list you can vote for the candidate that you wish.
>
> Citizen, Power, Influence, and Justice are in union. Division engenders weakness and anarchy. For this, inscribe yourself on the Turkish list so that you prevail and are strong.
>
> Citizen, Inscribe yourself on the Turkish list because its badge, whose predominance was achieved at Geneva, has for its goal to assure the independence and the prosperity and equal rights of all.[5]

The appeal to lofty goals of justice, independence, and equal rights was now combined with a more immediate promise: if enough people inscribed "as" Turks, the citizens of Hatay would have prosperity and prestige. The pamphlet warned against the alternative: the opposition intended to make the Sanjak's citizens into slaves.

Registrations proceeded calmly in Alexandretta that first morning, but at noon some two hundred Turcophiles went to an inscription bureau that had just opened in the predominantly Alawi Yenişehir quarter. "The Turks having begun to make speeches, the Arabs, approximately 400 in number, did the same," wrote the Security Services official, "and a serious incident between the two groups was only avoided by the arrival of the commander of the gendarmerie force and the chief of security who, by their mildness, succeeded in dispersing the two groups calmly." Electoral operations began again at one o'clock, protected by troops that the bureau's president had requested. French officials decided it would be necessary to recall troops to Alexandretta.[6]

The threat of violence accompanied the bureau's opening the next day, May 4, when a group of Alawis, the Arab nationalist activist Nadim Ward, and members of Antioch's League of National Action destroyed the hat of an Alawi Turcophile.

As one of the many Turcophiles pursuing the Leaguers reached for something in his belt, an Arab struck him on the head with his stick. Nadim Ward took out his gun, pointed it at the group, and asked them to back away. As the growing crowd of Turcophiles shouted "He pointed a weapon!" a Kemalist leader drew his own Parabellum revolver. Nadim Ward fled in the direction of the vegetable markets, firing his weapon. Police and gendarmes soon arrived and dispersed the crowd. Although Garreau claimed it wasn't clear who fired the first shots, police reported that the Kemalist leaders had begun the shooting. They had fled immediately after the incident and had not returned to Alexandretta the next day.[7]

The Turkish Foreign Ministry responded immediately. "No Turk can approach the bureau of inscription without risk," they protested, accusing local police of standing by and watching the attacks on Alexandretta's Turks without doing anything to stop them. The Ankara regime accused French officials of actively working against their interests in the election, claiming that local authorities were preferentially seeking to register Alawis and even arresting Turkish leaders solely to keep them from inscribing.[8]

Throughout the discussions in Geneva over the electoral regulations, and repeatedly during their conversations with French diplomats, Turkish leaders had emphasized the ambiguous nature of communal identities and their intention to convince members of the other listed groups to register "as Turks." The Turkish government had focused on the Alawis for many months, and the resulting division had led to tremendous acrimony within the Alawi community. Although there was an "Alawi" category in which they could inscribe, the League of National Action (headed by Alawi Zaki al-Arsuzi) insisted that the Alawis were Arabs, while the Halkevi claimed that the Alawis were the original Turks whose Arabic language was merely the result of historical accident. Divisions in the Alawi community had become particularly acute by the end of April, when Alawi religious leaders met with Nasib al-Arsuzi and leaders of the League of National Action. Two hours after that meeting, a Kemalist Alawi shaykh summoned Nasib to a meeting with the president of Alexandretta's Halkevi, some prominent Turcophiles, and a number of other Alawi shaykhs. The Halkevi president told al-Arsuzi, "The Turks are very powerful, they are in agreement with the French government, the French will leave the Sanjak soon and the Turks will govern it." Al-Arsuzi responded, "The Alawis are not Turks and those among them who vote Turkish will no longer be admitted in the Alawi community." Nasib al-Arsuzi's threatened banishment was contested by Kemalist Alawis, who rejected Zaki al-Arsuzi as the Affan quarter's Alawi delegate to observe election proceedings. "The man has publicly declared that he does not belong to the Alawi community but to the Arab community," and as a result, Kemalist Alawi leader Sadek Maruf argued, the people had no confidence in him to represent them.[9]

The Sanjak's Kurdish-speakers had come under heavy pressure from local Kemalists as early as January 1937, when Muhammad Ali, chief of the Atmali tribe, and Kojo, chief of the Sinemili tribe, protested to the high commissioner and the secretary-general of the League of Nations, seeking protection against Turkish efforts to "bring over Kurdish votes." "The present situation of Kurds in the Sanjak of Alexandretta," they wrote, "is rendered precarious as a result of the leaders of Turkish organizations who search in every way to strip away our rights and brush us aside."[10] The beginning of voter inscriptions escalated pressure on the Kurds still further, as Kemalists worked to increase Turkish numbers by insisting that Kurdish-speakers register "as" Turks. On the morning of May 5, 1938, Khalil Ali Kullo appeared at the Aktepe bureau of inscription requesting a confidential interview. When the chief of the bureau took him to a separate room, the Kurd confided that people affiliated with the Halkevi had told him, "We will put you in contact with Murselzade İnayet Bey, president of the Halkevi at Kirikhan. If you inscribe X people on the Turkish list [the writer forgot the number specified], we will pay you 750 Syrian pounds." Khalil Ali Kullo went the next day to Kirikhan, where the Halkevi president wrote and signed a confidential letter addressed to Cevat Bey. "Pay Khalil Ağa, immediately, 130 Syrian pounds, after taking the inscription card numbers of sixty-five people who will inscribe on the Turkish community list." Khalil Ali Kullo brought the letter with him to the inscription bureau as he filed his grievance against this effort to pressure Kurdish-speaking voters.

Reprisals against Khalil Ali Kullo were immediate. A charcoal seller, he had stored some of his goods in a ravine outside Aktepe while waiting for them to dry out after recent rains. The night of May 6–7, someone set the charcoal on fire; by morning, the pile had been reduced to cinders. The rest of his pile of charcoal had been dispersed in such a way as to make it impossible to gather up. Memduh Selim, representative of the local Kurdish community, believed there was a clear connection between this incident and Khalil's giving the letter to the electoral commission: "It is not necessary to search to know why and for whom this charcoal had been destroyed because it is easy to establish that Khalil Ali Kullo submitted to the consequences of the denunciation he made to Your Honorable Commission and it is clear that this deed was carried out against him by the men affiliated with the Turkish Halkevi. This matter is very characteristic." The consequences, according to the Kurdish representative, were severe. The victim was the father of many children and the charcoal his only resource, leaving the family open to starvation. Moreover, since Khalil had shown the letter to electoral commission, he had been threatened with ruin and with death, the first part of which had been realized. Memduh Selim worried that his house might be set ablaze next.

Memduh Selim's outrage was clear in his letter to the president of the League of Nations electoral commission. Turkish authorities were offering money and issuing threats in order to attain more registrants. He summarized the threats that had been circulating: "Turkish troops are concentrated on the border and are ready to march. They vow to slaughter those who do not want to march with the Turks. The Kurdish community, the Kurdish nation, Kurdish rights are so many hollow words. Those who put themselves on the Kurdish lists are condemned in advance to death. If you inscribe yourselves as Turks you will gain money and your life will be safe." The Kurdish leader continued, "We cannot imagine that these details could escape the notice of the Bureau of Inscription, because the threats, the distribution of funds, the machinations are so plain and clear that they could not escape even the eyes of a stranger who knows none of the languages of the country." He claimed that most of those coming to the registration bureaus were inscribing as Turks, having completely lost their liberty under the twin inducements of threat and reward. The letter Khalil had exposed was clear proof. "One could not as a consequence claim as free either the inscriptions made in these conditions or the elections to be supported on such fraudulent basis." As far as Memduh Selim was concerned, the inscription operations carried out until now should be considered null and void. He requested intervention by the League of Nations electoral commission, challenged the validity of inscriptions made under these circumstances, and demanded that decisions taken in the future be made in a way that would assure the required liberty for these operations.[11] Four days later, Memduh Selim followed up by pointing out that İnayet Bey, the person responsible for providing the cash for votes, was touring the inscription bureaus with the consul of Turkey, "continuing to deceive and to threaten the electors." The Turks, he claimed, had not stopped threatening Kurds. He demanded an inquiry, hoping to safeguard Kurds' own lives and the liberty of the elections.[12]

Threats turned into open warfare on May 6 when the polls opened in Aktepe, a town in the northern part of the Sanjak. Two Kemalist activists began to pressure Muhammad Hajo, a fifty-two-year-old charcoal seller, arguing that the Turks were right on the border, the French were to leave soon, and the Turks would take over. When Muhammad Hajo insulted all those who had begun wearing hats and had betrayed the Kurds, one of the Turcophiles hurled a stone at him, and panic erupted. "The cry of 'To Arms!' rung out, everyone took refuge in neighboring houses, and gunshots came from all sides for ten minutes." Prosecutor Pierre Burnier, attached to the Special Tribunal called for in the electoral regulations to hear cases connected with the elections, arrived at the scene soon after the incidents, and watched as the gendarmerie commander gathered the local men into a meadow and ordered that each be searched. No arms were found either on the people or in their homes; and inspections showed that none of the weapons of the rural guards had been discharged. Testimony before the Special Tribunal suggested that sixty to seventy shots had been fired.

Called to testify before the Special Tribunal, one witness after another described coercion. Kurdish-speakers recounted being offered money for registering as Turks while they waited to register at the Aktepe bureau on May 6; if they refused they were informed that the Turkish army was right across the border, the French would be leaving within a few days, and those who refused would be killed. When the men refused to "become Turks," as they put it, the activists scattered, and shooting broke out. The court fined two Turcophile activists 100 Syrian liras each and sentenced them to six months in prison for having disturbed the electoral proceedings and provoked a fight. Three other Kemalists received fines or prison time for having fired at the crowd or at the gendarmes. Muhammad Hajo had left town immediately after the altercation, suspecting some violence might follow, and was not accused. Turkish officials and the Kemalists' defense attorney insisted that these Turcophiles were innocent, and that all responsibility for the shooting lay with the local authorities, who had been trying to deny local Turks the free exercise of their rights. They insisted that the only people with weapons were the officials, that the local administrator was biased against the Turks, and that the court testimony was unreliable. Indeed, they claimed that it was the Kurds who had fired the shots in an effort to prevent fellow Kurds from realizing their own desire to register as Turks.[13]

That same evening, events in Antioch turned bloody. One man was injured during a quarrel among Alawis in the city's Dört Ayak quarter. As gendarmes approached the scene, they met sustained gunfire from the front of a nearby café. Two of the gendarmes, whom French police identified as a Turk and a Kurd, were killed; a third found cover and began to fire on the assailants while the captain and fifth gendarme went to find help. Citing the "extreme tension" in the Sanjak, French officials speculated the attack was premeditated.

The incident as reported by local Kemalists was quite different. They claimed that Turks had been the victims of a politically inspired attack during which the League of National Action and the non-Kemalist Sanjak Union fired on Turks and Alawi Turcophiles. The gendarmes who arrived at the scene, commanded by an Armenian, first mistreated the injured Turk and then fired on the clients of the café. *Yeni Gün* claimed that "the shots fired by the Arabs mortally wounded two of the Turkish gendarmes while the commandant of the gendarmerie and the other non-Turkish gendarmes were not struck."[14] In this Kemalist narrative the identity of the participants was based neither on language nor on religion. Anyone who had registered as a Turk, or who might indicate his desire to stand with the Turks, was henceforth classified as a Turk. Alawi-on-Alawi violence had become an Arab (Alawi) attack on a Turk (Alawi). Local security forces had become anti-Turkish partisans ready to shoot the patrons of the local café on the orders of their Armenian commander. One of the dead "Turkish" gendarmes was a Kurdish-speaker. Reformulated under these rules, the local forces of order had participated in the premeditated slaughter of Turks. Garreau was so disturbed by the events that he canceled his planned trip to Beirut and demanded armored cars and a Moroccan battalion as quickly as possible.[15]

Within hours of the deadly shootings in Antioch, local Turks set up roadblocks at Beylan, the top of the mountain pass commanding the road between Alexandretta and Antioch. They stopped and searched cars traveling in both directions, seeking members of the League of National Action. All traffic was impeded until reinforcements arrived from Kirikhan hours later to shut down the operation. Davis, Aleppo's British consul, traveling in a hired car from Aleppo to Alexandretta with his wife and young child, was held up "by a band of Turks armed with cudgels who behaved in a threatening manner and submitted me to an interrogation before they would allow me to continue my journet [*sic*]." Although not subjected to "ill treatment," Davis was displeased with having "an enforced stop in the pouring rain and the indignity of explaining my identity and movements to unauthorized interrogators," whose "menacing attitude" alarmed his family.[16] Italy's vice consul at Alexandretta registered a formal complaint on behalf of an Italian merchant living in Antioch who was detained, "forced to submit to an interrogation by a 'terrorist tribunal' and mistreated."[17]

French authorities struggled both to maintain unrestricted movement in the Sanjak and to restrain activists traveling to organize opposition and conduct propaganda. Soon after the Beylan roadblock had been cleared, for example, Garreau intercepted young men from the League of National Action leaving Antioch for Alexandretta to "make propaganda." The larger problem, however, was the continuing massive influx of Turkish men into the Sanjak. According to the statue, Sanjak citizens who were currently residing in Turkey and Syria could return to participate in the elections. On April 30, 145 passengers arrived from Turkey and were met at the train station by hundreds of Turcophiles.[18] Another one hundred passengers arrived from Turkey on May 3.[19] As the influx accelerated, Garreau questioned the legitimacy of their connections with the Sanjak. "The day before yesterday," Garreau wrote the high commissioner, "by the same train that returned me from Ankara, 283 young men arrived at Alexandretta, of whom the most part had no attachment with the Sanjak and came from all regions of Turkey. They had been suddenly invited to go to a rallying point where they were given a passport and the money for the cost of the trip. This evening another 150 young men are being awaited who will be followed, according to various indications given to us, by approximately a thousand others." The scenes at the train station were difficult enough, as the new voters were welcomed by hundreds of Turcophiles with demonstrations that included the destruction of fezzes, the singing of Turkey's national anthem, and cries of "Long

Live Atatürk!" Garreau was even more alarmed by "the dangers presented to public security by this abnormal influx of young men who comport themselves in the streets of Alexandretta and Antioch as in a conquered country." Garreau claimed that the electoral commission, when they wrote the rules, could not have envisaged "without disquiet" the large numbers of men seeking Sanjak nationality "who, from all evidence, have no right to it."[20]

As Garreau began his inquiries, it seemed increasingly clear that not all those arriving in the Sanjak held the special French visas allowing their return as citizens. Most of the legitimate visas had originated in Adana, and recipients were generally farmers of mature age, none of whom had left by the Taurus Express, from which crowds of young men were now disembarking.[21] The Foreign Ministry in Paris instructed Ambassador Ponsot to convey to the Turkish government the dangers that would result from the massive "invasion of shady elements," and to remind them that the French would strictly maintain order and assure all peaceful exercise of the rights that were defined by the Statue and Fundamental Law.[22]

Rejecting any Turkish responsibility for the recent violence, Turkish Consul Karasapan visited Garreau, informing him that all the confidence the Turkish government had placed in him after his recent trip to Ankara had been shaken by the troubling news from the Sanjak. Karasapan blamed the latest incidents on propaganda being disseminated by agents of both the Damascus government and the League of National Action, as well as on the anti-Turkish spirit of "certain French officials" and the Arabic-speaking authorities. Karasapan read Garreau a

Turkish Revolution Belongs to the Turks. Courtesy of Mihrac Ural.

note he had received from Menemencioğlu calling for much stricter measures. First, the attitudes of "certain Arabic-speaking and French functionaries" must be changed, as they had agreed at Ankara. Second, maintaining order and conducting the electoral operations well would require repression of "the terrorism," and, according to the Turks, it was urgent that Garreau arrest those who had provoked the incidents. Mandatory authorities must convince the population of the need to maintain public order, and not tolerate any acts that might disturb the peace. People in the Sanjak must know, Menemencioğlu insisted, that, "in every case, liberty of conscience, as well as the safeguarding of the life and property of the population, will be completely assured." Ankara accused the Sanjak's Arab nationalists of wanting the population to feel threatened by bloody events in order to convince them that the newly independent state would be unable to restrain acts of terrorism. Menemencioğlu's note reassured Garreau of Turkey's collaboration if needed. Garreau affirmed that all necessary measures would be taken to preserve order and the good functioning of electoral operations. At the same time, Garreau asked the Turkish consul to tell Menemencioğlu "how much I count on the moderating and pacifying actions that he promised me to exercise on the Turkish population of the Sanjak to facilitate my task."[23]

When France's ambassador to Turkey met Menemencioğlu in Ankara the next day, the Turkish diplomat claimed that the bloody events could have been prevented had mandatory officials anticipated trouble and taken serious steps to avoid it; if local authorities had taken energetic measures at the start, he argued, there would have been no new incidents and no new victims. Now, the local authorities were not even taking measures to arrest and punish those responsible for the incidents. In addition to arresting all the responsible parties at this point, Menemencioğlu demanded the dismissal of Hassan Jabara, the Sanjak's long-term financial officer, whom the Turks held responsible for many of the problems. The Turkish government persisted in blaming anti-Turkish agitators and officials; nonetheless, Turkish officials insisted, even if the perpetrators had been Turks, this behavior would be simply a reflection of the extreme conditions to which they had been subjected.

> The conditions and circumstances in which the last incident of Antioch occurred must be deeply studied. Even in the case where, for an instant, one agrees to recognize that it was Turks and not provocateurs of another community who brought about this incident, this only confirms the result of an impossible situation that we have tried to present to M. Garreau during the course of our interviews of Ankara. One could even say that the non-application of the severe measures that he had promised us following the first incidents . . . created an atmosphere of mistrust and anxiety that the [Republican] People's Party itself had not

the possibility and the power to control. It is this state of things that could finally lead the Turks, disciplined as they are, to react.

Menemencioğlu refused to acknowledge that this incident could be used to legitimize "draconian measures against the Turks and against those who claim to be Turks." If one included the new Moroccan troops, the current level of forces in the Sanjak had reached the maximum allowable according to previous discussions between the two governments.[24] Moreover, Menemencioğlu argued, Turkey had the same claim as France to assure the integrity of the Sanjak. The provocateurs of these continuing incidents were impostors who found their backing from outside the Sanjak. According to the Turkish government, mandatory officials had been much too tolerant of wrongdoing, and their actions must be seen as "the consequences of an attitude likely to frighten and to demoralize the Turks and those who support them. The military occupation of the city of Antioch can only produce the same effect."[25]

Menemencioğlu asked for clarification of the current French position: Were the mandatory authorities still seeking to arrive at the goal on which the Turks and French had agreed in their bilateral talks in Geneva the previous May, that is to say the gain for the Turks of twenty-two seats? Was France fearful that the number might be even greater, and was France, as a result, working to put brakes on the very great activity of Turkey's partisans? If this were the case, shouldn't this at least be known at Ankara? He answered his own questions by suggesting instead that important French authorities inside the Sanjak still did not understand the necessity of the Franco-Turkish collaboration. He believed that it was crucial that this collaboration rapidly become a reality, and insisted that all the foreign "fomenters of trouble" in the Sanjak be alerted without delay that their maneuvers of intimidation would not be tolerated. The Turkish diplomat insisted that Garreau attend to Turkey's concerns, hoping that the situation would change and that the presence of new troops in the Sanjak would put an end to regrettable incidents and permit the Sanjak population to prepare themselves in complete tranquility for the elections that would assure them a calm and happy future.[26] However, the Turkish diplomat ended with a veiled threat: if things did not improve, perhaps the entire resolution might need to be reconsidered. "Leaving things as they are would make us act to reopen the question of the Sanjak, with consequences that would be impossible to predict now. We want to convince ourselves that M. Garreau understands the situation well and that he will do what is necessary to make the direction of the Mandatory administration conform to the arrangements between us. The realization of this can no longer be a question of a month or a week, but a question of a day and hours."

High Commissioner Martel instructed his deputy in Damascus to talk with the Syrian government in an attempt to satisfy Ankara's demands. Jamil Mardam listened while the French official emphasized the necessity of détente with Ankara, of assuring Turkish preponderance in the Sanjak, and of removing "the two functionaries most representative of the previous regime": Alaeddin, secretary-general of the Sanjak administration, and financial chief Hassan Jabara. Jamil Mardam had likely been briefed before the discussion, and, while completely deploring the situation, he nevertheless admitted that it would be impossible for Syria to oppose it. Nonetheless, he insisted that Syria should have a strong interest in participating in the negotiations that would be opening at Ankara, especially the negotiations on renewing the frontier accord.[27] On May 11, Garreau signed a set of orders to placate the Turkish government. Jabara, Ankara's chief target, was furloughed along with Alaeddin and Salahaddin, the administrator of the Antioch district. Two other high officials, both on Turkey's list of undesirables, were retired, and two local administrators against whom Turkey had lodged complaints were fired. The Aktepe administrator, an Alawi, would be replaced by a Turk, and the disarmament of the rural guards would continue.[28]

As the Sanjak's Republican People's Party and the League of National Action squared off in their efforts to recruit the most voters, the men appointed by the League of Nations to supervise each of the bureaus filed reports detailing intimidation and fraud by both groups. The president of the bureau in Reyhanlı, site of the fatal confrontation in front of the League observers a few months earlier, relayed complaints he received from Arab villagers that their village leaders were preventing them from coming to the bureau to register. The next day, Arabs fled as a local landowner threatened them and fired his pistol.[29] On May 10, a group of Turks complained to the president of another bureau that a criminal who had been condemned to death in Turkey was spreading anti-Turkish propaganda and trying to keep Turks from inscribing, calling them infidels and threatening to kill them. Officials received notice of fraud as well, including a note claiming that Turks were using registration cards that belonged to Sanjak residents who had already died in Turkey.

By May 9, voters had begun inscribing themselves as "Sunni Muslims," despite the intervention of the Turkish consuls and Kemalist leaders. Since this "Sunni Muslim" was not a category included on the list of seven communities, they were claiming to belong in the "Other" category. Turkish representatives walked out of the electoral bureaus in protest, claiming these registrations were contrary to the regulations and the result of outside agitation.[30] They demanded that the question posed should be "To which nationality do you belong," not "To which community." When the president of one bureau asked one voter to which community he belonged, the villager handed him a piece of paper on which was written "inscribe me in the community 'other communities.'" To this official, a Swedish attorney, the attempt at secrecy reflected the very strong propaganda to which the villagers had been subjected.[31]

Turkish consul Karasapan sent his protests to the secretary of the League of Nations, the president of the ad-hoc Committee of the Council, and to French delegate Garreau objecting that Turks should not be permitted to register as Sunni Muslims in the "other communities" designation. He argued that Committee of Experts who had written the Fundamental Law had envisioned "other communities" as a collection of defined, recognized minority communities. "This grouping had been agreed on by the technical committee in Geneva in order to provide small communities (Circassians, Jews, Catholics, Maronites, etc.) with the possibility that they could jointly elect representatives. . . . The Electoral Bureau could not for example inscribe in the list of the 'other communities' a voter who claimed to belong to the Mormon community." Someone whose community was already listed should not be allowed to be inscribed in the "other communities" category, he argued, without specifying the minority group to which they belonged, one included on the list of recognized minorities.

Karasapan blamed local authorities for encouraging people to inscribe themselves in a Muslim Sunni community as a way to divide the Turkish community of the Sanjak into two parts, thereby preventing the Turks from being the "majority that it would have been by right." Initially, he claimed, the electoral commission had declined to register these people in a category that had not been approved by the Fundamental Law; it was only because of French urging that these Sunni Muslims were now being permitted to inscribe in the category "other communities." Karasapan insisted that registering Turks in this "Other" category was in clear contravention of the Fundamental Law. Sunni Muslims had no statutory existence and, indeed, should not, since they constituted the great majority in the Sanjak, accounting for some 85 percent of the Turks and 15 percent of the Arabs. Karasapan pointed out that it was this very separation *within* the Sunni community that the Fundamental Law rested on. He concluded, "The false application of these Geneva decisions can have no other goal or consequence except to destroy the great Turkish majority," and he demanded that the practice be stopped. Garreau denied accusations that the French were encouraging this sort of registration. On the contrary, he pointed out that he personally had tried to encourage the cohesion of the Turkish community, even to the point of encouraging dissident Turks to reconcile with the Kemalists.[32] The "other communities" crisis, though minimal in its real impact (only 291 individuals by May 16) suggested the limitations to Ankara's insistence that each voter be free to choose his community.

Despite the continuing efforts of the Turcophiles, early registration results showed registrations almost evenly divided between Turks and non-Turks; this worried French officials who understood Ankara's expectations.[33] Garreau wrote with evident relief that the May 11 registrations in the northern section of Kirikhan had gone smoothly: the local population of Turks and Kurds had registered largely as Turks. Even an anti-Kemalist deputy "surrendered to the offers of the Halkevi and went to Dörtyol where a sum of 4,000 livres was to be paid him to accelerate the conversion of the anti-Kemalist elements in his area."[34] Karasapan traveled to Aktepe to reproach Turcophile Kurds and the notables of the nearby villages for the large number of people who had not yet inscribed on the Turkish list; indeed, he castigated them by pointing out that some had inscribed on the Arab list. The consul left promising to arrange the freedom of those who had recently been arrested at Aktepe for troubling the public order.[35]

Nonetheless, with Turkish registrations at 50 percent by the morning of May 13, Turkish authorities were alleging serious tampering by the mandatory authorities to explain the unexpectedly low registration numbers. Karasapan protested against what he called the sabotage of the elections and claimed that Franco-Turkish collaboration was at risk.[36] French ambassador Ponsot claimed that Numan Menemencioğlu was similarly disturbed by the results, which he believed should by then have assured at least 55 percent Turks. "He continues to blame the support given by the authorities to propaganda inspired by religious fanaticism, which detached some Sunni Turks, but above all prevents Alawis from inscribing as Turks." Menemencioğlu feared that if the current pressure continued, the Turkish majority could be reduced to a minority, and insisted that Garreau must behave "in the spirit of the accord of March 10."[37]

The registration process presented technical challenges to the League of Nations representatives. On May 13, Kirikhan bureau president C. V. Dodgson reported that he had expelled the Turkish representative for having, over the course of the past three days, challenged the inscription of every Armenian who appeared. Six days later, Dodgson became convinced that there was "an organization among the Armenians for the production of certificates and identity cards" whose leader had the support of local village headmen and priests.[38] Jonas Lie, a Norwegian law professor who had previously helped to administer the Saar Plebiscite, drew a particularly challenging task: many of the villagers from his section were migrants, either as agricultural laborers or herders. The list provided by the local government bore little resemblance to the people who came to register in the election bureau, there were no birth date records, and many voters even arrived without the necessary certificates from the village head. When Lie decided to inscribe the villagers on the basis of the verbal declarations of village elders, the Turkish representative began to contest the registrations of all those who appeared without identity cards or an official receipt for payment of taxes, even if he knew the people. In the end, Lie claimed that there were almost three hundred Arabs he was unable to register, since they produced neither identity cards nor any other documents.

When Turks were a minority at 49 percent on May 14,[39] Menemencioğlu spread the blame widely, attributing responsibility not only to French colonial administrators but also to the League of Nations electoral commission and local anti-Turkish officials. He was particularly concerned about Sunni Turks not registering as Turks, which he claimed was a result of propaganda, of intervention in the bureaus' operations, and of "the triple filtering barrier" at the entrances of the registration bureaus. Turkey's prime minister, Celal Bayar, alleged publicly that France was engaged in various maneuvers to sow discord among the Turks. He claimed that the Sanjak's Turcophiles were being subjected to inadmissible treatment with the knowledge and tolerance of the mandatory administration. According to Bayar, French authorities were engaging in violence, suppressing pro-Turkish demonstrations, and using the bayonet to subject the people of Hatay to Paris's own agenda. Turkey's prime minister recommended that the Turcophiles should await developments with the composure that characterizes people certain of their rights, explaining that necessary measures were being taken.[40]

Kemalist efforts to bring non-Turkish voters to register "as Turks" continued to get mixed results. Turkish activists managed to split the Circassian community of Reyhanlı, paying a Circassian lycée teacher and two others to encourage people to inscribe as members of the Turkish community. Although prominent Circassians accepted invitations to meet with local Turcophiles, they refused to register as Turks.[41] Alawis continued to be divided. After an earlier parting, the Turkish consul managed to reconcile with Ali Ağa, head of Abajili village, on May 16 and kissed the older man's beard, exclaiming "all that has happened has happened. The task is for the events not to begin again, and to turn aside the ideas that divide us." The rapprochement was effective: that day, only area Turcophiles inscribed.[42] Also on that day, however, an estimated one hundred Alawi women and children walked through Alexandretta's Yenişehir quarter crying for long life to (dismissed financial officer) Hassan Jabara and down with the Alawi Kemalists. Local officials alleged that the demonstration had been instigated by a local Arab nationalist, who had promised to distribute flour and two francs to each participant.[43]

As registrations continued to reflect uncertainty, both sides complained of unfair pressure. Turcophiles protested in Reyhanlı on May 17 when armed Kurdish activists ambushed a group of peasants forty meters from the election bureau. According to Karasapan, neither the gendarmes nor the militiamen nor the soldiers intervened, despite the victims' appeal for help, and no one was arrested for the attack. Reimers and Anker were in the Turkish consul's office when the victims arrived, he continued, and the men "saw with their own eyes the pitiable state of the victims." Turkish and Kurdish villagers had stayed away from the bureau, unreassured about their safety despite the local commander's arrival with his entire available force. The Turkish delegation had left the bureau in protest, while Arabs continued to register.[44] A fight broke out in front of a Kirikhan electoral bureau two days later when an Arab leader slapped an Arab who had inscribed as a Turk.[45]

As Turkish officials complained about the unfair suppression of the Turkish vote, French and League of Nations officials were hearing escalating charges of a well-coordinated Turkish campaign of intimidation. Lugt was conducting registration operations in the villages around Kirikhan on May 18 when he received a complaint that the head of the registry office was preventing local Arabs from getting their identity cards. In another incident, a group of Turks had gone to a neighboring non-Turkish village, firing their weapons; the villagers had fled. Officials reported that Turkish consul Karasapan told his Kirikhan audience, "It is Turkey that commands here. What are the French and the Arabs doing here?"[46]

On the evening of May 18, Turkish registrations were only at 47.6 percent. Martel described the unsavory situation in which he found himself to the Foreign Ministry. The Ankara regime insisted that a Turkish majority existed in the Sanjak, and, despite Paris's agreement, it appeared increasingly unlikely that the electoral registrations would reflect one. The Turkish government had already rejected French ambassador Ponsot's suggestion that elections be adjourned and another means used to choose representatives. Martel feared that it was becoming increasingly unlikely that the Turkish proportion of registrations would increase, because the areas already registered were those with the highest Turkish population. France had accepted "Turkish preponderance" in principle "by the memorandum of March 10," but it now appeared that the promised Turkish majority would be unattainable. In the circumstances, Martel feared, Turkey could use the current conditions to threaten a "coup de force." Martel recommended that France change its interpretation of its March 10 promise. "It is important that we disengage as fast as possible from this formula on pain of seeing the Turks, in the shelter of our accepting the principle, exploit against us the least incident, in case of need, to resort to extreme solutions."[47]

Although he was growing certain that the Turks would not attain a majority of registrations, Martel ordered his delegates to establish barriers on the access routes to the Sanjak to prevent non-Turks from entering. Only those with permits provided by French officials would be allowed entrance, and Sanjak natives who were qualified voters would be given passes.[48] The president of the electoral commission, Reimers, complained that military forces were barring the routes between the Sanjak and Syria—allegations confirmed by a group of Armenians and Greek Orthodox would-be voters—while at the same time leaving the northern border with Turkey open. Reimers objected to the French efforts to interrogate people wanting to enter the Sanjak from Aleppo and Latakia, reminding Garreau that, according to the terms of the electoral regulation, it was the electoral commission alone that was competent to decide if a person qualified for Sanjak citizenship. He insisted that the mandatory authorities take no measure to obstruct people's freedom to inscribe and vote.[49]

As Reimers tried to assure equal access to the elections, and Martel contemplated ways to increase the proportion of Turkish registrations, the ad hoc Committee of the Council met in Geneva on May 21 to consider Turkey's scathing denunciation of the electoral commission. The Ankara government insisted that Turks should not be allowed to register in the "other communities" category, in which, they maintained, the writers of the revised electoral regulations had intended to include the members of specific, enumerated communities: Latin, Maronite, Melkite, Israelite, Druze, Ismaili, and Circassian. Reginald J. Bowker, the British representative on the committee, marveled at the Turkish inconsistency. It was the Turkish government that had insisted on the ability of each elector to register in any community he chose, and the Turkish delegate to the Committee of the Council had always insisted on a "strict and literal interpretation of the Fundamental Law." But, as Bowker pointed out, "there is nothing in the Fundamental Law to say that persons registering under 'other communities' shall specify the subgroup to which they belong." In this case, the Turkish government was trying precisely to restrict the free choice of registrants by claiming that it had been the "intention" of the revised regulations that each member of the "other communities" category must define the community to which he belonged. In the end, the Committee of the Council in Geneva decided to accept the registrations already made; in the future, however, each person inscribing in the "other communities" must indicate the community he claimed.[50]

Registrations at the end of May 22 showed Turkish inscriptions at 47 percent. Some in Turkey advocated an occupation of Hatay as the only way to resolve the situation, when faced with what they deemed French actions and procrastination. Atatürk's decision not to engage in military action over Alexandretta seemed no longer certain.[51] The Ankara administration blamed the French for anti-Turkish bias, and censured the electoral commission for unfair behavior. The Turkish government insisted that the earlier separation from the Sanjak of five districts (Bahir, Bassit, El Akrad, Jerablus, and Jazirah) with their estimated sixty thousand Turkish-speakers was responsible for the apparent lack of a Turkish majority.[52] Nonetheless, Atatürk's government continued to insist that the Turks still comprised the majority in the Sanjak, and if the registration figures did not reflect that reality, it must be the result of manipulation and French scheming. Instead of subverting Turkish registration, the Ankara regime insisted, the French must fulfill their "gentleman's agreement."

The alarm of the British grew as they watched the registration results. So far, not only had the Turks been unable to bring along the other communities to register as Turks, but, indeed, some of the Sanjak's Turkish-speakers had been refusing to do so. Moreover, they were hearing rumors of a secret agreement by which the French had promised Turkey a majority of the seats in the new Sanjak Assembly, a promise made before the registrations had even begun.

Percy Loraine, British ambassador in Ankara, reported on May 20 that his French counterpart acknowledged "the bargain." Although it was "a bad one," he concluded, "[it] must be fulfilled." Loraine summarized the informal Franco-Turkish agreement this way: "If on June 10th the French mandatory Power fails to deliver promised goods namely viz: a pro-Turkish majority of 55 percent at least a most unpleasant situation will arise. Turks will consider French Government [to] have broken faith and that this failure releases them from all obligations they have accepted vis-à-vis French, including partition of mandated territory and all agreements including that relating to their southern frontier." Both Loraine and his French counterpart Ponsot were convinced that the Turkish government would not use force, despite rumors of a pending rupture in diplomatic relations. On the other hand, Foreign Minister Aras told Loraine that if there was no pro-Turkish majority on June 10, "there would be nothing left for him but suicide: his personal responsibility was engaged up to the hilt that the French would fulfill their side of the bargain; he could not survive the shame of being let down." Loraine summarized the electoral situation: "French maintain that pro-Turkish majority does not exist and cannot be produced. Turks maintain local French action supported by military has deliberately prevented registration of pro-Turkish voters by violence and intimidation. And Doctor Aras tells me that he can produce chapter and verse for a large number of cases of this sort." According to the British diplomat, Turkey's press was publishing violently anti-French articles. The government in Ankara was "absolutely convinced that they have made every possible concession" and tolerated a great deal in order to keep alive the prospect of Franco-Turkish friendship but could suffer nothing more.[53]

As the British Foreign Office learned the details of the secret agreement that Turkey was accusing France of violating, they found themselves in an awkward position. From Geneva, Bowker summarized the situation:

> As a member of the League and a participator in the work of the Committee of Five, His Majesty's Government naturally wish to see the elections carried out fairly and properly. Moreover, they are not a party to, nor can they be expected to have any official knowledge of, an agreement reached between the Turks and the French behind the back of the League and of the United Kingdom, which settled beforehand the result of the elections, the operation of which had been entrusted to the League.

Bowker now found himself, the Committee of the Council, and his government compromised by a deal that would preclude the honest functioning of the League's electoral program.

When the Turkish prime minister officially informed the British ambassador about the "private arrangement" they had made with the French at Geneva in March, C. W. Baxter at the London Foreign Office called the agreement "quite indefensible." "Its substance was that the elections, somehow or other (presumably by fair means or foul), should result in a Turkish majority." This agreement had rendered "almost useless" the electoral commission's work in trying to run the elections according to the regulations. According to Baxter, if the two countries had agreed on a new parliament with a Turkish majority, they should have set it up without bringing in the League of Nations. "Nor was there any need to go through the farce of holding elections." Baxter was furious:

> The fact that these sham elections, whose result is determined semi-secretly in advance, are being held under the auspices of the League may enable the French and Turks to escape some of the responsibility for their shady bargain, but it will confer no credit on the League to have been used for such a purpose. . . . It will be noticed that the Turks are quite unrepentant. Their one fear is that the elections may, in spite of their efforts, go against them and that the French will not be able to secure for them the promised Turkish majority.[54]

The Foreign Office seemed astonished that, having abused the League of Nations for their own purposes, the Turkish government now had the audacity to seek British support. "In the circumstances, I find it inadmissible that Turkish Government should now expect His Majesty's Government to appreciate force of a complaint that French Government are dishonouring their bargain in failing to see that elections produce a Turkish majority."[55] Turkish foreign minister Rüştü Aras claimed that he thought the French had informed the British about the March 10 agreement, and was "astonished" that they had not. In any case, Aras insisted that Turkey had not and would not intentionally act behind the backs of His Majesty's government. For Turkey's government, however, the most urgent goal was attaining that majority among the Sanjak's registered voters.[56]

As it was becoming increasingly clear to French administrators that the Turks could not command a majority in the Sanjak, Kemal Atatürk took to the road once again to demonstrate the urgency of Turkey's claim. The Turkish president's train journey in January 1937 had brought immediate results, encouraging France to acquiesce to Turkey's demands in Geneva. Now, Atatürk embarked on a train to Mersin on May 19, and traveled on to Adana on May 24. So ill that he had trouble even standing, Atatürk took salutes at military parades for hours in each city, and made a tour of the military bases in these provinces close to Antakya. Like that earlier trip, Atatürk's journey had been intentionally designed to make the greatest impression on France at a pivotal moment, this time by creating the impression that Turkey was preparing "an *Anschluss*."[57]

Violence on the ground in the Sanjak itself escalated from intimidation through murder as each group tried to recruit its majority and keep its members from defecting.[58] A shooting took place outside the electoral bureau in Alexandretta, Turkish landowners threatened their Arab workers in the Reyhanlı area, and allegations that voters were being blocked from access to the registration bureaus became common. Roland Gorgé, presiding over Kirikhan registrations, reported that the Turkish representatives had been absent for three days, which he attributed to the fury of the city's Arabs after the recent murder of a local Arab. Despite Gorgé's efforts to reassure Turks and encourage their presence at the bureau, a Turkish representative informed him that the Turks had lost confidence in the gendarmerie and the League of Nations electoral commission and claimed that the Turks would no longer participate in the inscriptions in the district. Gorgé objected, noting that Turkish village leaders were circulating freely in the city, and one had even come to register in the bureau.[59] In Antioch, groups of Turks tried to search Alawi and Arab passersby on May 23, creating a "certain nervousness" in the city. Turkish consul Karasapan explained to Garreau that their intent had been "to assist the authorities in discovering arms carried by the members of the League of National Action and the Sanjak Union." Panic in the Arab-owned shops led the suq to remain closed all day.

"The Arab village of Kuchuk Ayranji situated in the plain of Amık was attacked tonight by Turkish elements," the police report that night began. "The village head was killed and three inhabitants injured . . . the home of the headman set on fire and a child burned alive." The armed band of Turks and Kurds was pursued by two platoons of cavalry, and officials began searching homes and making arrests. Garreau accompanied Burnier, prosecutor of the Special Tribunal, who accompanied local police as they searched the Halkevi of neighboring Reyhanlı and seized its papers. Garreau wrote to Martel that he hoped this behavior would have "the effect of stopping at least momentarily the increasingly frequent aggressions and violent acts of the Turks." Garreau then met with excited Arab leaders, urging calm. The Arab shops, closed as a sign of mourning, reopened, and Garreau dispatched a section of machine-gunners to the area. Karasapan left Antioch for Reyhanlı to begin his own inquiry.[60]

Turkey's continuing efforts to enroll Alawis met with limited success. Garreau assigned extra security to Antioch's predominantly Alawi Dört Ayak quarter, anticipating violence when the electoral bureau opened on May 23. The area had been the site of many previous skirmishes as Kemalists tried to increase the number of Alawis registering as Turks. Garreau expected Karasapan to keep a low profile amid the tension in the quarter; instead, the Turkish consul drove his car through a very dense crowd, flying a Turkish flag. Karasapan complained to

Garreau that someone spat on him as he passed, accusing the mandatory authorities of being unable to assure order.[61] The Turkish representative at the electoral
bureau in Antioch's Affan quarter informed electoral bureau president Fernand
Houssa that a local Alawi shaykh had received death threats for wanting to
inscribe as a Turk. Houssa refused the Turkish representative's demand that the
shaykh be inscribed at another bureau, instead calling the police chief and
making him personally responsible for the shaykh, even ordering that the shaykh
be accompanied back to his home after his inscription. Houssa then turned to
the shaykh, and asked him to declare the community to which he belonged.
When the shaykh responded, "to the Alawi community," the Turkish representative protested that this inscription was made "under the pressure of the street"
and threatened to leave. Houssa asked if the Turkish representative wished to
register a formal complaint, but he refused and walked out.[62] Local Kemalists
and the Turkish government saw the episode as proof of the bias of the electoral
commission: a bureau president had refused a request to change the shaykh's
electoral bureau.

Despite Atatürk's journey and escalating Kemalist efforts, Turkish inscriptions remained stubbornly below 48 percent. Foreign Minister Aras addressed
the Grand National Assembly on May 27, accusing France of doing everything it
could to prevent Turkish success in the Sanjak's elections. Turkey had excellent
relations with all countries except France, he claimed.[63] While the Ankara regime
was accusing France of thwarting Turkey's goals and subverting their agreement,
Turcophile leaders in the Sanjak were now blaming the electoral commission for
the failure of Kemalists' propaganda with the non-Turkish communities. Commissioners reported the "increasingly menacing attitude" of the local Turks, who
were accusing them of colluding with the mandatory authorities "to prevent the
people of the Sanjak from freely exercising their pro-Turkish aspirations."[64]

"The massacre continues," Menemencioğlu told Ponsot on May 30. "At
Antioch in the Dört Ayak quarter, six Turks were injured this morning with the
knowledge and in view of the authorities. At Reyhanlı the situation is no less
dangerous. In the whole country one learns of new crimes and the population
lives in terror." The secretary-general of Turkey's Foreign Ministry claimed that
pickets of ten to fifteen armed men were surrounding the voting bureaus and
keeping Turcophiles from getting access. Menemencioğlu complained that in
the days since Turkey had received formal assurances from Paris on May 24, the
situation had deteriorated. "For reasons that escape us, it is clear that since the
March 10 accord the orders of the French government have not been obeyed."
Despite it all, he claimed, the increasingly frustrated Turks of the Sanjak had
remained calm under orders from Atatürk, in the face of their inequitable treatment and the threats against them. Ponsot warned Paris that the Turkish government might make "a decision" soon, as the prime minister was scheduled to

return to Istanbul, where he could confer with Atatürk, who was staying at the Dolmabahçe palace.[65]

By May 30, the French had made their decision. Martel informed the Foreign Ministry that he had transmitted its orders to Garreau, along with his own emphasis on the "unavoidable nature of the obligations assumed regarding the Turks." Martel gave his assurance that his delegate understood the situation. Garreau would emphasize the aggressive tone of Aras's speech before the Turkish Grand National Assembly when the French delegate met with the heads of the various non-Turkish communities to urge them to encourage "the massive defections required to assure the Turkish majority."[66]

Garreau asked the League of Nations electoral commission to support his new instructions from the high commissioner. Although he had previously insisted on a policy of nonintervention with the electoral commission, Garreau now explained the requirements of the current situation to commission secretary Anker. Garreau asked for the commissioners' backing in order to avoid the serious complications to be expected if Turkey did not get its anticipated representation. Garreau believed that Anker both understood his arguments and was "disposed to favor various adjustments" that would help attain the necessary outcome: a Turkish majority in the registrations. Garreau listed the required steps: First, the electoral commission should reopen the electoral bureau of Aktepe for some four hundred "moderate" Turks who had previously abstained, and Garreau would work to encourage their registration as Turks. Second, Garreau urged the bureaus to inscribe more than five hundred Turks coming from Turkey without insisting on rigorous proof of their rights to Sanjak nationality. On the other hand, he asked that the bureaus be very strict in permitting the inscription of the many Arabs and bedouins in the Amık region, many of whom originated or resided part of the year outside the Sanjak. Finally, the electoral bureaus should favor appeals by Turks, and move into Turkish villages some of the bureaus currently in non-Turkish villages. Garreau promised Martel that he and Anker "will together look for all other means susceptible to raise the number of Turks inscribed compatible with the duties of the commission."

Garreau was less sanguine about the outcome of his discussions with Karasapan. When Garreau informed the Turkish consul of his new instructions and their need to work together to achieve the desired outcome, Karasapan first demanded apologies "for the alleged laceration of the portrait of Atatürk at the Halkevi at Reyhanlı in my presence and for the outrage of which he claimed to have been the victim in the streets of Antioch." Garreau reminded Karasapan that he had already expressed his regrets for the incident in Antioch, but denied that the photograph of Atatürk had been desecrated.[67] Karasapan conveyed his hope that registrations be suspended for five days "so that in the meantime the situation in the Sanjak would be completely modified." Garreau suggested that

Abdurrahman Melek, Kemalist leader of Antioch, be named director of the interior, a position from which he might be able to influence the registration process to favor the Turks. He was stunned when Karasapan immediately demanded instead that Melek be made head of a provisional government, "with full latitude to lay off immediately all the undesirable officials, to purge the gendarmerie, and to welcome a certain number of Turkish gendarmes." Garreau refused, claiming to be unable to effect such a dramatic reorganization in the administration of the Sanjak. Karasapan exploded. "The farce has continued long enough." If Garreau did not act immediately to form a provisional government, Karasapan threatened to move his family to Turkey for their safety, and concluded by asking Garreau for an escort to accompany him and his family to the frontier immediately.[68] Relations between Garreau and Karasapan had by then deteriorated so far that Karasapan insisted on circumventing Garreau completely. He telegraphed the Sanjak's military commander, Philibert Collet, within minutes to reassure him that he would keep his family at Alexandretta and his own journey over the border to Dörtyol would be only to communicate with his government.[69] Collet recognized that these conversations were actually an effort to set the military and civil authorities against each other in hopes of creating misunderstandings he could exploit.[70]

Garreau appealed to the electoral commission to suspend operations for five days, as Karasapan had requested. Violence had become rampant, and the Turkish numbers were still hovering below 50 percent. Garreau explained to the commissioners that the intent was "to permit local authorities to take measures necessary to maintain order and for the ultimate smooth running of the electoral operations."[71] Suspension of the inscriptions was effective May 31 at noon. That day, Garreau met with Armenian, Greek Orthodox, and Alawi notables, trying to convince them that they must abstain from registering "in order to avoid the worst." Encountering "a very lively resistance," especially among the Armenians, Garreau decided his next step would be to speak with the spiritual leaders of the various communities.[72] Martel instructed Garreau to provide Melek with all the functions requested as head of a provisional Sanjak government, reserving only the French role in providing security.[73]

The last day of May was bloody in the Sanjak; two Turks were killed by bandits, one Alawite was murdered by a Turkish crowd, and an Arab was killed while taking part in an attack against Turks.[74] The violence added to the renewed wave of Turkish pressure on French authorities in Antioch, Beirut, Ankara, and Paris. Garreau's meeting with Karasapan was, surprisingly, the most cordial of these encounters. Garreau informed the Turkish diplomat that the electoral commission had just agreed to suspend registration, and he thought he had brought the commissioners around to understanding the necessity for a Turkish majority. To facilitate this goal, the electoral commission had agreed to reopen the Aktepe bureau so that Turks who had previously refused to register could now inscribe. Moreover, the commissioners had, according to Garreau, agreed to liberally register immigrants from Turkey, and to hold the transient Arab population to a very high standard of proof before accepting their Sanjak citizenship. At the same time, Garreau told Karasapan about his lack of success in convincing leaders of the non-Turkish communities to abstain from voting, and then turned to the new status of Ankara protégé Melek, recently appointed director of the interior and administrator of the Sanjak, who would have control over both the police and the gendarmerie.

High Commissioner Martel's meeting with Akdur in Beirut was testier. While informing him of recent bloody events in the Sanjak, Martel emphasized the danger of Turkey's "systematically alarming interpretation" of such incidents. Martel warned the Turkish representative against using the recent conflicts and assassinations as a pretext for "even a symbolic Turkish military intervention." Turkey's consul responded that only the registration results were important. He asked Martel for formal assurances, noting that although recent measures seemed to help toward that goal, in the end, "the results would not depend exclusively on us."[75]

That evening, French foreign minister Georges Bonnet met the Turkish ambassador to Paris and recounted the actions his government had taken. "I reminded him one by one of the successive tangible proofs we had given his government of our determination to push the spirit of conciliation to its extreme limits." Bonnet then expressed his hope that this attitude would be returned, but that so far the French felt that their "desire for friendship" had been met only with Ankara's new demands. Turkish ambassador Davaz insisted that tensions in the Sanjak were growing hourly, and the Turkish population was increasingly the victim of acts that even included assassination. Referring to the recent violence, Davaz claimed that the biggest problem for the future would be protecting public order. Bonnet concluded, "It is obvious that Turkey is orienting itself toward the exploitation of this new source of strife."[76]

While Garreau, Bonnet, and Martel spoke with Turkish officials abroad, Ponsot met in Ankara first with Menemencioğlu and then with Aras. Menemencioğlu complained vehemently. "Despite assurances given, situation hasn't stopped getting worse, three Turks killed today at Antioch. Complete insecurity at Amık. He has come to fear massacres," Ponsot telegraphed. Menemencioğlu complained that the collaboration with Garreau "is proved to be impossible from now on." The Turks proposed military collaboration to provide the equality of effective forces for maintaining order.[77]

In his meeting with Aras, Ponsot emphasized the steps France had taken to appease Turkey's demands. He notified the Turkish foreign minister that Paris had now agreed to a suspend the registrations "to allow the Kemalist Party the persuasive effort necessary to return sentiments to a healthier appreciation of the forces and the dangers present, and, essentially, to reestablish the electoral game to its own profit." At the same time, France had assigned Turkey's chosen candidate as interior minister of the Sanjak. Finally, in deference to what they called Karasapan's "extreme demand," Garreau had given up his control over the local police. After calling Aras's attention to these "new indications of our confidence and good faith," Ponsot insisted that if these public actions were unable to win détente over the Sanjak, the Turkish government would be revealing "general dispositions irreconcilable with their professed sentiments" of Franco-Turkish friendship. Responsibility would then be exclusively on the Turkish government. Although officials in Paris continued to hope for improved relations, he said, they were becoming increasingly frustrated, and beginning to consider whether Turkey might have other motives.

> The dispositions shown day to day by the Kemalist authorities in the Sanjak of Alexandretta, despite the efforts that we multiply to give them satisfaction, are of a nature to shed doubt on the sincerity of Turkey's friendly and pacific protestations toward us. The forbearance that we have not ceased to provide in response, in a manner as comprehensive and effective as possible, to all the wishes formulated by Turkey seems only to encourage it to show herself each day more irreconcilable. If the clear evidence of our desire for entente encounters in exchange only a growing aggravation of the Turkish attitude, we must consider that the designs of the Government of Ankara are other than those that— despite all appearances—we have wanted to ascribe to her until now.[78]

Aras denied that Turkey had wanted a suspension of electoral operations, and asserted that "none of the measures envisaged at Paris, apologies, arrest of those responsible, communication to the press, have been accepted by M. Garreau, and that is why he appears today little qualified to be the agent of the desired improvement." According to Aras, nothing had changed since the new orders had arrived from Paris on May 24. Instead, he claimed, "the situation gets worse day by day in an atmosphere of anarchy and terror. None can dispute that since the beginning of electoral operations 30 Turks have been killed and one thousand were the object of cruelty on the part of the bands organized under cover of the Sanjak Union, nor the reports that, fearing massacres, refugees have begun flowing toward the border. No protection has been assured them. In these conditions, in whom could one place confidence?" Aras declared that his government refused any responsibility in this situation, "which it has denounced from the first day while offering cooperation which has not been accepted." Aras went one step further, claiming that the only way to restore order and allow the return of confidence would be through friendly military collaboration, in the spirit of the recent agreement between the two General Staffs, a joint military project with equal troops supplied by France and Turkey.[79]

When Ponsot learned of the Turkish Foreign Ministry's demand, he urged that, if the French government was willing to consider the possibility of military collaboration, Paris should take the initiative and propose an immediate meeting to discuss practical ways to carry it out.[80] Martel, on the other hand, was extremely alarmed at the prospect of Turkish military action, even if it was conducted jointly with France. He insisted in his telegram to the Foreign Ministry in Paris that the Turkish government was using the current insecurity in the Sanjak to make France "recognize the necessity of an entry of Turkish forces for a joint action." As far as Martel was concerned, this was to be avoided at all costs. Once they had found a pretext to send troops, he argued, they would refuse to retreat, and could then cite a variety of pretexts justifying a continuing Turkish military presence. Their presence would have catastrophic consequences, according to Martel, who claimed that after Turkish troops arrived, either the electoral operations would continue and the minorities voting against the Turks would immediately suffer reprisals or the Turkish troops would themselves prevent the minorities from voting, if necessary to the point of massacre. "In either case," he continued, "we would be associated with these excesses against Christian minorities with no possibility of disengaging our responsibilities."[81] Although Martel was willing to contrive to increase the Turkish proportion of registrants, he was unwilling to tolerate sharing power with Turkey or to participate in direct intimidation or violence against Christians in the Sanjak.

Martel seemed willing to go to almost any lengths to avoid this end. He reassured the French Foreign Ministry that, in order to avoid giving the Turks an excuse to invade the Sanjak, he would proclaim a state of siege, placing all the security forces under the orders of Commander Collet. "Moreover," he wrote, "the only argument that we could currently make with the minorities to obtain their abstention and create a Turkish majority is the need to avoid the worst, which is to say, precisely, the entry of Turkish troops." "For now," he told Paris, "I am taking the following tactic: exercising the maximum pressure on the minorities of the Sanjak before the reinstitution of inscriptions." To avoid a Turkish military invasion and to protect Christians, then, Martel was willing both to impose military rule and to pressure the Sanjak's minorities into giving up the rights provided by the Statute and Fundamental Law.[82]

Pressure from Turkish officials overshadowed French concerns with the League of Nations electoral process. When electoral commission president Reimers notified Garreau that the commissioners had agreed to suspend operations as Garreau had requested, Reimers insisted that the delay was intended to "permit local authorities to take all necessary measures to maintain order and for the ultimate best progress of the electoral operations." Reimers notified Garreau at the same time that the commissioners were quite concerned about the news being disseminated in the press, flying through the population, and being reported by delegates of many communities. "These reports indicate a psychological state of genuine anguish," which tended to make credible the declarations from various groups that voters' freedom of choice was being compromised. Since article 3 of the regulations gave the electoral commission the right "to take measures necessary to assure the free exercise of the right of inscription of every person," Reimers insisted on the commissioners' right to judge whether the new conditions "respond to the spirit and to the letter of the texts elaborated at Geneva" before recommencing registration.[83]

The commissioners sent League of Nations secretary-general Avenol a report on the secret agreement concluded between France and Turkey, and insisted that they could not associate themselves with pressure tactics. Instead, they suggested modifying the Fundamental Law to assure the Turks a majority, twenty-two seats of the forty in the Assembly. Martel thought this solution would be consistent with the March 10 Franco-Turkish understanding, but he was dubious that "this subterfuge" would satisfy the Turkish government. "It does not respond to their essential preoccupation, which is to make a Turkish majority appear in the Sanjak." In any case, Martel explained, Peter Anker was on his way back to Geneva, and the electoral commission was willing to delay inscriptions while awaiting a response from the League Council about amending the electoral law.[84]

Having acted as the midwife for the official agreements between France and Turkey, the British government found itself in an awkward position. Diplomat Bowker recognized that the secret Franco-Turkish agreement could lead to the resignation of the League of Nations electoral commission, but he did not consider that to be such a bad thing. "From the League point of view this would really be the best thing so they could then be able to say that their efforts to settle the dispute had been rendered vain by the actions of the two parties concerned who would thenceforward be responsible for finding their own solution. It seems most undesirable that the League should continue to sponsor what will now inevitably be blatantly 'cooked' elections and that the French and Turks should now themselves bear the responsibility for their dishonest behavior."[85]

The March 10 agreement, now in the open, had provided the framework under which French officials in the Sanjak had been operating for months. To fulfill Paris's secret agreement with Ankara, the colonial administration in the Sanjak had sought any methods that might increase the percentage of people registering as Turks. By late May, Garreau had visited the leaders of most of the non-Turkish groups in the Sanjak. When he asked them to abstain from registering as the last means to avoid a Turkish military invasion, they refused. "Since the cause is desperate and the Turkish invasion is inevitable, we refuse to give it a juridical base and we will vote," they replied. Garreau concluded that even if half of the Arabs, Armenians, and Alawites still unregistered inscribed as Turks, it would still be difficult for the Turks to attain 50 percent, let alone the 55 percent needed to acquire the promised twenty-two deputies. Garreau would clearly be unable to produce the results Paris sought.

Numan Menemencioğlu telephoned French ambassador Ponsot late in the evening on June 2, to verify news from the Sanjak. Was it true, he asked, that officials thought it would be almost impossible for the Turks to register more than 45 percent. Were the reports accurate that the commissioners had received protests against the actions of the French authorities who sought to assure a Turkish majority and were considering submitting their resignations? Would Garreau have to discontinue the arrests of Armenians that Commander Collet had begun? Menemencioğlu claimed that the villages were insecure and Arab bands were continuing to flow into the Sanjak so that despite Ponsot's efforts and the assurance of French officials, the situation remained unchanged.[86]

High Commissioner Martel asked Garreau whether he could produce a Turkish majority from the inscriptions. When Garreau acknowledged he could not, the high commissioner turned to Colonel Collet. If both military and civil powers were to be concentrated in Collet's hands, he asked, would it "permit him to employ more radical methods, in the hope of producing among the Alawi community a more accentuated slide?" When Collet answered in the affirmative, Martel turned Garreau's power over to the military commander and decided to declare martial law. Martel explained to the French foreign minister that "this measure, permitting action more expedient for justice, and also [producing] the absence of any incident for two days, will allow Your Excellency to refute the insecurity argument that the Turks would likely make to justify their demand to send troops to the Sanjak."[87] Unable to get the agreed-on Turkish majority under the conditions specified by the Sanjak's new laws, and unwilling to entertain the prospect of sharing military power with Turkey, the French imposed martial law on the Sanjak's population.

7

Martial Law

At ten o'clock in the morning on June 3, Commander Collet took over all of Garreau's powers, consolidating in his own hands both civil and military authority in the Sanjak. Two hours later, he declared martial law.[1] Despite the escalating murders, arson, and assaults that had accompanied voter registration for the first elections to the assembly of the newly independent Sanjak, French high commissioner Martel had not considered security generally threatened. He had instituted martial law to convince the Turkish government that French mandatory officials were taking serious action to stem the violence that Ankara insisted was rampant. Martial law seemed the last recourse to prevent Turkish military intervention during the elections.[2]

Collet's objective was quite different from the goals of the League of Nations electoral commission. Commander Collet had been given complete power over the Sanjak by promising to produce a Turkish majority in the inscriptions; the electoral commission was charged with carrying out equitable and fair registrations, free of coercion. Nonetheless, Collet reassured electoral commission president Reimers that French officials would comply with all of the electoral regulations. Reimers was skeptical, fearing the kinds of steps that would be required to transform the Turks, currently inscribing 48 percent of the Sanjak's voters, into the majority on which the French and Turkish governments had secretly agreed. Citing the recent Romanian precedent, Reimers suggested that France and Turkey modify the electoral regulations to guarantee the Turks a majority of the seats instead of relying on an unlikely turn in the registrations. Although France's representative on the electoral commission agreed that such a change in the electoral regulations would allow the commissioners to pursue the inscription process in an equitable way, Ankara refused to revise the process. If the electoral commission was to carry out the elections as planned, Reimers stated, it would insist on French mandatory authorities providing the requisite freedom and security. Collet provided those assurances.

The commissioners responded a bit skeptically to a request for a second suspension of their operations, pointing out that both France and Turkey had recently emphasized the importance of completing the process as quickly as possible. Although acquiescing to the new delay until June 9 to ensure security, the electoral commission refused responsibility for the consequences of the new schedule. Commission president Reimers noted Collet's assurances that registrations would resume "under conditions of the most complete impartiality and without any pressure, direct or indirect, being tolerated on any elements of the population." The commissioners demanded that martial law not infringe the liberty of the electoral operations; if the principle of free, uncoerced registration was infringed, "we will have nothing more to do here." In addition to the broader concerns, Reimers insisted on allowing free access to the Sanjak for everyone claiming the right to vote. According to the electoral regulations, he reiterated, only the electoral commission could establish who had that right. Although French mandatory authorities could require a simple verification of identity to enter the Sanjak, they must allow anyone claiming to be a citizen to appear at the election bureaus, and let the commissioners evaluate their claims. Collet reassured Reimers vaguely that the liberty of the inscription process would be assured "in the same conditions as previously," promising to study the question of free access for all who wanted to register. Collet reported himself skeptical that Reimers was convinced.[3]

In the same letter in which Collet relayed his promises to Reimers for the complete impartiality of the registration process, he outlined for Martel the measures he planned to assure the Turks a majority in the Antioch district. Collet installed Ankara's protégé Abdurrahman Melek as governor of the Sanjak, appointed sympathetic mayors to Süveydiye and Harbiye, recruited fifty Circassian gendarmes (under the command of noncommissioned Turkish and Circassian officers) to assure the protection of electoral bureaus, arranged for Moroccan units to provide surveillance, and replaced the representatives chosen by the Alawi community with pro-Turkish Alawis. Collet worried that it would be difficult to be discreet while engaging in propaganda among the minorities, especially the Alawis. As he reflected on the discrepancy between his plans and his promises, Collet wondered if the commissioners "would consider these measures as means of pressure and will carry out their threats of this morning." Nonetheless, the commander informed his superior that he would pursue these measures unless the high commissioner sent other instructions.[4]

French promises and French policies infuriated the Syrian government. "When word spread in Damascus that the Turks would be assured 22 of 40 seats in the new Sanjak Parliament in any case," wrote Martel, "indignation against France translated itself into demonstrations." Martel's deputy Count Stanislas Ostrorog spoke with Syrian prime minister Jamil Mardam on June 5 to enlist his aid in controlling the anger on the street. Mardam was "extremely emotional" about the turn of events in the Sanjak. He acknowledged that he had hardly anticipated a resolution that would be favorable to Syria, but it was with "the most painful surprise" that he watched France "deliberately propping up Turkish pretensions," initiating action intended to "assure the Turks a fictitious majority." Pointing out that the Turks had obtained recognition of certain rights in the Sanjak since 1921, Ostrorog reminded the Syrian prime minister that Martel had warned him repeatedly during the 1936 negotiations about the "inevitable manifestation of Turkish ambitions in the Sanjak." Ostrorog portrayed French promises to Turkey as a favor the Paris government had provided to protect the Syrians: "in the current situation France rendered an important service to Syria, favoring a peaceful solution that avoids catastrophe." Ostrorog continued, "It is only by a politics of flexibility and conciliation that one could settle objectively the relations between Turkey and Syria, and it was the French government's job to assume a responsibility, however painful, to assure in the greatest measure the defense of the real interests of Syria." Mardam responded that Syrian public opinion would hold France completely responsible for the loss of the Sanjak, and because of the National Bloc's collaboration with the French, Mardam himself would be found guilty. He already had to defend himself against a variety of grievances, including the anarchy prevailing in Jazira, and the continuing delays in the ratification of the treaty, which were fueling a growing defiance against France and France's National Bloc collaborators. Criticized even by his friends and his colleagues, Mardam was finding his authority and his prestige eroding day by day. This could not continue, he predicted, anticipating that the moment would come soon "when his efforts would be in vain or when he would be forced to concede to the pressure of public opinion." The National Bloc had nothing to show for its policy of honorable cooperation with the colonizers: the Franco-Syrian Treaty, on which they had predicated all of their actions, had not even been submitted to the French Parliament, and now the French had betrayed their promises regarding the Sanjak.

Across Syria, demonstrators took to the streets in opposition to not only Turkey and France but also to the National Bloc government. Markets were closed in Syria's four largest cities, Aleppo, Damascus, Homs, and Hama. Thousands protested in Damascus against French "treason" and the National Bloc's powerlessness.[5] The director of Aleppo's Special Services concluded that France had few supporters in his district. "One could affirm," he concluded, "without resorting to pessimism, that we have the whole of the population against us: the Muslims reproach France for bad faith, the Armenians, who remember the abandonment of Cilicia, put no confidence in us, predicting a new abandonment of the Sanjak to the Turks; as for the Christians, seeing the events rushing toward the advantage of the Turks, they regret having made vows toward France, drawing on themselves the animosity both of the Syrian nationalists and of the Turks. With this state of emotions . . . one could expect violent and serious reactions."[6] In Syrian eyes, France had betrayed the people it had sworn to protect: not only the Syrians it had promised to tutor but also the Armenians and other Christians who had constituted the supposed cause for French interventions in the region for the previous century.

Revelations of the secret March 10 Franco-Turkish agreement evoked fear among some of the Sanjak's population. British subjects requested official permission to fly the British flag "in case of need." An estimated two hundred families left the Sanjak immediately, becoming refugees in Aleppo. According to the mandate's director of security in Beirut, these were Armenian, Christian, and Muslim families fearing a Turkish invasion. To French officials' horror, refugees and students made their way to Aleppo's Italian consulate, asking for Italy's intervention in the Sanjak. The Italian consul was said to have responded by telling them "to appeal to their loving mother," and reassuring them that "in case France takes no further interest in their destiny, Italy would intervene, even militarily, if necessary."[7]

The electoral commission was "furious at 'Gentlemen's Agreement' made by France and Turkey at Geneva behind the back of League and of which they were entirely unaware until recently," wrote British consul Davis from Aleppo. "They were congratulating themselves on the progress made with registration of electors, of whom 28,000 out of total of 50,000 had been inscribed without any visible pressure before operations were suspended on May 31st. British members of the Commission now request that His Majesty's Government should recall them unless some satisfactory 'whitewashing' expedient . . . can be advised."[8] The secret March 10 Franco-Turkish agreement had made a mockery of the electoral process, and the League's commissioners, as well as the project they were implementing, seemed now irredeemably compromised.

Three members of the electoral commission visited Collet on June 5. Commission president Reimers informed the French commander that three Alawi shaykhs had called on the commissioners to complain that Collet had summoned them to convince them of the Alawis' Hittite origins. Reimers insisted that such pressure was unacceptable and would make the electoral commission's mission impossible. Collet responded that he had been charged with a mission by the French government, and he was using the same means as his predecessor to accomplish his task. Collet explained his conduct with the Alawi shaykhs as condescension: "faced with the inadequacy of the average intelligence of this morning's Alawi visitors, I satisfied myself with explaining to them the necessity for their community to maintain friendly relations with the Turkish majority." Reimers reiterated his demand that the inscription process could continue only under conditions of complete impartiality; they could tolerate neither direct nor indirect pressure by any group.[9] After meeting with Turkish consul Karasapan to convey his discussion with Reimers as he had promised, Collet inquired about recent rumors predicting the imminent entry of Turkish troops. Karasapan reassured him that the Turkish commander at Dörtyol was one of his friends, and that any troop movements on the border would simply be standard practices for the season.[10]

Reimers began submitting objections to Collet immediately on the reopening of some of the electoral bureaus. Armenians alleged that French authorities were refusing to permit Armenians originally from Kesab to enter the Sanjak to register for the elections unless they agreed to inscribe in the Turkish community.[11] Reimers wrote Collet the same day asking him to investigate reports that Turks living around Kesab were threatening local Alawis, trying to prevent them from registering.[12] According to Collet, the fault was with the leaders of the Armenian community, who were trying to dissuade Armenians from participating. He promised to apprise the high commissioner of the problems.[13]

Martel insisted that security had been restored to the Sanjak. "Calm continues to reign at Alexandretta and Antioch," he informed Paris. "Designation of [new Antioch governor] Abdurrahman Melek was received well and suqs were reopened." The same confidence informed his response to the Armenian apostolic delegate who visited his office to inform him of the Armenian community's anxiety and their belief that Turkish troops would soon be entering the Sanjak. Martel reassured him that order was not troubled, that French forces were maintaining security, and that the Sanjak was being discussed by Ankara and Paris in a congenial way that did not confirm his fears. Nonetheless, the apostolic delegate persisted: If Turkish influence were to prevail, the Sanjak's Armenians would emigrate. Were they ready to receive them in Lebanon or somewhere else? Martel responded that the question had not yet arisen because order and security had been assured.[14]

Commander Collet's plan to replace administrators with successors who would be more enthusiastic about ensuring a Turkish majority was showing results. The Alawi representative who accompanied bureau president Jean Lecomte to meet a newly appointed local administrator seemed "very anxious, even terrorized," and explained that the new officials had counseled voters to inscribe themselves as Turks because there was an accord between France and Turkey. "It is thus in their interest to inscribe themselves as Turks; if not they will risk being massacred. Everyone who returns from the bureau with a card from another community will be arrested and taken to prison and even hanged." Lecomte insisted "that each of the electors would have the right to inscribe in the community to which he belongs, as well as to lodge complaints in front of the Commission for acts of violence or threats." Lecomte told the new administrator that he had come to inform him that the inscriptions would resume on Thursday,

June 9, and to arrange to call villages to register. The new administrator reassured Lecomte that calm reigned in his district, that the voters would have all liberty to inscribe as they wanted, and that the villages would be regularly convoked. The same day, Collet expelled Syria's official representative from the Sanjak, along with his driver and his two secretaries.[15]

Reimers wrote to Collet on June 8 to register an official "most energetic" protest against six French policies they considered inconsistent with France's commitment to enforce freedom of choice in the electoral registrations. First, they objected that all of the high officials recently appointed came exclusively from the Republican People's Party, the group that controlled the Halkevleri, and some of them had been actively engaged in propaganda. Second, lower ranking officials had been dismissed without any cause on the eve of the recommencement of registration procedures. Reimers claimed that those dismissed came from places with a well-known non-Turkish majority, and that "there was no doubt, in the eyes of the Commission, that the goal of these firings was none other than the intimidation of the local populations to lead them to inscribe themselves in a different community from that to which they would have [inscribed] at the beginning of the operations." Third, Collet had called together the leaders of non-Turkish groups to overtly pressure them to urge the members of their communities either to abstain or to inscribe in a different community from the one to which they "in fact" belonged. Fourth, Turkish gendarmes had been "systematically sent to places where inscriptions were about to take place and where non-Turks constituted the majority." Fifth, only the non-Turkish press had been suspended. Finally, authorities had made it difficult for non-Turks living outside the Sanjak to enter in order to register with the electoral bureaus. "The Commission had not known until today the extent to which all this pressure would, in fact, have repercussions on the free choice of the people. It now states, from today, that these pressures have created an atmosphere of intimidation, which has sown panic in one part of the population, to the point of provoking an exodus among them."

As an example, the commissioners cited events on June 8, 1938, the day before inscriptions were to recommence, in which a group of gendarmes beat the Arabs of Mashrafiye village near Reyhanlı; the villagers had fled, abandoning their belongings.[16] Kurdish and Arab representatives petitioned the electoral commission, claiming that "the Turks and the gendarmes, aided by the authorities, are coercing the Arabs and the Kurds, by cruelties and false acts, to inscribe themselves in the Turkish community. The Turkish assassins of the Arabs circulate publicly at Reyhanlı. Women and children are in terror. Goods and souls are threatened. We implore you to put an end to the aggressions and partisanship. Save us before it becomes too late."[17] Reimers warned that, although the commissioners had decided to resume electoral operations, they would "reserve to themselves at any moment to give the order to stop the registration operations in case they reach the conclusion that the pressures in question have risen to the point where they systematically affect, in certain regions, the free choice of people wanting to avail themselves of the arrangements of the electoral regime."[18] Recognizing that the growing coercion now appeared to have the approval of French authorities, the League of Nations electoral commission nonetheless persisted in the project of supervising the elections.

The electoral commission wrote the same day to the French and Turkish governments announcing that the two suspensions would be expiring that evening, June 8 and noting that non-Turkish communities in the Sanjak were being pressured to abstain or limit the number of inscriptions. After mentioning its previous two letters to Collet earlier in the week calling the attention of the authorities to the need to strictly respect the free determination of electors, the electoral commission now "makes all reservations in case these conditions would not be fulfilled, and refuses any responsibility for the situation created by this pressure." The electoral commission insisted that the current situation was very grave and that its own position was becoming more and more difficult.[19]

Turkey's ambassador in Geneva, Necmettin Sadak, was scathing in his response. In a letter to League of Nations secretary-general Avenol, Sadak expressed his government's "profound surprise" at the electoral commission's description of the current situation in the Sanjak. The commissioners had made no similar protests in the face of the "extremely grave events" at the end of May, when the Sanjak's Turks had been exposed to "the most violent pressure and terrorism on the part of the authorities, whose attacks by force were committed daily against them by bands assured of impunity." Sadak accused the commissioners of having kept silent while Turks were "molested, wounded and killed with no provocation nor reaction on their part" but raising protests now "when these acts of terror and pressure have been stopped or decreased." According to Ambassador Sadak, the previous administration had been the period of terror and false election results. He denied that non-Turkish voters were being refused their freedom. "It is only the Turkish element that until today has submitted to the lack of recognition of its rights," he said, and claimed that the electoral commission's complaint constituted a new kind of pressure against those rights— pressure emanating from the League of Nations itself. Sadak impugned the electoral commission's impartiality, and accused it of hindering the joint efforts of the Turkish and French governments to work together toward appeasement; being placed under the jurisdiction of the League of Nations had become the "aggravating circumstance." For this reason, the Turkish government would brook no delay in the registration process, "this critical phase that the two interested governments want to see achieved as quickly as possible."[20]

As registrations were about to resume on the morning of June 9, the electoral commission distributed a new communiqué (Communiqué 14) to leaders of the various Sanjak communities, reminding the public that the electoral operations had been suspended at the request of both the French authorities and the Turkish consul general at Antioch in order "to permit the reestablishment of order and to assure conditions of complete liberty and security in the registration of the electors." The communiqué continued, "The electoral commission has established that during this period of suspension, one part of the population had been the object of pressure and intimidation that, in its opinion, was contrary to the goals envisioned by the authorized suspension." Despite this situation, the electoral commission had authorized the reopening of electoral bureaus that had been functioning before the suspension, while protesting "most energetically with the responsible authorities." Communiqué 14 reminded the Sanjak's population that, according to the electoral regulations still in force, each voter must inscribe himself and had the absolute freedom to decide his community. Finally, the commissioners stipulated that if the recent pressures on one part of the population prevented their registering freely, the electoral commission would be forced to consider ending the process.[21]

Collet claimed that Communiqué 14 from the electoral commission went too far. Although he understood the telegram as an expression of the commissioners' "legitimate concern to affirm its neutrality and to make reservations about the future," this communiqué seemed instead an effort to subvert his hard work. Collet complained to Martel that Communiqué 14 constituted, "in fact, a call to resistance to my propaganda, already sufficiently injured by the maneuvers of Syrian agents, by setting the minorities against the Turks. And this the same day when, without claiming to have persuaded the Alawis of their Turkish ethnicity, I had acquired the belief that the minorities, aware of their real interests, had begun to reconcile with their adversaries of yesterday and their future rulers." Instead of supporting Collet's efforts, the commissioners were insisting on the old rules of electoral freedom, not the new rules requiring everyone to agree to become reconciled to Turkish domination in the Sanjak. Collet confided to Martel that he had considered simply refusing to circulate Communiqué 14, citing the needs of martial law, but he worried about the implications such an act would have on the relations between France and the League of Nations. Publishing Communiqué 14 had seemed so urgent to the commissioners that they had already begun to distribute copies in French. After three hours of discussion, however, Collet convinced the commissioners not to publish Communiqué 14 officially. Martel was convinced, however, that the diffusion of the copies already delivered was inevitable, and would "galvanize the resistance of the minorities."[22]

Collet seemed surprised that the electoral commission would take such a step at this point, when he believed the commissioners to have remained passive in the face of the assassinations in the Harbiye area during the last week of May. He claimed that the commissioners knew that no incidents had taken place during his first week in the job, and that Communiqué 14 would hardly improve the "state of spirits," and even less facilitate his task. Not only would there be increased security issues as a consequence of what he viewed as a "provocation of minority attitudes" but also Communiqué 14 would add a new element to Collet's already contradictory projects. As he saw it, he wrote to Martel, he had first to create a Turkish majority in the remaining areas "to avoid the Kemalist government's imposing military collaboration on us"; he had to "take care of the scruples" of the electoral commission to keep it from leaving the Sanjak; and at the same time, he would have to avoid provoking a rising by the Arab population, who had been "encouraged to resist by the attitude of the Commission and the propaganda directed by the Syrian authorities of Aleppo and Latakia." Indeed, he had recently been notified that bands were being recruited in Harim, and that an "intense pan-Arab propaganda" was being carried out "destined to raise the Arab population of Kuseyr against all attempts at 'Turkicization.'" Collet concluded that these contradictory projects would require him to obfuscate his interventions, which would make them less effective.[23]

Ambassador Necmettin Sadak registered an energetic protest against the electoral commission on behalf of the government of Turkey, calling its behavior "extremely grave provocations" and "intolerable meddling." After the difficulties of establishing order in the Sanjak and at a time when people were still agitated by the "remarkable encouragements" from the recently dissolved Syrian administration, "the proclamation [Communiqué 14] will reanimate emotions and even bring about bloody troubles." Turkey refused any responsibility for this "provocation" or for the bloodshed likely to result from this "unfortunate and dangerous initiative." Sadak pointed out that the commissioners had provided copies of Communiqué 14 to "anti-Turkish organizations" before the authorities could decide whether or not to publish it, a clear indication, he claimed, of how little qualified the commissioners were to carry out their mission impartially.[24] As far as the Turkish government was concerned, the commissioners were now interfering in a political question outside the limits of its jurisdiction. "The electoral commission must limit itself to controlling and registering the facts," and should not be intervening in the political relations between Turkey and France, whose efforts to pacify the current situation went beyond the responsibilities of the commissioners.[25] Both the French and Turkish governments worried that Communiqué 14 would result in the empowerment of minorities; indeed, that was precisely what the electoral commission had intended. The commissioners had signed on to a project, advocated by Ankara, in which each voter could declare any affiliation he chose; they were now dedicated to carrying out that assignment, long after the French and the Turkish governments had settled on a different mission.[26]

British authorities were becoming increasingly concerned about the situation in the Sanjak. On the one hand, the position in which the electoral commission found itself threatened to compromise the integrity of the League of Nations; on the other, the British worried about the possible repercussions if the Turks failed to achieve their majority. "There was some very dirty work between the French and Turks and the former will be faced, I feel, by an infuriated Turkish Government," wrote one Foreign Office official. "The French, far from extricating themselves from the difficulties which they have made for themselves, seem to be drifting into a worse and more dangerous position," wrote another British diplomat. A third speculated on France's next moves. "Although the probable resignation of the League Commission may be welcome to the Turks I cannot believe that the French will acquiesce in it without a struggle. They have always insisted on the necessity for having the League as a cover for their agreements with the Turks. If, therefore, the Commission does resign it is more than likely that the French Government will evolve some other means of securing a League cover."[27]

While French, Turkish, and British diplomats fretted about the implications of Communiqué 14, the effects of government-tolerated coercion were evident at the electoral bureaus. The League-appointed president of each electoral bureau reported daily incidents, and the reports, read collectively, paint a picture of daily violence and intimidation. On June 9, an Arab representative in Reyhanlı announced that the Arabs would not be coming to register because "military authorities and police had received an order to favor Turkish voters coming to the electoral bureau; if there was a fight 'it would be necessary above all to strike the Arabs.'" Reyhanlı electoral bureau president E. Polet claimed the next day that it was not possible to work in the conditions that existed. "The Arab and Armenian populations are terrorized, many are seeking to flee, abandoning their belongings." An Arab representative had been imprisoned, and another was in flight. The new administrator of the village of Shaykh Hassan demanded that the villagers be called to register immediately, before they renounced their agreement to enroll as Turks. Fifteen of the Alawis inscribed as Turks, but, "evidently under pressure," most preferred to abstain.[28] When Dragoljub Pavkovitch reopened his bureau at Wadi Jarab in the Süveydiye district on June 9, none of the villagers called had appeared. The headman from one of the villages had warned the electoral commission that gendarmes were preventing the voters from coming.

Nonetheless, inscription results as of June 9 were hardly encouraging for those working to produce the promised Turkish majority. Of a total of 31,680 registered, Turks accounted for 13,955, only 44 percent. According to Collet, nearly ten thousand qualified voters from the city of Antioch and its environs had not yet registered, and the same number again had yet to register from the center of the Sanjak. Hundreds of Turcophiles, he claimed, remained uncounted at Reyhanlı. Nonetheless, even including the Turks not yet registered, Collet could not imagine that more than 47 percent of the inscriptions would be in the category "Turk."[29]

On the afternoon of June 10, a car carrying local Turkish landowners appeared in the village of Ayranji Sharki. That night, an armed band entered the village, firing guns and setting fire to some of the village houses inhabited by Arab laborers. The Arabs left the village, taking all of their belongings, afraid to return.[30] Reyhanlı electoral bureau president Polet's district included not only the site of the June 10 arson but also Mashrafiya, where police had attacked would-be Arab voters two days earlier. Citing "the terror existing among the Arab inhabitants and the impossibility of continuing the inscriptions in these conditions," Polet suspended operations on June 11.[31]

Only Turkish representatives were present at the electoral bureau at Osmaniye, in the Antioch district, on June 10. Despite repeated invitations, the representatives of the other communities stayed away. More than seventy of the Alawis and Greek Orthodox residents summoned to register did not appear, and fewer than fourteen Arabs, Alawis, or Christians inscribed. One of the Arab soldiers serving the mandatory regime "showed signs of terror": the previous evening, an Arab who had inscribed as an Arab had been brutally beaten and taken to the hospital.[32] Abdulgani Türkmen appeared with three of his companions at the electoral bureau near Karamurt. Bureau president E. de Plomgren insisted that the Turkish leader could not enter the bureau, and that if he wanted to talk with the Turkish representatives, he should do it outside. Soon afterward, Plomgren noticed that Alawis coming to register were always accompanied by one of Türkmen's three companions, and Plomgren refused to allow them to enter. Türkmen left soon after. The next day, Plomgren learned that local gendarmes were searching Alawis for weapons while allowing Turks to pass, which he feared had discouraged voters from coming to register. Two Alawis had been arrested without explanation, and one, on entering the electoral bureau, was threatened by the gendarmes, who claimed that they would drive him from his home unless he registered as a Turk. "Such incidents are frequent," Plomgren added. When he protested, the gendarme corporal responded that he was acting under orders from his superior.[33]

Nonetheless, it was becoming apparent that the efforts at intimidation were enjoying limited success. When electoral bureau president Lie objected to a uniformed policeman's demand that the Alawi representative leave the bureau and go with him, the policeman claimed he was acting under orders. The representative returned half an hour later, claiming that he had been taken to see Commander Collet, who had inquired about the number of Alawis and Turks who had inscribed. When Collet asked him why the Alawis were not inscribing as

Turks, he had responded that voters had the right to inscribe in the community of their choice. At the end of the day, Lie counted registrations for 660 Alawis and 170 Turks. Gendarmes and Turks stood a few meters from the entrance to Lecomte's electoral bureau the next day, insulting and threatening the Alawis inside. Defiantly, Alawis inscribed as Alawis, and five Sunni Muslims inscribed as Arabs, "to the surprise of the Turkish representative, who wanted to contest the inscription." Upon their making the required solemn declaration, the Turkish representative had to drop his contest. [34]

Although reports of Turks intimidating Alawis abound in the records of the Special Tribunal, an increasingly pessimistic Martel confirmed to Paris on June 13 that many Alawi voters continued to inscribe in the Alawi community. Some of the Alawi shaykhs had rallied behind the Turkish propaganda effort, but the others had been encouraged, he claimed, by the electoral commission's efforts to count the non-Turks, "thus annulling Commander Collet's efforts to have them decline."[35] Indeed, Martel blamed Communiqué 14 for the new atmosphere; by empowering the other groups, he claimed, the electoral commission's "clandestine diffusion" of Communiqué 14 had encouraged "the spirit of resistance to the Turkish enterprise." Martel blamed the "clumsy pressure" exerted by the Halkevi's propaganda; worse, the new Kemalist governor had ordered Halkevi leaders to search the homes of three Alawis, a project intended—unsuccessfully—to intimidate. According to Martel, these sorts of incidents obviously disturbed the minorities; the high commissioner tried to impress on the governor the dangers inherent in these sorts of actions which, in any case, "yielded no result."[36] Although Turkish consul Karasapan still hoped that the Arabs of Kuseyr could be brought along, Collet no longer shared that optimism. Indeed, Collet decided to encourage the Turkish General Staff delegation to consider possible alternatives when it arrived in Antioch for talks with French mandatory officials on June 12. Martel hoped that the Turkish officers would treat the news "more objectively" than if it came from Garreau, because of Collet's reputation as a Kemalist supporter.[37] Huntziger, head of the French General Staff, presented Consul Karasapan and members of the Turkish General Staff with the latest registration numbers. The Turkish group concluded that all hope had not yet been lost and decided to telegraph Ankara with the news. Collet suspected that Karasapan would inform Ankara that "the current direction of the inscriptions is imputable to the partiality of the League of Nations Commission," and that its departure following the arrival of the Turkish troops in the Sanjak would demonstrate the existence of a Turkish majority.[38] For Karasapan, the League of Nations electoral commission was the cause of the Turks' inability to reach the majority they clearly deserved.

The bloody events of June 13 provided Karasapan's opening. At eight o'clock that evening, a Turk was stabbed in Antioch's Christian quarter. Unable to arrest the perpetrators, Collet instead imprisoned two of the Sanjak's "anti-Kemalist" leaders, Zaki al-Arsuzi and Beylouni. The next morning, voters protested by staying away from the Awakiye electoral bureau. A very large crowd tried to overrun the government offices, and three people were injured when police shot into the air to repel the attack.[39] A procession of Alawi women arrived at the Tourism Hotel to implore the electoral commission to release al-Arsuzi. Hearing them, electoral commission president Reimers, commissioner Lagrange, and Pierre Burnier, prosecutor of the Special Tribunal, came to the front of the hotel to get information. The women cried out to them, "Zaki al-Arsuzi was unjustly arrested, we demand that he be freed." The head of Special Services described the commissioners' response: "The Delegates sought to calm the crowd, asking each [woman] to return to her home. They claimed that they would investigate the affair the next day." When he went back inside, Reimers asked the hotel to close the fences and turn off the lights.[40]

Karasapan's version of the events reflected the animosity with which he viewed the electoral commission: Reimers had gone out on the balcony of the Tourism Hotel to harangue Alawi demonstrators who had come to demand the liberation of their leader Zaki al-Arsuzi, and incited them to persevere in the affirmation of their rights. Collet tried to verify Karasapan's "somewhat sensational information" and was informed that it was baseless. For the Turkish consul, however, the electoral commission's very purpose was anathema. Empowering voters to implement their right to register in any community they wished, as the Turks had demanded at Geneva, was no longer acceptable. Indeed, for Karasapan, anything less than blatant support for a Turkish majority would make the electoral commission suspect. Thus, Reimers's reassurance to an Alawi group was, on its face, an act of treachery.

For the Turkish regime, Reimers's speech was the last straw. Ponsot wrote from Ankara that, following the most recent incidents at Antioch "during which the President of the electoral commission and his two colleagues publicly took the position of the crowd who wanted to surround the government building," the Turkish government was lodging a formal complaint with Geneva; Ankara planned to end all collaboration with the commissioners. The Turkish government claimed that a deposition about Reimers's speech provided by a Circassian gendarmerie commander corroborated its assertions. Collet denied that any Circassian officer had made a report on the subject.[41]

In an effort to dispute Turkey's angry missive, the electoral commission sent an "energetic protest" to the secretary-general of the League of Nations, debunking Turkey's accusations on a wide range of topics.[42] They responded to Turkey's disparagement of the electoral delays by explaining the technical causes, and insisting that the requests for the two temporary suspensions had come from both the French and the Turkish representatives in the Sanjak. The commissioners emphatically disavowed Ambassador Sadak's accusation that their silence during the last weeks of May illustrated their anti-Turkish partisanship. Instead, they claimed, the electoral commission had received twenty-five complaints from representatives of the Republican People's Party, and thirty-two from Arabs or Alawis. They had forwarded most of these to the Special Tribunal for inquiries or punishments, or transmitted them to the local authorities. During those last two weeks of May, the electoral commission had sent two letters to Garreau demanding that order be enforced. It was in response to the electoral commission's intervention that Garreau had promulgated the May 27 decrees that prohibited strangers from staying in the districts where registrations were proceeding, and forbade the circulation of automobiles at night. Moreover, the Turkish consul had regularly visited the commissioners, spoken of various questions related to the electoral operations, even claimed during his last visit on May 23 that "he had never doubted the perfect impartiality of the Commission." During all of that time, the commissioners insisted, Karasapan had made no allusions to "the most violent terrorization on the part of the authorities." Even after that date, the Republican People's Party had sent representatives to the electoral commission, which had encouraged them to submit their complaints in writing so the commissioners could take necessary measures. Following one of these visits, three commissioners had presented Garreau with the Turkish complaints and demanded an immediate inquiry. Turks and non-Turks had thanked the League of Nations election staff for their impartiality, both verbally and in writing. In sum, the electoral commission insisted it had been neither partisan nor passive and demanded Ankara's evidence.

To counter Sadak's claim that "acts of terror or pressure" had stopped or become less frequent since the beginning of June, the commissioners argued that the opposite situation now prevailed.

> In the opinion of the Commission, the expression "acts of terror or pressure" can be applied more properly to acts of intimidation and pressure that have been systematically organized, since the beginning of the month of June, by the authorities against one part of the population little inclined to inscribe themselves as Turks. The Commission can affirm, in effect, that the announcement of France's commitment according to which she assures Turkey a slight majority to the Turkish element in the future Sanjak Parliament, coincided with a change in attitude of the mandatory authorities in the Sanjak, an attitude illustrated by the declaration made to the Commission on 30 May by the Delegate [Garreau] of the High Commissioner according to which he had received instructions to assure this majority "by all means."

Daily reports from delegates and electoral bureau presidents had "indisputably established the responsibility of local authorities and especially the gendarmerie" in the situation created in the Sanjak. The electoral commission concluded that, although its mandate did not permit meddling in politics, article 3 of the regulation required it to take "necessary measures" in the case of any sort of pressure during the elections. They insisted that Communiqué 14 neither was a provocation nor contained "any declaration that could risk provoking bloodshed."[43]

While the electoral commission renewed its commitment to implementing its assigned task, the mandatory regime repeatedly tried to obstruct its efforts. By mid-June, Turcophiles were in control of much of the registration process, intimidating and arresting voters with the apparent approval of the Kemalist appointees who now held most of the offices in the Sanjak. Petitions and accusations poured into the electoral commission with complaints of voter tampering, intimidation, and violence by local officials. Gendarmes harassed voters, stole their money, barred their routes, even assaulted them physically.[44] Gendarmes stopped cars bringing Arab villagers to register. Gendarmes searching villagers at Hamam Sharki beat them; one who had received a serious head injury was presented at the election bureau the next morning covered with blood. In places where the official violence became too severe, electoral bureau presidents closed registrations. Electoral bureau president Polet concluded that "the inscriptions done in these conditions have no value and in no way represent the opinion of the people." Polet was sent by the commissioners to investigate claims that the villages of Middle Kuseyr (Batrum, Deir, Filinjar) were witnessing "systematic terror against the Arabs by the military forces, the gendarmerie, and Turkish propagandists." Dodgson, presiding over Middle Kuseyr's electoral bureau, noted the absence of Arab representatives, who, he soon learned, had been arrested and accused of "creating disorders and making propaganda." One group of villagers arrived without their headman, who remained behind in concern for his family when twenty soldiers set themselves up in his village. Despite the intimidation and harassment, 227 of the 280 villagers who appeared inscribed as Arabs or Alawis.[45]

Official intimidation was more effective in the villages of Lower Kuseyr to be registered by Bennewitz, president of the local electoral bureau. When he protested against the arrest of the village head and some local Arabs, he was informed that the order had been received from Antioch's new district administrator. Arab and Alawi voters refused to register in protest. Soon, an officer arrived in the village with twelve gendarmes "to keep order." Turkish representatives claimed that they would no longer be attending the inscriptions if the Arab representatives continued to be present. The Arab villagers who had been called to register did not arrive. In their place, a Turkish village that had not yet been called appeared at the electoral bureau.[46] At the neighboring electoral bureau, where only Turkish representatives were present, local Greek Orthodox villagers who had been called did not appear. Days later, the curé and the village head arrived asking to be released from the responsibility to inscribe because their village was located in the middle of fifty-two Arab and Turkish villages that had been soliciting the Greek Orthodox to inscribe themselves as Arab or Turk.[47] Alawi representatives at one of the electoral bureaus in the Süveydiye district refused to continue working when gendarmes arrived at a local village and threatened the Alawi inhabitants. When the president of the electoral bureau asked why the village heads of most of the villages in his district had been arrested and imprisoned by order of the district administrator, the local official claimed to know nothing about the reasons for the arrests. Unable to proceed without the presence of the village heads, the president closed his bureau. When inscriptions resumed, the local administrator, the chief of the gendarmerie post, and most of the gendarmes had been replaced by Turks, and the electoral bureau president noted "considerable pressure exercised by the authorities on the villagers."[48]

Despite the collaboration of mandatory officials, Turkish registrations barely reached 42 percent by mid-June. The Turkish consul demanded "energetic action by the mandatory authorities before it is too late," and before "it becomes necessary to proceed to a surgical operation."[49] Collet, gave Karasapan his repeated assurances that he was giving "all my support to the Turkish element," but the French delegate was becoming increasingly pessimistic about achieving the outcome he had promised the high commissioner. His hands were tied by the presence of the League commissioners. "I am paralyzed by the incessant presentations of the electoral commission, which complains of the pressure exercised by functionaries of the authorities and gendarmerie and even inquires about the slightest troop movement." In the meantime, Collet complained, Turkey's consul and the Halkevleri continued to distrust French authorities.

Registrations were nearly complete, with the electoral bureaus operating even on Saturdays and Sundays to finish their work before the scheduled elections. Collet argued that the French had little time left. In the current situation, he could not fulfill French promises to Turkey. If they were to "still attain the necessary 55 percent, it is necessary to provoke the departure of the electoral commission without waiting longer, to undertake the operations on our account in agreement with Ankara." If, on the other hand, the 55 percent objective were to be abandoned, Collet claimed, he would continue acting as he had been, "giving pledges of our good will to the Turks and at the same time the maximum appeasements to the commission, which are often incompatible." Collet warned that this balancing game carried its own dangers, bringing bloodshed to Antioch,

Süveydiye, and Harbiye "between the populations set one against the other by opposing propaganda." Collet claimed that the risks of violence were still greater in the Arab villages of the Kuseyr region, which he claimed had been "profoundly worked up by Syrian agents and League of Nations delegates overtly encouraging minorities to not inscribe as Turks." Collet worried that the military means he had employed so far would become inadequate, and asked for instructions about how to carry out his mission.[50]

Collet's efforts were inadequate to mollify Ankara's demands. Karasapan presented him with a telegram edited by Foreign Minister Aras, based on consultation with Atatürk. It began with a series of complaints about French administration, expressing Turkey's shock that the man who killed a Turk on the evening of June 13 had still not been apprehended, and inquiring whether sanctions had been taken against a low-ranking French official who had "dared call his dog Mustafa Kemal," Atatürk's name. The telegram registered Ankara's surprise at the continuing action of the Sanjak Union and the League of National Action, and incomprehension that high-ranking former officials like Garreau had been allowed to remain in the Sanjak after their dismissal—they were even continuing to participate in many meetings, in contradiction to the politics of Franco-Turkish friendship. The telegram ended, "We await the final result to be able to make the decision on the situation we will impose. You must tell Colonel Collet that our impressions are pessimistic and that we have the sense that the intrigues and provocations against our interests continue." The threat was hardly veiled, and was accompanied by an accusation that Collet was actively working against Turkish interests. Karasapan seemed apologetic about having to deliver such a message to his friend. Collet realized that he was the subject of these reproofs because, "contrary to the accords of March, we hesitated to Turkify the minority populations of the region with blows of sticks, volleys of rifles." Collet denied the allegations of bad faith, responding to each of the accusations by illustrating his continuing efforts to appease Turkish demands. The assassination case was being handled by the prosecutor of the Special Tribunal; the dog owner had been transferred; and the leaders of the offending organizations had been arrested.[51] Despite his protestations, Collet's efforts to circumscribe the electoral commission's cherished electoral freedom received no recognition from the Turkish government.

Ankara's anger was conveyed to French foreign minister Bonnet in three official notes dated June 18. Together, the notes accused the French administration in the Sanjak of inciting a climate of anti-Turkish terror, tolerating "the campaign of excitement led by the agents provocateurs," and harboring the killers of the Turk murdered in Antioch on June 13. The Turkish ambassador demanded a joint investigation. Claiming that attacks against Turks were increasing daily, he insisted that there had been no amelioration in the Sanjak.

Despite the friendly assurance of the French government, the Sanjak Authorities continue always to be animated by an anti-Turkish state of
mind. The authorities of the Sanjak act following the directives of
M. Martel whose anti-Turkish sentiments are known. The replacement
of M. Garreau by Colonel Collet has produced no change in the situation
of the Sanjak. It is thus that the members of the Party of National Unity
and the Usbajis [League of National Action members] continue to benefit from the same protection and organize, in view of the whole world,
armed bands. Neither those who insulted President Atatürk nor the
assassins of the Turkish chauffeur Osman have been arrested until now.

The Turkish notes accused French officials of ignoring the increasing activity of
Syrian armed bands while they continued to persecute Turkish activists, and
blamed former officials of collaborating with the June 13 killings. The Turkish
government accused Reimers of exacerbating the violence: "President of the
Commission, M. Reimers, addressing himself to the aggressors, pronounced a
discourse in which he claimed, notably, that the majority of the population was
with them and that they had a right to react against the arrests. M. Reimers took
thus a great responsibility in provoking the emotion and the excitement among
the population."[52]

The Turkish notes addressed future options directly. French commander
Huntziger had informed Turkish officials that the agreed number of Turkish deputies could not be assured. He had suggested that France and Turkey assume
direct control of electoral operations without recourse to the League of Nations
electoral commission, establishing a system similar to that used in the recent
Romanian elections. Turks would attain the most seats for having a relative
majority. Ankara refused this offer, insisting on the promise France had made,
and the "categorical assurances of the French government." The Turkish note offered three different alternatives, each requiring the introduction of Turkish
troops and Franco-Turkish military cooperation; the options differed only on
the extent of Turkish participation in the election process and which government would be responsible for its outcome. The first option would be to bring
Turkish troops into the Sanjak immediately to enforce public order, send the
electoral commission back to Geneva, and have France and Turkey jointly assume the commissioners' role in controlling the elections. In this case, France
would remain solely responsible for the electoral results and the application of
the secret March 10 Franco-Turkish agreements. In the second option, responsibilities would be shared. Turkey would collaborate with France not only in maintaining order but also in administering the Sanjak, taking on some of the rights
and responsibilities of the mandatory power. Both France and Turkey would
share responsibility for the results of the elections. In the third scenario, France

would "provisionally transmit to Turkey the mandate for the Sanjak," with all rights and responsibilities that ensued becoming solely the responsibility of Turkey. The Turkish note claimed that it had been proved "that public order is completely troubled in the Sanjak" and that the French effort was "insufficient to assure the security of the country." The only way to avoid the "return of bloody incidents" would be to introduce Turkish troops at the lowest level needed to assure public order, the note insisted, cautioning that a weak contingent would be "at the mercy of surprises and could not meet the situation in the Sanjak."

As France considered these options, the League of Nations electoral commission took strong exception to Turkey's accusations. They began by insisting that Reimers had not even been in Antioch on June 13 and 14 when the Turkish government accused him of making speeches there. They noted that Collet's inquiries had shown that "these rumours were baseless and that it was impossible to publish a denial in the Turkish newspaper." The electoral commission claimed to be "astonished" that Ankara was giving credence to such "fantastic reports," castigating the Turkish government for including the electoral commission in its official communications without first verifying the information.[53]

While Turkey's government objected to the "reign of terror" against the Sanjak's Turks, local officials continued trying to prevent the registrations of the other groups. Alawi representatives to the Harbiye electoral bureau were arrested, the home of one surrounded by twenty gendarmes and Moroccan soldiers. The gendarmerie commander responded to requests for their release by saying that he had received his orders directly from Colonel Collet himself. The electoral bureau president reported many complaints by villagers telling of violence, threats, and gendarme searches: "The pressure against the Alawis to force them to inscribe as Turks has not succeeded even though a considerable number abstained from inscribing, having been stopped on the road and having returned to the village."[54] On his way to open a new electoral bureau on June 20, Lecomte saw cars full of Turkish propagandists coming from Antioch, and concluded that the prohibition against circulating freely in the areas where inscriptions were proceeding was being enforced only against Arabs. On his arrival at Filinjar, Lecomte noted three armored cars, a group of Moroccan sharpshooters, a squadron of cavalry, and a dozen gendarmes. A group of villagers met him and asked if the inscription would be free. When he responded affirmatively, they told him how they had been threatened by armed men.[55] Süveydiye bureau president Pavkovitch encountered a crowd of several hundred women stopped by Syrian soldiers on the road from Harbiye to Antioch. After stopping to listen to their complaints, he continued to the Tourism Hotel to inform the electoral commission.[56] Collet complained that Pavkovitch had photographed the group, objecting that this act had itself been dangerous to his project. "There is no doubt that such an attitude must be of a nature to excite simple minds to persevere in resistance." Collet spoke with Reimers by phone, threatening to "exercise the rights conferred on me by the declaration of martial law in the Sanjak" if the commissioners were to "persist in thoughtlessly encouraging demonstrations."[57]

Martel sounded as if he was making a terrible accusation when he wrote to Paris that the League of Nations electoral commission remained intent on observing its mission, which he described as "assuring by all means the liberty of conscience of the minorities." "The facts," he wrote, "prove it," citing examples including Reimers's journey to a Christian village that had decided to abstain from inscribing. Reimers had even established electoral bureaus in the Arab villages of Kuseyr so that those "refractory to Turkish propaganda" would not have to submit to pressure. The government of Turkey was now refusing all further collaboration with electoral commission, claiming that its actions "constitute contempt for the resolutions of Geneva and a denial of justice and right with which Turkey can in no way associate herself." Martel was convinced, though, that even if the commissioners were informed about the Turkish objection, they would not stop their work, "animated as it is by its mystique and its desire to make it appear that the Turks are a minority." Martel suggested that Paris take advantage of the tone of the recent Turkish note to call on the electoral commission to suspend its work immediately. "This would have the advantage for us of making Turkey solely responsible for the departure of the commission." Failing that, Martel requested authorization to permit Collet, under the pretext of martial law, to stop the inscriptions—before they were completed—to keep the electoral commission from "officially verifying the Turkish defeat." There was great urgency here, he insisted, because inscriptions were to end in just a few days.[58]

"Collet was summoned today by the commission, who received him seated in plenary meeting," Martel telegraphed on June 21. The commissioners warned Collet that threats were becoming more and more animated, that the free choice of voters was not being respected, that the military forces Collet had sent to the Kuseyr region seemed to be intimidating voters, and that Sanjak officials were excepting Turkish propagandists from the interdiction against travel in places where electoral registration was taking place. The commissioners demanded written reassurance from Collet that he would "carry out remedies to this state of things, failing which the Commission would suspend its work." If Collet gave the electoral commission the assurances they demanded, Martel opined, "we would be risking grave complications from the Turkish side." Instead, Martel instructed Collet to retreat "behind the need to maintain order" to explain to the commissioners his inability to provide the assurances they sought.[59]

Unsatisfied, Reimers wrote Collet later the same afternoon to demand an official response. He outlined the obstacles impeding the functioning of the electoral bureaus, especially in the three districts of Kuseyr. Reimers listed the remedies necessary for the electoral commission to continue its task, demanding that Collet free the representatives of the communities and the village heads participating in the electoral bureaus, discipline gendarmes responsible for violence against the population, enforce prohibitions on travel in order to limit intimidation, stop systematically arresting the notables of the villages on the eve of registration, and equitably carry out the orders summoning villagers to register. In addition, Reimers asked Collet to keep troops and machine guns away from the electoral bureaus, "in any measure compatible with security." Reimers ended his letter asking Collet, "given the gravity of the situation," to respond by informing the electoral commission of his intentions as early as the same evening, to allow the commissioners to decide whether it would be possible for them to continue their activity.[60]

The electoral commission sent a telegram to the League of Nations Council the same day castigating the mandatory administration for its actions, which were interfering with registrations "and gravely prejudice the freedom of choice of part of the population." The telegram claimed that measures adopted since May 31 "constitute means of pressure and intimidation which are more than mere guidance to the population, as indicated by the mandatory authorities, and are incompatible with the Electoral Regulations."[61]

The events of June 21 shocked the commissioners and alarmed the League of Nations. Dodgson knew the situation was tense at his new Babtrun electoral bureau even before he traveled to the neighboring village of Deir to find out why the villagers had not arrived to register. Dodgson inquired of the new village administrator about the soldiers standing on a nearby hilltop, and about reports that seven Deir residents had been arrested and four others required to present themselves to the gendarmes. The administrator responded that he had given those orders because the men had mistreated a Turk who had been living in Deir. On his return to Babtrun, in recognition of the disquiet between the people of Babtrun and the villagers of Deir, Dodgson instructed the local administrator and the chief of the gendarme post that everyone in Babtrun must remain in their homes during registrations and that all the people of the other villages would not be authorized to remain at Babtrun. If these instructions were not followed, the responsibility for any disturbance would be solely on the gendarmerie and the administrator.[62]

That night, some twenty soldiers went to the neighboring village, Baksanos, to inform the population that if they did not inscribe as Turks they would be beaten or even shot. As electoral bureau president Polet traveled to monitor Dodgson's bureau the next morning, he encountered some Arabs from Deir, who had been turned back by Turkish activists. Polet persuaded them to return, but as he was speaking with Dodgson about the situation, the Arabs were again chased away from the electoral bureau. When 150 voters from Baksanos arrived, men standing at the door of the electoral bureau seized and beat an Arab voter. At eleven o'clock in the morning, Dodgson ordered the gendarme to arrest the Turkish activists who had come to his electoral bureau in order to seize and beat the Arab voters. The gendarme fled. "At this time, I saw some 15–20 civilians armed with sticks and dressed as French near my bureau, but on my approach they all fled." Dodgson went to the gendarmerie station and ordered the soldiers there to guard his bureau and keep away everyone except the villagers of Baksanos, who were in the process of registering. Returning from the station, he ordered the arrest of a Turcophile activist who was standing outside the bureau warning voters that it was dangerous to vote and that the inscriptions were about to be stopped. At 11:20, Babtrun's administrator informed Dodgson that if the inscriptions were not stopped, "serious events would take place"; Dodgson sent an urgent message to the electoral commission describing the situation and requesting them to send one of the commissioners.

Things happened quickly. "Around 12:15, my bureau was attacked on all sides by 30–40 civilians dressed in French clothing and armed with sticks and pistols. Many gunshots were fired and I ordered all the electors to enter my bureau (at the mosque) for security, and I gave the order to the two gendarmes present to guard the door to the courtyard and not to let anyone enter. In every case, they allowed many of these propagandists to enter the courtyard. One Arab received a serious head injury and many other Arabs small injuries. One of the attackers indeed entered the mosque, while I was at the door preventing the Arabs from leaving, and fired many pistol shots very close to me." Dodgson was furious that the gendarme had not arrested the intruder either when he entered or when he left. Neither of the gendarmes at the electoral bureau did anything to stop the attack. "The attack continued in my bureau for 15 to 20 minutes, and about 150 shots total had been fired."[63] When Nicol arrived in response to Dodgson's urgent call, he saw three buses "full of young Turks" coming from Babtrun. The voters from Baksanos remained shut inside the mosque guarded by a gendarme at the door, and a soldier at the entrance to the courtyard. Nicol encouraged Dodgson not to end the inscriptions, since that was what the aggressors had been seeking. After the registrations were completed, the voters left together, accompanied to their village by a cavalry squadron.

When Kemalist leader Abdulgani Türkmen arrived that afternoon and, "under the pretext of conferring with the Turkish representative," entered as far as the door to the mosque, Nicol ordered him to leave, "telling him he had no right to enter the bureau. Türkmen responded, 'I have the right to go where I want,' and added 'The work that you do here is in any case arbitrary,' then went outside to confer with the Turkish representative." Nicol concluded his report: "Two things are striking from these incidents: the courage of the Arabs who refuse to be intimidated or influenced by the threats; and the unfitness of the gendarmerie who, one must conclude, acted in this manner [refusing to arrest anyone who had entered the mosque and fired the gunshots near M. Dodgson] in conformance with the orders of the Authorities."[64]

In response to the attack on the electoral bureau, the commissioners suspended all electoral operations for four days and referred the whole situation to the League of Nations. The electoral commission was considering leaving despite the five thousand electors who remained unregistered. The Babtrun incident seems to have been "the last straw."[65] The same day, seeking to mollify Ankara, Collet officially outlawed the League of National Action and the Sanjak Union, claiming the organizations were "the origin of the demonstrations that troubled public order."[66]

On June 22, the day after the attack on voters at Babtrun, Suad Davaz handed the French foreign minister a note. Because of the electoral commission's attitude and the bias it had shown against the Turks, the Turkish government was notifying the League of Nations that it would no longer cooperate with the electoral commission. Turkish ambassador Davaz insisted that the French government intervene with either the League or the commissioners to demand the suspension of electoral operations for fifteen days. "It is, at the present hour, indispensable that the electoral operations be immediately suspended and that the commission of the League of Nations be immediately sent back in order to avoid Turkey's finding itself in a situation whose consequences could be irreparable." The French and Turkish governments, he suggested, would create a new procedure after the electoral commission left. The General Staffs must conclude their discussions quickly, he urged, and arrive at an agreement that included Turkey sending an infantry regiment.[67]

French foreign minister Bonnet updated Martel on the current diplomatic situation and rehearsed its antecedents in a long telegram the same day. Before a general Franco-Turkish military accord could be signed, he wrote, the two countries still had to determine the circumstances under which the agreed-on arrangements would come into force. What had been complicating the agreement, however, was that its execution would be dependent on three things: the conclusion of a friendship treaty, a convention of good-neighborliness, and resolution of "the Sanjak affair." In all of these, Bonnet wrote, including questions of the generally disputed frontier, "the fundamental problem is of the Sanjak. Concerned with disarming Turkish irredentism, whose pressure weighs so heavily on the whole of the frontier, we occupied ourselves with channeling and cantoning this threat. After having determined the impossibility of bringing the adverse party to any other solution, we have conceded that, by the accords of 1921, we have implicitly recognized the call to political dominance. In return, Ankara affirmed its territorial disinterest. These two engagements, rigorously interdependent, had taken shape in the friendly entente of March 10 last."

At the same time, the foreign minister confirmed his belief that the secret March 10 agreement had been inspired by France's goal of acting in "the best interests of our pupils and at the same time enlightening and orienting them." The French government's responsibility to advise, he observed, had become more urgent as the crisis became more serious. "In our opinion, carefully managing the politics of accommodation was the only way out that appeared permanent and viable. It seemed to offer the best exchange for avoiding armed interference. We have scrupulously kept our word." Though the French had not managed to carry out the elections with their anticipated result, the foreign minister found a silver lining: "The groups among which the population of the Sanjak is divided are themselves incapable of governing the country if they are handed it. The mandate until the present has compensated for this weakness." In the French government's eyes, the electoral process had reinforced the notion that the Sanjak's residents remained unfit for self-government, further legitimizing the continuing French mandate.

Foreign minister Bonnet went on to consider the choices Turkey's ambassador had offered in his June 18 note. Bonnet refused the proposed association of the two powers, which implied a "dismemberment of our mandate under pain of giving a very serious blow to our authority." It would only be possible to accept collaboration with the Turkish government as required to maintain order, and the collaboration would have to be made with negotiated guarantees. Nonetheless, he recognized that it was becoming increasingly difficult each day to resolve the Alexandretta affair on electoral grounds. It was essential that the French abstain from getting involved in the dispute between the Turkish government and the League of Nations. The French foreign minister suggested that perhaps the League would revisit the entire question of the Sanjak. At the same time, he had asked Ponsot to encourage the Turkish government to ask for the suspension of the electoral commission's work. Bonnet suspected that the Ankara government would try to make France responsible for such a suspension, and asked Martel to examine "very urgently with Colonel Collet the most expedient ways to provoke this interruption . . . such that we can in a certain measure defend ourselves before Arab opinion."[68]

Despite facing Turkish hostility and Collet's refusal to provide the commissioners the assurance they demanded, the electoral commission had not followed through on its threat to leave the Sanjak before finishing its work. Martel was frustrated. He took matters into his own hands by arranging a confidential meeting between Anker, the electoral commission's secretary, and Antioch's Commander Bonnet. Bonnet was to inform Anker that if the electoral commission continued to work despite the "violent Turkish protest at Geneva and the unsuccessful ultimatum to Collet, the Commission would discredit itself." After the conversation, the commissioners suspended electoral operations, and Anker decided to leave the next day for Geneva. Martel was still concerned about how to "orchestrate at Geneva the departure of the Commission." The electoral commission's presence deprived French officials of "the liberty of action that we need." Martel insisted that "it is well understood" that the electoral results France had promised to Ankara "could be attained only in the absence of all international control."[69]

Martel did not have long to wait. On June 23, the electoral commission sent a telegram to the League of Nations Council. As a result of conditions in the Sanjak, Collet's refusal to assure the freedom of elections, and the attack on the electoral bureau at Babtrun, the electoral commission had recognized the impossibility of carrying out the electoral regulations and had decided to suspend the registrations. In the absence of other instructions from the League of Nations Council, the electoral commission would inform delegates and interpreters, and make arrangements to leave the Sanjak within a week.[70] Martel no longer had to worry about how France could "extract ourselves from the commission without putting us in a delicate situation vis. a vis. Geneva." Martel asked authorization from the Foreign Ministry to allow Collet to begin electoral operations on France's responsibility. This would be consistent, he noted, with the first proposal in Davaz's note of December 18. They could thus preserve the French mandate, and safeguard "the juridical base of the Statute and the Fundamental Law with the only exception the commission." In this context, the introduction of Turkish troops into the Sanjak would be "a voluntary gift," subordinate to the conclusion of the current negotiations.[71]

The National Bloc government in Damascus, still trusting international institutions and relying on the rule of law, was delighted with the electoral commission's decision to end registration operations. Syria's Arab nationalists were hopeful that the gesture of the commissioners would underline their own legal argument, thereby strengthening the Arabs' cause. The Syrian government hoped to benefit from the situation by increasing its protests about the Sanjak situation, and sent a delegate to Antioch to invite the commissioners to Damascus to show them the "recognition and profound esteem" that their attitude had evoked.[72]

The electoral commission's decision to leave the Sanjak did not end the violence. In the Süveydiye district, Turkish gendarmes and civilian Alawi Kemalists went to the home of Said Franji to arrest his brother. When they couldn't find him, the group began searching the houses in the village, stabbing a woman, and beating one of the farmers while he was working in his field; another woman was injured by two gunshots to her legs when she refused to obey a Turkish gendarme's order. They killed Said Franji when they found him in the market. Süveydiye's markets were closed, and the local administrator sought refuge in the court, where he was being guarded by the gendarmes. Armored cars were in the streets.[73]

Reimers wrote to Collet on June 26 to inform him that, as a result of his inability to provide the electoral commission with the assurances it had requested, it had decided that the conditions "will not any longer permit a part of the population to freely exercise the right of inscription provided by the electoral regulations." As a result, all electoral operations had been suspended on June 22, and were now pronounced definitively ended.[74]

For Martel, however, the problem had not been resolved. He pointed out to the French Foreign Ministry that they were still up against the problem of people refusing to inscribe as Turks. Even if the leaders of non-Turkish groups were willing to recognize the need for Turkish preponderance, they were unwilling to make individuals follow their lead. Moreover, when the inscriptions were interrupted, Turks made up 46 percent of the inscriptions with only five thousand voters left to register. Two solutions were possible: begin again or finish the work. Collet reported that Karasapan would recommend to his government that they simply finish the process the electoral commission had almost completed. This would mean inscribing the remaining villages and reopening the electoral bureaus where "one would find enough Turks to arrive at the percentage." Without the electoral commission, Collet was estimating "that this result could be easily obtained." Karasapan visited Collet full of optimism about the future of Franco-Turkish relations. "He insisted especially on the will of his government and its local representatives to work toward reconciling the communities and calming the eagerness of the Halkevis, especially prohibiting them from intervening in the administrative affairs of the Sanjak."[75]

Turkish prime minister Celal Bayar addressed Turkey's Grand National Assembly on June 29 as talks continued in Ankara, Paris, and Antioch. He insisted that the Sanjak would remain Turkish, and informed the Assembly that the League of Nations electoral commission had left the region. Turkey's friendship with France would be reestablished after its severe test. "A softer wind was blowing," Bayar declared, predicting a friendly arrangement in which the Sanjak would have a government "within the framework" of a Turkish majority. The Grand National Assembly provided full powers to the prime minister to take any necessary steps during its upcoming recess.[76]

Turkish foreign minister Aras agreed that inscriptions in the Sanjak should continue where they had left off, and willingly agreed to wait twelve days before resuming electoral operations. Ponsot had underscored the importance of this waiting period, to provide time after the entry of Turkish troops during which the population could be reassured. Operations could then be resumed in a way that would permit the League of Nations Council, when they returned in September, to exonerate them.[77]

French foreign minister Bonnet appeared in Paris on July 1 with Turkish ambassador Suad Davaz at his side to inform the press that negotiations between their two countries had concluded successfully. France accepted that the 1921 Ankara Treaty implied a special position for the Sanjak's Turks, and Turkey had confirmed her "territorial disinterestedness." The military agreement between France and Turkey defined the parameters of their joint guarantee of the Sanjak, and the new protocol just signed by their General Staffs fixed their methods of cooperation. In addition, they were in the process of drawing up a tripartite convention to regularize the frontier between Turkey and Syria. Finally, a new treaty of friendship was soon to be signed by France and Turkey to consolidate "the existing equilibrium in the Eastern Mediterranean."[78]

The German newspaper *Deutsche diplomatische-politische Korrespondenz* applauded the settlement of the Sanjak question.

> Whatever may have been the motives—and they were not simple— leading to a settlement, the fact remains that France, admittedly with an eye to the necessity of not endangering her good relations with Turkey, has now *de facto* recognized the right of the Turks in all circumstances to take active part in shaping the destiny of their "Volksgenossen" [race comrades] in the Sanjak. If France, in opposition to the terms of treaties that are more tyrannical than just, furthers and assists developments that correspond better to the moral claims of peoples, naturally such action will rouse no opposition in countries where understanding of true justice exists.[79]

Turkish Colonel Şükrü Kanatlının Enters Hatay. Courtesy of Mihrac Ural.

Regardless of Turkey's claims about its lack of territorial intentions, the German newspaper had drawn the obvious conclusions. The Ankara regime had been successful in its irredentist claims to intervene on behalf of fellow Turks within another country. The Turkish government had put one more nail in the coffin of the compromise represented by the League of Nations minorities treaty system.

On July 4, 1938, the governments of France and Turkey signed a Treaty of Friendship, with a representative of Syria looking on. According to the treaty, neither power would engage in political or military acts against the other, and if either were the victim of aggression, the other would provide no assistance to the aggressor. If there were any threat to the Sanjak's territorial integrity, the two countries promised to collaborate in carrying out their obligations under the Franco-Turkish Agreements they had signed in Geneva on May 29, 1937. A joint declaration followed their signing the new Treaty of Friendship, in which France and Turkey committed their countries "to put into execution the Statute of the Sanjak and Fundamental Law," but in the "spirit" of the Ankara Treaty of 1921, "which recognized a preponderance of the Turkish element in the Sanjak." At the same time, the declaration "affirmed that the question of the Sanjak was not a territorial one for Turkey."[80]

Davis, the British ambassador to Aleppo, described the scene as Turkish troops entered the Sanjak on July 4, 1938. "The popular welcome accorded to the Turkish troops appeared to be tremendous. Every town and village in the Sanjak was decorated with triumphal arches in the Turkish national colours, portraits of Kemal Atatürk and other Turkish leaders, Turkish flags, and addresses in the new Turkish script hailing the 'liberators' of the Sanjak. . .. Every car, every bicycle on the road was decorated with red and white streamers and bore a Turkish flag. The French flag was hardly to be seen anywhere, the Syrian flag nowhere at all."[81]

Conclusion

While living in Aleppo in 2007, I found myself in a taxi driven by a red-haired young man. "Where are you from?" I asked him. "I'm from Antioch," he responded. "Really? Have you been there?" I asked. "No," he responded. "My grandparents left after 1938, but they've told me all about it. I want to go visit some day."

Violence had been unleashed in the Sanjak of Alexandretta, the unforeseen consequence of a convergence of international, regional, and local impulses: the League of Nations' project to protect minorities left large sectors of the Sanjak's population defenseless, France's existential fear led Paris to refuse to consider any but its own colonial and regional interests, and Turkey's nationalist agenda created an education in animosities still unfamiliar in the cosmopolitan province. In the name of popular sovereignty, and for quite different, self-interested reasons, France and Turkey collaborated in dividing the citizens of the Sanjak, dissolving its connection to Syria and imposing new leadership. An estimated 80 percent of the Sanjak's various Christians emigrated between 1938 and 1940, rendering a remarkably diverse population much more homogenous. The exodus included thousands of others as well—Turks who rejected the ideology of the modern Turkish republic, Arabs who refused to acquiesce to the new situation.[1] Two generations later, the Sanjak question provides a source of family lore, nationalist pride (and humiliation), nostalgic memory, and diplomatic conflict. The map on the Syrian Parliament's Web site home page still shows the Sanjak to be part of Syria, and even as the two countries have opened the border in both directions, diplomatic agreements in 2010 continued to be hung up on Syria's unwillingness to officially relinquish its claim to the province.[2]

The end came quickly for the Sanjak's independence. After many months in which High Commissioner Martel tried every possible course to keep the Ankara regime out of the Sanjak, he was forced to welcome Ankara's envoy to assist with the resumption of elections.[3] Cevat Açıkalın arrived on July 15 as

"Turkish envoy extraordinary" with the same powers wielded by Martel's delegate Collet; administrative decrees would now be issued jointly. On July 22 the two men issued a communiqué announcing their joint supervision of the first general elections for the new, independent Sanjak Assembly. The French-Turkish Electoral Commission would accept the existing inscriptions, complete the process of registration, and hear all appeals.[4] Meeting Ankara's registration goals became much easier under the new circumstances: French officials closed operations in Arab villages, and the proportion of Turks rose in the remaining districts as other groups abstained, "anxious about eventual retaliation," according to Martel. French officials expected registrations to be finished within days, and claimed that the elections of both the first-stage electors and of the Assembly members would take on the "character of simple formalities."[5]

When results were announced on August 2, the Turks were allocated twenty-two seats in the new forty-person legislature, the Alawis nine, the Armenians five, the Arabs two, and the Greek Orthodox two.[6] The results of the elections were entirely predictable: leaders of each community submitted the lists of electors for the first stage, and since the number of electors from each community had already been decided, all were successful in their bids. These men, in their turn, voted for the members of the new Sanjak Assembly from the lists that had been formulated, again, by the leaders of each community. Each list had the exact number of candidates as seats that had been allocated.[7] Days before the members of the new Assembly were officially announced, and before the Assembly had met to make any decisions about future leadership, Açıkalın called on Collet to notify him of the composition of the Sanjak's new government:

> Turkey, guarantor power, concerned to assure the successful function of the future government, has chosen as President of the Sanjak, Tayfur Bey [Sökmen], as President of the Assembly, Abdulgani Türkmen, as president of the Executive Council, Abdurrahman Melek, current Governor. For the four other members of the Council, three will be Turks and one could be a minority chosen by the French authorities. In addition, the heads of the services intended to work under the aegis of the members of the council could be chosen from the minorities.

Açıkalın claimed that all the decisions about the Sanjak were being made by Atatürk himself.[8]

France's Foreign Ministry could hardly object. According to the Fundamental Law, the majority would have the right to appoint all the highest positions in the Sanjak. Nonetheless, the French thought it would have been better to reserve two seats on the Council as well as the presidency of the Assembly for minority members, in recognition of their demographic predominance and to help Turkey reinforce the good will it had been trying to exhibit since its forces had entered the Sanjak on July 4.[9]

The first session of the Assembly met in an old cinema on September 2, 1938. Although Arabic was an official language according to the Committee of Experts, the entire proceeding was conducted in Turkish and with the results that the Turkish government had anticipated. "Colonel Collet and Turkish Minister Açıkalın went together to the opening. French and Turkish companies did the honors. The Turkish national anthem and the Marseillaise were played. The session was opened with Muhammad Adali, the oldest member, presiding. Abdulgani Türkmen was unanimously elected [Assembly] President. The Chamber named two Vice-Presidents: [Shaykh] Maruf, Alawi; Vedi Munir, Turk. As expected, the choice of the chamber was unanimous for Tayfur Bey [Sökmen] for the post of President of the Sanjak."[10] The cabinet they appointed was composed entirely of Turks.[11] The Assembly immediately adopted the name Hatay for their republic, took the Turkish national anthem as their own, and created a flag that added one star to the Turkish flag. In January 1939, the Republic of Hatay adopted the Turkish criminal and penal codes, import policies, postage stamps, and money. The president and prime minister of the Sanjak both had seats in Turkey's Grand National Assembly.[12]

Neither the entrance of Turkey's troops nor the election of the new Assembly, however, resolved the legal status of the Sanjak. Turkey had intervened ostensibly

Flying the Hatay Flag, Antioch, circa 1940. Courtesy of Mehmet Saplama.

to help restore order so that the elections could be completed. Once finished, however, the Sanjak did not revert to the Statute and Fundamental Law that had been created by the Committee of Experts and approved by the League of Nations Council on May 29, 1937. Although the Statute of the Sanjak specified the use of Syrian currency and a connection to Syria in a customs union, the new Hatay government quickly outlawed the use of any currency except the Turkish lira, and abolished customs barriers with Turkey. At the same time, mandatory officials imposed "foreign" tariffs at the border for all Hatay goods entering Syria, as they tried to divert Syrian trade away from the port at Alexandretta and toward Latakia and Tripoli. Although passports were required to travel from Hatay to Syria, the border was opened for free travel between the Sanjak and Turkey. Finally, according to the Statute on behalf of which the Turks had claimed to be intervening, a high commissioner of French nationality and responsible to the League of Nations was to administer the Sanjak alongside the newly elected Parliament.[13] Instead, Turkey's Foreign Office seemed to be in charge.

Having acquiesced to Turkey's demand for the Sanjak, the French Foreign Ministry found itself uneasy about the fate of its remaining Syrian territories. Officials worried and wrote with increasing suspicion that the Turks would continue to incorporate border areas. Turkey's renewed claim on the three contested districts of Bayır, Bujak, and Hazine rejected by the League of Nations only two years earlier seemed to corroborate their fears. French prime minister Édouard Daladier was writing by June that Turkey was interested not only in Syria, but even in retaking Turkey's former territories now part of Iraq.[14]

In the Sanjak itself, a new animosity had been cultivated alongside the European insistence on a politics of identity. The intercommunal violence that had begun with the 1936 Syrian electoral contest did not cease at the creation of an independent Hatay. French reports for the fall of 1939 continued to detail violence, shootings, and attacks on villages based on the collective language or religion of the inhabitants. As in Europe, where identity politics had been displacing communities, this method of defining politics led to large numbers of refugees. Jakob Kunsler wrote a report from Syria documenting the exodus that began in June 1938, when Turkish troops entered the Sanjak. "The huge Amık plain, with its hundreds of Arabic, Kurdish and Armenian villages, was almost deserted. Despite the prospect of harvest, Christians and Muslims (Arabs, Alawis, and Kurds) hurried over the frontier. From Reyhanlı, fifty-four out of sixty families migrated immediately, and in the same way Kirikhan and other villages were left by the Armenians." Many sent their families away on the initial entry of Turkish troops, but emigration accelerated in the fall with the murder of a French soldier in October, the entry of many new Turkish troops, the creation of a customs barrier at the Syrian border, and the increasing monopoly of Turks over all official positions. This time, those leaving included "many of the prosperous class," who sold or took with them their possessions. "During the last days of October, it was difficult to find enough lorries and motor cars to carry away the families with their belongings." The report suggested that two-thirds of the Sanjak's Armenians had emigrated out of fear of the Turks and economic uncertainty, headed toward Aleppo, southern Syria, and Lebanon. The new customs boundary between the Sanjak and Syria made people worry that the steamers that had previously called at Alexandretta were now likely to abandon the port, making jobs and income scarce.[15]

Today's Turks tell a story of victorious "restitution." Turkish ambassador Güçlü described the aftermath in his 2000 book, *The Question of the Sanjak of Alexandretta*:

> The non-Turk local elements, on their part, remained calm and aspired only to preserve their rights, their liberty of worship and their properties. Everywhere in the Sanjak the Turkish flag waved beside the French colours. Manifestations of the Franco-Turkish friendship were finally seen and the Deputy Delegate of the High Commissioner [Collet] was at last able to decree the lifting of the martial law. On July 14, the French National Day, a Turkish detachment took part in the review. Thus, the Turks had achieved their immediate object—they were well established within the borders of the Sanjak.[16]

The triumphal narrative takes no notice of the refugees, the disenfranchisement of non-Kemalists within the government of Hatay, the effects of the separation of the population from former family and commercial networks, or the redirection of the Sanjak's trade away from its centuries-old connections with the now separate countries to the south and east.

In October 1938 Catton, the British representative at Mersin on the Turkish coast, reported that things were not going well in the new Hatay. Turks now occupied all of the Sanjak's offices, those of not only the department heads but even the minor officials, creating some resentment among non-Turks. According to Aleppo's British consul, Davis, traffic at the Alexandretta port had shrunk an estimated 60–70 percent as a result of the Syrian customs duties that France was now imposing at the new border between the Sanjak and Syria. The loss of income made it more difficult for Hatay to pay salaries; some officials had not been paid for two months.[17] By May 1939, he reported that the economic changes were resulting in widespread disillusionment. "The declarations made in such glowing terms to the Turkish Press by the President and Prime Minister of the Hatay State appear grossly to exaggerate the unanimity and joy with which the introduction of the new regime based on Kemalist principles has been received by the population of the Hatay." Davis claimed that "considerable discontent" existed among Arabs, Christians, and even Turks. The new government, in imposing both the Turkish currency and Turkish exchange control, had created a great deal of confusion among the commercial classes and made it much more difficult for people to make payments abroad for medical cures, education, holidays, and life insurance. In addition to the new customs duties, the Hatay government had imposed a heavy consumption tax. "Imported goods have tripled in price, local products such as fruit, vegetables, etc. have doubled in price, and many commodities have become absolutely unobtainable." At the same time, wages and salaries were remaining steady, resulting in what Davis called "a serious decline in purchasing power and in the general standard of living of the population of the Hatay." Fear that union with Turkey would reduce the number of government jobs and introduce conscription added to the mounting discontent. The president of Alexandretta's Halkevi created an angry scene in the Hatay Assembly, protesting that the government had introduced many new measures without consulting the Halkevleri.[18]

The international status of Hatay still remained unresolved. No longer consonant with the stipulations of the Statute and Fundamental Law of May 29, 1937, that had defined its independence, Hatay's existence had to be normalized in some way. Negotiations between France and Turkey reverted to their previous level of discord, as the two governments proved unable to settle their remaining issues. The events at Munich in October 1938 changed French policy in the Balkans and made the French less willing to give up territory in the eastern Mediterranean at the same time that they increasingly needed Turkey's support—or at least neutrality.[19] The French government had divided between pragmatists, who saw no way out except to concede the territory finally to Turkey, and the colonial front, who insisted on maintaining French territories overseas, especially in light of the oncoming rush to war in Europe. The new high commissioner, Gabriel Puaux, who replaced Martel, opposed ceding Hatay and gained support for his position when French senator Gustave Gautherot toured Hatay in the spring of 1939. Senator Gautherot found the French military presence quite weak, and wrote a letter to the Foreign Ministry in early May demanding to know "Are we abdicating?"[20]

Treaties were the sought-after prize by 1939, and England's discretion throughout the diplomatic maneuverings of the Sanjak crisis finally bore fruit. In May 1939, Great Britain signed a Mutual Aid Agreement with Turkey, which protected each country from aggression by the other; London loaned the Ankara regime 16 million pounds to buy armaments. The treaty became tripartite when talks finally concluded between Turkey and France. On June 23, 1939, the French and the Turks signed a treaty making the boundary between Syria and Hatay the new border between Turkey and Syria. French troops were to be

Downtown Antioch, circa 1940. Courtesy of Mehmet Saplama.

withdrawn during the next month. The Hatay Assembly met for the last time on June 30, 1939. During June and July, thousands of Armenians crossed into Syria and Lebanon, along with hundreds of Turks opposed to the Kemalist regime. Hatay officially became the sixty-third province of the Republic of Turkey.[21]

Yusuf Öcal, born in Antioch in 1926, remembered the momentous events he witnessed as a boy.

> After the annexation, the revolutions reverberated through us [our lives]. I will always remember, my father wore a fez and my mother a veil and black chador. Yet in a single day my father threw his fez away and my mother took her veil and black chador off. She did not cover her head and [wore] normal clothing. Not only her, but almost everyone in Antioch followed [the rules]. Those who did not follow [the new dress code] went to Syria.
>
> All the people of Antioch got together in front of the barracks that day. Women, men, children, everyone. Everyone rushed in front of the gate of the barracks and the flags were raised and lowered ceremoniously and the national anthems chanted. After their soldiers [the French] left—they went to Aleppo—I and everyone else saw the inside of the barracks for the first time. All the people rushed forward towards the barracks and filled them. The people cleansed the barracks all over. Women, children, all of us cleaned them up altogether.[22]

The people of Hatay claimed the new barracks to implement the transition.

People Opposing the Annexation of Hatay. Courtesy of Mihrac Ural.

When the Sanjak became Hatay, the sixty-third province of the Republic of Turkey, it incorporated many Arabic-speakers, joining the thousands already living in other southern provinces of Turkey. Many of those who left, and their descendants, like my driver, still speak with longing of the homes they lost. The government of Syria long refused to acknowledge the new situation: the maps the Syrian participants handed out at the 2000 Berlin International Tourism Fair included the Sanjak within the borders of Syria.[23] In the particularly tense days of 1998, when Turkey accused Syria of supporting a Kurdish separatist group and Syria claimed Turkey was diverting too much water from the Euphrates River on which both depended, Syria's ambassador to the United States referred to Hatay as Syria's stolen province, and Turkish troops mobilized on the border.

The narrative on the other side of the border is significantly different. In 2002, on the anniversary of Hatay's "joining the motherland," Turkish president Ahmet Necdet Sezer described the process: "With the unanimous decision by the parliament of Hatay our citizens from Hatay who were tied to the motherland from their hearts claimed their past and chose their own style of living and national identity."[24] With few exceptions, today's Turks "know" that Hatay became part of Turkey through a plebiscite, and "without one bullet being fired."[25]

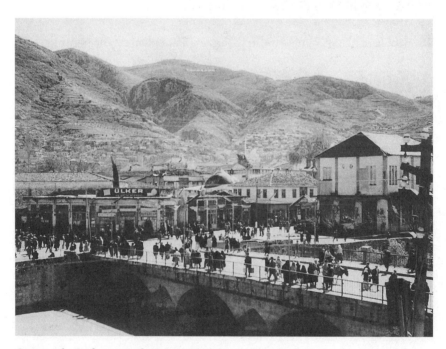

Crossing the Bridge, Antioch, circa 1940. Courtesy of Mehmet Saplama.

Turkey's celebratory narrative has occasionally been countered by historians and legal scholars claiming that the resolution of the "Sanjak question" was illegal: that France abdicated its responsibilities to both the League of Nations and to the Syrian government in behavior that was irreconcilable with previous decisions of the League of Nations. Instead of preserving Syria's territorial integrity as required by the mandate, France signed a treaty for its own benefit, essentially purchasing Turkey's mutual security pact with the currency of the Sanjak. Moreover, France's acquiescence to Ankara's irredentist claim on the Sanjak was particularly incomprehensible because Paris was simultaneously rejecting the very same German argument that Danzig, with its overwhelmingly German-speaking majority, should be returned to Germany.[26]

Turkey's claim to the Sanjak was not based only on irredentism, however. After all, hundreds of thousands of Turkish-speakers lived in Bulgaria, but Turkey made no claim to that territory. Turkey had two reasons to insist on controlling the Sanjak, one strategic and the other political. Strategically, the Turks' fear of invasion was paramount. Italians had invaded Anatolia by way of the Sanjak after World War I, and Turkey considered itself quite vulnerable through that port; both British and French military planners agreed with Turkey's strategists on this.[27] Second, Turkey was in the process of consolidating a revolutionary state. By 1936, the Kemalist regime in Ankara had committed itself for one whole decade to a nationalist project that sought to write "Turk" onto the entire population of Anatolia. That its program was running into obstacles and losing steam became evident not only in the aborted 1930 attempt at multiparty democracy, an experiment the government considered a catastrophe and in response to which it lowered a curtain of political conformity. Limits on the success of this nationalist project could also be seen even more clearly—and violently—in the 1937 uprising in Dersim and the military brutality employed to suppress it. Those risings, by Kurdish Alevis seeking to retain their autonomy against a centralizing state, showed the shallowness with which Turkification had rooted. Film, radio, and the press provided the outlets through which the government mobilized the Sanjak question as a popular nationalist cause in the Turkish republic. In this context, the Sanjak became the new backdrop against which a nationalist drama could play out, allowing the regime in Ankara to rewrite the history of Turkey, to reformulate the Alawis as Hittites (the original Turks), to refocus attention on a stage where the struggle for identity and Turkishness became a spectacle showcasing the ideology and power of the newly consolidating republic.

That Turkey's ambitious goals were facilitated by the policies of France and the recommendations of the League of Nations, regardless of the legality or custom of the time, requires a review of the broader context in which the League was functioning. Recognizing the role played by a member of a separatist group in bringing about World War I, U.S. president Woodrow Wilson reframed what had appeared to be a colonial conflict as a war for liberty and self-determination. Indeed, the Versailles Treaty that ended World War I created new states for some of the aggrieved nationalist groups and revised European borders to accommodate the demands of others. It soon became clear, however, that it would be impossible to create nation-states in Europe such that all linguistic groups could be collected within the borders of homogenous states. Many Germans remained outside Germany's new borders; Basques lived in parts of France and Spain. Fearful that those groups that the League of Nations was unable—or unwilling—to satisfy by creating a state of their own might destabilize the insecure peace, the League created an intermediate system. The Minorities Treaties were designed as a consolation prize for groups unable to achieve their own states, imposing a set of expectations on the newly created or expanded countries that hosted minority linguistic groups, insisting that these minorities be respected and given rights to develop their separate cultures within the framework of the existing state. The first of the Minorities Treaties, with Poland in 1919, served as the model for the rest, going beyond simple tolerance to an insistence that the languages and cultures of Polish minorities must be accommodated in public places, courts, and schools. Article 8 reads: "Polish nationals who belong to racial, religious or linguistic minorities shall enjoy the same treatment and security in law and in fact as the other Polish nationals. In particular, they shall have an equal right to establish, manage and control at their expense charitable, religious and social institutions, schools and other educational establishments, with the right to use their own language and to exercise their religion freely therein." In the first major test of the new Minorities Treaties system, the League of Nations refused to allow the Aaland islanders either to secede from Finland or to join Sweden, insisting instead that a minority treaty would protect their Swedish culture within the framework of the state of Finland. Moreover, the League of Nations made it clear that the privileges to be afforded members of minority groups applied to them as individuals; the group had no separate, collective legal standing. "They do *not* . . . encourage the existence of distinct national groups within the State."[28]

The 1921 Ankara Treaty ending hostilities between France and Turkey had included language similar to other minority treaties in its article 7: "A special administrative regime shall be established for the district of Alexandretta. The Turkish inhabitants of this district shall enjoy every facility for their cultural development. The Turkish language shall have official recognition." Alexandretta was to become a "special administrative district" within an Arabic-speaking Syria; promising the Turkish-speaking population special recognitions was consistent with European practice at the time. The language and the promise were consistent with Minorities Treaties because the Turkish community of the

Sanjak was recognized as the same sort of minority that existed throughout Europe at the end of the Versailles process.

If the goal of the Minorities Treaties regime had been to prevent the proliferation of small nation-states, it remains unclear why the League of Nations agreed so readily to the Sanjak's independence. Many in Europe agreed with the Balkan Entente's assessment that revising the borders established at the end of World War I would endanger the stability of the very system that had been established to avoid further war. The League of Nations had agreed to few demands to revise borders; the Saar Plebiscite, which assigned the disputed Saarland to Germany, was not the result of German demands but had already been stipulated in the 1918 Versailles Treaty. Indeed, the other border revisions Germany demanded were refused, which led, in part, to Germany's resignation from the League.

I spoke Turkish with the driver as I left Aleppo in October 2007. "Why do you speak Turkish?" I asked. "Because I'm a Turk," he responded. As we crossed the Syrian border into Turkey, the driver conversed with the guards in Arabic. "Why is it that you speak Arabic?" I asked. "Because I am an Arab," the driver responded.

Once having agreed to the Sanjak's independence, the League of Nations adopted what appears to be a novel form of representation there. Proportional representation had become common by World War I as a way to make certain that varied segments of the population would have their voices heard in a democratic system. Most were like the one adopted in the United States, where geography determined proportions in the lower house. In nineteenth-century Denmark, the middle class used proportional representation to reserve representation to their group in the face of the onslaught of universal male suffrage.[29] In the Sanjak, however, the Committee of Experts appears to have introduced an apparently new form of proportional representation that would be based on the linguistic or religious identity of the population.

This book has documented the consequences of this new form of proportional representation in the Sanjak. The project of registration *by community* produced devastating results. Although one could argue that the violence, arson, assault, and murder were a result of the Turkish government's insistence on revising the method of proportional representation suggested by the League of Nation Committee of Experts, it seems quite clear that the revised regulations only exacerbated existing problems. The Sanjak was cosmopolitan. Its people were not blind to their differences; indeed, rural villages were frequently dominated by one religious or linguistic group, as were many of the city's residential quarters. Nonetheless, the Sanjak's population had previously viewed their variations as something that would not necessarily require resolution, let alone conflict. Indeed, for many that variety had been an asset, not a liability; those trying to escape identity-based conflict had relocated to the Sanjak.

The Committee of Experts, in creating its novel formula for a new kind of democratically elected assembly for the Sanjak, was trying to implement the kind of protections that underlay the Minorities Treaties. The League of Nations, by guaranteeing seats for each of the communities it recognized as important, was enforcing the rights of diverse communities. In many ways, this new form of proportional representation was consistent with the long-term policies of the French government. Fearful of the power of a unified Sunni state, the mandatory regime had formulated and inculcated a politics of identity since the beginning of the mandate, a politics that had actually been born nearly a century earlier with France's interventions in Ottoman Syria on behalf of "minorities." The European powers at Geneva codified this politics of identity in the electoral regulations for the Sanjak, just as they would write it into the political charter of the new Lebanon. Their insistence on registration by "communities" cohered not only with the League's concern for the dangers of unreconciled minorities but also with European notions about Islam and Muslims' quest for control over non-Muslims. European fears of Muslims' treatment of Christian minorities had, after all, provided the legitimization for the wars of conquest that Europeans called the Crusades; that France and Britain had both used to insist on intervening in the Ottoman Empire; and that they offered as rhetorical justification for their colonial presence. Claiming that the Muslims would inevitably persecute the Christians or—a corollary claim— that the "communities" could not coexist peacefully allowed Europeans repeatedly to invade the Middle East in order to provide "protection." Once there, they enforced the divisions that provided their legitimation, allowing them more easily to dominate the conquered. In the Sanjak of Alexandretta, this very insistence on "protecting" minorities by guaranteeing them seats in the new Sanjak Assembly led not only to horrific violence but also to the dismemberment of a cosmopolitan society.

It was Turkey that demanded that the League of Nations disconnect politics from identity. Ankara claimed that it was impossible to actually divide the people of the Sanjak into groups because they had coexisted for so long. Motivated by their own desire to dominate the Sanjak, however, the Turks did not seek to dismantle the divisive electoral regulations but merely to modify them so that people could actually "change" their identities, could "become" Turks, or at least register as Turks. The Ankara regime utilized the underlying value structure represented in the new electoral regulations to create new facts. Recognizing that identities were malleable, Turkey manipulated the system to realize its own political agenda. The Sanjak episode enabled Turkey to put Kemalist nationalism on stage, providing Ankara with a venue for claiming entitlement to the allegiance of Alawis and Kurds as Turks, for displaying the nascent ideology for a home audience still not completely behind the Kemalist program, and for creating, at the same time, the Turkish majority necessary to comply with the League of Nations' electoral regulations. As League of Nations officials had predicted, however, allowing individual choice of identity registration could lead to tremendous violence.

In the end, it was not the freedom of individual choice demanded by Ankara that was so devastating for the safety of the residents of the Sanjak but the registration project itself. There might, perhaps, have been less violence if that free choice had not opened the door to coercion. Nonetheless, the Committee of Experts had defined categories as exclusive even though they were, in fact interdependent. Most residents of the Sanjak could have claimed more than one identity, especially if, as many demanded, Sunni Muslim had been included as an option. Alawis and Greek Orthodox residents spoke Arabic, so each could have registered in two groups. Nearly all of the people registering in linguistic groups could have also registered in religious groups, and vice versa. Recognizing the porous nature of identity in the Sanjak, the Turkish government rejected essentialist identities while at the same time denouncing the logical corollary of that rejection: the desire of some Turkish-speakers to oppose a Kemalist agenda. The consequence of the Turkish insistence on individual identity choice was violence and coercion that, as the League of Nations electoral commission noted, soon came to be systematically used to control and persecute the non-Turks of the Sanjak. The project of inscriptions under the revised electoral regulations led to divided villages and communities.

Indeed, it would be quite possible to argue that the project imposed by the Committee of Experts began the process of creating the kind of exclusionary identity that historian Peter Sahlins defines as nationalism.

> The definition of national identity does not depend on natural boundaries, nor is it defined by a nuclear component of social or cultural characteristics—an essential, primordial quality of "Frenchness" or "Spanishness." National identity is a socially constructed and continuous process of defining "friend" and "enemy," a logical extension of the process of maintaining boundaries between "us" and "them" within more local communities. National identities constructed on the basis of such an oppositional structure do not depend on the existence of any objective linguistic or cultural differentiation but on the subjective experience of difference.[30]

It was both a national identity and a political ideology that local Kemalists and the Ankara regime brought to the Sanjak; the Damascus regime was in the process of transforming an anti-imperial movement into a distinctively Syrian nationalism. The struggle over the Sanjak, by dividing the population and creating those boundaries between "us" and "them," helped in the development of the League of National Action, whose ideologue Zaki al-Arsuzi would become one of the theoreticians behind the new Arab Socialist Renaissance Ba'ath party that has ruled Syria since the 1960s.

> Queen of Hearts: Now then, are you ready for your sentence?
> Alice: But there has to be a verdict first.
> Queen of Hearts: Sentence first! Verdict afterwards.

Like the Queen of Hearts, the Ankara regime insisted that a Turkish majority be recognized before inscriptions even began. It is clear from the French documents that not only were the Turks never a majority in the Sanjak, but that French officials never actually believed them to be. French officials frequently referred to the 1921 Ankara Treaty to legitimize their acquiescence to Turkish demands, suggesting that they had previously recognized Turkish predominance in an instrument that was based, ironically, on the Minorities Treaties system. However, once Paris agreed that the Turks constituted a majority, it was faced with the challenge of actually implementing that recognition in the absence of an actual Turkish majority. Turkish officials blamed the French, the League of Nations electoral commission, and the detachment of supposedly Turkish-majority districts from the Sanjak, adamantly refusing to acknowledge the existing demographic situation. Paris consistently refused to renege on the French government's March 10 secret agreement with Ankara promising Turks a majority of seats in the new Sanjak Assembly. The sentence had been imposed months before the demographic verdict was in.

What France sought was Turkey's friendship, a guarantee that Turkey would not enter an upcoming war as an ally of Germany as the Ottoman Empire had done in World War I.[31] Italy had been making inroads into the region by presenting itself as an alternative to the hated French colonialists, especially through its creation of an Arabic-language broadcaster, Radio Bari.[32] France was unwilling to do anything to defend the Sanjak militarily, as the British repeatedly pointed out and as the Turks clearly understood, especially after France's failure to intervene to protect its interests much closer to home. Refusing to fight for the Sanjak of Alexandretta, and, in any case, needing a guarantee of Turkey's loyalty in the strategically important eastern Mediterranean, France judged cession of the Sanjak a small price to pay.

Syria's National Bloc government had neither the means nor the interest to prevent the alienation of the Sanjak. French control over Syria and the Sanjak prohibited an organized resistance. But paramount was the politics of the still unsigned Franco-Syrian Treaty promising Syrian independence. French politicians repeatedly warned the Damascus regime that its obstinacy over the Sanjak would endanger that treaty of independence. By the time Hatay became part of Turkey, that treaty was no longer even being discussed in Paris, and the National Bloc had itself been discredited and rendered ineffectual.

In the end, the population of the Sanjak was educated into a kind of polarized collective identity. Many resisted, including villagers who did not want to register because they refused to exacerbate local divisions, and Turks who rejected the nationalist Kemalist project and insisted on registering in a broader collective as Sunni Muslims. It is here that the Sanjak question provides its most important lessons. Implicit in the League's assumption was a conviction that the Sanjak people's religious and linguistic identities were singular (each man would have only one language or one religion), mutually exclusive (more than one identity could not coexist in one voter), and timeless (identities remained the same forever). Once the relative proportions were set, the Sanjak's new Statute and Fundamental Law assumed they would stay that way forever. Men (and only men were considered voters) would be represented as Turks, Kurds, Arabs, Orthodox, Armenians, Alawis, or others. Their class interests, professional needs, and ideological commitments were not considered "significant." Unlike in Europe or the United States, for example, where Armenians were considered whole persons whose political affiliations could be toward the left or right, and whose votes would be determined by a whole range of concerns, the Sanjak system insisted that the needs of Armenians in the Middle East were atavistic, timeless, and concerned with identity above all else. Many of the residents of the Sanjak responded as political people instead of engaging in identity politics. Turks who did not support the Kemalist political project insisted on registering as something other than "Turks," because it was clear that this category had been redefined by the Ankara regime to mean not a language but a political ideology that they could not support. Similarly, non-Turkish-speakers supporting the Kemalist reforms registered "as Turks." The system that had been intended to protect minorities, ironically, became an opening for the creation of animosity based on language or religion. The politics of difference enshrines identity as the most important political attribute, reifying language and religion as the determinative element of political affiliation, and justifying the indefinite leadership of elites who are defined by their inherent separation from one another.

The statesmen sifting through the ashes of the old Europe found their explanation for the origins of World War I, but did not realize that their forensic evidence provided clues only for the fires they had been investigating. They brought their evidence to the rest of the world instead, introducing into the Middle East the very processes which they had judged to have been the causes of World War I. Their forensic work concluded that it was the politics of identity that had divided Europe, and it was the politics of identity which could, paradoxically, prevent the next cataclysm. The populations of the world, divided into identity groupings, would determine their own collective future; those who differed from the dominant identity group would be guaranteed minority rights.

The electoral system the Committee of Experts introduced into the Sanjak of Alexandretta offered the best answer Europeans had yet discovered to provide rights to "minorities," in the process creating a new kind of politics in the Sanjak in which one's identity would pit him against members of the other groups in a competition for resources and power. Syria thus became an unwilling bystander suffering the brutal consequences when the League of Nations Committee of Experts decided that the only way to protect the population was to divide it. The identity groups that the Committee of Experts imposed on the Sanjak were illogical and therefore untenable; they could be made viable only by creating exclusions and drawing sharp divisions where none had existed and by purging (often violently) the liminal elements that illustrated the incoherence of the identity-politics project. Paradoxically, self-determination—the justification the European government used for the destructive process that took place in the Sanjak of Alexandretta—did not even matter in the end. The resolution of the Sanjak question reflected instead the strategic needs of the French government as Paris faced the renewed threat posed by a rearming Europe still in the throes of its own unresolved nationalism and irredentism.

The politics of identity, as introduced by European statesmen in their efforts to prevent another global conflagration like the first world war, has left a legacy of violence in urgent need of its own forensic investigation. Having failed to avert a second world war, identity politics has nonetheless acquired credibility as a respected way to "resolve" conflicts outside Europe. Across Africa and Asia, infernos have been ignited as "minorities," defined and set apart by colonizing or post-colonial outsiders, square off against former neighbors.

The larger region remains fraught with the repercussions of the League of Nations' efforts, both personal and political. My red-haired driver still identifies himself with a city to which he can no longer "belong." Identity politics has been codified in Lebanon's constitution, for example, where the "leaders" of each community spent decades thriving on the power they derived by maintaining the division of Lebanon's people into the groups that had been defined by a colonizing France as being incapable of political cooperation. Even further from the Sanjak, Bagdad faced its own horrific ethnic cleansing in 2006 after centuries as a city intertwined. While foreign media provided endless inaccurate and ahistorical analyses of the inability of Sunnis and Shi'is to coexist, Iraqi refugees responded to the United Nations High Commissioner for Refugees' "identity question" with a peevish "Why do you Europeans always ask that?"[33] When I asked my twenty-something Iraqi student about this supposedly all-important identity marker in 2004, she had pondered for a moment before admitting she did not know and promising to ask her mother. Nonetheless, as warfare emerges in places where ethnic and linguistic differences had not previously elicited a violent response, outsider experts persist in the kind of forensic analysis that hands power—and, metaphorically, matches—to those purporting to be leaders of "their communities."

Appendix I

TREATIES (CHRONOLOGICAL ORDER)

National Pact (Misak-ı Milli, also called National Oath) was created by the Ottoman Parliament in its final meeting on January 28, 1920. The National Pact claimed territories inhabited by non-Arab Muslim majorities as part of its state, while relinquishing control over the Ottoman Empire's Arab provinces.

San Remo Resolution of April 25, 1920, emerged from the meeting of the Supreme Allied Council (representatives of Great Britain, France, Italy, and Japan) in San Remo, Italy. The Resolution allocated mandates in the former Ottoman territories, although the delineation of the boundaries was not determined until the Sèvres Treaty.

Sèvres Treaty, whose full name is Treaty of Peace between the Allied and Associated Powers and Turkey, was signed in the Paris suburb of Sèvres on August 10, 1920. The Sèvres Treaty created a small Turkish state in the center of the defeated Ottoman Empire, to be surrounded by proposed Kurdish and Armenian states in the east and Greek-controlled areas on the Aegean coast. Remaining Ottoman territory in Europe was to become part of Greece, and the Ottoman Arab provinces were assigned to Britain and France. The Sèvres Treaty was never enforced, replaced by the Treaty of Lausanne at the end of the Turkish War of Independence.

Ankara Treaty, signed October 20, 1921, in Ankara, ended hostilities between Turkey and France that had been ongoing since World War I. It is also called the Franco-Turkish Agreement of 1921, and the Franklin-Bouillon Treaty, even though the Franklin-Bouillon who signed on behalf of France represented only one side. Yusuf Kemal signed the treaty on behalf of Turkey. The Ankara Treaty made special provisions for the Turkish population of the Sanjak of Alexandretta.

Mandate for Syria and Lebanon, approved on July 24, 1922, assigned control over the Ottoman territories to France as part of the Mandates system, to be administered under the supervision of the League of Nations Permanent Mandates Commission.

Treaty of Lausanne was signed on July 24, 1923, by Turkey, Great Britain, Greece, France, Italy, Japan, Romania, and the Serb-Croat-Slovene State. It ended hostilities that had been ongoing since World War I (though France had earlier signed a separate peace) and replaced the 1920 Sèvres Treaty, which had been overturned by the continuing warfare between Turkish nationalist forces and European armies of occupation. The Treaty of Lausanne provided international recognition to the new Republic of Turkey.

Franco-Syrian Treaty of 1936, also called the Franco-Syrian Treaty of Independence and the Franco-Syrian Treaty of Friendship and Alliance, was negotiated by France's Popular Front government and Syria's National Bloc representatives in Paris in September 1936 and signed by Viénot and Mardam in Damascus on December 22, 1936. Ratified three months later by the Syrian Parliament, it was never submitted for ratification to the French body.

Sandler Report was approved by the League of Nations Council on January 27, 1937. It sketched the outlines of an independent Sanjak, redefining the region from part of the Syria mandate to a "distinct entity" that was to be federated with Syria.

Statute of the Sanjak, created by a Committee of Experts and approved by the League of Nations Council on May 29, 1937, codified the structures of the new state, delineated its boundaries, and described its relations with neighbors and France.

Fundamental Law of the Sanjak, created by a Committee of Experts and approved by the League of Nations Council on May 29, 1937, described a government with three branches and the electoral basis for the creation of a legislative assembly.

Franco-Turkish Agreements were signed May 29, 1937, at the acceptance of the League of Nations Council's resolution accepting the Sanjak Statute and Fundamental Law. In the agreements, the two governments committed themselves to its joint defense, guaranteed the independence of Syria and Lebanon, and stipulated the boundaries between Syria and Turkey.

Treaty of Friendship was signed by the governments of France and Turkey on July 4, 1938, with a Syrian representative looking on. The two countries promised to work together to guarantee the Sanjak's territorial integrity and promised not to engage in political or military attacks on each other.

Appendix II

PARTIES AND COMMISSIONS (ALPHABETICAL ORDER)

Active Committee of the National Turkish Party, headed by Abdulgani Türkmen, was established at the beginning of 1937 but seems to have dissolved into the Republican People's Party.

Committee of Nationalist Youth and Students was likely the Aleppo chapter of the Arab nationalist youth organization affiliated with the National Bloc government.

Committee for the Defense of the Sanjak was headed by Syrian opposition leader Abd al-Rahman Shahbandar.

Committee of the Defense of the Liwa of Alexandretta and Antioch was an Arab nationalist ad hoc group that appeared with the distribution of brochures in 1937.

Hatay Committee was formed at the beginning of 1937, and seems to have become part of the Republican People's Party.

International Mission of Observers to the Sanjak of Alexandretta was a three-person delegation agreed on by the League of Nations Council at its meeting on December 16, 1936. Its mission was to inform the Council on the situation in the Sanjak without inquiring into the "substance" of the dispute or intervening in events.

League of National Action was the Arab nationalist party that led both the anti-colonial struggle and the effort to keep the Sanjak within Syria's orbit.

League of Nations Commission for the Organization and Supervision of the First Elections in the Sanjak of Alexandretta (electoral commission) drew up regulations for the elections, visited the Sanjak under the leadership of President

Reid, and returned to supervise the elections in April 1938 under the leadership of Reimers.

League of Nations Committee of Experts was appointed by the League of Nations Council to draw up the Statute and Fundamental Law for the Sanjak.

League of Nations Committee of the Council, also called the Committee of Five, was an ad hoc committee of five members (representing Sweden, Great Britain, Belgium, France, and Turkey) formed to revise the electoral regulations that had been created by the League of Nations Commission for the Organization and Supervision of the First Elections in the Sanjak of Alexandretta.

League of Nations Permanent Mandates Commission was to provide a supervisory role for all of the League of Nations mandates.

National Bloc was the nationalist political group that rose to power in opposition to French rule in Syria by the 1930s. After signing the Franco-Syrian Treaty that, they hoped, would achieve Syria's independence, they entered into a policy of "honorable cooperation" with the mandatory regime.

National Union, created at the end of 1937, hoped to unify the Sanjak's population and bring peace and prosperity in connection with Syria and within the framework of the Statute and Fundamental Law.

Republican People's Party was the ruling party in Turkey. It was represented in the Sanjak by local chapters and by People's Houses (*halkevleri*, sing. *halkevi*).

Sanjak Union, created at the beginning of 1938, may have been connected with the National Union. It sought to bring together Arabs, non-Kemalist Turks, and others, eliciting the animosity of the Sanjak's Kemalists.

Society for Annexation to Turkey was established by Captain Refik Bey in October 1936. It seems to have disappeared soon after, its activities apparently folded into the work of the Republican People's Party.

NOTE ON SOURCES

French government records and League of Nations archives related to these events are now open to researchers. Besides the Turkish government, these two were the active groups determining not only the outcome but also the day-to-day situations on the ground in the Sanjak. The new Syrian government had little influence on decisions, on institutions, or even on the lives of those in the Sanjak, and I have not made use of their records for this work. At the same time, the memoirs of important Syrian government leaders remain silent about the Sanjak Question, most likely because its outcome proved a fatal embarrassment for their rule. The major exception is in the works of Zaki al-Arsuzi, an opponent of the Syrian regime as well as the French occupation, for whom the Sanjak Question served as a foundational experience for his later philosophy and political activism.

The other major party to the dispute, the government of Turkey, has refused access to government records of these events. Dr. Yücel Güçlü, who served as Turkey's ambassador to Italy while writing *The Question of the Sanjak of Alexandretta: A Study in Turkish-French-Syrian Relations*, wrote, "The study of Turkish foreign policy should ideally be based on Turkish archives. But unfortunately this is not possible as the archives of the Ministry of Foreign Affairs of Turkey dealing with the post-1918 period are still closed to private research" (p. viii). Needless to say, they were also unavailable to me. I have been able to view scattered documents from the Turkish Interior Ministry, deliberations of Turkey's parliament toward the end of the incidents, and varied Turkish documents in both the French and League of Nations archives. I hope that future researchers are able to revise the findings of this book when access to Turkish records becomes available.

ABBREVIATIONS USED IN NOTES

AA	Paris and Nantes: Ministères des affaires étrangères. Series: Ankara
AEGR	Turkey: Ankara Embassy General Records (AEGR) 751, State Department Central Files, Record Group 59 (RG 59); National Archives at College Park, MD (NACP)
CP	Paris and Nantes: Ministères des affaires étrangères. Series: Syrie-Liban Cabinet Politique (CP)
CSG	An abbreviation for the Chief of General Security
DSG	An abbreviation for the individual Director of General Security who signed many of the event summaries found in the mandatory archives in Nantes.
FO	London: National Archives (formerly Public Record Office), Foreign Office 371 (Syria)
IEGR	Turkey: Istanbul Embassy General Records (IEGR) 751, State Department Central Files, Record Group 59 (RG 59); National Archives at College Park, MD (NACP)
MAE	Minister of Foreign Affairs, France
NACP	College Park, Maryland: National Archives and Records Administration
RG	Record Group, State Department Central Files, U.S. National Archives, College Park, Maryland
SecState	Secretary of State of the United States
SDN	Geneva, Switzerland: League of Nations Archives (Société des Nations). Includes: **S** League of Nations Secretariat: Political Section and Mandates Section, Registry Files; and **C** League of Nations External Fonds: Electoral Commission for the Sanjak of Alexandretta and Archives of the Special Tribunal (1919–1947)

NOTES

Introduction

1. Audience of June 9, 1938, League of Nations External Fonds, Electoral Commission for the Sanjak of Alexandretta and Archives of the Special Tribunal (Hereafter C) 1041, Geneva, Switzerland: League of Nations Archives (Société des Nations) (hereafter SDN).
2. Woodrow Wilson, *Woodrow Wilson: Essential Writings and Speeches of the Scholar-President*, ed. Mario R. D. Nunzio (New York: New York University Press, 2006), 412–13.
3. For an introduction to some of the literature on Arab nationalism, see Rashid Khalidi, "Arab Nationalism: Historical Problems in the Literature," *American Historical Review* 96 (1991): 1363–73; Philip S. Khoury, *Syria and the French Mandate: The Politics of Arab Nationalism, 1920–1945* (Princeton, NJ: Princeton University Press, 1989); James P. Jankowski and Israel Gershoni, *Rethinking Nationalism in the Arab Middle East* (New York: Columbia University Press, 1997); James Gelvin, "Modernity and Its Discontents: On the Durability of Nationalism in the Arab Middle East," *Nations and Nationalisms* 5 (1999): 71–89.

Chapter 1

1. Pierre Bazantay, *Enquête sur l'artisanat a Antioche* (Beirut: Imperimerie Catholique, 1936), 13.
2. Ahmet Faik Türkmen, *Mufassal Hatay: Tarih, cografya, ekalliyetler, mezhepler, edebiyat, içtimai durum, lengüistik durum, folklor, etnografya ve Hatay davcasini ihtiva eden 4 cild* (Istanbul: Cumhuriyet Matbaasi, 1937), 49–87.
3. Pierre Bazantay, *La pénétration de l'enseignement dans le sandjak autonome d'Alexandrette* (Beirut: Imprimerie Catholique, 1935), 7.
4. Keith Watenpaugh, *Being Modern in the Middle East: Revolution, Nationalism, Colonialism, and the Arab Middle Class* (Princeton, NJ: Princeton University Press, 2006), 32.
5. Watenpaugh, *Being Modern in the Middle East*, 143–44. Robert B. Satloff, "Prelude to Conflict: Communal Interdependence in the Sanjak of Alexandretta 1920–1936," *Middle Eastern Studies* 22 (1986): 147–80.
6. Yücel Güçlü, *Question of the Sanjak of Alexandretta: A Study in Turkish-French-Syrian Relations* (Ankara: Türk Tarih Kurumu, 2001), 330.
7. Sarah Shields, "Convivencia and Muslims," *Pacem* 4 (2001): 39–53.
8. For the French division of the Syrian mandate, see Philip S. Khoury, *Syria and the French Mandate*; and Itamar Rabinovich, "The Compact Minorities and the Syrian State, 1918–45," *Journal of Contemporary History* 14 (1979): 693–712. Martin C. Thomas,"French Intelligence-Gathering in the Syrian Mandate, 1920–1940," *Middle Eastern Studies* 38 (2002): 1–32.

9. Bazantay, *La pénétration de l'enseignement,* 5–6.
10. Seda Altuğ, "Popular Nationalism in Antioch during the French Mandate: The Making of the Sanjak of Alexandretta," *Chronos* 13 (2006): 231–75.
11. Durieux to Martel, October 15, 1936, Paris and Nantes: Ministères des affaires étrangères. Series: Syrie-Liban Cabinet Politique (hereafter CP), 973
12. Howard Lee Eissenstat, "The Limits of Imagination: Debating the Nation and Constructing the State in Early Turkish Nationalism," Ph.D. diss., University of California at Los Angeles, 2007. Selim Deringil, "The Ottoman Origins of Turkish Nationalism, Namik Kemal to Mustafa Kemal," *European History Quarterly* 23 (1993): 165–91.
13. Despite the Republic's emphasis on secularism, the identity of Turk was tied to being Muslim. Ahmet İçduygu and Özlem Kaygusuz, "The Politics of Citizenship by Drawing Borders: Foreign Policy and the Construction of National Citizenship Identity in Turkey," *Middle Eastern Studies* 40 (2004): 26–50.
14. Filliet to Special Services Inspector, December 11, 1934, CP 973.
15. Conseiller Adjoint to High Commissioner, December 12, 1934, CP 973, folder 7.
16. Report, April 10, 1936, CP 973.
17. James Gelvin, *Divided Loyalties: Nationalism and Mass Politics in Syria at the Close of Empire* (Berkeley: University of California Press, 1998).
18. Khoury, *Syria and the French Mandate,* 122–23.
19. Keith Berriedale, "Mandates," *Journal of Comparative Legislation and International Law* 4 (1922): 71–83.
20. Edmund Burke III, "A Comparative View of French Native Policy in Morocco and Syria, 1912–1925," *Middle Eastern Studies* 9 (1973): 175–86. Martin Thomas, *The French Empire between the Wars: Imperialism, Politics and Society* (Manchester: University of Manchester Press, 2005). Martin C. Thomas, "French Intelligence-Gathering in the Syrian Mandate, 1920–1940," *Middle Eastern Studies* 38 (2002): 1–32. Khoury, *Syria and the French Mandate.* N. E. Bou-Nacklie, "Les Troupes Spéciales: Religious and Ethnic Recruitment, 1916–1946," *International Journal of Middle East Studies* 25 (1993): 645–60. Michael Provence, *The Great Syrian Revolt and the Rise of Arab Nationalism* (Austin: University of Texas Press, 1925). Gelvin, *Divided Loyalties.* Elizabeth Thompson, *Colonial Citizens* (New York: Columbia University Press, 2000).
21. See William B. Cohen, "The Colonial Policy of the Popular Front," *French Historical Studies* 7 (1972), 368–393, on French policy.
22. *La République,* September 24, 1936, enclosed in Lescuyer to Delbos, September 25, 1936, CP 516.
23. Lescuyer to Delbos, September 27, 1936, CP 516.
24. *La République,* September 25, 1936, enclosed in Lescuyer to Delbos, September 25, 1936, CP 516.
25. Martel to French foreign ministry (hereafter MAE), October 3, 1936, CP 516. The Halkevi (plural Halkevleri), or People's Houses—a government-sponsored center whose mission was to inculcate Turkishness in the population (discussed in chapter 2).
26. Lescuyer to Delbos, September 27, 1936, CP 516. Martel to Delbos, October 3, 1936, CP 516. Selim Deringil discussed the role of Turkey's press in *Turkish Foreign Policy during the Second World War: An "Active" Neutrality* (Cambridge: Cambridge University Press, 1989), 7–11.
27. Lescuyer to Delbos, September 14, 1936, CP 508.
28. Martel to MAE, October 3, 1936, CP 516.
29. Millot to Meyrier, September 25, 1936, CP 516.
30. To Martel, September 23, 1936, included with Durieux to Martel, October 5, 1936, CP 523.
31. Keith Watenpaugh, "'Creating Phantoms': Zaki al-Arsuzi, the Alexandretta Crisis, and the Formation of Modern Arab Nationalism in Syria," *International Journal of Middle East Studies* 28 (1996): 363–89.

32. Director of General Security (hereafter DSG) Beirut Information 3634, October 6, 1936, from Alexandretta Security, October 5, 1936, CP 564.
33. Intelligence report, October 7, 1936, CP 564. Al-Barazi to al-Jabiri, October 6, 1936, CP 523.
34. Intelligence report, October 7, 1936, CP 564. Police report 745, October 5, 1936, CP 523. Gacon to Durieux, October 16, 1936, CP 523.
35. CP 524.
36. MacMurray to Secretary of State of the United States (hereafter SecState), December 1, 1936, 751.67/106, RG 59, NACP.
37. Martel to MAE, January 8, 1937, CP 516.
38. DSG Beirut Information 3724, October 12, 1936, CP 524.
39. Telegram, DSG Information 3772, October 13, 1936, CP 524. The French used "liwa," the Arabic equivalent for the Turkish-origin "sanjak" (sancak), a province or subsection of a province.
40. Provence, *Great Syrian Revolt*, 61. Peter Shambrook, "Bypassing the Nationalists: Comte Damien de Martel's 'Administrative' Reforms of January 1936," in *France, Syrie et Liban 1918–1946: Lies ambiguités et les dynamiques de la relation mandataire*, edited by Nadine Méouchy (Damascus, 2002), 233.
41. On France's efforts to divide the population according to ethnicity, see Khoury, *Syria and the French Mandate*; and Rabinovich, "The Compact Minorities and the Syrian State."
42. John M. VanderLippe, *The Politics of Turkish Democracy: Ismet Inonu and the Formation of the Multi-party System, 1938–1950* (Albany: State University of New York Press, 2005), 16–17. Soner Çağaptay, "Race, Assimilation and Kemalism: Turkish Nationalism and the Minorities in the 1930s," *Middle Eastern Studies* 40 (2004): 86–101. İlker Aytürk, "Turkish Linguists against the West: The Origins of Linguistic Nationalism in Ataturk's Turkey," *Middle Eastern Studies* 40 (2004): 92–108.
43. Quoted in Andrew Mango, *Atatürk: The Biography of the Founder of Modern Turkey* (Woodstock, NY: Overlook Press, 1999), 434.
44. Annex to Durieux to Martel, October 24, 1936, CP 523, annex by Gacon dated October 16, 1936. DSG Beirut Information 3887, October 19, 1936, from Alexandretta Security, October 15, 1936, CP 524.
45. DSG Beirut Information 3775, October 13, 1936, from Alexandretta Security, October 10, 1936, CP 524.
46. Garabed Summary, October 4, 1936, CP 523. Telegram, Martel to MAE, October 5, 1936, CP 523. Telegram, Durieux to Martel, October 5, 1936, CP 523. Service de Police No. 745, Antioch, October 5, 1936 also emphasized the role of the Istanbul press, CP 523.
47. Alexandretta Security Information 3772, October 10 and 13, 1936, CP 524.
48. Martel to Durieux, October 9, 1936, CP 508.
49. Ponsot to Martel, October 7, 1936, CP 524.
50. Telegram, October 8, 1936, CP 516.
51. Al-Barazi to Minister of the Interior, attached to Fiey to Martel, October 15, 1036, CP 523.
52. Durieux to Martel, October 5, 1936, CP 523.
53. Durieux to Martel, October 5, 1936, CP 523.
54. Durieux to Martel, October 5, 1936, CP 523.
55. Khoury, *Syria and the French Mandate*, 469.
56. Police 745 to Antioch Police, October 5, 1936, CP 523.
57. Martel to MAE, October 6, 1936, CP 508.
58. Telegram sent October 3, 1936, enclosed with DSG Beirut Information 3772, October 13, 1936, from Alexandretta Security, October 10, 1936, CP 534.
59. Telegram, Martel to MAE, October 11, 1936, CP 523.

60. Annex to Durieux to Martel, October 24, 1936, CP 523, annex by Gacon dated October 16, 1936.

61. Annex to Durieux to Martel, October 24, 1936, CP 523, annex by Gacon dated October 21, 1936.

62. Soner Çağaptay, "Race, Assimilation and Kemalism," quoting Galip, 88–89.

63. DSG Beirut Information 3891, October 19, 1936, from Alexandretta Security, October 16, 1936, CP 524. DSG Beirut Information 4002, October 20, 1936, from Alexandretta Security, CP 524.

64. Annexes to Durieux to Martel, October 24, 1936, CP 523, annexes by Gacon dated October 16 and 21, 1936.

65. On the role of the French security services, see Thomas, "French Intelligence-Gathering in the Syrian Mandate," 1–32.

66. Pourcel to Durieux, October 14, 1936, CP 523.

67. Pourcel to Durieux, October 14, 1936, CP 523.

68. Durieux to Martel, October 24, 1936, CP 523.

69. Durieux to Martel, Message no. 50, forwarded October 30, 1936, CP 523. Telegram, parents to Martel, November 2, 1936, CP 523.

70. Annex to Durieux to Martel, October 24, 1936, CP 523, annex by Gacon dated October 20, 1936.

71. Gacon to Durieux, October 26, 1936, CP 523.

72. Gacon to Durieux, October 26, 1936, CP 523.

73. Gacon to Durieux, October 21, 1936, CP 523.

74. Gacon to Durieux, October 21 and 26, 1936, CP 523. Husni al-Barazi, in his letter to the Syrian interior minister on October 6, took many of the same positions. He claimed that the Turkish press campaign had become shrill, and accused Turkish agents of working to foment trouble. He also presented a fascinating alternative view of the October 4 market strike, claiming that the Turks had been carrying prohibited weapons, and that the choice of Sunday to close the markets reflected the new policy within Turkey of taking Sunday as a day of rest. Al-Barazi to Interior Minister, October 6, 1936, CP 523. For more on al-Barazi and his participation in nationalist politics in Syria, see Khoury, *Syria and the French Mandate.*

75. Durieux to Martel, October 24, 1936, CP 523. Gacon to Durieux, October 26, 1936, CP 523.

76. Telegram, MAE to Martel, November 7, 1936; Damascus to Martel and Telegram, Durieux, CP 523. Telegram, Martel to MAE, November 5, 1936, CP 523.

77. MacMurray to SecState, December 1, 1936, 751.67/106, RG 59, NACP. See also Güçlü, *Question of the Sanjak,* 109–10, and Yilmaz Öz, *Quotations from Mustafa Kemal Atatürk* (Ankara: Ministry of Foreign Affairs, 1982), 1936.

78. Güçlü, *Question of the Sanjak,* 110.

79. Brock Millman, "Turkish Foreign and Strategic Policy 1934–42," *Middle Eastern Studies* 31 (1995), 485–486.

80. MacMurray to Hull, May 19, 1937, AEGR.

81. Güçlü, *Question of the Sanjak,* 112–113.

82. Durieux to Martel, October 24, 1936, CP 523.

83. Annex to Durieux to Martel, October 24, 1936, CP 523, annex by Gacon dated October 21, 1936.

84. Durieux to Martel, October 31, 1936, CP 523.

85. Official Denial, Durieux, November 10, 1936, CP 523.

86. Telegram, Durieux to Martel, November 11, 1936, CP 523.

87. Pourcel to Dureiux, November 16, 1936, CP 524.

88. Telegram, Durieux to Martel, November 11, 1936, CP 523.

89. Telegram, Martel to MAE, November 13, 1936, CP 523. Telegram, Durieux to Martel, November 13, 1936, CP 523.

Chapter 2

1. The French estimated participation at 40 percent in Alexandretta, 45 percent in Antioch, and 51 percent in Kirikhan. In Damascus, 36 percent voted; Aleppo had the highest rate at 59 percent. In 1931, more than 70 percent of eligible Sanjak voters had participated. Telegram, Martel to MAE, November 24, 1936, CP 523. Martel noted that the Antioch figure included the countryside. In the Turkish quarters of the city, the vote was "insignificant." According to the Turkish press, only 4.5 percent of voters had gone to the polls at Antioch, 9 percent at Reyhanlı, 12.5 percent at Beylan, and 21 percent at Kirikhan. Telegram, Ponsot to Martel, November 21, 1936, CP 523. The boycott had varied effects. In the Kirikhan area, local officials wrote, "first day of elections took place in the most complete calm. Only the district of Aktepe could finish. The result obtained went beyond the provisions of the past two days, 1,295 votes of 1,503, 86.1 percent." On the other hand, voting places in Karaçağil and Muratpaşa towns received only a few voters, and the towns of Beylan and Kirikhan had Armenian votes and a few Sunni voters. "Reyhanlı will have a satisfying result altogether. Turkish element voted en bloc in the district of Aktepe, in very few numbers at Karaçail and Muratpaşa; they abstained entirely at Kirikhan, Belan and Reyhanlı." Enclosure 4: Pourcel to Durieux, November 15, 1936, with Durieux to Martel, November 19, 1936, CP 524.
2. Durieux to Martel, November 17, 1936, CP 524.
3. DSG Aleppo Information 1211, November 13, 1936, enclosed in Durieux to Martel, November 19, 1936, CP 524. Telegram, Martel to MAE, November 20, 1936, CP 523. Delegate Damascus to Martel, November 21, 1936, CP 523.
4. DSG Aleppo Information 1211, November 13, 1936, enclosed in Durieux to Martel, November 19, 1936, CP 524. Delegate Damascus to Martel, November 21, 1936, CP 523.
5. Durieux found himself unsure which Alawi candidate to support: Shaykh Sadek Maruf, "a crook," was running against Zaki al-Arsuzi, "an anarchist/communist." The governor arrested al-Arsuzi later that day for obstructing the freedom of the elections. Durieux to Martel, November 17, 1936, CP 524. Telegram, Durieux to Martel, November 17, 1936, CP 523. Pourcel to Durieux, November 16, 1936, enclosed with Durieux to Martel, November 19, 1936, CP 524.
6. Telegram, Durieux to Martel, November 20, 1936, CP 523. Durieux repeated his accusations that Turcophiles had taken these measures to obstruct the polling in an interview with Turkey's consul Feridun Erkin, at Aleppo on December 10, 1936. Durieux to Martel, December 11, 1936, CP 524.
7. Telegram, Martel to MAE, November 21, 1936, CP 523.
8. Telegram, Martel to MAE, November 25, 1936, CP 523. Summary of December 10 interview with Feridun Erkin.
9. Accounts of the riots on November 30 and December 1 are taken from Garabed Summary 902, December 3, 1936, CP 524. Also Martel to MAE, December 1, 1936, CP 523. Telephone message, DSG Alexandretta to DSG Beirut and Damascus, December 1, 1936, CP 523. Gacon to Special Services Alexandretta, December 3, 1936, CP 523. Telephone message, DSG Alexandretta to DSG Beirut and Damascus, December 1, 1936, CP 523. Durieux to Damascus Delegate, December 1, 1936, CP 523. Telephone message, DSG Alexandretta and Antioch to DSG Beirut and Damascus, December 1, 1936, CP 523. Telegram, Bonnot to Martel, December 2, 1936, CP 523. Telegram, Martel to MAE, December 4, 1936, CP 523. Telegram, Durieux to Martel, December 8, 1936, CP 523. Durieux to Martel, December 7, 1936, CP 523. Telegram, Durieux to Martel, November 30, 1936, CP 523.
10. Philip S. Khoury, *Syria and the French Mandate*, 389.
11. Only one Turcophile notable, Vedi Munir, was present.
12. DSG Beirut Information 4781, December 4, 1936, based on Aleppo Security, December 2, 1936, CP 524.

13. League of Nations, *Official Journal 1937*, 53. SDN C.538.M.348.1936, S 1644. Güçlü makes the same claims for rampant violence and French coercion in *The Question of the Sanjak of Alexandretta*, 116–18, 124n, but unfortunately does not provide sources.
14. League of Nations, *Official Journal 1937*, 53–54.
15. Paullepistre to Martel, December 4, 1936 CP 516.
16. Arvengas to Delbos, December 4, 1936, CP 516.
17. In his note of October 10, 1936, Turkey's ambassador to Paris, Suad Davaz, made the Turkish position clear. The Sanjak's "autonomy was therefore understood to come within the framework of the French mandate and not of Syrian independence. The incorporation at one time of Alexandretta and Antioch in Syria constitutes an act of authority which can be explained by the requirements of the mandatory administration, but which cannot constitute a right acquired for Syria"; League of Nations, *Official Journal 1937*, 42.
18. League of Nations, *Official Journal 1937*, 24–29. Gilbert, the U.S. consul in Geneva, summarized the French case in a telegram to the secretary of state, December 15, 1936, 84/350/69/21/5, Foreign Service Post Files, Record Group 84 (hereafter RG 84) NACP. He offered his own analysis: "The chief of the League of Nations Section of the British Foreign Office has told me, what indeed appears to be obvious, that in the Council both Turkey and France are exploiting their legal positions for its effect on general opinion letting the practical issues remain in the background. He believes the problem to be difficult of solution. He confirms that the Turks discussed with the British the presentation of the Case to Geneva but asserts that this does not mean that Great Britain gave its endorsement to the Turkish position. He stated that France could not consent to the Sanjak becoming Turkish or to its independence which would presumably mean Turkish tutelage, for strategic reasons. He said that London held views similar to Paris in this respect and that he had reason to believe that a 'Turkish Alexandretta' was likewise opposed by Rome."
19. League of Nations, *Official Journal 1937*, 31–34.
20. Telegram, Martel to Lescuyer, December 18, 1936, CP 523.
21. Lescuyer to Martel, December 22, 1936, CP 524.
22. According to the U.S. ambassador in Paris, the French "feel that the mission of the three neutral observers to be sent to the Sanjak by the League will probably develop into an inquiry into the activities of the Turkish agents in the Sanjak who have been provoking disorders." Telegram, Bullitt to SecState, December 18, 1936, 350/69/21/5, RG 84, NACP.
23. Martel to MAE, January 1, 1937, CP 516.
24. Martel to MAE, January 1, 1937, CP 516.
25. Telegram, Durieux to Martel, December 30, 1936, CP 516.
26. Telegram, Martel to MAE, January 1, 1937, CP 516. Telegram, Bonnot to Martel, January 1, 1937, CP 516.
27. DSG Beirut Information 32, January 4, 1937, based on Azaz Security, December 28, 1936, CP 524. DSG Beirut Information 34, January 4, 1937, based on Alexandretta Security, January 2, 1937, CP 524. DSG Beirut Information 36, January 4, 1937, based on Alexandretta Security, CP 524. Martel reminded Durieux that international agreements foresaw a special pavilion for the Sanjak, but the official emblem not yet having been defined and the authorities not having been called to sanction it, it would be appropriate to consider as seditious all emblems except the Syrian national flag. Telegram, Martel to Durieux, December 31, 1936, CP 516.
28. Examples include trips by Antioch's Turcophiles to Kilis, in Turkey, to provide information and to be present at the inauguration of the new Club Hatay. DSG Beirut Information 170, January 12, 1937, based on Aleppo Security January 9, 1937, CP 524. DSG Beirut Information 89, January 8, 1937, based on Aleppo Security January 5, 1937, CP 524. DSG Beirut Information 73, 74, January 6, 1937, based on Aleppo Security January 4, 1937, CP 524. Martel to Viénot, January 8, 1937, CP 516.
29. Telegram, Martel to MAE, December 22, 1936, CP 508.

30. Kemal H. Karpat, "The People's Houses in Turkey: Establishment and Growth," *Middle East Journal* 17 (1963): 55–67. M. Asım Karaomerlioğlu, "The People's Houses and the Cult of the Peasant in Turkey," *Middle Eastern Studies* 34 (1998): 67–91. Sefa Şimşek, "'People's Houses' as a Nationwide Project for Ideological Mobilization in Early Republican Turkey," *Turkish Studies* 6 (2005): 71–91. As Karaomerlioğlu described the project (p. 69), "the People's Houses were supposed to create a mass society which in turn would serve to create the true nation."

31. The Turkish consul in Aleppo sent instructions to Antioch emphasizing the importance of people wearing the hat, which would "demonstrate to the Observers that the Sanjak is Turkish." Beirut DSG Information 74, January 6, 1937, based on Aleppo Security January 4, 1937, CP 524. Lynn Hunt discussed the importance of clothing as symbols of political identity in *Politics, Culture and Class in the French Revolution* (Berkeley: University of California Press, 1984); see especially chap. 2, "Symbolic Forms of Political Practice."

32. The officer provided remarkable detail for the distribution, Trojani Information 30, January 11, 1937, CP 524. Martel claimed that emissaries were sent daily into the Sanjak from Turkish Kilis. He had heard that the fifteen hundred hats to be distributed free in the frontier villages were a symbol of the Azaz district's coming attachment to Turkey. Telegram, Martel to MAE, January 14, 1937, CP 524. The same group seemed to be pressing for Kürt Dağ's connection to Turkey, calling it Türk Dağ. DSG Beirut Information 182, January 13, 1937, based on Aleppo Security January 11, 1937, CP 524. DSG Beirut Information 203, January 15, 1937, based on Aleppo Security January 13, 1937, CP 524. Trojani Information, January 11, 1937, CP 524.

33. DSG Beirut Information 202, January 15, 1937, based on Aleppo Security CP 524. DSG Beirut Information 303, January 20, 1937, based on Aleppo Security January 18, 1937, CP 524. DSG Beirut Information 301, January 20, 1937, based on Aleppo Security January 18, 1937, CP 524. On the same day, Saydo Diko was reported to be circulating around Kürt Dağ with fifty horsemen, threatening death to any person not wearing a hat. The Turkish consul in Aleppo was reportedly told that the French gendarmerie commander in Kürt Dağ ordered the Kurds to renounce the wearing of hats, failing which the new head coverings would be confiscated and burned. A number of Kurds, on this intervention, were said to have reclaimed their former head coverings.

34. Telegram, Martel to MAE, January 4, 1937, CP 516. Information 58, January 5, 1937, CP 516.

35. DSG Beirut Information 151, January 11, 1937, based on Alexandretta Security January 7, 1937, CP 524.

36. DSG Beirut Information 160, January 11, 1937, based on Alexandretta Security January 7, 1937, CP 524. DSG Beirut Information 228, January 15, 1937, based on Aleppo Security, January 12, 1937, CP 524.

37. League of Nations, *Official Journal 1937*, 36–55.

38. Viénot to Ponsot, December 31, 1936, Paris and Nantes: Ministères des affaires étrangères. Series: Ankara (hereafter AA), 158.

39. MacMurray to SecState, January 8, 1937, 751.67/128, RG 59, NACP. Gilbert to Hull, January 22, 1937, 751/67/126, RG 59, NACP.

40. Güçlü, *Question of the Sanjak*, 124–32. "Turks Warn Paris of War for Rights," *New York Times*, January 7, 1937. The *Times* story states that the Turkish government was claiming that 80 percent of the Sanjak population was Turkish.

41. Quoted by Güçlü, *Question of the Sanjak*, 133.

42. Telegram, Puaux to Ponsot, January 9, 1937, SDN 581. Telegram, Viénot to Martel, January 11, 1937, CP 516. The U.S. press interpreted this meeting at Eskişehir as an indication that the Turks were talking about going to war. Istanbul to SecState, January 9, 1937, 751.67/118, RG 59, NACP, and Telegram, Moore to Embassy, January 9, 1937, Turkey: Ankara Embassy General Records, State Department Central Files, Record Group 59; National Archives at College Park, MD (hereafter AEGR) 1937, vol. 5, box

12, 710. MacMurray noted that local Nazi leader and German teacher Herr Krechler, having spent ten years in Turkey and with close connections in the Turkish community, "has been strongly propagating the idea that only by entering and occupying the territory can Turkey get any satisfaction for her claims as regards the Sanjak, and that she is in a position to do so with impunity, as France would not in the present situation risk war by armed resistance. In telling my informant of his activities in this matter, Herr Krechler added that if Turkey were to do the intelligent thing instead of relying upon the League of Nations, it would create a situation in which Germany could immediately take possession of Danzig." MacMurray to Hull, January 8, 1937. Attaché's Report, 751.67/135, RG 59, NACP.

43. Telegram, Martel to Viénot, January 12, 1937, CP 508.
44. Telegram, Martel to Viénot, January 12, 1937, CP 508.
45. MacMurray to Hull, January 8, 1937, 751.67/128, RG 59, NACP.
46. Although Güçlü agrees with this assessment, he argues that Ataturk's late night ride did not indicate a conflict with other government figures but was instead part of a calculated effort to convince the French that he was serious about the significance of the Sanjak, *Question of the Sanjak*, 132–37. U.S. officials produced an unsigned memorandum, "Strife between the President and the Cabinet," dated January 29, 1937, that asserts that Atatürk had been "preparing a military demonstration against the French-Syrian State in connection with the Anti-Sanjak deadlock." Atatürk was discouraged by the prime minister and three other ministers and called back to a cabinet meeting. "It transpires that he was called back in order to avoid a provocative move on his part against the French while very delicate and intricate negotiations were going on between the French and Turkish Governments and the League of Nations. This remonstrance did not please him and he left the capital for Istanbul to show his dissatisfaction." The memorandum continues: "There is no doubt that the method of procedure adopted in calling back the President from Konia is an unprecedented one. It amounted in the opinion of many to an order." According to Major Royden Williamson, acting U.S. military attaché in Turkey, troop movements toward Alexandretta did coincide with the nocturnal Konya conference. Williamson memorandum, "Some Military Aspects of the Alexandretta Dispute," May 18, 1937, NACP. MacMurray to Hull, January 16, 1937, 751.67/122, RG 59, NACP.
47. DSG Beirut Information 111, January 8, 1937, based on Aleppo Security January 6, 1937, CP 524.
48. Telegram, Martel to Viénot, January 3, 1937, CP 516. DSG Beirut Information 26, January 4, 1937, based on Aleppo Security, December 31, 1936, CP 516. Aleppo Information, January 4, 1937, CP 516. DSG Beirut Information 113, January 8, 1937, based on Aleppo Security, January 6, 1937, CP 516. Telegram, Bonnot to Martel, January 2, 1937, CP 516. DSG Beirut Information 187, January 13, 1937, based on Aleppo Security January 11, 1937, CP 516. Martel to Levant Commander, January 13, 1937, CP 516. Information, Bertschy, January 11, 1937, CP 516. Information, January 13, 1937, CP 516. DSG Beirut Information, January 25, 1937, CP 516. Telephone message, Commandant Kirikhan sector to Commandant Alexandretta, January 15, 1937, CP 516. League of Nations official Peter Anker, traveling with the International Mission of Observers to the Sanjak of Alexandretta, reported that local military leaders seemed divided on the importance of the raids. Some were preoccupied with them, convinced they would increase during the Geneva discussions, while others saw them as presenting no immediate danger. All worried about the possibility of serious incidents as soon as the League of Nations Council made its decision. Anker to Haller, January 15, 1937, SDN S1646 No. 2.
49. Antioch Summary, January 9, 1937, CP 523. Telegram, Durieux to Martel, January 9, 1937, CP 523. Mentque to Durieux, January 9, 1937, CP 516. Garabed Summary, January 9, 1937, CP 523. Telegram, Martel to MAE, January 9, 1937, CP 523. DSG Beirut Information 144, January 11, 1937, based on Alexandretta Security January 9 1937, CP 524. Anker to Haller, January 13, 1937, SDN S 1646 No. 2.

50. Garabed Summary, January 9, 1937, CP 523. Telegram, Martel to MAE, January 9, 1937, CP 523. DSG Beirut Information 144, January 11, 1937, based on Alexandretta Security January 9, 1937, CP 524. Anker to Haller, January 13, 1937, SDN S 1646 No. 2.

51. Garabed to Councillor for the Alexandretta Police, January 6, 1937, CP 516.

52. Anker to Haller, January 13, 1937, SDN S 1646 No. 2. Kirikhan Summary, January 11, 1937, CP 516. Garabed to Councillor for the Alexandretta Police, January 10, 1937, CP 516. Yahya Summary, January 10, 1937, CP 516. Telephone message, Jamil, January 8, 1937, CP 516. Telegram, Martel to Viénot, January 10, 1937, CP 516.

53. Letter from Türkmen and all to Gacon, January 10, 1937, CP 516.

54. Telegram, Martel to Viénot, January 10, 1937, CP 516. Arabic speeches were translated into French; one speaker read his speech in English. Garabed Summary, January 11, 1937, CP 523.

55. Telegram, Durieux to Martel, January 11, 1937, CP 523. Garabed Summary, January 11, 1937, CP 523. Councillor for the Alexandretta Police, January 11, 1937, CP 516. Anker to Haller, January 13, 1937, SDN S 1646 No. 2.

56. Aleppo Information 5, January 12, 1937, CP 524.

57. Garabed Summary, January 11, 1937, CP 523.

58. Garabed Summary, January 12, 1937, CP 524. Durieux estimated the number of demonstrators at ten to fifteen thousand. Telegram, Durieux to Martel, January 12, 1937, CP 523.

59. Garabed to Councillor for the Alexandretta Police, January 12, 1937, CP 524.

60. Anker to Haller, January 13, 1937, SDN S 1646 No. 2.

61. Durieux to Martel, January 12, 1937, Martel to MAE, January 12, 1937, CP 523. Anker to Haller, January 14, 1937, SDN S 1646 No. 2.

62. Note attached to Martel to Ponsot, January 25, 1937, AA 159. The author of the note pointed out that although the Kemalists were a minority, they were much more disciplined than the other groups and could make an impression that convinced the Observers of a consensus on their position. Citing Alisan Bayiramyan, *Qadiyyat liwa al-Iskandaruna* (Damascus, 1970), Dalal Arsuzi-Elamir provides different figures: of 117,600 Arabs (49 percent of the population), two-thirds were Alawis, 20,000 were Orthodox Christians, and the rest were Sunni Muslims. There were 55,000 (23 percent) Turks, and 43,000 (18 percent) Armenians; the remaining 2 percent included the rest. "Zaki al-Arsuzi and Syrian-Arab Nationalism in the Periphery: The Alexandretta Crisis of 1936–1939," in *From the Syrian Land to the States of Syria and Lebanon*, edited by Thomas Philipp and Christoph Schumann (Beirut: Orient-Institut der DMG Beirut, 2004), 308.

63. Anker to Haller, January 15, 1937, SDN S 1646 No. 2.

64. Anker to Haller, January 15, 1937, SDN S 1646 No. 2.

65. Undated petition, Semih Azmi and all, CP 523.

66. Reyhanlı mayor and all to the Commission, January 9, 1937, CP 523.

67. DSG Beirut Information 387, January 25, 1937, CP 524 reports on a meeting that had taken place on January 15 in which a group of Turcophiles had drawn up a petition asking for Aleppo's annexation to Turkey. This was reportedly to have been delivered to the Turkish consul.

68. Martin C. Thomas, "French Intelligence-Gathering in the Syrian Mandate."

69. Arnal to Delbos, January 14, 1937, *Documents diplomatiques français 1932–1939*, series 2, vol. 4 (Paris, 1972), 501–4. Anker asked that documents on Danzig be sent to the Sanjak so the observers could look at models of agreements on minorities, Anker to Haller, February 3, 1937, SDN S 1646 No 2. Robert J. Young, "The Aftermath of Munich: The Course of French Diplomacy, October 1938 to March 1939," *French Historical Studies* 8 (1973): 305–22.

70. Telegram, Viénot to Ponsot, January 11, 1937, AA 158. Thierry (Bucharest), January 9, 1937, SDN 581.

71. Sarah Shields, "The US and the Sancak Question: Navigating a New Relationship in a Rapidly Changing Context," forthcoming. MacMurray to SecState, December 14, 1936, 751.67/120, RG 59, NACP.
72. Atherton, January 11, 1937, 751.67/133, RG 59, NACP.
73. The text of Blum's letter is available in app. 6 in Güçlü, *Question of the Sanjak*, 348–49.
74. League of Nations, *Official Journal 1937*, 118–23. Telegram, Gilbert to SecState, January 22, 1937, NACP AEGR 1937, vol. 5, box 12, 710.

Chapter 3

1. Telegram, Martel to MAE, January 27, 1937, CP 508.
2. There was some speculation that the opposition Syrian Popular Party and the League of National Action were behind the demonstrations. The Syrian official telling the students to find weapons was al-Barudi. Sources for the description of events disagree on details. They include Information 30/S, Damascus, January 26, 1937, CP 508; CSG Damascus to DSG Beirut, January 26, 1937, CP 508; Telegram, Damascus to Martel, January 25, 1937, CP 508; Telegram, Martel to MAE, January 25, 1937, CP 508 (estimated the number of demonstrators at four thousand); the midday Damascus Information, January 26, 1937, CP 508. This last report presents a slightly different version of the exchange with Mardam, claiming it was the incident most retold by the public: students stopped the car of the president of the Council as it passed through the street near the Turkish consulate. "We want to know immediately what you will do." "We have no demands to receive from you," responded the official.
"The people are above you," came the students' reply.
"Return to class," came the rejoinder. "We have until now run the country well, we will continue."
3. Fain to Martel, January 25, 1937, CP 508.
4. Telegram, Martel to MAE, January 25, 1937, CP 508. Telegram, Martel to Durieux, January 25, 1937, CP 508. Telegram, Martel to Fain, January 25, 1937, CP 508. According to the U.S. representative in Geneva, the members of the French delegation to the League seemed to disagree over the settlement. While one delegate's comments to Gilbert reflected Martel's optimism, another felt the "agreement is only an expedient facade and furthermore may easily be subject to the play of great power politics." Gilbert to SecState, January 27, 1937, 751.67/130, RG 59, NACP.
5. Telegram, Fain to Martel, January 26, 1937, CP 508.
6. Khoury, *Syria and the French Mandate*, 458–59.
7. Damascus to DSG Beirut, January 26, 1937, CP 508.
8. Damascus Information, January 26, 1937, CP 508.
9. Damascus Information 30/S, January 26, 1937, CP 508.
10. Damascus Information 34/S, January 27, 1937, CP 508.
11. Telegram, Fain to Martel, January 27, 1937, CP 508.
12. Telegram, Fain to Martel, January 26, 1937, CP 508.
13. Telegram, Martel to MAE, January 25, 1937, CP 508. Telegram, Martel to Durieux, January 25, 1937, CP 508. Telegram, Martel to Fain, January 25, 1937, CP 508.
14. Telegrams, Viénot to Martel, January 26, 27, 1937, CP 508.
15. Damascus Information 35/S, January 28, 1937, CP 508. Although their leaders gave in at the last minute, thousands of students, not yet notified of the change, continued the separate demonstration as planned.
16. Damascus Information 37/S, January 28, 1937, CP 508. Fain to Martel, January 28, 1937, CP 508. There had been a small pro-Arab demonstration in Alexandretta on January 27, attended by an estimated three hundred people. Shops were closed in both Antioch and Alexandretta. Telegrams, Durieux to Martel, January 27, 1937, CP 523.

17. Damascus Information 38/S, January 28, 1937, CP 508.
18. Anker to Haller, January 29, 1937, SDN S 1646 No. 2.
19. Fain to Martel, January 28, 1937, CP 508. Rumors from Damascus claiming that the Sanjak was to be given to Turkey had elicited a minor protest at Dayr al-Zur. Delegate Dayr al-Zur to Martel, January 27, 1937, CP 508.
20. The report itself took more than a week to arrive in the Sanjak. The League Observers received a copy on Monday, February 1, 1937. Anker claimed that even Martel in Beirut did not have a copy. Anker to Haller, February 3, 1937, SDN S 1646 No. 2.
21. Telegram, Martel to Ponsot, February 6, 1937, CP 508. Ponsot to Martel, February 7, 1937, CP 508.
22. Anker to Haller, January 29, 1937, SDN S 1646 No. 2.
23. Anker to Haller, February 3, 1937, SDN S 1646 No. 2.
24. Anker to Haller, February 3, 1937, SDN S 1646 No. 2.
25. Damascus Information 62/S, February 16, 1937, CP 508.
26. Martel to MAE, February 5, 1937, CP 508.
27. Chaylard to Ponsot, February 2, 1937, AA 158. The U.S. ambassador in Turkey was not impressed with the outcome. "Although the terms of settlement of the Sanjak question seem to have been substantially determined by the 25th they have been only cautiously dribbled out to the public here in a form suggesting a portentous victory for the Turkish viewpoint and only yesterday did the press publish any concrete information as to the terms. Even then the announcements slurred over the fact that the fundamental question of the relationships between the Sanjak and Syria are held over for later consideration. The announcement was accompanied by fulsome exchanges of congratulations between Ataturk and the Prime Minister and Minister for Foreign Affairs which however do not dispel the impression that the mountain has given birth to a mouse. I gather that the French Embassy feels relieved that an annoying trifle has been disposed of, and the Turks seem happy that they have saved their faces in the affair." MacMurray to Hull, January 29, 1937, 751.67/132, RG 59, NACP.
28. DSG Beirut Information 650, February 6, 1937, based on Aleppo Security February 4, 1937, CP 524.
29. In light of the importance of the Alawis for this argument, the sentence on translators is notable for leaving them out: "Toutefois, les individus ne comprenant pas cette langue ou ne désirant pas l'employer peuvent, devant le Tribunaux par exemple, recourir à des traducteurs. L'on s'exprimera en arabe, l'arménien en arménien, le juif en hébreu, le kurde en kurde, ce qui permettra de ne pas gêner bon nombre de personnes qui ne comprennent pas l'arabe." Martel suggested in his cover letter that this suggestion of French might be intended to get the experts writing the statute to agree to "sacrifice" Arabic. Martel to MAE, February 5, 1937, CP 508. Durieux claimed that 60 percent of the population spoke Arabic.
30. Patrick Seale, *Asad: The Struggle for the Middle East* (Berkeley: University of California Press, 1990): 9–11. Mahmud A. Faksh, "The Alawi Community of Syria: A New Dominant Political Force," *Middle Eastern Studies* 20 (1984): 133–36. Hanna Batatu, "Some Observations on the Social Roots of Syria's Ruling, Military Group and the Causes for Its Dominance," *Middle East Journal* 35 (1981): 333–36.
31. Batatu, "Some Observations," 333–36. See also Zeynep Turkyılmaz, "Anxieties of Conversion: Missionaries, State and Heterodox Communities in the Late Ottoman Empire," Ph.D. diss., University of California at Los Angeles, 2009.
32. Khoury, *Syria and the French Mandate*, 100–102.
33. Itamar Rabinovich, "The Compact Minorities." Michael Provence, *The Great Syrian Revolt*.
34. Quoted in Keith D. Watenpaugh, "'Creating Phantoms,'" 367. See also Hiroyuki Aoyama and Malek Salman, "A Biography of Zaki al-Arsuzi," in *Spiritual Father of the Ba'th: The Ideological and Political Significance of Zaki al-Arsuzi in Arab Nationalist Movements* (Tokyo: Institute of Developing Economics, Japan External Trade Organization, 2000),

5. Dalal Arsuzi-Elamir, "Zaki al-Arsuzi and Syrian-Arab Nationalism in the Periphery," 307–27.

35. Aoyama and Salman, "Biography of Zaki al-Arsuzi," 5. Watenpaugh, "'Creating Phantoms,'" 368, 371–75. Arsuzi-Elamir, "Zaki al-Arsuzi and Syrian-Arab Nationalism," 307–27.

36. Arsuzi-Elamir, "Zaki al-Arsuzi and Syrian-Arab Nationalism," 307–27.

37. Aleppo Information 123, April 9, 1937, CP 524. Zannardi to Inspector General of Police, Beirut, April 17, 1937, CP 524. Martel to MAE, April 26, 1937, CP 524. Lacroix to Special Services Chief at Beirut, April 14, 1937, CP 524.

38. Aleppo Information 127, April 12, 1937, CP 524. DSG Beirut Information 1866, April 9, 1937, based on Aleppo Security April 7, 1937, CP 524.

39. Aleppo Information 130, April 15, 1937, CP 524.

40. Ramzi to Commander of Aleppo-North Company, April 10, 1937, CP 524.

41. Telegram, Martel to Ponsot, May 10, 1937, CP 524. Alexandretta Security, May 5 and 7, 1937, CP 524. Telegram, Durieux to Martel, May 8, 1937, CP 524. DSG Beirut Information 2364, May 8, 1937, based on Alexandretta Security May 5, 1937, CP 524. Alexandretta Information 883, May 21, 1937, CP 524. Director of Antioch Agency, Bank of Syria and Greater Lebanon to Direction of Agencies, Bank of Syria and Greater Lebanon, May 15, 1937, CP 524.

42. DSG Beirut Information 2510, May 18, 1937, based on Alexandretta Security May 14, 1937, CP 524. For a fictionalized autobiographical account of the economic conditions for some of the area's peasants and silk-growers, see Hanna Mina, *Fragments of Memory: A Story of a Syrian Family*, trans. Olive Kenny and Lorne Kenny (Northampton, MA.: Interlink Books, 2004).

43. Colombani Information 2236, April 29, 1937, based on Azaz Security April 25, 1937, CP 524.

44. CSG Damascus Information, April 13, 1937, CP 524. CSG Aleppo Information 108, April 1, 1937, CP 524. There was considerable anxiety among the Amk population in the spring of 1937 about a rumored invasion of bedouin tribes driven by drought toward the sea. The rumors, whose origins the local officials did not know, were seriously alarming landowners, who bitterly remembered the previous passage of the nomadic tribes in 1932. Imaginations were taking over, according to French officials, as Kemalist leaders saw an evil eye at play and harbored the hope that Turkey would intervene to restore order in the country where there would inevitably be serious engagements between the nomadic Arabs and the sedentary Turks. Others floated the idea of opposing the invasion by their own means. The villagers of the frontier district of Aktepe were so nervous that they demanded that the authorities take all possible steps to prevent the bedouin intrusion. French officials claimed that the Turkish press was using the rumors to allege a French campaign to augment the number of Arabs in the Sanjak. Durieux to Martel, April 3, 1937, CP 516.

45. Martel to MAE, March 3, 1937, AA 159.

46. David to Martel, January 6, 1937, CP 516. DSG Beirut Information 40, January 4, 1937, based on Derik Security December 24, 1936, CP 516. The American ambassador in Beirut shared his concern. Marriner, May 3, 1937, 751.67/160, RG 59, NACP.

47. DSG Beirut Information 1450, March 17, 1937, based on Arab-Pounar Security March 12, 1937; 1488, March 19, 1937, based on Muslimiya report March 17, 1937; 1510, March 20, 1937, based on Muslimiya report March 18, 1937, French officials were confused that the Turks made no complaint about an incident at the point farthest east of their joint boundary. On March 28, nine Syrian Christians of al-Qamishli crossed into Turkish territory under the pretext of visiting their family, when they clashed with Turkish soldiers and killed two. They escaped pursuing Turkish villagers and managed to reenter Syria. One month later, when General Jacquot interviewed the governors of the neighboring Turkish provinces, they "systematically avoided" any discussion of the incidents. Telegram, Martel to MAE, April 24, 1937, CP 509.

48. Ponsot to Delbos, April 13, 1937, AA 158. Turkish Ambassador to the French Ministry of Foreign Affairs, April 3, 1937, AA 158. For the political uses of animal theft, see Sarah D. Shields, "Sheep, Nomads and Merchants in Nineteenth-century Mosul: Creating Transformations in an Ottoman Society," *Journal of Social History* 25 (1992): 773–89.
49. Martel to Erkin, April 7, 1937, CP 524.
50. Courson to Minister of Defense, April 12, 1937, AA 158.
51. Mardam to Delegate (undated, received April 19, 1937), CP 509.
52. Damascus Information 684/S, December 7, 1936, CP 524. DSG Beirut Information 1220, May 8, 1937, from Aleppo Security May 3, 1937, CP 524.
53. Barazi to Mentque, March 17, 1937, CP 516. Mentque to Barazi, March 20, 1937, CP 516. Bazantay to Mentque, March 18, 1937, CP 516. Mentque to Martel, March 26, 1937, CP 516. Gacon to Inspector of Special Services of the Mohafazat, March 19, 1937, CP 516. Philip Khoury, *Syria and the French Mandate*, 421, 474.
54. Director General of Posts and Telegraphs of the Syrian Republic (Damascus) to Inspector General of Posts and Telegraphs of the States of the Levant under French Mandate (Beirut), March 1, 1937, CP 516.
55. Posts and Telegraphs, High Commissariat of the French Republic to Secretary-General, March 2, 1937, CP 516. President of the Council of Ministers to the Damascus Delegate, March 3, 1937, CP 516. Martel explained that, having not been consulted by the Damascus authorities, he could not oppose the practice. Telegram, Martel to MAE, March 2, 1937, CP 516. Delegate Damascus to Martel, March 5, 1937, CP 516. The system was overturned in December, when Garreau sent formal instructions to the receivers of the posts of Alexandretta and Antioch to stop returning the letters carrying the Hatay destination, even though "this geographic appellation has not been consecrated by the international accords in force, it does not constitute an attack on public order, but, on the contrary, the systematic returning of mail, though specified, presents a character of vexation that seems to me difficult to tolerate long-term." Garreau to Secretary General of the Sanjak of Alexandretta, December 28, 1937, CP 516.
56. "Conversation entre Istanbul et Ankara avec le President du Conseil Syrien, le 5 Avril 1937," CP 511. The Syrian government paid close attention to Turkish efforts to woo Alawis. CSG Damascus Information, April 13, 1937, CP 524. Marriner to SecState, May 11, 1937, Turkey: Istanbul Embassy General Records 751, State Department Central Files, Record Group 59; National Archives at College Park, MD (hereafter IEGR 1937), box 22. Local anxieties about Turkish intentions were exacerbated by a map sent from Turkey. "The news has been diffused lately at Aleppo that the Turks will come soon to occupy the city since an official map of the Sanjak of Alexandretta edited in Turkey contains Aleppo in the limits of this territory." Martel sent the map in question, observing: "The apprehension of the Aleppo populations is clearly excessive. The map does not indicate in an explicit way that the city of Aleppo will be incorporated into the Sanjak. But the complete disappearance of all administrative divisions, and even of the frontier with Turkey, could give the impression to an uneasy reader that Turkey intends to see included in the Sanjak all the territory contained in the rectangle, including the city of Aleppo. I gave Aleppo advice of quieting. Perhaps Your Excellency estimates it opportune to call the attention of the Turkish authorities to the consequences of sending to Turkey or to the Sanjak documents likely to excite political passions." A few weeks later, Turkish authorities noticed that the Hatay maps being sold at Aleppo did not include the villages of Bayer and Bujak, and pulled them from circulation, intending to perfect them. Martel to MAE, February 18, 1937, CP 516. DSG Beirut to Martel, February 18, 1937, CP 516. DSG Beirut Information 1435, March 10, 1937, from Aleppo Security March 8, 1937, CP 516. Mardam pointed out that League of Nations observers had already denied Ankara's allegations about Turkish majorities in the three disputed districts.

57. Dilek Barlas, "Friends or Foes? Diplomatic Relations between Italy and Turkey, 1923–1936," *International Journal of Middle East Studies* 36 (2004): 231–52. Yücel Güçlü, *The Question of the Sanjak of Alexandretta*, 142–47.

58. "Note: Point de vue du Département de la Marine sur la question du Port d'Alexandrette," December 28, 1936, AA 158. Gilbert to SecState, May 21, 1937, 751.67/159, RG 59, NACP.

59. League of Nations, *Official Journal 1937*, 248.

60. "Societé des Nations, Comité d'experts chargé d'étudier le statut et la loi fondamentale du Sandjak d'Alexandrette, Compte Rendu du premier séance, tenue à Genève le 25 février 1937," SDN S 1642 No. 1.

61. "Societé des Nations, Comité d'experts chargé d'étudier le statut et la loi fondamentale du Sandjak d'Alexandrette, Compte Rendu du deuxième séance, tenue le vendredi, 26 février 1937," SDN S 1642 No. 1.

62. League of Nations, *Official Journal 1937*, 574. See SDN S 1642 for memoranda on currency, customs, posts, and ports and the expert reports on which these were based.

63. Marriner to SecState, May 11, 1937, 751.67/169, RG 59, NACP.

64. CSG Alexandretta Information, May 21, 1937, CP 511.

65. Telegram, Durieux to Meyrier, May 20, 1937, CP 516. DSG Beirut Information 2602, May 22, 1937, from Alexandretta Security May 20, 1937, CP 516.

66. CSG Alexandretta Information, May 21, 1937, CP 511. Telegram, Durieux to Martel and Damascus Delegate, May 22, 1937, CP 511.

67. Telegram, Durieux to Meyrier, May 20, 1937, CP 516. Telegram, Durieux to Martel and Damascus Delegate, May 22, 1937, CP 511.

68. CP 511.

69. CSG Alexandretta Information, May 21, 1937, CP 511.

70. Telegram, Türkmen, May 23, 1937, CP 524.

71. Telegram, Durieux to Martel and Damascus Delegate, May 22, 1937, CP 511. Zannardi to Bouchede, May 24, 1937, CP 511. Alexandretta Security to Beirut Security and Damascus Security, May 22, 1937, CP 511. Colonel Bringuier Summary, May 22, 1937, CP 511. Durieux Message, May 22, 1937, CP 511. Meyrier to MAE, May 22, 1937, CP 511 claims three arrests were made and that the police did not use their arms.

72. Zannardi to Bouchede, May 24, 1937, CP 511, claims the actual prohibition of the demonstration came from Governor al-Barazi.

73. CSG Alexandretta Information, May 24, 1937, CP 516. DSG Beirut Information 2690, May 27, 1937, from Alexandretta Security May 24, 1937, CP 516. DSG Beirut Information 2634, May 24, 1937, from Alexandretta Security May 21, 1937, CP 516.

74. William Cohen summarized the fate of the treaty: "Viénot's greatest success was the signing of the Franco-Syrian treaty of December 22, 1936. Although almost every French government for more than a decade had promised to negotiate a treaty giving Syria independence, none had been concluded. While signing the treaty with Syria, Viénot nevertheless was a hard bargainer. Instead of granting immediate independence his treaty gave Syria self-government for three probationary years after which the country would gain full independence. Also the Syrian negotiators had to accept a twenty-five-year political and military alliance with France. In spite of the favorable clauses parliamentary opposition to the treaty was powerful, and the Blum government therefore decided not to submit it for ratification. Nearly two years later, however, the treaty was finally considered by the foreign affairs commission of both houses of parliament. The two reporters on the bill for the senate commission declared their hostility to the treaty on December 14, 1938. It was clear that the Daladier government was also opposed to the bill, for on the same day the minister of foreign affairs, Georges Bonnet, told the foreign affairs commission of the Chamber of Deputies that the government did not "at the present time" want to see the bill presented to parliament. And so Viénot's treaty died." William B. Cohen, "The Colonial Policy of the Popular Front," 379.

75. Meyrier to Durieux, May 22, 1937, CP 511.
76. CSG Alexandretta Information, May 27, 1937, CP 511.
77. League of Nations, *Official Journal 1937*, 580–89. Güçlü, *Question of the Sanjak*, 183.
78. League of Nations, *Official Journal 1937*, 332–33.
79. Gilbert to SecState, May 21, 1937, 751.67/159, RG 59, NACP. League of Nations, *Official Journal 1937*, 332.
80. League of Nations, *Official Journal 1937*, 332. Despite Delbos's assurance that this outcome would be in the Syrians' interest, he seemed less than pleased with the results. Writing to Martel on May 20, he claimed: "I sharply regret that Jamil Mardam could not accompany me to Paris and Geneva; during the discussion which precedes the final settlement of the Sanjak affair the presence of the head of the Syrian government is especially indicated. His absence risks weakening the import of the arguments that the representatives of France will develop before the Council of the League of Nations." Telegram, MAE to Martel, May 20, 1937, CP 511.

Chapter 4

1. Shaw to SecState, June 12, 1937, 751.67/174, RG 59, NACP.
2. Telegram, Ponsot to MAE, June 15, 1937, AA 157.
3. Shaw to SecState, June 12, 1937, 751.67/174, RG 59, NACP.
4. Telegram, Meyrier to MAE, May 30, 1937, CP 511. Telegram, Durieux to Meyrier and Damascus Deputy, May 31, 1937, CP 511. Aleppo Deputy to Martel, June 2, 1937, CP 511. Telegram, Meyrier to French delegation, June 1, 1937, CP 511. Meyrier to MAE, June 9, 1937, CP 511.
5. Telegram, Durieux to Meyrier, June 3, 1937, CP 511. Telegram, Dayr to Meyrier, June 3, 1937, CP 511. CSG Damascus, June 3, 1937, CP 511. Telegram, Meyrier to MAE, June 3, 1937, CP 511. Telegram, Meyrier to MAE, June 4, 1937, CP 511. Meyrier to MAE, June 9, 1937, CP 511. The new committee is described in Information 289, June 14, 1937, CP 523. Farrell, June 15, 1937, 751.67/177, RG 59, NACP. Khoury, *Syria and the French Mandate*, 539.
6. President of the Council of Ministers of the Syrian Republic to the Deputy of the High Commissioner, Damascus, June 7, 1937, CP 511. Farrell, June 15, 1937, 751.67/177, RG 59, NACP.
7. Marriner to SecState, June 9, 1937, 751.67/178, RG 59, NACP.
8. Marriner to SecState, June 9, 1937, 751.67/178, RG 59, NACP.
9. Türkmen to Durieux, June 3, 1937, CP 511. Türkmen to Durieux, June 5 and 6, 1937, CP 517. Durieux to Meyrier, June 8, 1937, CP 517.
10. Mentque to Meyrier, June 4, 1937, CP 511.
11. Mardam referred to Aaland as an example.
12. "Memorandum adressé à Son Excellence Monsieur le Ministre des Affaires Etrangères de France concernant la résolution prise à Genève en date du 29 mai 1937 au sujet du Sandjak d'Alexandrette," attached to Mardam to Martel, October 4, 1937, CP 516.
13. Telephone message, Alexandretta Security to Beirut and Damascus Security, June 4, 1937, CP 511. Meyrier to MAE, June 7, 1937, CP 517. Telegram, Lescuyer to Meyrier, June 8, 1937, CP 511. Telegram, Lepissier to Meyrier, June 12, 1937, CP 511. Meyrier to Lescuyer, June 9, 1937, CP 511. Meyrier to Lepissier, June 14, 1937, CP 511.
14. Al-Quwwatli to Fain, June 7, 1937, CP 517. The *Times* continued, "A painful impression has been produced throughout Syria by news broadcast by the Turkish wireless that two divisions of the Turkish Army had been sent to the frontier. The population is greatly excited. Nationalist leaders harangued a large meeting at Damascus. All business premises in Syrian towns have been closed in protest against the League of Nations' adoption of the Alexandretta agreement." Farrell, June 15, 1937, 751.67/177, RG 59, NACP. Marriner to Secretary of State, June 5, 1937, claimed that four people were killed and twenty wounded in Antioch on June 4, 751.67/165, RG 59, NACP.

15. Fain to al-Quwwatli, June 7, 1937; al-Quwwatli to Fain, June 7, 1937, CP 517.
16. The letter to Durieux, dated June 7, 1937, was signed by Abdulgani Türkmen and others, CP 511. Türkmen to Durieux, June 3 and 6, 1937, CP 517.
17. Meyrier to MAE, June 7, 1937, CP 517. Mentque to Meyrier, June 8, 1937, CP 511. Mentque to Martel, June 7, 1937, CP 523. Meyrier to MAE, June 9, 1937, CP 511.
18. "In accordance with the Council's resolution of January 27th, 1937, it will rest with France, until the termination of the mandate, to bring the new regime into operation as far as is compatible with the exercise of her mandate. It is understood that the appointment of the League of Nations delegate will take place on the expiry of the mandate." Collection of Texts Concerning the Sanjak of Alexandretta, SDN C.282.M.183.1937, 4.
19. Telegram, General Deputy Beirut to Deputy Alexandretta, June 6, 1937, CP 517.
20. Telegram, Viénot to Martel, June 7, 1937, CP 517.
21. Meyrier to MAE, August 11, 1937, CP 523. Meyrier to Mentque, July 28, 1937, CP 523. Mentque to Türkmen, July 31, 1937, CP 523.
22. Meyrier to Damascus Deputy, June 7, 1937, CP 517.
23. Durieux to Meyrier, June 8, 1937, CP 511. Meyrier to MAE, June 9, 1937, CP 511.
24. Minister of National Defense and War to MAE, June 29, 1937, CP 523.
25. MAE to Minister of War, July 15, 1937, CP 523.
26. Telegram, Durieux to Martel, July 2, 1937, CP 523.
27. Telegram, Martel to MAE, July 6, 1937, CP 523. Khoury, *Syria and the French Mandate*, 398, 505. "Annual Report, Economic (A), for 1937," *Records of Syria, 1918–1973*, ed. J. Priestland (Slough, UK: Cambridge Archive Editions, 2005), 253. "Conversation entre Istanbul et Ankara avec le President du Conseil Syrien, le 5 Avril 1937," CP 511. Martel claimed that the Damascus government sought to rally Armenians to their position through the Communist Party.
28. Telegram, Durieux to Martel, July 2 and 3, 1937, CP 523. Telegram, Aleppo Delegate to Martel, July 6, 1937, CP 523. Telegram, Martel to Durieux, July 7, 1937, CP 523.
29. Martel to MAE, July 14, 1937, CP 523.
30. Extract from *L'Orient*, July 14, 1937, CP 523.
31. Martel to MAE, July 21, 1937, CP 523.
32. Martel to MAE, July 21, 1937, CP 523.
33. Martel to MAE, July 21, 1937, CP 523.
34. Telegram, Ponsot to Martel, July 15 and 16, 1937, CP 523, quoting *La République*. Telegram, Martel to Durieux, July 7, 1937, CP 523.
35. Mentque to Martel, July 25, 1937, CP 517. Mentque to Meyrier, August 10, 1937, CP 517. Mentque to Makhian and Radouan, August 10, 1937, CP 517.
36. Martel to Mentque, July 28, 1937, CP 517. Meyrier to MAE, August 11, 1937, CP 523. Meyrier to Mentque, July 28, 1937, CP 523. Mentque to Türkmen, July 31, 1937, CP 523.
37. Türkmen to Martel, July 25, 1937, CP 523. Telegram, Türkmen to Martel, July 25, 1937, CP 523. Meyrier to MAE, August 29, 1937, CP 523.
38. Salaheddine Information, August 11, 1937, AA 157. Zannardi Information, August 11, 1937, AA 157.
39. Garabed summary, August 9, 1937, AA 157. Garabed summary, August 10, 1937, AA 157. Depositions from August 9, 1937, AA 157. Telegrams, Mentque to Meyrier, August 9 and 10, 1937, CP 523. Telegram, Meyrier to MAE, August 9, 1937. Meyrier, consistent with years of French terminology that labeled pan-Arab activists "radicals," referred to the original disputants as "moderate Alawis and Alawi partisans of the League of National Action." Garabed, Police Chief of the Sanjak, disparaged the suspect Kör Sabet as "an individual belonging to a dangerous extremist party," previously convicted of many crimes, and the "executioner in the pay of the Turkish partisans of Antioch," one who would unhesitatingly make an attempt on the lives of local or French mandatory authorities in return for pay. Telegram, Mentque to Meyrier, August 12, 1937, CP 523 claims Kör Sabet was on the payroll of the Halkevi.

40. Meyrier to MAE, August 12, 1937, CP 523. Telegram, Meyrier to MAE, August 9, 1937, CP 523. See also Telegram, Paris to Beirut, August 11, 1937, CP 523.
41. Telegram, Mentque to Durieux, August 9, 1937, CP 523.
42. Garabed, August 10, 1937, AA 157. Garabed summary, August 10, 1937, AA 157.
43. Mentque to Meyrier, August 10, 1937, CP 523. Telephone message, Special Services Antioch, August 10, 1937, AA 157. Salaheddine, "Report of Incident," August 12, 1937, AA 157.
44. Meyrier to MAE, August 12, 1937, CP 523.
45. Telegram, Meyrier to MAE, August 10, 1937, CP 523. Telegram, Meyrier to Ponsot, August 10, 1937, CP 523. Telegram, MAE to Martel, August 11, 1937, CP 523.
46. Garabed Summary, August 11, 1937, AA 157.
47. Mentque to Mesney, August 11, 1937, CP 523.
48. Mesny, Note de Service, August 11, 1937, CP 517.
49. Telegram, Türkmen and all to Martel, August 13, 1937, CP 523. Telegram, MAE to Martel, August 15, 1937, CP 523 and AA 157.
50. Attached to Zannardi, August 12, 1937, AA 157 and CP 517.
51. Garabed Summary, August 14, 1937, AA 157. Meyrier to MAE, August 13, 1937, CP 523.
52. Garabed Summary, August 14, 1937, AA 157.
53. Garabed summary, August 13, 1937, AA 157. Although he considered the results "rather weak," Police Chief Houel wrote on August 13 that the searches had a huge impact on the situation. In the two intervening days, he wrote, individual aggression and fights had stopped. All those arrested had been released on their own guarantees except Kör Sabet and one Muhammad ibn Ahmed, in whose home the searchers had uncovered two revolvers, a stock of tools for an arms factory, and some spare parts for shotguns. Houel report, August 13, 1937, CP 517. Mesny to General Commander of Troops of Northern Syria, n.d., AA 157. Mentque to Meyrier, August 11, 1937, CP 523. Telegram, Mentque to Meyrier, August 11, 1937, CP 523. Mentque to Meyrier, August 12, 1937, CP 523.
54. Garabed Summary, August 14, 1937, AA 157.
55. Antioch Information, August 19, 1937, AA 157. Telegram, Mentque to Meyrier, August 19, 1937, CP 523. Mentque, "Weekly Information Bulletin 34," August 24, 1937, CP 523. On May 28, Aleppo Security claimed that the Turkish consul had sent a messenger to inform Adana authorities that the Antioch Republican People's Party leadership had squandered 60,000 Turkish lira that had been provided to them for propaganda. CSG Aleppo Information 196, May 28, 1937, CP 516. Queru Information, August 16, 1937, AA 157.
56. Dubecq Information 280, August 13, 1937, AA 157.
57. Houel to Durieux, August 12, 1937, AA 157. Pourcel to Mentque, August 11, 1937, AA 157.
58. Queru Information, August 16, 1937, CP 524.
59. Queru Information, August 16, 1937, CP 524. Petition, AA 157. The French official forwarding the petition claimed that mandatory authorities had not been previously informed about this initiative.
60. Telegram, MAE to Meyrier, August 14, 1937, quoting telegram from Ponsot, CP 523. Telegram, MAE to Meyrier, August 14, 1937, CP 523.
61. Ponsot's tone seems almost incredulous. He ended his letter asking if the wolves of Jazira are sheep in the Sanjak. Ponsot to Delbos, August 17, 1937, CP 524.
62. Telegram, Ponsot to Meyrier, August 19, 1937, CP 523. Telegram, Meyrier to MAE, August 19, 1937, CP 523.
63. Telegram, Meyrier to Ponsot, August 20, 1937, CP 523. Ponsot to Meyrier, August 14, 1937, CP 523.
64. Telegram, Ponsot to Meyrier, August 24, 1937, CP 523.
65. Ponsot to Delbos, August 31, 1937, AA 157.

66. Alexandretta Information, August 19, 1937, CP 524. Mentque, "Weekly Information Bulletin 34," August 24, 1937, CP 523. Meyrier's report to Paris that had characterized the Sanjak as quiet did point out that "The least incident between the Turkish elements and Arabs creates a mob, and a closing of the shops." The army, he said, remained in Antioch to restore order. Meyrier to MAE, August 18, 1937, CP 523.

67. "Traduction d'un manifeste publié le 17 August au soir par les turcs a Antioch," sent by Zannardi, August 19, 1937, CP 524. "We have received their firm attitude, their conception of truth and of evidence, their sentiment of love and of justice, with appreciation and admiration. . . .. We have regret and sadness to note that some still pursue shadows and arrogance, departing from logic and wisdom."

68. Mentque to Meyrier, August 24, 1937, CP 523. Telegram, Meyrier to MAE, August 23, 1937, CP 523. Telegram, Meyrier to MAE, August 19, 1937, CP 523. Meyrier to MAE, September 1, 1937, CP 523.

69. Zannardi to Mentque, August 23, 1937, CP 523.

70. Meyrier to MAE, September 1, 1937, CP 523.

71. Only the driver was arrested and handed over to the prosecutor, however. In an effort to stop future illegal border crossings, police were instructed to install a checkpoint between Alexandretta and Payas and to begin demanding identification for people entering and leaving Turkey. Zannardi Information, August 13 and 14, 1937, AA 157. Elias résumé, August 13, 1937, AA 157. Mentque to Meyrier, August 12, 1937, CP 523.

72. Mentque to Meyrier, August 24, 1937, CP 523. Telegram, Meyrier to MAE, August 23, 1937, CP 523. Telegram, Meyrier to MAE, August 19, 1937, CP 523. Meyrier to MAE, September 1, 1937, CP 523. Mentque, "Weekly Information Bulletin 34," August 24, 1937, CP 523.

73. Telegrams, Meyrier to MAE, September 7, 8, and 15, 1937, CP 523.

74. Yücel Güçlü, *The Question of the Sanjak of Alexandretta*, 194. Mentque, "Weekly Information Bulletin 34," August 24, 1937, CP 523.

75. CSG Alexandretta Information, October 6, 1937, CP 524.

76. "Turkey: Activity in the Sanjak," October 30, 1937, CP 514.

77. Telegram, MAE to Martel, November 2, 1937, quoting Ponsot, CP 511. Kelley, November 16, 1937, 751.67/196, RG 59, NACP.

78. Telegram, Martel to MAE, November 10, 1937, CP 511.

79. League of Nations, October 6, 1937, S1544 No. 10. The president of the League Council was, at this time, the French representative, and he deferred to the secretary-general (representing Ecuador) to make the appointments. Ponsot to Delbos, October 21, 1937, CP 523.

80. "Texte de l'allocution prononcée par M. Reid," attached to Martel to MAE, May 24, 1937, CP 513.

81. Translation of *Yeni Gün* article, November 13, 1937, SDN S 1643, No. 6.

82. President of the Commission to Garreau, November 15, 1937, SDN S 1643 No. 6.

83. Gacon Information 1671, November 17, 1937, SDN S 1643 No. 6.

84. Martel to MAE, November 24, 1937, CP 513.

85. Martel to MAE, November 27, 1937, CP 513. In the end, the Turkish consul suggested that no flags be flown.

Chapter 5

1. "Arcs de triomphe" were placed in front of the Hatay Garage, at the exit of the Uzun Çarşı, in front of the Hatay Oven in the Habib Necuar quarter, near the Halkevi, in Süveyka, in Cuma Pazar, at the Yeni Cami door, and in the Carpenter's Suq.

2. The speeches were translated into Arabic by Remzi ibn Ismail, originally from Dayr al-Zur, who was the editor of the Arabic part of *Yeni Gün*, and Jalal Abu El Mutaleb, an Alawi Turcophile originally from Latakia, former clerk of the head of the Latakia tribunal, who had lived in the Sanjak for some months.

3. Description of the events from Summary, November 30, 1937, CP 511. Zannardi to DSG Beirut, December 2, 1937, CP 511.

4. DSG Beirut Information 6587, December 2, 1937, from Aleppo Security November 30, 1937, CP 511. DSG Beirut Information 6585, December 2, 1937, from Aleppo Security November 30, 1937, CP 511. Telegram, Martel to MAE, December 2, 1937, CP 511. DSG Beirut Information 6613, December 3, 1937, from Aleppo Security December 1, 1937, CP 511.

5. DSG Beirut Information 6616, December 3, 1937, from Dayr al-Zur Security November 29, 1937, CP 511. Before dispersing, the students sent two telegrams that illustrated their interest in two simultaneous nationalist issues. The first, to the French delegate in Damascus, the French Foreign Ministry, and two local journals, read "The Students of the Euphrates, on strike, protest against the application of the statute of Alexandretta. Please address our protest to the competent authorities." The second was sent to the British consulate in Damascus and two Syrian journals. "Your ignominy against an aged combatant increases our attachment to the Arabism of Palestine. History will record a scandalous stain on your justice."

6. Telegram, Radouan to Martel, December 2, 1937, CP 511.

7. Kelley to Hull, December 13, 1937, 751.67/200, RG 59, NACP.

8. Davaz to MAE, December 2, 1937, AA 157. Text repeated MAE to Martel, December 4, 1937, CP 511. Ponsot to Delbos, October 21, 1937, CP 523.

9. Telegram, Martel to MAE, December 4, 1937, CP 511. Telegram, Martel to MAE, December 3, 1937, CP 511.

10. Telegram, MAE to Martel, October 23, 1937, CP 517. Claiming that conditions this year were quite difficult, the Turkish government thought the French would agree about the "importunity" of such a measure on the eve of elections. They asked the Paris government to send urgent instructions to Martel for a one-year respite. When Martel told the Turkish consul that his request was interference with internal affairs, the consul left off. Telegram, Martel to MAE, October 23, 1937, CP 517.

11. Text of Turkish Telegram, Antioch, CP 511.

12. Telegram, Martel to MAE, December 3, 1937, CP 511.

13. Telegram, MAE to Martel, December 4, 1937, CP 511. Chautemps to Aras, December 18, 1937, 751.67/207, RG 59, NACP.

14. Aras to MAE, December 24, 1937, 751.67/207, RG 59, NACP.

15. Antioch Security Information, December 8, 1937, CP 524. Beirut DSG Information 67111, December 11, 1937, based on Alexandretta Security December 8, 1937, CP 524.

16. Telegram, Martel to MAE, December 4, 1937, CP 511.

17. Alexandretta Information, December 8, 1937, CP 517. DSG Beirut Information, December 10, 1937, from Alexandretta Security December 7, 1937, CP 517.

18. CSG Alexandretta Information, December 10, 1937, CP 517. "Weekly Information Bulletin 50," December 6–13, 1937, CP 524. Antioch Security Information, December 8, 1937, CP 524.

19. Those connected with the Turkish Consulate in Aleppo claimed that France instigated Sa'dallah al-Jabiri's declaration at the Syrian Parliament that the Syrian government rejected the decision of the League of Nations on the new statute. Aleppo Security Information 446, December 6, 1937, CP 524.

20. "Weekly Information Bulletin 50," December 6–13, 1937, CP 524. Muhammad Ali Zarka and Yusuf Elian were arrested with al-Arsuzi; Elian was released later the same day.

21. Antioch Security Information 41, December 19, 1937, CP 518.

22. Ponsot to Delbos, December 20, 1937, *Documents diplomatiques français 1932–1939*, vol. 7 (Paris, 1972), 763–65.

23. Kelley to Hull, December 30, 1937, 751.67/202, RG 59, NACP.

24. Daladier to Delbos, January 29, 1938, *Documents diplomatiques français 1932–1939*, vol. 8 (Paris, 1972), 143–45.

25. Philip S. Khoury, *Syria and the French Mandate*, 486–88.
26. Lorraine, January 1, 1938, London: National Archives (formerly Public Record Office), Foreign Office 371 (Syria) (hereafter FO) 371/21909.
27. Kelley to Hull, December 30, 1937, 751.67/202, RG 59, NACP.
28. Telegram, Loraine, January 1, 1938, FO 371/21909.
29. Davis to Foreign Secretary, December 30, 1937, FO 371/21909. Williams, from the Foreign Office staff, noted on the cover: "So long as the Syrian Parliament maintains uncompromising opposition to the Alexandretta settlement I cannot see that the French are likely to ratify the Franco Syrian Treaty." Kelley to Hull, December 30, 1937, 751.67/202, RG 59, NACP.
30. DSG Beirut Information 3, January 3, 1938, from Antioch police December 29, 1937, CP 518.
31. Davis to Foreign Secretary, December 23, 1937, FO 371/21909.
32. According to Reid in Geneva, the League Secretariat was estimating that fifteen thousand Turks were entering the Sanjak, not all of whom he believed were "rightfully electors." Williams, record of telephone conversation with Reid, January 17, 1938, FO 371/21909.
33. Kelley to Hull, December 30, 1937, 751.67/202, RG 59, NACP.
34. Kelley to Hull, January 25, 1938, 751.67/207, RG 59, NACP.
35. According to League Secretariat member Paul Anker, now acting as secretary for the electoral commission, the commission actually met with Aras himself on November 18, and on November 20 with the Turkish consul-general in Antioch. They tried repeatedly, until they left the Sanjak, to meet again with the Turkish consuls there, only to be informed each time that he was unavailable. Anker letter extract with note from Rendel, January 12, 1938, FO 371/21909.
36. Williams, "Alexandretta," January 17, 1938, FO 371/21909.
37. Rendel, January 26, 1938, FO 371/21909. Kelley to Hull, January 25, 1938, 751.67/207, RG 59, NACP.
38. Rendel, January 27, 1938, FO 371/21909.
39. Henderson (Berlin) to Eden, January 25, 1938, FO 371/21909.
40. Kelley to Hull, January 25, 1938, 751.67/207, RG 59, NACP.
41. Rendel, January 26, 1938, FO 371/21909
42. Rendel, January 28, 1938, FO 371/21909.
43. The Committee of Three reminded Rendel of the committee formed a few months earlier to discuss Palestine. Rendel, January 28, 1938, FO 371/21909. Rendel, January 30, 1938, FO 371/21909. The Turkish consul in the Sanjak brought back instructions earlier in the month that Turks should boycott the registrations if their demands were not met. DSG Beirut Information 64, January 6, 1938, from Alexandretta Security, CP 524.
44. Rendel, January 30, 1938, FO 371/21909.
45. Rendel, January 30, 1938, FO 371/21909. Under the circumstances, Rendel suggested that a less senior diplomat should participate. Stevenson's note agreed that "we are committed to capitulation to the Turks."
46. *League of Nations Official Journal 1938*, 115–17.
47. Davis to Foreign Secretary, January 6, 1938, FO 371/21900.
48. Antioch Security Information 52, February 5, 1938, CP 517.
49. Garabed Summary, February 7, 1938, CP 523. Zannardi, Alexandretta Security, February 7, 1938, CP 523. Telegram, Martel to MAE, February 9, 1938, CP 523.
50. Zannardi, February 8, 1938, CP 523.
51. Telegram, Martel to MAE, February 9, 1938, CP 523. Martel wrote that he had no objection to the appointment, which, he pointed out, had the additional advantage of exiling this activist (whose activities incriminated him in the eyes of the British) from Damascus and the Palestinian refugees.
52. Antioch Security Information, February 23, 1938, CP 517 and 524.
53. Antioch Security Information 67, February 10, 1938, 517.

54. Marty, Information, February 28, 1938, CP 517.
55. Telegram, Martel to MAE, December 4, 1937, CP 511.
56. Antioch Security Information, February 23, 1938, CP 517 and 524. One of the French informants who had been observing the shadow system was threatened by heads of the alternative police force, "obliging him to end all contact with my [French] service." The "annexes" were to be found in "Alexandretta, Kirikhan, Reyhanlı, El-Urdu, Shaykh Koy, Kuseyr, etc." Agents listed were as follows. From Alexandretta to Antioch: Alkaya Memduh Şakir; from Kirikhan to Antioch: Mursel family; from Reyhanlı to Antioch: Mursel Family; from El Urdu to Antioch: Mahmud Ağa; from Shaykh Koy to Antioch: Mahmud Ağa; from Süveydiye to Antioch: Maruf family (İzeddin); from Antioch to Aleppo: Vedi Munir, Şükrü Balcı, Semih Azmi.
57. Yücel Güçlü, *The Question of the Sanjak of Alexandretta*, 205.
58. Rendel, March 7, 1938, FO 371/21909. Telegram, Rendel, March 9, 1938, FO 286/869.
59. Rendel, "Alexandretta: Geneva Proceedings, March, 1938. Note No. 2." Telegram, Rendel, March 9, 1938, FO 286/869.
60. Telegram, Rendel, March 9, 1938, FO 286/869.
61. This prediction was months before Munich. Telegram, Rendel, March 9, 1938, FO 286/869. "Alexandretta, Proceeding of the Committee of the Council appointed to revise the Draft Electoral Law, March 1938. Note No. 7. Confidential Record by Mr. G. W. Rendel," March 18, 1938, FO 286/869. Rendel seemed quite certain that intimidation would follow these decisions, describing "what was obviously the intention of the Turks, i.e., that the majority of the Alawites and Arabs should be compelled by every form of illegitimate pressure to register as Turks, but should do so without fully realising the consequence of their action." Rendel described the proposed system of color-coded cards indicating which community a voter had claimed. "It is easy to see how those who bring back from the registration stations cards not of the Turkish colour will be penalised by Turkish landlords, agents from Angora, &c. I confess that I shall be surprised if more than a very small number of Alawites and Arabs register as anything but Turks under this system."
62. Rendel, January 18, 1938, FO 371/21909.
63. "M. Rüştü Aras does not think that Germany anticipates war and believes that she is ready at this moment for an effort of détente. The relations of Turkey with that country are not bad and Germany has made it known to her that these good relations are completely compatible with all the accords, especially with France, England, and even the USSR, that Turkey could have in the meantime." "Note d'audience du Ministre: Entretien avec M. Rustu Aras," January 30, 1938, in *Documents diplomatiques français*, vol. 8 (Paris, 1972), 149–50.
64. Courson to Daladier, March 28, 1938, in *Documents diplomatiques français*, vol. 9 (Paris, 1974), 126–27.
65. "Note du Commandant Supérieur des troupes du Levant relative aux accords militaires à etablir avec la Turquie," February 19, 1938, in *Documents diplomatiques français*, vol. 8 (Paris, 1972), 419–21.
66. League of Nations, "Report of the Commission for the Organization and Supervision of the First Elections in the Sanjak," August 20, 1938, 32–33. SDN C. 261.1938.

Chapter 6

1. Ponsot to Martel, May 6, 1938, CP 512.
2. Kelley, May 7, 1938, 751.67/217, RG59, NACP.
3. Kelley, quoting *Tan*, May 7, 1938, 751.67/217, RG 59, NACP.
4. DSG Beirut Information 2376, May 5, 1938, based on Alexandretta Security May 2, 1938, CP 524.
5. DSG Beirut, May 5, 1938, from Alexandretta Security May 2, 1938, CP 524.

6. DSG Beirut, May 7, 1938, from Alexandretta Security May 4, 1938, CP 524. Telegram, Alexandretta Administrator to Martel, May 4, 1938, CP 513.

7. DSG Beirut Information 2470, May 9, 1938, based on Alexandretta Security May 5, 1938, CP 514.

8. "Note au sujet des incidents . . . qui, selon les Turks, se seraient produits recemment dans le Sandjak d'Alexandrette," May 17, 1938, CP 513. The next day, they opened an additional seven bureaus, all in the neighboring Kirikhan kaza. Communiqué of the Commission of the League of Nations for the First Elections in the Sanjak of Alexandretta, CP 514. Telegram, Alexandretta Administrator to Martel, May 4, 1938, CP 513. Telegram, Martel to MAE, May 4, 1938, CP 513.

9. DSG Beirut Information 2255, May 2, 1938, CP 524. Request No. 36, April 26, 1938, SDN C 1077.

10. Mehmed Ali and Kojo to Martel and Secretary-General of the League of Nations, January 20, 1937, CP 513.

11. Memduh Selim to Reimers, May 7, 1938, SDN C 1041. "Summaries of the Reports," attached to "Report to President of the Commission of the League of Nations for the First Elections in the Sanjak of Alexandretta on My activity at Rihanie and at Miskhane," SDN C 1077 (hereafter "Summaries of the Reports").

12. Memduh Selim to Reimers, May 11, 1938 (letter 36), SDN C 1041.

13. Deposition, May 6, 1938, Affair 16.1, SDN C 1041. Affaire d'Aktepe, Conclusions et Requisitions, and trial transcript, SDN C 1041. See also "Note au sujet des incidents . . . qui, selon les Turcs, se seraient produits recemment dans le Sandjak d'Alexandrette," 17 May 1938. Note edited based on information provided by Rifki Refik Pasin, Chef de Section aux Affaires Etrangeres, CP 513. The representative of the Turkish community claimed that the Halkevi had been fired on, and the whole incident was created by Kurds who refused to accept those who wanted to register as Turks. Garreau telegraphed Martel and the French Foreign Ministry, "The Special Tribunal of the Electoral Commission just pronounced verdict re: Turkish aggressors of Aktepe of May 6. Three of them were acquitted at the former session. Two accused judged today were condemned to six months in prison." May 19 and 20, 1938, CP 513.

14. Garreau to Martel, May 6, 1938, CP 513. Telegram, Martel to MAE and Ponsot, May 6, 1938, CP 513.

15. Garreau to Martel, May 6, 1938, CP 513. Telegram, Martel to MAE and Ponsot, May 6, 1938, CP 513.

16. Davis, May 7, 1938, CP 513.

17. Cortese to Garreau, May 7, 1938, CP 513.

18. DSG Beirut Information 2375, from Alexandretta Security, May 5, 1938, CP 524.

19. DSG Beirut Information 2376, May 5, 1938, Alexandretta Security, May 2, 1938, CP 524.

20. Garreau to Martel, May 7, 1938, CP 513. Telegram, Alexandretta Administrative Councillor to Martel, May 4, 1938, CP 513. Telegram, Martel to MAE, May 4, 1938, CP 513. In this summary, Martel claims that three people were injured.

21. Telegram, Ponsot to Martel, May 9, 1938, CP 513.

22. Telegram, MAE to Martel, May 9, 1938, CP 513. Serri, Commander of the Gendarmerie Force of the Sanjak, No. 4009/33, May 4, 1938, CP 514.

23. Garreau to Martel, May 7, 1938, CP 513.

24. Ponsot to Martel, May 10, 1938, Martel to MAE, May 10, 1938, CP 513.

25. Hassan Jabara was the official who elicited the most demands by the Turks, "especially Jabara, who had celebrated in the Sanjak the festival of martyrs, 'victims of Turkish terrorism during the war.'" Ponsot to Martel, May 10, 1938, interview with Menemencioğlu.

26. Summary of an interview with Numan Menemencioğlu, May 7, 1938, with Ponsot to MAE, May 9, 1938, CP 513.

27. Telegram, Martel to MAE and Ponsot, May 11, 1938, CP 513.

28. Telegram, Martel to MAE and Ponsot, May 12, 1938, CP 513. Garreau to Martel, May 19, 1938, with copy of Edhem Cevelek letter to Martel, May 12, 1938, CP 513. Ponsot to Martel, May 13, 1938, CP 513.

29. The villages were Kercaoğlu, Karavaoğlu, Jinjinkli. "Summary of the Reports." Karasapan claimed that "Arab propagandists and terrorists" were in Reyhanlı that same day, "terrorising the population with pistols." Annex to the letter of the Consul General of Turkey, May 11, 1938, CP 513.

30. Alexandretta Information, May 15, 1938, CP 514.

31. "Summaries of the Reports."

32. Karasapan to Garreau, May 17, 1938, and enclosures, CP 513. Garreau to Martel, May 18, 1938, CP 513.

33. Telegram, Garreau to Martel, May 11, 1938, Turks 4292, others 4276, CP 513.

34. Garreau described him as "until this day an irreducible adversary of Kemalism and to whom I had given the counsel of moderation," Telegram, Garreau to Martel, May 12, 1938, CP 513.

35. Alexandretta Information, May 17, 1938, CP 514.

36. Telegram, Martel to MAE, May 18, 1938, CP 513.

37. Telegram, Ponsot to Martel, May 10, 1938, Telegram, Ponsot to Martel, May 13, 1938, CP 513.

38. "Summaries of the Reports."

39. Telegram, Martel to Paris, May 6, 1938, CP 513.

40. Extract of a bulletin of Agence d'Anatolie, May 17, 1938, CP 513. Ponsot to Martel, May 18, 1938, CP 513.

41. DSG Beirut, May 3, 1938, from Alexandretta Security April 30, 1938, CP 524.

42. Munir to Commander of the Sanjak Gendarmerie Forces, May 16, 1938, CP 513.

43. Information, Alexandretta, May 16, 1938, CP 514.

44. "Summaries of the Reports." Karasapan to Garreau, May 17, 1938, CP 513. Response in the note to Garreau by Queru, May 27, 1938, CP 513. Latour, Chief of Forest Service, Response, May 24, 1938, CP 513.

45. "Summaries of the Reports."

46. "Summaries of the Reports." Documents confiscated by French police indicate a well-organized Turkish effort to keep Turkish voters in line. They had reports of registrations, and inquired into individual instances where Turks were not voting as they "should." In addition, they notified representatives of the positions taken on issues such as registrations as Sunni Muslims. See Committee for the Independence of Hatay, Dörtyol to President of the People's Party Alexandretta, May 13, 1938, and other attachments with Zannardi to DSG Beirut, May 17, 1938, CP 524. See also attachments to DSG Beirut to Martel, May 14, 1938, CP 513.

47. Telegram, Martel to MAE, May 18, 1938, CP 513.

48. Telegram, Martel to Aleppo Deputy, May 20, 1938, CP 513. Telegram, Martel to Latakia Deputy, May 20, 1938, CP 513.

49. Reimers to Garreau, May 24, 1938, CP 513.

50. Notes on Mr. Walter's telephone call on interpreting article 17, May 17, 1938, FO 371/21911. Bowker, "Further meeting of the League Committee of Five which drew up the Revised Regulations for the Elections in the Sanjak of Alexandretta," May 23, 1938, FO 371/21911. Telegram, MAE to Martel, May 23, 1938, CP 513.

51. For information on Atatürk's January 1937 consideration of war for Alexandretta, see Mango, *Atatürk*, 508–9.

52. Ponsot to Martel, May 18, 1938, CP 513.

53. Telegram, Loraine, May 20, 1938, FO 371/21911.

54. Notes in response to telegram from Loraine of May 22, 1938, FO 371/21911.

55. Foreign Office to Loraine, May 30, 1938, FO 371/21911. The British, receiving appeals for assistance from both France and Turkey, were considerably annoyed. "It would certainly

be wrong for us to urge on the French the importance of 'cooking' the elections, when the League Electoral Commission (and thus we ourselves) are responsible for seeing that they are properly carried out," wrote the Foreign Office's Baxter. Notes with Loraine telegram, May 28, 1938, FO 371/21911.

56. Bowker note, June 1, 1938, FO 371/21911.
57. Yücel Güçlü, *The Question of the Sanjak of Alexandretta*, 218–19.
58. Response in Queru to Garreau, May 27, 1938, CP 513.
59. "Summaries of the Reports."
60. Telegram, Martel to MAE, May 25, 1938, CP 513. Memo, no date, included between letter of president of the electoral commission to Garreau, May 24, 1938, and telegram from MAE to Martel May 23, 1938, CP 513. Telegram, Davis, May 25, 1938, FO 371/21911.
61. No date, included between letter of president of the electoral commission to Garreau, May 24, 1938, and telegram from MAE to Martel May 23, 1938, CP 513.
62. "Summaries of the Reports."
63. Telegram, Loraine, May 28, 1938, FO 371/21911.
64. Martel, May 27, 1938, CP 513.
65. Ponsot to Martel, May 30, 1938, CP 513.
66. Telegram, Martel to MAE and Ankara, May 30, 1938, CP 513.
67. Telephone message, Garreau to Martel, May 30, 1938, CP 513. "As far as the search made at the Halkevi of Reyhanlı following the murders committed by a Turkish band in the village of Ayranji Kharki [*sic*], it was made by the Procureur General in my presence and that of the Procureur with the Special Tribunal of the Electoral Commission in the most regular and completely correct conditions. I do not need to tell you that he did not touch the portrait of Ataturk. The photograph taken after our departure showing the effigy of the Ghazi thrown on the ground does not constitute a witness to support the version adopted by the Turkish government." Telephone message, Garreau to Martel, May 30, 1938, CP 513.
68. Telephone message, Garreau to Martel, May 30, 1938, CP 513. Telegram, Martel to MAE, May 30, 1938, CP 513.
69. Telephone message, Garreau to Martel, May 30, 1938, CP 513.
70. Telegram, Martel to MAE and Ankara, May 30, 1938, CP 513.
71. Telephone message, Garreau to Martel, May 30, 1938, CP 513. Telegram, Martel to MAE and Ponsot, May 30, 1938, CP 513. Garreau to Reimers, May 31, 1938, CP 513. "Report of the Commission for the Organisation and Supervision of the First Elections in the Sanjak," SDN C 261.1938, 44.
72. Telegram, Martel to MAE and Ponsot, May 31, 1938, CP 513.
73. Telephone message, Garreau to Martel, May 30, 1938, CP 513. Telegram, Martel to MAE, May 30, 1938, CP 513.
74. Telegram, Martel to MAE, June 1, 1938, AA 160.
75. Telegram, Martel to MAE, June 1, 1938, AA 160. Telegram, Martel to MAE, June 1, 1938, CP 513. Garreau related his instructions to try to convince the leaders of the non-Turkish communities to the Committee of the Council of the League of Nations on June 10–11, 1938, Bowker note, June 14, 1938, FO 371/21911
76. Telegram, Bonnet to Martel, June 2, 1938, CP 513.
77. Ponsot to Martel, May 31, 1938, CP 513.
78. Telegram, MAE to Ponsot, June 1, 1938, AA 160.
79. Telegram, Ponsot to MAE, June 1, 1938, AA 160. Telegram, Ponsot to Martel, May 31, 1938, CP 513.
80. Telegram, Ponsot to Martel, June 1, 1938, CP 513.
81. Telegram, Martel to MAE, June 2, 1938, CP 513. Martel wished to avoid firing Garreau.
82. Telegram, Martel to MAE, June 1, 1938, CP 513. Martel the next day reiterated his belief that the Ankara regime was set on finding a pretext to invade. Telegram, Martel to MAE, June 2, 1938, CP 513. Telegram, Martel to MAE, June 2, 1938, CP 513. For Foreign

Minister Bonnet, a Turkish military presence would also imply that France was delegating her mandate. Telegram, Bonnet to Martel, June 1, 1938, CP 513.

83. Reimers to Garreau, June 1, 1938, CP 513.
84. Telegram, Martel to MAE, June 2, 1938, CP 513. In addition to fearing that it would not meet Turkish demands, Martel feared that "in associating ourselves with this procedure we risk seeing the Turks profit by accusing us one more time of looking for a way to shun our obligations."
85. Bowker note on Walter's conversation, June 1, 1938, FO 371/21911.
86. Ponsot to Martel, June 3, 1938, CP 513.
87. Telegram, Martel to MAE, June 2, 1938, CP 513.

Chapter 7

1. Decree of High Commissioner, June 3, 1938, CP 513. Telegram, Martel to Garreau, June 1, 1938, CP 513.
2. Decree of June 3, 1938, CP 513. Telegram, Martel to MAE, June 3, 1938, CP 513. Telegram, Martel to French officials in Cairo, Bagdad, Jerusalem, June 3, 1938, CP 513.
3. Reimers to Collet, June 4, 1938, CP 513. Collet to Martel, June 4, 1938, CP 513.
4. Collet to Martel, June 4, 1938, CP 513.
5. Telegrams, Martel to MAE, June 5, 1938, CP 513.
6. Colombani to DSG Beirut, June 3, 1938, CP 513.
7. DSG Beirut Information, June 9, 1938, CP 521. Telegram, Davis, June 6, 1938, FO 371/21911. The British consul in Aleppo claimed that the refugees were mostly Armenian. DSG Beirut Information, June 10, 1938, CP 518, claimed that one hundred people from varied communities came in five vehicles to Aleppo on June 7 to take refuge, fearing a Turkish invasion.
8. Telegram, Davis, June 4, 1938, FO 371/21911.
9. Collet to Martel, June 5, 1938, CP 513. Telegram, Martel to MAE, June 5, 1938, CP 513. Reimers to Collet, June 4, 1938, CP 513. Collet to Martel, June 7, 1938, CP 513. Martel to MAE, June 7, 1938, CP 513.
10. Collet to Martel, June 7, 1938, CP 513.
11. Reimers to Collet, June 7, 1938, CP 513.
12. Reimers to Collet, June 7, 1938, CP 513.
13. Collet to Reimers, June 10, 1938, CP 513.
14. Telegrams, Martel to MAE, June 7, 1938, CP 513.
15. Collet to Martel, June 8, 1938, CP 513.
16. "Summaries of the Reports."
17. Telegram, Khurail and all to Martel, June 9, 1938, CP 513.
18. Reimers to Collet, June 8, 1938, CP 513. League of Nations, "Report of the Commission for the Organization and Supervision of the First Elections in the Sanjak," August 20, 1938, SDN R 4143 6A/3465/29161.
19. Commission to Collet, June 8, 1938, CP 513. This last suspension was not to be observed in the two districts of Kesab and Jabal Musa or the final unregistered bureau of the Alexandretta region.
20. Sadak to Avenol, June 10, 1938, CP 513.
21. Commission des Première elections dans le sandjak d'Alexandrette, Communiqué No. 14, June 9, 1938, CP 513. Reimers to Collet, June 9, 1938, CP 513.
22. Telegram, Martel to MAE, June 10, 1938, CP 513.
23. Collet to Martel, June 10, 1938, CP 513.
24. Sadak to Avenol, June 11, 1938, SDN R 4140. Ponsot to Martel, June 10, 1938, CP 513.
25. Sadak to Avenol, June 11, 1938, SDN R 4140.
26. Reimers, "Memorandum of the Commission of the League of Nations for the First Elections in the Sanjak of Alexandretta," June 28, 1938, CP 513.

27. Baxter, Stevensen, and "L" notes, June 15, 1938, FO 371/21911. The comments of official "AC" are particularly instructive. "I had ten years' experience of Geneva, but this shocks even me. I don't know whether to accord more sympathy to the French member for the embarrassing position in which he finds himself, or admiration for his blatancy. . .. I don't see how the French or Turks are going to get out of this mess without trouble or with any remaining shred of decency. If the Commission resigns, I really see nothing for us but to refuse to have anything more to do with this dirty business. What capital the Germans and Italians could make out of it!"
28. "Summaries of the Reports."
29. Collet to Martel, June 11, 1938, CP 513.
30. "Summaries of the Reports." SDN C 1040, file 9, case 119.
31. "Summaries of the Reports."
32. "Summaries of the Reports."
33. "Summaries of the Reports."
34. SDN C 1041, file 3.
35. Martel to MAE, June 10, 1938, CP 513. Martel to MAE, June 13, 1938, CP 513. Collet to Martel, June 14, 1938, CP 513.
36. Collet to Martel, June 17, 1938, CP 513. SDN C 1040, file 9, case 119.
37. Telegram, Martel to MAE, June 14, 1938, CP 513. Yücel Güçlü, *The Question of the Sanjak of Alexandretta*, 222.
38. Collet to Martel, June 14, 1938, CP 513.
39. Telegram, Martel to MAE, June 14, 1938, CP 513.
40. Gacon to Collet, June 14, 1938, CP 513. "Summaries of the Reports."
41. Ponsot to Martel, June 16, 1938, CP 513. Communication of Collet, n.d., CP 513. Telegram, Martel to MAE, June 19, 1938, CP 513: "No Circassian officer of the gendarmerie made a report on the subject of the incident. It confirms that the Turks were looking for a pretext to exploit against the Commission."
42. Reimers to Lagarde, June 13, 1938.
43. Reimers, "Memorandum of the Commission of the League of Nations for the First Elections in the Sanjak of Alexandretta," June 28, 1938, CP 513.
44. "Summaries of the Reports."
45. "Summaries of the Reports."
46. "Summaries of the Reports."
47. "Summaries of the Reports."
48. "Summaries of the Reports."
49. Collet to Martel, June 16, 1938, CP 513.
50. Telegram, Collet to Martel, June 15, 1938, CP 513.
51. Collet to Martel, June 18, 1938, CP 513. Telegram, Martel to MAE, June 20, 1938, CP 513.
52. Morgan to Halifax, June 18, 1938, FO 371/21912, claims that the Turkish government was redirecting its most venomous attacks from the French to the League of Nations, hoping that they would "efface themselves" and leave the Sanjak so the French and Turks could together produce the electoral outcome they had agreed to.
53. "First Elections in the Sanjak of Alexandretta," June 23, 1938, FO 371/21912.
54. "Summaries of the Reports."
55. "Summaries of the Reports."
56. Pavkovitch report, June 20, 1938, to Reimers. "Summaries of the Reports."
57. Communication of Collet, n.d. [copy on stationery dated June 20], CP 513.
58. Telegram, Martel to MAE, June 20, 1938, CP 513.
59. Telegram, Martel to Ponsot, June 21, 1938, AA 158.
60. Reimers to Collet, June 21, 1938, CP 513.
61. League of Nations, June 23, 1938, FO 371/21912.
62. Report of Mr. Dodson, Section of Babtrun, June 20, 21, 1938, SDN C 1061.
63. Report of Mr. Dodson, Section of Babtrun, June 21, 1938, SDN C 1061.

64. Report of Mayor Nicol on the events of Babtrun, of June 21, 1938, SDN C 1061.
65. Telegram, Davis, June 23, 1938, FO 371/21912.
66. Collet, Arreté, June 21, 1938, CP 513.
67. Note given by M. Suad Davaz to M. Georges Bonnet, June 22, 1938 CP 513.
68. Telegram, MAE to Martel, June 22, 1938, CP 513.
69. Telegram, Martel to MAE and Ponsot, June 22, 1938.
70. League of Nations, June 23, 1938, FO 371/21912.
71. Telegram, Martel to MAE, June 23, 1938, AA 158.
72. DSG Beirut Information 64, June 25, 1938, CP 513.
73. DSG Beirut Information, June 29, 1938, CP 521.
74. Reimers to Collet, June 26, 1938, CP 513.
75. Martel to MAE, June 27, 1938, CP 513. Collet to Martel, June 27, 1938, CP 513.
76. Telegram, Davis, June 30, 1938, FO 371/21912. Güçlü, *Question of the Sanjak*, 230–31.
77. Ponsot to Martel, June 30, 1938, CP 513.
78. Telegram, Phipps, July 1, 1938, FO 371/21912.
79. Telegram, Henderson, July 4, 1938, FO 371/21912.
80. Telegram, Morgan, July 5, 1938, FO 371/21912. According to Güçlü, *Question of the Sanjak*, 231, the military agreement was signed July 3 and provided for six thousand troops to be stationed in the Sanjak: one thousand local troops, twenty-five hundred each from France and Turkey—until the Statute began functioning normally. Turkish troops would maintain order in those areas with a largely Turkish population until the end of the emergency, at which point both French and Turkish troops would be withdrawn and the territory would be policed by a local gendarmerie. Turkish troops would not be under the orders of a French officer, but the highest Turkish officer would be a colonel. Both sides agreed that this was not to be considered a limitation or a dismemberment of the French mandate.
81. Telegram, Davis, July 11, 1938, FO 371/21912.

Conclusion

1. Georges Araman, "L'issue dramatique de la première guerre mondiale pour les Chrétiens de la region d'Antioche de Syrie." *Chronos: Revue d'Histoire de l'Université de Balamand* 13 (2006): 337–77.
2. http://www.parliament.gov.sy/ar/syria.php and http://www.todayszaman.com/tz-web/news-196473-102-pm-vows-to-build-model-partnership-with-syria.html (accessed September 11, 2010).
3. Telegram, Ponsot to Martel, July 11, 1938, CP 513. Telegram, Martel to Ponsot, July 12, 1938, CP 513.
4. Yücel Güçlü, *Question of the Sanjak*, 236. Electoral decrees and lists are found in CP 513.
5. Telegram, Martel to MAE, July 30, 1938, CP 513.
6. Turks, 35,847 (twenty-two seats); Alawis 11,319 (nine seats); Armenians 5,504 (five seats); Orthodox 2,098 (two seats); Arabs 1,845 (two seats), Other Communities 359. The electoral regulations had guaranteed a minimum number of seats for five communities, Turks eight, Alawi six, Arab two, Armenian two, Greek Orthodox one. The number of electors to be determined in the first stage (the electors of the second degree who would make the decisions) would be 358 Turks, 113 Alawi, 55 Armenians, 18 Arabs, and 20 Greek Orthodox. Commission of Elections of the Sanjak of Alexandretta, Decision No. 15, August 2, 1938, CP 513. Mehmet Tekin counts the final results as thirty-one seats for Turks, including the nine Alevis. *Hatay Devlet Reisi Tayfur Sökmen* (Antakya: Mustafa Kemal Üniversitesi, 2002), 82.
7. Meyrier to MAE, August 23, 1938, CP 513.
8. Meyrier to Istanbul, August 10, 1939, AA 161. See also Tayfur Sökmen, *Hatay'ın Kurtuluşu İçin* (Ankara: Türk Tarih Kurumu Yaınları, 1992), chapter 6.
9. Telegram, Paris to Beirut Delegate, August 12, 1938, CP 513.

10. Telegram, Meyrier to Istanbul, September 2, 1939, AA 161.

11. Cemal Alpar, Minister of Public Works and Agriculture, Cemal Yurtman, Minister of Justice, Setir Cemil, Minister of Finance, Ahmet Faik, Minister of Public instruction and Hygiene. Walter Bandazian, "The Crisis of Alexandretta," Ph.D. diss., American University, 1967), 129–30.

12. MacMurray to Hull, March 15, 1939, MacMurray to SecState, December 7, 1938, AEGR 1938, box 18, NACP. Bandazian cited *La République*, April 25, 1939, which quoted Sök-men, who traveled to Turkey to be sworn in as a deputy: "Although, formally, I am the Chief of State of the Hatay I am, in reality, only an officer appointed to the Hatay in order to apply and execute the orders of the Eternal Chief Atatürk and of President İsmet İnönü." *Yeni Gün*, September 3, 1938.

13. Telegram, MAE to Martel, October 26, 1938, CP 513. Language in the school—Arabic to be abolished, Meyrier to Istanbul, August 26, 1938, AA 161. Davis to Secretary of State, November 14, 1938, FO 371/21913. The Hatay government responded by reducing their own customs tariffs on imports by 40 percent. Davis thought this was to compensate for tariffs the French had imposed at the Syrian border, "the effect of which has been to render virtually impossible the transport by road of merchandise from Alexandretta to Aleppo, with disastrous results to the shipping and transit trade of the Hatay. With the Customs tariff at twenty-five percent ad valorem in Syria and only fifteen percent in the Hatay it is anticipated that smuggling from the Hatay into Syria will become a profitable enterprise calculated to bring back to the port of Alexandretta the traffic which it has temporarily lost through the suspension of its traditional transit trade." Davis to Secretary of State, November 14, 1938, FO 371/21913.

14. Martel to MAE, October 19, 1938, CP 512. Telegram, Ponsot to Martel, October 31, 1938, CP 513. Daladier feared Von Papen had gotten to the Turks. Telegram, Ponsot to Martel, October 31, 1938, CP 513.

15. "Assyrians and Armenians, Report from Syria by M. J. Kunsler (Oeuvre Suisse pour les Refugies, Beyrouth), November 8th 1938," FO 371/21913. Kunsler wrote that the Armenian Protestant churches were recommending that their members remain, and the pastors of the Alexandretta church were building a wall, an indication of their plan to stay. Khoury writes, "Just two months after the Sanjak's transfer, Syria had already received some 50,000 refugees. The largest number were Armenians—as many as 22,000—who fled their homes even before the French troops had pulled out, many for a second time in less than 20 years. In addition, some 10,000 Alawites, 10,000 Sunni Arabs (including tribes), and 5,000 Christian Arabs also left. Those who chose to remain were Sunnis and Alawite peasants who were attached to the land and who, unlike the merchant and artisanal communities, had few opportunities to resettle in Syria." *Syria and the French Mandate*, 513. Avedis Demirci, one of those Armenians, told an interviewer in the spring of 2002 that half of those in his village of 120 households left when the French withdrew in 1939. The Turkish government claimed that the Armenians were leaving because of the work of propagandists. Interview with Nüvis. Telegram, MAE to Martel, December 23, 1939. *New York Times*, July 26, 1939.

16. Güçlü, *Question of the Sanjak*, 232.

17. Davis to SecState, December 13, 1938, FO 371/21911.

18. Davis to SecState, May 18, 1939, *Records of Syria 1918–1973*, 786–88. The French Foreign Ministry was informed by the Turkish Ambassador in Paris that "a propaganda hostile to the Ankara government was currently developing in Hatay. It is practiced in Muslim circles by the intervention of imams who take their orders to the direction of the Evkaf." Telegram, MAE to Martel, December 23, 1938, CP 513.

19. Robert J. Young, "The Aftermath of Munich," 305–22.

20. Philip S. Khoury, *Syria and the French Mandate*, 512–13. The new British Ambassador in Ankara, Knatchbull-Hugessen, claimed that the negotiations were foundering over things like the French schools, and Turkey's refusal to allow French possession of their

war cemetery. "They continue to bring forward new demands all the time," telegraphed British Ambassador Phipps from Paris, June 14, 1939, FO 371/23278. Knatchbull-Hugessen, June 14, 1939, FO 371/23278. The Turkish government had repeatedly claimed they would not annex the Sanjak, and would comply with the Geneva Statute approved in May 1937. Davis to Secretary of State, November 14, December 13, 1938, FO 371/21913.

21. MacMurray to Hull, August 21, 1939, AEGR 1939, box 29, NACP. Bandazian, 133–134. On June 24, the *New York Times* published the text of the French-Turkish mutual assistance pact signed in Paris on June 23. *New York Times*, July 1, 1939. "By unanimous vote the Kamutay (Parliament) today ratified the French-Turkish convention and its annexes about the cession of Hatay (formerly the Sanjak of Alexandretta) to Turkey. Yesterday the Assembly of Hatay at Antioch held its last sitting and evacuation of the French troops was begun."

22. Nüvis Interview, spring 2002. *New York Times*, July 24, 1939.

23. Roberta Micallef, "Hatay Joins the Motherland," in *State Frontiers: Borders and Boundaries in the Middle East* (London: I. B. Tauris, 2006), 141.

24. Micallef, "Hatay Joins the Motherland," 149.

25. Micallef, "Hatay Joins the Motherland," 152.

26. Majid Khadduri, "The Alexandretta Dispute," *American Journal of International Law* 39 (1945): 406–25. Bazandian, 138–39.

27. Von Papen recalled the Ankara regime's anxieties about Italy after its invasion of Albania, and his efforts to intervene to reassure Turkey about Axis intentions. Franz Von Papen, *Memoirs*, trans. Brian Connell (New York: Dutton, 1953), 446–50.

28. Blanche E. C. Dugdale and Wyndham A. Bewes, "The Working of the Minority Treaties," *Journal of the British Institute of International Affairs* 5 (1926), 79, emphasis in original.

29. Charles Seymour, *How the World Votes: The Story of Democratic Development in Elections* (Springfield, MA: A. Nichols, 1918), 175–80.

30. Peter Sahlins, *Boundaries: The Making of France and Spain in the Pyrenees* (Berkeley: University of California Press, 1989): 270–71.

31. Turkey had extensive economic relations with Hitler's Germany; Weinberg points out that Turkey could use the Sanjak situation to refuse a treaty with Germany, wanting to avoid alienating France with the Sanjak resolution pending. Gerhard L. Weinberg, *Hitler's Foreign Policy: The Road to World War II 1933–1939* (New York: Enigma Books, 2005), 321, 575–77.

32. Khoury, *Syria and the French Mandate*, 514. The French feared Italy, the Italian military presence on the Dodecanese islands, Italy's Arabic propaganda through print and wireless media, Italy's consulates, and Italy's philanthropic, educational, and financial organizations. "The role of Radio Bari and of radical Syrian politicians with ties to Italy, such as Shakib Arslan, caused the Quai d'Orsay and the High Commission considerable worry in the late 1930s." See also Thomas, "French Intelligence-Gathering," 20.

33. Conversation with Sybella Wilkes, United Nations High Commissioner for Refugees office, Damascus, Syria, 28 November 2007.

BIBLIOGRAPHY

Government Documents and Unpublished Sources

League of Nations Archives, Geneva. Series: Mandates, Political, and Commission on the Elections in the Sanjak of Alexandretta, 1937–1938

League of Nations. "Report of the Commission for the Organisation and Supervision of the First Elections of the Sanjak." Geneva: 1938

France, Archives des affaires étrangères, Paris and Nantes. Series: Syrie-Liban Cabinet Politique Ankara

Turkey, Başbakanlık arşivi, Ankara. Series: Dahiliye

Türkiye Büyük Millet Meclisi

United Kingdom, National Archives, London. Series: Foreign Office, Colonial Office

United States, National Archives, College Park, Maryland. State Department Central Files

League of Nations, Official Journal 1936, 1937, 1938

Records of Syria, 1918–1973. Edited by J. Priestland. 15 vols. Cambridge: Archive Editions, 2005

Commission de publication des documents relatifs aux origines de la guerre 1939–1945. Documents diplomatiques français. Series 1936–1939. Paris: Imprimerie Nationale, 1963–

MacMurray Papers, Seeley G. Mudd Manuscript Library, Princeton University

Yeni Gün (Atayolu)

Interviews Conducted by Nüvis, Fall 2002

Published Sources and Dissertations

Alexandre, M.A. "Le conflict Syro-Turc du Sandjak d'Alexandrette d'octobre 1936 à juin 1937, vu d'Antioche." Entretiens sur l'évolution des pays de civilisation arabe 2 (1938): 105–41.

Altan, Cemren. "Populism and Peasant Iconography: Turkish Painting in the 1930s." Middle Eastern Studies 41 (2005): 547–60.

Altuğ, Seda. "Popular Nationalism in Antioch during the French Mandate: The Making of the Sanjak of Alexandretta." Chronos: Revue d'histoire de l'université de Balamand 13 (2006): 231–75.

Anderson, Benedict. Imagined Communities: Reflections on the Origins and Spread of Nationalism. London: Verso, 1983.

Angell, Elizabeth. "Inventing Hatay: Turkish Nationalism, Minority Politics, and the Sanjak of Alexandretta Dispute." MA thesis, St. Antony's College, 2005.

Anghie, Antony. "Colonialism and the Birth of International Institutions: Sovereignty, Economy, and the Mandate System of the League of Nations." *New York University Journal of International Law and Politics* 34 (2002): 513–633.

Aoyama, Hiroyuki, and Malek Salman. "A Biography of Zaki al-Arsuzi." In *Spiritual Father of the Ba'th: The Ideological and Political Significance of Zaki al-Arsuzi in Arab Nationalist Movements*. Middle Eastern Studies Series, no. 49. Tokyo: Institute of Developing Economics, Japan International Trade Organization, 2000.

Araman, Georges. "L'issue dramatique de la première guerre mondiale pour les Chrétiens de la region d'Antioche de Syrie." *Chronos: Revue d'histoire de l'université de Balamand* 13 (2006): 337–77.

Archibugi, Daniele. "A Critical Analysis of the Self-determination of Peoples: A Cosmopolitan Perspective." *Constellations* 10 (2003): 488–505.

Ari, Eyal. "The People's Houses and the Theatre in Turkey." *Middle Eastern Studies* 40 (2004): 32–58.

Arsuzi-Elamir, Dalal. "Zaki al-Arsuzi and Syrian-Arab Nationalism in the Periphery: The Alexandretta Crisis of 1936–1939." In *From the Syrian Land to the States of Syria and Lebanon*, edited by Thomas Philipp and Christoph Schumann, 307–27. Beirut: Orient-Institut der DMG Beirut, 2004.

Aswad, Barbara. *Property Control and Social Strategies: Settlers on a Middle Eastern Plain*. Ann Arbor: University of Michigan Press, 1971.

Aydın, Ertan. "Peculiarities of Turkish Revolutionary Ideology in the 1930s: The Ülkü Version of Kemalism, 1933–1936." *Middle Eastern Studies* 40 (2004): 55–82.

Aydın, Mustafa. "The Determinants of Turkish Foreign Policy, and Turkey's European Vocation." *The Review of International Affairs* 3 (2003): 306–31.

Aytürk, İlker. "Turkish Linguists against the West: The Origins of Linguistic Nationalism in Ataturk's Turkey." *Middle Eastern Studies* 40 (2004): 92–108.

Bandazian, Walter. "The Crisis of Alexandretta." Ph.D. diss., The American University, 1967.

Barbaro, Jean Elie. *La Question du sandjak d'Alexandrette*. Aleppo: Imprimerie Rotos, 1941.

Barlas, Dilek. "Friends or Foes? Diplomatic Relations between Italy and Turkey, 1923–1936." *International Journal of Middle East Studies* 36 (2004): 231–52.

Batatu, Hanna. "Some Observations on the Social Roots of Syria's Ruling, Military Group and the Causes for Its Dominance." *Middle East Journal* 35 (1981): 331–44

Bazantay, Pierre. *Enquète sur l'artisanat a Antioche*. Beirut: Imperimerie Catholique, 1936.

Bazantay, Pierre. *La pénétration de l'enseignement dans le sandjak autonome d'Alexandrette*. Beirut: Imprimerie Catholique, 1935.

Bendiner, Elmer. *A Time for Angels: The Tragicomic History of the League of Nations*. New York: Alfred A. Knopf, 1975.

Bennett, Brian C. "Consequences of the War in Croatia at the Village and Urban Professional Levels." In *Neighbors at War: Anthropological Perspectives on Yugoslav Ethnicity, Culture, and History*, edited by Joel Martin Halpern and David A. Kideckel, 203–88. University Park: Pennsylvania State University Press, 2000.

Berriedale, Keith. "Mandates." *Journal of Comparative Legislation and International Law* 4 (1922): 71–83.

Bieber, Florian, and Stefan Wolff, "Introduction: Elections in Divided Societies." *Ethnopolitics* 4 (2005): 359–63.

Bitterlin, Lucien. *Alexandrette, le "Munich" de l'orient, ou, Quand la france capitulait*. Paris: Jean Picollec, 1999.

Bonnet, Georges. *Défense de la paix*. Vol. 2: Fin d'une Europe. Genève: Éditions du Cheval Ailé, 1946–48.

Böröcz, József, and Melinda Kovács. "Empire's New Clothes: Unveiling EU Enlargement." *Central European Review*, 2001. http://www.ce-review.org.

Bou-Nacklie, N. E. "Les Troupes Spéciales: Religious and Ethnic Recruitment, 1916–1946." *International Journal of Middle East Studies* 25 (1993): 645–60.

Brown, Nathan. "Iraq's Constitutional Process Plunges Ahead." *Carnegie Endowment Policy Outlook*, July 2005. http://www.carnegieendowment.org/publications/index.cfm?fa=view&id=17206.

Bruinessen, Martin Van. "'Aslını inkar eden haramzadedir!' The Debate on the Ethnic Identity of the Kurdish Alevis." Working paper, Centre for the Study of Asia & the Middle East, Deakin University, Malvern, Victoria (Australia).

Bruinessen, Martin Van. "Genocide in Kurdistan? The Suppression of the Dersim Rebellion in Turkey (1937–38) and the Chemical War against the Iraqi Kurds (1988)." In *Genocide: Conceptual and Historical Dimensions,* edited by George J. Andreopoulos, 141–70. Philadelphia: University of Pennsylvania Press, 1994.

Burke, Edmund III. "A Comparative View of French Native Policy in Morocco and Syria, 1912–1925." *Middle Eastern Studies* 9 (1973): 175–86.

Çağaptay, Soner. "Passage to Turkishness: Immigration and Religion in Modern Turkey." In *Citizenship and Ethnic Conflict: Challenging the Nation-state,* edited by Haldun Gülalp, 61–82. London: Routledge, 2006.

Çağaptay, Soner. "Race, Assimilation and Kemalism: Turkish Nationalism and the Minorities in the 1930s." *Middle Eastern Studies* 40 (2004): 86–101.

Choueiri, Youssef M. *Arab Nationalism: A History.* Oxford: Blackwell, 2000.

Coakley, John. "Approaches to the Resolution of Ethnic Conflict: The Strategy of Non-Territorial Autonomy." *International Political Science Review* 15 (1994): 297–314.

Cohen, William B. "The Colonial Policy of the Popular Front." *French Historical Studies* 7 (1972): 368–93.

Çolak, Yılmaz. "Language Policy and Official Ideology in Early Republican Turkey." *Middle Eastern Studies* 40 (2004): 67–91.

Criss, Bilge, and Pinar Bilgin. "Turkish Foreign Policy toward the Middle East." *Middle East Review of International Affairs* 1 (1997). http://www.biu.ac.il/SOC/besa/meria/journal/1997/issue1/jv1n1a3.html.

Dawisha, Adeed. *Arab Nationalism in the Twentieth Century: From Triumph to Despair.* Princeton, NJ: Princeton University Press, 2003.

Demir, Ataman. *Through the Ages Antakya.* Istanbul: Akbank, 1996.

Deringil, Selim. "The Ottoman Origins of Turkish Nationalism, Namik Kemal to Mustafa Kemal." *European History Quarterly* 23 (1993): 165–91.

Deringil, Selim. *Turkish Foreign Policy during the Second World War: An "Active" Neutrality.* Cambridge: Cambridge University Press, 1989.

Dugdale, Blanche E. C., and Wyndham A. Bewes. "The Working of the Minority Treaties." *Journal of the British Institute of International Affairs* 5 (1926): 79–95.

Eberhard, Wolfram. "Nomads and Farmers in Southeastern Turkey: Problems of Settlement." *Oriens* 6 (1953): 32–49.

Eissenstat, Howard Lee. "The Limits of Imagination: Debating the Nation and Constructing the State in Early Turkish Nationalism." Ph.D. diss., University of California at Los Angeles, 2007.

Ersanlı, Büşra. "History Textbooks as Reflections of the Political Self: Turkey (1930s and 1990s) and Uzbekistan (1990s)." *International Journal of Middle East Studies* 34 (2002): 337–49.

Faksh, Mahmud A. "The Alawi Community of Syria: A New Dominant Political Force." *Middle Eastern Studies* 20 (1984): 133–53.

Farley, Lawrence T. *Plebiscites and Sovereignty: The Crisis of Political Illegitimacy.* Boulder, CO: Westview Press, 1986.

Fink, Carole. "Minority Rights as an International Question." *Contemporary European History* 9 (2000): 385–400.

Gageby, Douglas. *The Last Secretary General: Sean Lester and the League of Nations.* Dublin: Town House Press, 1999.

Garces, Laura. "The League of Nations' Predicament in Southeastern Europe." *World Affairs* 158 (1995): 3–17.

Gellner, Ernest. *Nations and Nationalism.* Ithaca, NY: Cornell University Press, 1983.

Gelvin, James L. *Divided Loyalties: Nationalism and Mass Politics in Syria at the Close of Empire.* Berkeley: University of California Press, 1998.

Gelvin, James. "The League of Nations and the Question of National Identity in the Fertile Crescent." *World Affairs* 35 (1995): 35–43.

Gelvin, James. "Modernity and Its Discontents: On the Durability of Nationalism in the Arab Middle East," *Nations and Nationalisms* 5 (1999): 71–89.

Gilquin, Michel. *D'Antioche à Hatay: L'histoire oubliée du Sandjak d'Alexandrette*. Paris: L'Harmattan, 2000.

Güçlü, Yücel. "The Controversy over the Delimitation of the Turco-Syrian Frontier in the Period between the Two World Wars." *Middle Eastern Studies* 42 (2006): 641–57.

Güçlü, Yücel. *The Question of the Sanjak of Alexandretta: A Study in Turkish-French-Syrian Relations.* Ankara: Türk Tarih Kurumu, 2001.

Gudelevičiūtė, Vita. "Does the Principle of Self-Determination Prevail over the Principle of Territorial Integrity?" *International Journal of Baltic Law* 2 (2005): 48–74.

Gülalp, Haldun. "Introduction: Citizenship vs. Nationality?" *Citizenship and Ethnic Conflict: Challenging the Nation-state*, edited by Haldun Gülalp, 1–18. London: Routledge, 2006.

Haddad, Mahmoud. "The Rise of Arab Nationalism Reconsidered." *International Journal of Middle East Studies* 26 (1994): 201–22.

Hannum, Hurst. *Autonomy, Sovereignty, and Self-Determination: The Accommodation of Conflicting Rights*. Philadelphia: University of Pennsylvania Press, 1996.

Heinrichs, Waldo H., Jr. *American Ambassador: Joseph C. Grew and the Development of the United States Diplomatic Tradition*. Boston: Little, Brown, 1966.

Hobsbawm, E. J. *Nations and Nationalism since 1780*. Cambridge: Cambridge University Press, 1990.

Hobsbawm, E. J., and Terence Ranger, eds. *The Invention of Tradition*. Cambridge: Cambridge University Press, 1983.

Hourani, Albert. *Emergence of the Modern Middle East*. Berkeley: University of California Press, 1981.

Hunt, Lynn. *Politics, Culture and Class in the French Revolution*. Berkeley: University of California Press, 1984.

İçduygu, Ahmet, and Özlem Kaygusuz. "The Politics of Citizenship by Drawing Borders: Foreign Policy and the Construction of National Citizenship Identity in Turkey." *Middle Eastern Studies* 40 (2004): 26–50.

Ireland, Philip W. "Turkish Foreign Policy after Munich." *Political Quarterly* 10 (1939): 185–201.

Jankowski, James P., and Israel Gershoni, *Rethinking Nationalism in the Arab Middle East*. New York: Columbia University Press, 1997.

Joffé, George H. "Disputes over State Boundaries in the Middle East and North Africa. In *The Middle East in Global Change: The Politics and Economics of Independence versus Fragmentation*, edited by Laura Guazzone, 58–75. New York: St. Martin's Press, 1997.

Kaplan, Sam. "Documenting History, Historicizing Documentation: French Military Officials' Ethnological Reports on Cilicia." *Comparative Studies in Society and History* 44 (2002): 344–69.

Kaplan, Sam. "Territorializing Armenians: Geo-texts, and Political Imaginaries in French-occupied Cilicia, 1919–1920." *History and Anthropology* 15 (2004): 399–423.

Karaomerlioğlu, M. Asım "The People's Houses and the Cult of the Peasant in Turkey." *Middle Eastern Studies* 34 (1998): 67–91.

Karpat, Kemal H. "The People's Houses in Turkey: Establishment and Growth." *Middle East Journal* 17 (1963): 55–67.

Karsh, Efraim, and Inari Karsh. "Reflections on Arab Nationalism." *Middle Eastern Studies* 32 (1996): 367–92.

Kasaba, Reşat. "Diversity in Antakya: A Historical Perspective." In *The Mediterranean World: The Idea, the Past and the Present*, edited by Kudret Emiroğlu, Oktay Özel, Eyüp Özveren, Süha Ünsal, 207–22. Istanbul: Iletişim, 2006.

Kasmieh, Khairia. "An Effort to Foster Arab Nationalism in the early 1930s: The League of National Action." In *From the Syrian Land to the States of Syria and Lebanon*, edited by Thomas Philipp and Christoph Schumann, 329–41 Beirut: Orient-Institut der DMG Beirut, 2004.

Khadduri, Majid. "The Alexandretta Dispute." *American Journal of International Law* 39 (1945): 406–25.

Khalidi, Rashid. "Arab Nationalism: Historical Problems in the Literature," *American Historical Review* 96 (1991): 1363–73.

Khalidi, Rashid, Lisa Anderson, Muhammad Muslih, and Reeva Simon. *The Origins of Arab Nationalism*. New York: Columbia University Press, 1993.

Khoury, Philip S. "Continuity and Change in Syrian Political Life: The Nineteenth and Twentieth Centuries." *American Historical Review* 96 (1991): 1374–95.

Khoury, Philip S. "A Reinterpretation of the Origins and Aims of the Great Syrian Revolt, 1925– 1927." In *Arab Civilization: Challenges and Responses. Studies in Honor of Constantine K Zurayk*, edited by George N. Atiyeh and Ibrahim M. Oweiss, 241–71. Albany: State University of New York Press, 1988.

Khoury, Philip S. *Syria and the French Mandate: The Politics of Arab Nationalism, 1920–1945*. Princeton, NJ: Princeton University Press, 1978.

Khoury, Philip S. "The Syrian Independence Movement and the Growth of Economic Nationalism in Damascus." *Bulletin (British Society for Middle Eastern Studies)* 14 (1987): 25–36.

Khoury, Philip S. "Syrian Urban Politics in Transition: The Quarters of Damascus during the French Mandate." *International Journal of Middle East Studies* 16 (1984): 507–40.

Khuri, Fuad I. "The Alawis of Syria: Religious Ideology and Organization." In *Syria: Society, Culture, and Polity*, edited by Richard T. Antoun and Donald Quataert, 49–61. Albany: State University of New York Press, 1991.

Knatchbull-Hugessen, Sir Hughe. *Diplomat in Peace and War*. London: John Murray, 1949.

Kramer, Lloyd. *Nationalism: Political Cultures in Europe and America, 1775–1865*. New York: Twayne Publishers,1998.

Lijphart, Arend. "Constitutional Design for Divided Societies." *Journal of Democracy* 15 (2004): 96–109.

Lijphart, Arend. *Democracy in Plural Societies: A Comparative Exploration*. New Haven, CT: Yale University Press, 1977.

Longrigg, Stephen Hemsley. *Syria and Lebanon under French Mandate*. London: Oxford University Press, 1958.

Lustick, Ian. "Stability in Deeply Divided Societies: Consociationalism versus Control." *World Politics* 31 (1979): 325–44.

Lynch, Allen. "Woodrow Wilson and the Principle of 'National Self-Determination': A Reconsideration." *Review of International Studies* 28 (2002): 419–36.

Makdisi, Ussama. "Ottoman Orientalism." *The American Historical Review* 107 (2002): 768–96.

Mango, Andrew. *Atatürk: The Biography of the Founder of Modern Turkey*. Woodstock, NY: Overlook Press, 1999.

Mazower, Mark. *Dark Continent: Europe's Twentieth Century*. New York: Vintage Books, 1998.

Mazower, Mark. "Minorities and the League of Nations in Interwar Europe." *Daedalus* 126 (1997): 47–64

McCarthy, Justin. *Muslims and Minorities: The Population of Ottoman Anatolia and the End of the Empire*. New York: New York University Press, 1983.

McBain, Howard Lee. *The New Constitutions of Europe*. New York: Doubleday, 1922.

McGarry, John, and Brendan O'Leary, "Iraq's Constitution of 2005: Liberal Consociation as Political Prescription." *International Journal of Constitutional Law* 5 (2007): 670–98.

Micallef, Roberta. "Hatay Joins the Motherland." In *State Frontiers: Borders and Boundaries in the Middle East*, edited by Inga Brandell, 141–58. London: I. B. Tauris, 2006.

Migdal, Joel S. "Mental Maps and Virtual Checkpoints: Struggles to Construct and Maintain State and Social Boundaries." In *Boundaries and Belonging: States and Societies in the Struggle to Shape Identities and Local Practices*, edited by Joel S. Migdal, 3–23. Cambridge: Cambridge University Press, 2004.

Millman, Brock. *The Ill-Made Alliance: Anglo-Turkish Relations, 1934–1940*. Montreal: McGill-Queen's University Press, 1998.

Millman, Brock. "Turkish Foreign and Strategic Policy 1934–42." *Middle Eastern Studies* 31 (1995): 485–86.

Mina, Hanna. *Fragments of Memory: A Story of a Syrian Family.* Translated by Olive Kenny and Lorne Kenny. Northampton, MA: Interlink Books, 2004.

Mizrahi, Jean-David. "La France et sa politique de mandat en syrie et au liban (1920–1939)." In *France, Syrie et Liban 1918–1946: Les ambiguités et les dynamiques de la relation mandataire,* edited by Nadine Méouchy, 35–65. Damascus, 2002.

Mizrahi, Jean-David. "Un 'nationalisme de la frontière': Bandes armées et sociabilités politiques sur la frontière turco-syrienne au début des années 1920." *Vingtième siècle* 2003: 19–34.

Morin, Aysel. "Crafting a Nation: The Mythic Construction of the New Turkish National Identity in Atatürk's Nutuk." Paper presented at the Cornell University Turkish Forum, "European Turkey: Modernization, Secularism, and Islam," December 3–4, 2004.

Musgrave, Thomas D. *Self-Determination and National Minorities.* New York: Oxford University Press, 2000.

O'Leary, Brandon. "Debating Consociational Politics: Normative and Explanatory Arguments." In *From Power Sharing to Democracy: Post Conflict Institutions in Ethnically Divided Societies,* edited by Sidney John Roderick Noel, 3–43. Montreal: McGill-Queen's Press, 2005.

Omar, Saleh. "Philosophical Origins of the Arab Ba'th Party: The Work of Zaki al-Arsuzi." *Arab Studies Quarterly* 18 (1996).

Öz, Yılmaz. *Quotations from Mustafa Kemal Atatürk.* Ankara: Ministry of Foreign Affairs, 1982.

Papen, Franz von. *Memoirs.* Translated by Brian Connell. New York: E. P. Dutton, 1953.

Preece, Jennifer Jackson. "Minority Rights in Europe: From Westphalia to Helsinki." *Review of International Studies* 23 (1997): 75–92.

Preece, Jennifer Jackson. *National Minorities and the European Nation-States System.* New York: Oxford University Press, 1998.

Pomerance, Michla. "The United States and Self-Determination: Perspectives on the Wilsonian Conception." *The American Journal of International Law* 70 (1976): 1–27.

Provence, Michael. *The Great Syrian Revolt and the Rise of Arab Nationalism.* Austin: University of Texas Press, 2005.

Puaux, Gabriel. *Deux Années au Levant: Souvenirs de Syrie et du Liban 1939–1940.* Paris: Hachette, 1952.

Quataert, Donald. "Clothing Laws, State, and Society in the Ottoman Empire, 1720–1829." *International Journal of Middle East Studies* 29 (1997): 403–25.

Rabinovich, Itamar. "The Compact Minorities and the Syrian State, 1918–45." *Journal of Contemporary History* 14 (1979): 693–712.

Richmond, Oliver P. "States of Sovereignty, Sovereign States, and Ethnic Claims for International Status." *Review of International Studies* 28 (2002): 381–402.

Rondot, Pierre. "L'experience du Mandat francais en Syrie et au Liban, 1918–45," in *Revue Générale de Droit International Public,* 18 (1947): 387–407.

Rosting, Helmer. "Protection of Minorities by the League of Nations." *American Journal of International Law* 17 (1923): 641–60.

Sahlins, Peter. *Boundaries: The Making of France and Spain in the Pyrenees.* Berkeley: University of California Press, 1989.

Sahlins, Peter. "State Formation and National Identity in the Catalan Borderlands during the Eighteenth and Nineteenth Centuries." In *Border Identities: Nation and State at International Frontiers,* edited by Thomas Wilson and Hastings Donnan, 31–61. Cambridge: Cambridge University Press, 1998.

Sanjian, Avedis K. "The Sanjak of Alexandretta (Hatay): Its Impact on Turkish-Syrian Relations (1939–1956)." *Middle East Journal* 10 (1956): 379–94.

Satloff, Robert B. "Prelude to Conflict: Communal Interdependence in the Sanjak of Alexandretta 1920–1936." *Middle Eastern Studies* 22 (1986): 147–80.

Schmitz, David F. *Thank God They're on Our Side: The United States and Right-Wing Dictatorships, 1921–1965.* Chapel Hill: University of North Carolina Press, 1999.

Scott, James C. *Seeing Like a State: How Certain Schemes to Improve the Human Condition Have Failed*. New Haven, CT: Yale University Press, 1998.

Seale, Patrick. *Asad: The Struggle for the Middle East*. Berkeley: University of California Press, 1990.

Seymour, Charles. *How the World Votes: The Story of Democratic Development in Elections*. Springfield, MA: C. A. Nichols, 1918.

Shambrook, Peter. "Bypassing the Nationalists: Comte Damien de Martel's 'Administrative' Reforms of January 1936." In *France, Syrie et Liban 1918–1946: Les ambiguités et les dynamiques de la relation mandataire*, edited by Nadine Méouchy, 230–33. Damascus, 2002.

Shambrook, Peter A. *French Imperialism in Syria 1927–1936*. Reading, UK: Ithaca Press, 1998.

Shennawy, Abdel Aziz. "The Restoration of Hatay, an Attempt Begun by Atatürk and Achieved by İnönü." *Büyük Zafer ve Sonuçları*. Istanbul: Boğaziçi Üniversitesi Yayınları, 1982: 223–47.

Sherrill, Charles H. *A Year's Embassy to Mustafa Kemal*. New York: Charles Scribner's Sons, 1934.

Shields, Sarah. "Convivencia and Muslims." *Pacem* 4 (2001): 39–53.

Shields, Sarah D. "Sheep, Nomads and Merchants in Nineteenth-Century Mosul: Creating Transformations in an Ottoman Society." *Journal of Social History* 25 (1992): 773–89.

Shields, Sarah. "The U.S. and the Sancak Question: Navigating a New Relationship in a Rapidly Changing Context," forthcoming.

Şimşek, Sefa. "'People's Houses' as a Nationnwide Project for Ideological Mobilization in Early Republican Turkey." *Turkish Studies* 6 (2005): 71–91.

Sluglett, Peter. "Aspects of Economy and Society in the Syrian Provinces: Aleppo in Transition, 1880–1925." In *Modernity and Culture: From the Mediterranean to the Indian Ocean*, edited by Leila Tarazi Fawaz and C.A. Bayly, 144–57. New York: Columbia University Press, 2002.

Sluglett, Peter. "Will the Real Nationalists Stand Up? The Political Activities of the Notables of Aleppo, 1919–1946." In *France, syrie et Liban 1918–1946: Les ambiguités et les dynamiques de la relation mandataire*, edited by Nadine Méouchy, 273–90. Damascus, 2002.

Sökmen, Tayfur. *Hatay'in Kurtuluşu İçin Harcanan Çabalar*. Ankara: Türk Tarih Kurumu Yayınları, 1992.

Stillwell, Stephen Joseph, Jr. *Anglo-Turkish Relations in the Interwar Era*. Lewiston, ME: Edwin Mellen Press, 2003.

Stokes, Martin. "Imagining 'the South': Hybridity, Heterotapias and Arabesk on the Turkish-Syrian Border." In *Border Identities: Nation and State at International Frontiers*, edited by Thomas Wilson and Hastings Donnan, 263–87. Cambridge: Cambridge University Press, 1998.

Tauber, Eliezer. "The Struggle for Dayr al-Zur: The Determination of Borders between Syria and Iraq." *International Journal of Middle East Studies* 23 (1991): 361–85.

Tekin, Mehmet. *Hatay Basınında Atatürk*. Antakya: Antakya Gazeteciler Cemiyeti, 1985.

Tekin, Mehmet. *Hatay Devlet Reisi Tayfur Sökmen*. Antakya: Mustafa Kemal Üniversitesi, 2002.

Tekin, Mehmet. *Hatay Tarihi*. Ankara: Atatürk Kültür Merkezi BaşkanlığıYayınları, 2000.

Temiz, Mine. "New Architectural Formations on the Mandate-Era Kurtuluş Street in Antakya." *Chronoc: Revue d'histoire de l'université de Balamand* 13 (2006): 181–230.

Thobie, Jacques. "Le nouveau cours des relations franco-turques et l'affaire du sandjak d'Alexandrette 1921–1939." *Relations internationales* 19 (1979): 355–74.

Thomas, Martin. *The French Empire between the Wars: Imperialism, Politics and Society*. Manchester: University of Manchester Press, 2005.

Thomas, Martin C. "French Intelligence-Gathering in the Syrian Mandate, 1920–1940." *Middle Eastern Studies* 38 (2002): 1–32.

Thomas, Martin. "Imperial Defence or Diversionary Attack? Anglo-French Strategic Planning in the Near East, 1936–40." In *Anglo-French Defence Relations between the Wars*, edited by Martin S. Alexander and William J. Philpott. New York: Palgrave Macmillan, 2002.

Thompson, Elizabeth. *Colonial Citizens*. New York: Columbia University Press, 2000.

Thornberry, Patrick. *International Law and the Rights of Minorities*. New York: Oxford University Press, 1993.

Tibi, Bassam. *Arab Nationalism: Between Islam and the Nation State*. New York: St. Martin's Press, 1997.

Trask, Roger R. *The United States Response to Turkish Nationalism and Reform, 1914–1939*. Minneapolis: University of Minnesota Press, 1971.

Türkmen, Ahmet Faik. *Mufassal Hatay: Tarih, cografya, ekalliyetler, mezhepler, edebiyat, içtimai durum, lengüistik durum, folklor, etnografya ve Hatay davcasini ihtiva eden 4 cild*, v. 1–2. Istanbul: Cumhuriyet Matbaasi, 1937.

Turkyılmaz, Zeynep. "Anxieties of Conversion: Missionaries, State and Heterodox Communities in the Late Ottoman Empire." Ph.D. diss., University of California at Los Angeles, 2009.

VanderLippe, John M. *The Politics of Turkish Democracy: İsmet İnönü and the Formation of the Multi-Party Sustem, 1938–1950*. Albany: State University of New York Press, 2005.

Veou, Paul du. *Le desastre d'Alexandrette*. Paris: Éditions Baudincine, 1938.

Walters, F.P. *A History of the League of Nations*. London: Oxford University Press, 1952.

Wambaugh, Sarah. *A Monograph on Plebiscites with a Collection of Official Documents*. New York: Oxford University Press, 1920.

Watenpaugh, Keith David. *Being Modern in the Middle East: Revolution, Nationalism, Colonialism, and the Arab Middle Class*. Princeton, NJ: Princeton University Press, 2006.

Watenpaugh, Keith. "'Creating Phantoms': Zaki al-Arsuzi, the Alexandretta Crisis, and the Formation of Modern Arab Nationalism in Syria," *International Journal of Middle East Studies* 28 (1996): 363–89.

Weinberg, Gerhard L. *Hitler's Foreign Policy, 1933–1939: The Road to World War II* . New York: Enigma Books, 2005)

Weisband, Edward. "The Sanjak of Alexandretta, 1920–1939: A Case Study." *Near East Roundtable*, 1967–68, edited by R. Bayly Winder. New York, 1969.

Weulresse, Jacques. "Antioch, essai de geographie urbaine." *Bulletin d'études orientales* 4 (1935): 27–79.

Whelan, Anthony. "Wilsonian Self-Determination and the Versailles Settlement." *International and Comparative Law Quarterly* 99 (1994): 99–115.

Winter, Stefan H. "The Nusayris before the Tanzimat in the Eyes of Ottoman Provincial Administrators, 1804–1834." In *From the Syrian Land to the States of Syria and Lebanon*, edited by Thomas Philipp and Christoph Schumann, 97–112. Beirut: Orient-Institut der DMG Beirut, 2004.

Yeğen, Mesut. "Citizenship and Ethnicity in Turkey." *Middle Eastern Studies* 40 (2004): 51–66.

Yeğen, Mesut. "Turkish Nationalism and the Kurdish Question." *Ethnic and Racial Studies* 30 (2007): 119–51.

Yerasimos, Stéphane. "Le sandjak d'Alexandrette: formation et intégration d'un territoire." *Revue des mondes musulmans et de la Méditerranée* (July 2004): 198–212.

Young, Robert J. "The Aftermath of Munich: The Course of French Diplomacy, October 1938 to March 1939." *French Historical Studies* 8 (1973): 305–22.

Zhivkova, Ludmila. *Anglo-Turkish Relations 1933–1939*. London: Secker and Warburg, 1976.

Zubaida, Sami. "The Fragments Imagine the Nation: The Case of Iraq." *International Journal of Middle East Studies* (2002): 205–15.

Zürcher, Erik-Jan. "From Empire to Republic—Problems of Transition, Continuity and Change." In *Turkey in the Twentieth Century*, edited by Erik-Jan Zürcher, 15–30. Berlin: Klaus Schwarz, 2008.

INDEX

Abdullah, King of Jordan, 113
Açıkalın, Cevat, 232–34
Active Committee of the National Turkish Party, 60, 253
ad hoc Committee of the Council, 164, 169–172, 175, 188, 192
Adali, Mohammad, 39, 50, 52, 234
Affan quarter, 128, 165–66, 179, 196
Ağa, Ali, 190
Akdur, Zihni, 135–36, 137
Aktepe, 180–82, 189, 197, 198–99
Alawis
    as Arabs, 179
    in Cilicia, 98
    demonstrations, 69, 72
    election boycott, 48
    emigration from the Sanjak, 235
    Franco-Turkish Agreements, 105
    hats, 178
    as Hittites, 207, 241
    identity, 34, 89–90, 125, 245
    Kemalists, support of, 151
    languages of, 88
    as linguistic group, 73
    as Muslims, 19
    opposition to independence, 73
    oppression of, 125
    registration as Turks, 173, 176, 189, 195, 203, 222
    Sandler Report, 86
    in Sanjak Assembly, 124, 233
    Turkish landowners, 38
    Turkish majority, 139, 151
    Turkish propaganda, 133
    as Turks, 40, 88–89, 167, 179, 245
    violence against, 125–26, 134, 182–83, 190
    voter registration, 178–79, 198, 208, 214–15
Aleppo, 19, 22
    protests in, 113, 145, 206

Sanjak refugees, 207, 236
Turkish claim to, 98, 160
Alexandretta
    Ankara Treaty, 20, 28, 29–30
    demonstrations, 69
    free trade zone, 80, 114
    history, 18–19
    port, 55, 236
    strategic importance, 99
    strike, 105
    voter registration violence, 195
Amık region, 140, 195, 197, 199, 235
Anatolia, 23–24, 26, 44, 99, 241
Ankara Accord (1926), 116
Ankara Treaty (1921), 20, 28–30, 46, 251
    Cilicia, 56
    Franco-Syrian Treaty, 56
    French mandate, 64, 76
    Sandler Report, 81
    Syrian-Turkish border, 55–56
    Turkish majority, 162–63, 231, 246
    Turks in Syria, 116, 242
Anker, Paul, 59, 72, 73–74, 86, 197
Antaki, Naim, 28–29
Antakya. See Antioch
anticolonialism, 22–24, 89
    League of National Action, 48, 90, 253
    National Bloc, 87, 106
    Syria, 9–10
Antioch
    demonstrations, 41, 69, 78, 105
    election boycott, 39
    Franco-Syrian Treaty, 36
    Franco-Turkish Agreements, 112
    Halkevi, 62, 126, 127, 133, 137
    hats, 25, 35, 151
    history, 17–19

Antioch (*continued*)
  independence celebration, 143–46
  protests, 74, 86, 133, 136
  religions, 19, 92
  Statute and Fundamental Law, 113
  Syrian mandate, 27–29, 31
  violence, 23, 47, 51–53, 58, 69–72, 116, 127,
    129, 152, 165–66, 182–83, 195–96, 199,
    215–16
  voter registration, 213
Antonescu, Victor, 76
Arab nationalism, 9, 79, 151. *See also*
  pan-Arabism
Arab Popular Front, 103
Arabs
  distrust of the French, 151–52
  elections, 165, 196, 197
  electoral violence, 213–14, 218, 220, 222–25
  emigration from the Sanjak, 232, 235
  in Hatay, 237
  identity, 247
  as linguistic group, 7, 34, 73
  registration as Turks, 157, 173, 203, 209
  Sandler Report, 86
  Sanjak Assembly, 233
  Sanjak Union, 254
  Statute and Fundamental Law, 152
  voter registration, 178, 197, 213, 215
Aras, Rüştü
  Alawis, 133, 134
  Balkan Entente, 45, 67, 76
  elections, 148, 175
  electoral commission, 157–59
  electoral violence, 199, 200
  Franco-Syrian Treaty, 29
  Franco-Turkish Agreements, 194
  observers, 57–58
  Statute and Fundamental Law, 150
  Turkish majority, 162
  Turks in the Sanjak, 54–55
Armenians
  in Antioch, 17
  as a community, 171
  demonstrations, 70–71
  electoral violence, 213
  emigration, 235–36, 239
  ethnic origins, 40
  fezzes, 121
  France and, 206–8
  identity, 9, 34, 247
  language, 73, 86, 88
  League of National Action, 151
  in Lebanon, 208, 236, 239
  registration as Turks, 203
  Sandler Report, 86
  Sanjak Assembly, 114, 233
  Turkey and, 39, 73, 134, 139

Turkish boycott, 40, 41, 48
Turkish majority, 130, 139, 151
voter registration, 170, 178, 189, 191, 198,
  203, 208
Arnal, Pierre, 75–76
Arsuzi, Nasib al-, 179
Arsuzi, Said al-, 166
Arsuzi, Zaki al-, 91, 125, 255
  Alawis, 89–90, 179
  arrest, 152, 216
  Ba'ath party, 10, 246, 255
  League of National Action, 31, 71, 90,
    135–36
  violence in Antioch, 115, 119, 166
Article 55, 110, 118, 148, 150
Arvengas, Gilbert, 53
Atasi, Hashim al-, 27, 28, 29, 81
Atatürk
  Hatay, 67, 88
  hats, 24, 25, 35, 63
  modern Turkey, 35, 62, 63
  nationalism, 9
  Sanjak as Turkish, 43–44
  Sanjak question, 66–68, 76, 93, 113, 138,
    154–55, 161, 233
  Syria, 154
  Turkish majority, 192, 194, 196. *See also*
    Kemal, Mustafa
Avenol, Joseph, 170–71, 172, 202, 210
Awakiye, 216
Ayranji Sharki, 140, 214
Azaz district, 32, 63
Azma, Nabih al-, 166
Azmi, Semih, 50

Ba'ath party, 10, 246, 255
Babatorun. *See* Babtrun
Babtrun, 218, 224, 225, 226, 228
Baksanos, 224–26
Balcı, Şükrü, 39, 42, 45, 50, 128
Balkan Entente (1934), 45, 67, 76
Barazi, Husni al-
  agitation, accusations of, 37, 96, 103, 115,
    117
  demonstrations, 105–06
  League of National Action, 123
  opposition to new status, 136, 156
Barudi, Fakhri al-, 84–85, 113, 117
Baxter, C. W., 194
Bayar, Celal, 190, 229
Bayır, 88, 236
Bazantay, Pierre, 17, 22
benevolent neutrality, 174
Bennewitz, 218
Beylan, 123, 140, 183
Beyluni, Albert, 166, 216

Bik Obassi, 63
Blum, Leon, 76–77, 97, 106, 154
Bonnet, Georges, 199, 226–27, 229
border, Syrian-Turkish, 54, 55–56, 191, 236
  customs, 235
  Hatay, 237
  Sandler Report, 83, 92–95
  tripartite convention, 230
  Turkish raids, 68, 130–31
Bourquin, Maurice, 101
Bowker, Reginald J., 192, 193, 202
Bujak, 88, 235
Burnier, Pierre, 181–82, 195, 216
Bytias, 135

Çakmak, Fevzi, 53, 67
Caron, L. J. J., 59
Çelenk, Selim, 25, 31, 88, 91, 128
Christians
  in Alexandretta, 9
  in Antioch, 17
  Arab-speakers, 22, 48, 73
  emigration from the Sanjak, 24,
    232, 235
  France and, 206, 207
  in Hatay, 237
  League of National Action, 151
  Muslim persecution of, 244
  propaganda, Turkish, 49
  pro-Turkish, 134
  violence against, 201
  voter registration, 214. *See also* Greek
    Orthodox Christians; Maronites
Cilicia
  Alawis, 98
  Ankara Treaty, 20
  Arabs in, 34
  Armenians in, 206
  France and, 54, 56, 99, 206, 207
  in Hatay, 237
  Muslim persecution of, 244
  Turkey and, 98, 154
  violence against, 201
  voter registration, 214
Circassians, 73, 139, 151, 188, 190, 192
circus riot, 23, 25
clothing, European, 35–36, 46, 63, 69–70, 121,
  225, 239
Collet, Philibert, 198, 201, 204–229, 233–34
colonialism, 5, 6, 11, 26, 30
Commission for the Organization and
  Supervision of the First Elections in the
  Sanjak of Alexandretta, 162, 174–75, 253.
  See also electoral commission
Committee for the Defense of the Liwa of
  Alexandretta and Antioch, 104, 253

Committee for the Defense of the Sanjak, 113,
  114, 117, 253
Committee of Experts, 101–2
  communities, 171–72, 188, 244
  electoral regulations, 158–59, 163, 169
  identity categories, 245, 248
  linguistic and religious preferences, 166
  minorities, 102, 188, 248
  proportional representation, 125, 243
  report to League of Nations Council, 107–10
Committee of Five, 164, 165, 193, 254
Committee of Nationalist Youth and Students,
  145, 253
Committee of Three, 163, 164
Communiqué 14, 211, 212, 215
Communist Party, 82, 103, 107, 115, 120,
  123, 146,
community, registration by, 156, 159, 170, 172,
  188, 243, 244

Daladier, Édouard, 235
Damascus, protests in, 78–80, 82, 84–85,
  113–14, 206
Danzig, 171, 241
Davaz, Suad, 45, 53, 127, 146–49, 199, 226, 229
Davis, British Consul, 155–57, 183, 207, 231,
  236–37
Dawalibi, Maruf al-, 96, 145
de Caix, Robert, 101
de Haller, Edouard, 73, 160, 161
Deir, 218, 224
Delbos, Yvon, 45, 52–53, 77, 110–11, 164
Dodecanese Islands, 44, 67, 99, 174
Dodgson, C. V., 189, 218, 224–25
Doğu Ayrancı. *See* Ayranji Sharki
Dört Ayak, 126, 128, 182, 195, 196
Druze, 19, 20–22, 34, 89, 192
Dunnett, James MacDonald, 101
Durieux, Pierre
  Arabs, 43
  demonstrations, 50, 51
  education, French colonial, 38
  election boycott, 48, 49, 50
  martial law, 51–52
  press, 36, 37
  Syrian elections, 45–46
  violence, control of, 103

Eden, Anthony, 77, 110–11, 162
Edhem, Haji, 50, 52
elections, Syrian (1937), 48–50, 66, 91
electoral commission, 139–41, 177, 207, 253
  community identity, 171–72, 188
  complaints to, 180–81, 184, 188, 190, 195–97,
    209, 217, 218

Eden (*continued*)
  electoral regulations, 163, 184, 192, 202, 205
    opposition to, 157–59, 192, 210, 212–13, 216,
      221–23, 226
    registration suspension, 198, 201, 226–29
    Turkish majority, 194, 204, 246
    voter registration, 177–78, 205. *See also*
      Communiqué 14
  electoral regulations, revision of
    ad hoc committee, 164, 169–70, 175
    communal identities, 179, 192, 245
    Turkish demands, 158–64, 244
    Turkish majority, 204. *See also* Committee of
      Five
  entité distincte, 102

Fain, 80–85
Faysal, King (Iraq), 26, 36, 91, 121
fezzes, 24, 35, 36, 47, 92, 239
  rejection of hats, 36, 136, 151
  violence over, 42, 51, 125, 133, 134, 183.
    See also hats; sedara
Fifth Levant Battalion, 136
Filinjar, 218, 222
Firuz, Consul, 137–39
flags, 60, 88, 121, 143–146, 234
France
  minorities, 20–22, 244
  Ottoman provinces, 24
  role in the Sanjak, 6, 118–19, 148, 149–50
  San Remo Resolution, 60
  Sandler Report, 57
  Syrian elections, 49–50
  Syrian independence, 154
  Syrian mandate, 6, 11–12, 20, 60, 241
  Syrian-Turkish border, 54, 55
  Turkey, 11, 98–99, 101, 177, 220–21, 246
Franco-Syrian Treaty (1936), 27–31, 39, 150,
    252
  France's role, 118–20, 149–50, 252, 254
  opposition to, 31, 36, 39
  ratification of, 57, 61, 87, 106–7, 154–55,
    166
  Sandler Report, 81, 83
  status of the Sanjak, 56, 81, 83, 113–14
  Syrian elections, 38, 47
  Syrian independence, 10, 80, 247
Franco-Turkish Agreements (1937), 112, 133,
    252
  demilitarization, 152
  electoral commission, 207
  France and, 118–19, 123, 146–47
  Syria and, 116
  Treaty of Friendship, 231
  Turkish majority, 193, 246
Franco-Turkish Treaty, 30, 32

Franji, Said, 228
Franklin-Bouillon Treaty (1921), 28, 162, 251.
    See also Ankara Treaty
French mandate, 27–28, 30, 45, 65, 227, 228
  Arabs, 74–75
  Armenians, 73
  border, 54
  Franco-Syrian Treaty, 27
  League of National Action, 91
  San Remo Resolution, 118
  Sandler Report, 77, 78
  Sèvres Treaty, 26
  Statute and Fundamental Law, 141
French-Turkish electoral Commission, 233

Gacon, Special Services chief, 41–43, 50–51,
    140–41
Galip, Reşit, 40
Garreau, Roger, 137, 141–42, 168
  electoral violence, 179, 183–87, 195
  persecution of Turks, 151, 157
  Turkish banners, 145, 146
  Turkish majority, 197–98, 203, 217
  Turkish opposition, 147–49, 200
  voter registration, 176–77, 188–89, 199, 201,
    202, 217
Gautherot, Gustave, 237
Germany
  Danzig, 171, 241
  territorial claims, 7, 53–54, 68, 75, 243
  Turkish ties to, 173, 246
Ghali, Shaykh Abdullah al-, 151
Gorgé, Roland, 195
Grand National Assembly
  creation of, 24
  Franco-Turkish Agreements, 112
  Hatay, Republic of, 234
  territorial claims, 44, 45
  Turkishness, 35
Great Britain
  electoral regulations revision, 164
  Faysal, 26
  Mosul, 49, 98
  Mutual Aid Agreement, 237
  Ottoman provinces, 24
  religious minorities, 20, 244
  Sanjak independence, 66
  Turkey, 67, 76, 160–61
Greece, 24, 251
Greek Orthodox Christians, 24, 121, 167
  in Antioch, 19, 92
  Arab-speaking, 22, 73
  Crimean War, 20
  Franco-Turkish Agreements, 105
  Sanjak Assembly, 113, 233
  Sanjak independence, 143

schools, 79, 85
Statute and Fundamental Law, 178, 247
Turkey, 134, 139
violence against, 117, 129
voter registration, 191, 198, 214, 219, 245

Hajo, Muhammad, 181–82
Halkevi (Halkevleri, plural)
activism, 123–24, 132, 133, 152, 229
Alawis, 125, 179
closure of, 129, 137
electoral violence, 197
flight to Turkey, 128, 129
Hatay Assembly, 237
manifesto, 134–35
non-Turkish speakers, 166–67
police raids, 127, 136, 149, 195
propaganda, 209, 215
Republican People's Party, 42–43, 62, 126, 254
Sanjak independence celebration, 143–44
shadow government, 168–69
Turkish majority, 150
Turkishness, 62
voter registration, 156, 178, 180, 189
Halkevleri, 62–63, 168, 254
activism, 123
closure of, 128
demonstrations, 91
distrust of the French, 219
Republican People's Party, 209
Hamam Sharki, 218
Harbiye, 135, 205, 212, 220, 222
Hatay
ancient Turks, 33
Atatürk, 67, 88
flags, 60, 88, 121, 146, 234
mail to, 96–97
occupation of, 192
as province of Turkey, 239–40, 247
Hatay Assembly, 239
Hatay Committee, 91, 253
Hatay Hamam. *See* Hamam Sharki
Hatay Party, 88
Hatay, Republic of, 234–39
Harim, 70, 212
hats
circus riot, 23, 25
Kemalists, 121
secularism, 24–25, 176
Turkish identity, 9, 25, 35–36, 40, 41, 63, 92
violence over, 3, 131, 169, 181. *See also* fezzes; sedara

Hazine, 235
Hittites, 33, 75, 89, 207, 241
Holstad, Hans, 59
Houssa, Fernand, 196
Huntziger, Charles, 152–53, 174, 221

identity, 8, 187
ethnic, 7, 30
Turkish, 24, 34
and voter registration, 187. *See also* linguistic identity; national identity; religious identity
identity politics, 12, 235, 244, 247–48
İnönü, İsmet, 67, 116
inscription. *See* voter registration
International Mission of Observers to the Sanjak and Alexandretta, 58–64, 71, 102, 253
identity, 69
League of Nations, 116
Sandler Report, 86–87, 175
Iraq, 6, 29, 53, 66, 68, 235, 248–49
irredentism, 7, 53–54, 65, 76, 161, 226, 241, 248
İskenderun. *See* Alexandretta
Italy, 67, 99, 241, 246
Anatolia, 99, 241
Great Britain, 66
refugees from the Sanjak, 207
threat to Turkey, 44, 152, 173

Jabara, Hassan, 131, 136, 151, 167, 185, 187, 190
Jabiri, Sadallah al-, 79–80, 103
Jazira, 206
Jedida, 126
Jews, 9, 17, 19, 20, 188

Kafa, Jema, 165
Karabadjakian, Katchadour, 41
Karamurt, 214
Karasapan, Turkish consul
border troops, 208
electoral commission, 229
electoral violence, 184–85, 190–91, 195, 197–98, 217
Sunni Muslims, 188, 189
Turkish majority, 215
Kaya, Şükrü, 67, 130, 133
Kemal, Mustafa, 6, 9, 24, 26, 93. *See also* Atatürk
Kemal, Namik, 24
Kemalists, 25, 31, 38, 117, 135
Alawis, 90
Arab voter registration, 157
demonstrations, 71, 74
electoral boycott, 42
electoral violence, 52

Kemalists (*continued*)
  fezzes, 151
  Franco-Syrian Treaty, 36
  hats, 35–36
  Syrian elections, 39. *See also* Halkevi; People's
    Houses
Kesab, 208
Kilis, 92
Kirikhan, 32, 46, 123
  Armenians at, 122, 235
  demonstrations, 69, 71
  electoral violence, 46, 191
  inscription, 180, 188, 189, 195
Kitchener, Horatio Herbert, 99
Kollewyn, R. A., 101, 102
Koray, Mehmet Sait, 92
Kuchuk Ayranji, 195
Kullo, Khalil Ali, 180
Kunsler, Jakob, 235
Kurds
  emigration from the Sanjak, 235
  identity, 34
  as linguistic group, 7, 73
  Turkish majority, 139
  as Turks, 245
  uprising, 241
  voter registration, 178, 180–82, 209
Kürt Dağ district, 32, 63, 68, 75, 93
Kürt Deresi, 126
Kuseyr, 133, 212, 215, 218, 220, 223
Kuseyri, Mustafa, 25, 42, 48, 50–52, 152

Lagarde, Ernest, 159–60, 162, 173
Lagrange, Jacques, 139, 216
language
  Arabic as official, 83, 88, 89, 108, 234
  as identity, 7, 8, 19, 151, 171, 235, 247
  Turkish as official, 20, 77–78, 81, 86, 88, 108,
    112, 242
  Turkish in the Sanjak, 6–7, 9, 56, 62, 75, 77,
    116. *See also* linguistic diversity; linguistic
    identity
Latakia, 22, 212, 235
  Alawis, 89
  Sandler Report, 78
  Statue and Fundamental Law, 113
  Turkish interest in, 93, 98
League of National Action, 31, 102, 123–24,
    182, 253
  Arab nationalism, 151
  election boycott, 48
  electoral violence, 195, 220
  flags, 144, 145
  Franco-Turkish Agreements, opposition to,
    113
  French colonizers, 107

hats, 178–79
history of, 90–91
International Mission of Observers, 62
national identity, 246
outlawed, 226
propaganda, 184
Sanjak as Syrian, 71
Sanjak independence, 97
sedara, 36
shut down, 135
Statute and Fundamental Law, opposition to,
    120
Turkish majority, 150
voter recruitment, 187
League of Nations, 5, 6, 7, 105, 244
  Bosphorus and Dardanelles, 44–45
  electoral regulations, 161, 163–64
  identity, 3, 245
  International Mission of Observers, 116
  mandates, 6, 8, 11–12, 26
League of Nations Council, 56, 117, 121, 159,
    165
  Committee of Experts, 101, 107–8, 254
  electoral commission, 224, 228, 229
  International Mission of Observers, 175, 253
  Sandler Report, 77, 175
  Statute and Fundamental Law, 112, 252
  Turks in the Sanjak, 54–55
League of Nations Permanent Mandates Com-
    mission, 26, 56, 98, 252, 254
Lebanon
  Armenians in, 208, 236, 239
  France, 34, 45, 65
  Franco-Syrian Treaty, 83
  Franco-Turkish Agreements, 252
  French mandate, 56, 60, 64, 251
  Great Britain, 20, 36
  politics of identity, 244, 248
  Syria, division of, 81, 105
Lecomte, 208–9, 222
Lie, Jonas, 189, 214, 215
linguistic diversity, 19, 22, 73, 121
linguistic identity, 7, 9, 12, 34, 242, 245, 247
  and politics, 159, 166
  proportional representation, 150, 243. *See also*
    language, as identity
Litvinov, Maxim, 110
Liwa, 34, 102–4, 252
Loraine, Percy, 193

MacMurray, John Van A., 45, 68, 76
Mahayri, Fahmi al-, 102
Mahli, Mustafa, 51
Mandate for Syria and Lebanon, 56, 60, 251.
    See also French mandate
Mardam, Jamil

border incursions, 95
demonstrations, 79, 106
France, 206
Franco-Syrian Treaty, 97, 154, 166
Sandler Report, 79–82, 85, 97–98, 101
Statute and Fundamental Law, 113, 115–16
Turkey, 98, 154–55, 206
Maronites, 19, 34, 188, 192
Marriner, J. Theodore, 114
Martel, Damien de
  Communiqué 14, 215
  elections, Syrian, 49
  electoral commission, 228
  electoral violence, 199
  French mandate, 77
  inscriptions, 229
  League of Nations observers mission, 59
  military intervention, 201
  minorities, 223
  press, 36–37, 47
  Sandler Report, 80, 83
  Sanjak independence, 146, 232
  state of siege, 58
  Statute and Fundamental Law, 121
  Turkish activists, 150
  Turkish claims, 74–75
  Turkish majority, 139, 148, 191–92
  Turkish threats, 67–68
  visit to the Sanjak, 121–22
martial law, 51, 117, 203, 204–31, 236
Maruf, Sadek, Shaykh, 40, 50, 125, 126, 133, 135, 179, 234
Mashrafiye, 209, 214
Mayakon, İsmail Müştak, 33
Mehmet, Tecirli, 50
Melek, Abdurrahman, 168, 198, 199, 205, 208, 233
Menemencioğlu, Numan
  Committee of Experts, 101–2
  community affiliation, 171–73
  electoral violence, 185–86, 196, 199
  Statute and Fundamental Law, 112
  Turkish majority, 176, 189–90, 203
Mentque, 115, 118, 123, 124, 126, 127, 135–37
Mesny, Col., 136
Meyrier, 106
Ministerial Declaration, 61–62
minorities, 54, 74, 247, 248
  Ankara Treaty, 20–22
  Arabization of, 134
  Committee of Experts, 102, 248
  Communiqué 14, 211, 212, 215
  and elections, 149, 201, 211, 223
  France and, 244
  Germany and, 75
  League of Nations and, 5, 8, 11, 231, 232, 242
  non-Turkish, 148

  Ottoman, 28, 34
  proportional representation, 125
  religious, 22
  rights of, 30, 201
  in Sanjak Assembly, 233, 244
  in the Sanjak, 72–73
  Turkey and, 93
  voter registration, 188, 205, 220
Minorities Treaties, 242–44, 246
Mosul, 6, 66, 68, 170
  Turkish claim to, 49, 75, 98, 160, 163, 170
Mottier, Charles, 59
Moumen, Ibrahim Edhem Bey al-, 25
Mount Lebanon, 20–22, 34, 45. *See also* Lebanon
Muhammad, Efendi Hoca Kurd, 25
Munir, Vedi, 25, 32, 50, 72, 128, 234
Murselzade, Abdullah, 32
Murselzade, İnayet, 180, 181
Musa Dağ, 70
Muslims, 9, 17, 22, 25, 41, 75, 89, 206, 244
  identity, 9, 24, 247
  inscription, 187–88, 215
  in Ottoman Empire, 19–20. *See also* Sunni Muslims

Nadi, Yunus, 47, 52, 122, 154
National Bloc, 26, 27, 31
  collaboration with France, 206
  Franco-Syrian Treaty, 61, 154
  Franco-Turkish Agreements, 113
  lack of resistance, 246–47
  Ministerial Declaration, 61–62
  Sandler Report, 82–85, 87, 105
  Statute and Fundamental Law, 114
  Syrian elections, 49
  Syrian independence, 80
  Turkish propaganda, 43
national identity, 9, 10, 19, 240, 245. *See also* identity; identity politics
National Pact (1920), 43–44, 74, 251
National Union, 165–66, 254
Nicol, A. P., 175, 225
Numan, Omar, 64, 94

Orontes River, 17, 36, 50, 51
Osmaniye, 214
Ostrorog, Stanislas, 102, 205–6
Ottoman Empire, 6–10, 17–20, 23–24, 134, 246, 251

Palestine, 20, 32, 53, 81, 99, 105
pan-Arabism, 73, 96, 97, 125, 212
Party of National Unity, 221
Pavkovitch, Dragoljub, 213, 222

Payas, 60, 68, 98, 130
People's Houses, 62, 91, 123, 176, 254. *See also*
  Halkevi; Halkevleri
plebiscite, 49, 160, 170, 172, 240
Plomigren, E. de, 214
Polet, E., 213, 214, 218, 224
Ponsot, Henri, 193, 200
  Alawis, 133
  electoral commission suspension, 227
  inscription, 229
  military intervention, 201
  Turkey, 132, 133, 153
  Turkish majority, 189
press, Arab, 36, 37
press, Syrian, 36–37, 58, 105
press, Turkish
  anti-French, 151, 193
  Arab-Turkish tension, 36, 37
  clothing, 36
  election boycott, 39, 40, 48, 52–53
  electoral commission, 157
  Franco-Syrian Treaty, 28–29
  League of Nations, 161
  Sanjak autonomy, 30
  Sanjak independence, 146, 147
  Turkish identity, 36
  violence in the Sanjak, 58, 59–60, 127, 132
  violent tone, 93–94
proportional representation, 125, 140, 150, 170,
  243–44
Puaux, Gabriel, 67, 237

Qadir, Abd al-, 103, 120, 131, 136
Queru, Captain, 125, 131
Quwwatli, Shukri al-, 85–86

Refik, Captain, 32, 154
Reid, T., 139–40, 158, 159, 171, 175, 253
Reimers, Herman, 139
  Alawis, 207–9
  Armenians, 208
  demonstrations, 216
  suspension, 201–2, 205, 229
  Turkish accusations, 221–24
  Turkish majority, 204
religious identity, 7, 9, 12, 22, 31, 34, 159, 166,
  243, 245, 247
Rendel, George William, 159–60, 170–73
Republican People's Party, 185–86, 254
  electoral commission, 217
  flight to Turkey, 128, 135
  Halkevi, 62, 126
  Hatay Committee, 91, 253
  mistrust of France, 151
  outlawed, 41–43

propaganda, 209
recruitment of voters, 187
Statute and Fundamental Law, 134–35
voter registration, 187, 209
women's suffrage, 98
Reyhaniye. *See* Reyhanlı
Reyhanlı, 3, 74, 121–22, 123, 187, 235
  Halkevi, 195, 197
  violence in, 69–70, 190, 195, 196, 209, 213
  voter registration, 190, 213–14
Riza, Effendi Ali, 40
Ruşdi, Kör, 94

Sabet, Kör (Sabet ben Hasan Şarbatcı), 126, 136
Sadak, Necmettin, 163, 210, 212
Şaho, Mustafa, Mevlevi Shaykh, 150
Samandağ. *See* Süveydiye
San Remo Resolution (1920), 26, 54, 55, 60,
  118, 251
Sandler Report (1937), 77–104, 175, 252
Sandler, Rickard J., 55, 57, 107
Sanjak Assembly, 113, 114, 124, 140, 165, 205,
  217, 233, 234, 244
Sanjak Union, 152, 182, 195, 200, 220, 226, 254
secret agreement. *See* Franco-Turkish
  Agreements
Secretan, Roger, 139
sedara, 36, 91, 131
self-determination
  Franco-Syrian Treaty, 30
  International Mission of Observers, 69
  League of Nations and, 5–6, 11–12, 242, 248
  majority in the Sanjak, 34, 78
  Turkey and, 169
Selim, Memduh, 180–81
Şemsettin, Fevzi, 128
Sèvres Treaty, 15, 20, 23, 24, 99, 251
Sezer, Ahmet Necdet, 240
shadow government, 168–69
Shahbandar, Abd al-Rahman, 102, 114
Shaw, G. Howland, 113
Society for Annexation to Turkey, 32, 254
Society of the Turco-Arab Conflict, 91
Sökmen, Tayfur, 127, 133, 233–34
Special Tribunal of the League of Nations,
  181–82, 215, 217, 220
Statute and Fundamental Law, 77, 101–2,
  107–110, 235
  communities, 178, 188
  demonstration, 105
  electoral law, 171–72
  electoral regulations, 158
  France's role, 118–120, 141, 149–50
  Hatay, 237
  individual rights, 124
  minority rights, 201

opposition to, 112–142
Syrian reaction, 78–83, 166
Treaty of Friendship, 231
Turkish majority, 163, 202
undermining of, 146, 147
Steel Shirts, 71, 82, 84–85, 113, 132–33
strikes
general, 26, 80–82, 105
student, 46, 69, 145–46
Sunni Muslims
and Alawis, 89, 167
in Alexandretta, 9, 38
as anti-Western, 22, 75
emigration from the Sanjak, 235
identity category, 244, 245, 247
inscription, 187–88, 190, 215
languages, 22, 73
Turkish majority, 139
Süveydiye, 125, 135, 205, 213, 219–20, 222, 228
Sykes-Picot Agreement, 26
Syria
anticolonialism, 9–10
claims to the Sanjak, 232, 240
Committee of Experts, 248
division of, 81
elections, 38–39, 40
French mandate, 241
independence, 6, 27
nationalist ideology, 33–34
religious minorities, 20, 22
Sandler Report, 78–83
Statute and Fundamental Law, 116–17, 120
uprising (1925), 34–35
violence in, 206. *See also* border,
   Syrian-Turkish; French mandate;
   Mandate for Syria and Lebanon
Syrian mandate. *See* French mandate; Mandate
   for Syria and Lebanon
Syrian Popular Party, 82, 83, 85

Transjordan, 81
Treaty of Friendship (1938), 230, 231, 252
Treaty of Lausanne (1923), 24, 29, 56, 116, 251,
   252
tripartite confederation, 64–65, 230, 237
Turkey
Alawis, 89–90
Committee of Five, 164
Communiqué 14, 212
electoral commission, 212
electoral regulations, 159, 160, 163, 204
France, 11, 98–99, 101, 177, 220–21, 246
Franco-Syrian Treaty, 39
identity, 6–7, 35
immigrants from, 199
imperialism, 93–94

International Mission of Observers, 60
invasion rumors, 68, 93, 131, 169, 181–82, 208
Iraq, 235
national holiday (1936), 41
nationalists, 34
role in the Sanjak, 137, 149
Sandler Report, 87–88
Statute and Fundamental Law, 112
and Syria, 6, 55, 64, 77, 111–12, 230, 237
territorial claims, 44, 45, 68, 76
tripartite confederation, 64–65. *See also* Mosul
Turkey, Republic of
Arab majorities in, 44
claim to the Sanjak, 6, 60
Hatay, 239–40
and Italy, 99
minorities in, 134
nationalism 9–10
recognized, 24
secularism, 35
students in, 22
Treaty of Lausanne, 24, 252
westernization, 35
Turkish Free Zone, 109, 114
Turkish majority, 193, 197–98, 202–4, 212–14
Ankara Treaty, 162–63
Atatürk, 112
elections, 148, 164, 191–95
electoral regulations, 245
France and, 176–77, 187, 188, 203
International Mission of Observers, 64
Syrian-Turkish border, 54
Turkey and, 192–93, 202, 246
Turkish military invasion, 201, 215
voter registration, 151, 191, 204, 208
Turkishness, 33–35, 41–42, 60, 62–63, 72, 125, 241
Turkmën, Abdulgani, 105, 115
Active Committee of the National Turkish
   Party, 60, 253
Antioch Halkevi, 168
demonstrations, 50–51
election boycott, 40
Executive Council, 139, 233, 234
flight to Turkey, 128
hats, 25, 92
rights of Sanjak's Turks, 124
voter registration, 214, 225

Uçgedik. *See* Awakiye
Union of Arabs, 151
United Front, 82
Usbajis, 221

Van der Mandere, H. Ch. G. J., 139
Van Wattenwyl, Charles, 59

Versailles Treaty (1918), 242, 243
Viénot, Pierre, 55–57, 64–65, 83, 119
voter registration, 176–203
  communities, 159, 210–11, 216
  Turkish majority, 151
  violence and, 195, 204. *See also* electoral
    commission; electoral regulations
Wadi Jarab, 213
Ward, Nadim, 178–79
Westman, Karl Ivan, 101, 160
Wilson, Woodrow, 5, 11, 242
women's suffrage, 98
World War I
  aftermath of, 3–5, 6, 11
  Ankara Treaty, 251
  borders, 45, 65, 243

causes, 247–48
demilitarization, 44
France, 20, 89
Germany, 246
Italy, 99, 241
minorities, 8
Ottoman Empire, 8, 9, 23, 111
Palestinian Mandate, 105
Treaty of Lausanne, 252
Versailles Treaty, 243

Yenişehir quarter, 178, 190

Zarka, Muhammad Ali, 151, 155